The Art of Earth Architecture

The Art of Earth Architecture
Past, Present, Future

Jean Dethier

Princeton Architectural Press
New York

Contents

Introduction **In Praise of Earth Architecture**	6

The Case for Raw Earth: An Ecological Material
    for a New Concept of the Built Environment   8
    Jean Dethier
The Ecological Merits of Raw Earth Construction   21
    Hubert Guillaud
Earth Architecture and Changes to the Social Paradigm   22
    Romain Anger
The Benefits and Limitations of Earth Architecture   24
    Dominique Gauzin-Müller
Maps   26

Chapter 1
Constructional Logic   28

An Overview of Traditional Methods of Raw
    Earth Construction   31
    Hubert Guillaud
Geology and Materials   35
    Patrice Doat
How Raw Earth Buildings Stand the Test of Time   36
    Hugo Houben & Henri Van Damme
Improving the Performance of Raw Earth
    While Retaining Its Ecological Benefits   38
    Hugo Houben & Henri Van Damme
Earth Architecture Gallery   40

Chapter 2
Archaeological Evidence   64

Earth Architecture in Antiquity   66
    Hubert Guillaud
What Archaeology Can Teach Us   70
    David Gandreau
Earth Architecture Gallery   72

Chapter 3
Historical Innovations   102

Revolutions in the Art of Earth Architecture   105
    Jean Dethier
Ending the Prejudice Against Earth Architecture:
    What Can History Teach Us?   106
    Ruth Eaton
Earth Architecture Gallery   108

Chapter 4
Vernacular Heritage   150

What Can We Learn from Vernacular Traditions?   153
    Anne-Monique Bardagot & Nathalie Sabatier
The Vernacular Spirit and the Builders of Today   154
    Hubert Guillaud
Earth Architecture Gallery   156
The Revival of Vernacular Traditions   267
    Jean Dethier
Earth Architecture Gallery   268
Earth Architecture in Africa: Development
    and Potential   290
    Sébastien Moriset
New Ways to Restore the Legacy
    of Earth Architecture   293
    Patrice Doat
Modernizing Building Cultures to Stimulate
    Local Development   294
    Hubert Guillaud

Chapter 5
Alternative Forms of the Modern:
1789–1968   296

The Quest for an Alternative Form of Modern
    Architecture: 1789–1968   298
    Jean Dethier
François Cointeraux: First Great Pioneer
    of Modern Earth Architecture   308
    Jean Dethier
Earth Architecture Gallery   310
Hassan Fathy: Second Great Pioneer
    of Modern Earth Architecture   334
    Jean Dethier
Earth Architecture Gallery   336

Chapter 6 — 356
Contemporary Creativity: 1970 to the Present Day

Half a Century of Evolution: 1970–2020 — 358
  Ariane Wilson
Overview of Contemporary Architectural Practices — 365
  Hubert Guillaud
Portraits of Three Pioneers — 368
  Francis Kéré — 368
  Wang Shu and Lu Wenyu — 369
  Hubert Guillaud
CRAterre: Pioneers of Modern Earth
  Architecture since 1979 — 370
  Jean Dethier
A Note from the Founders of CRAterre — 374
  Patrice Doat, Hubert Guillaud, & Hugo Houben
Earth Architecture Gallery — 376

Chapter 7 — 472
Perspectives on the Future

What is the Future of Earth Architecture?
  Obstacles and Gains — 474
  Jean Dethier
The Need for a Cultural and Educational Revolution — 476
  Patrice Doat
Building with Earth in an Urban Context:
  A Circular Economy for the Future — 478
  Hugo Gasnier
The Future of Earth Architecture: Six Viewpoints — 480
  S. K. Sharma — 480
  Martin Rauch — 482
  Anna Heringer — 483
  Sébastien Moriset — 484
  Lara K. Davis — 485
  Dominique Gauzin-Müller — 486
Warnings for the Future — 488
  Ron Cobb & Luc Schuiten

Conclusion — 490

About the Authors — 492
Bibliography — 496
Index of Architects and Other Creators — 502
Index of Illustrated Works by Country — 505
Member Institutions of the UNESCO Chair
  on Earthen Architecture — 506
Acknowledgments — 507
Picture Credits — 510

Introduction

In Praise of Earth Architecture

Earth samples collected by the Auroville Earth Institute, India (see pp. 384–385 and 481).

The Case for Raw Earth
An Ecological Material for a New Concept of the Built Environment

Jean Dethier

The primary purpose of this book is to combat a deep-rooted cultural neglect, a form of collective amnesia. An extraordinary global heritage has been forgotten: the history of architecture, settlements, and structures built from earth. More specifically, it is important to stress that we are talking about raw earth rather than fired or baked earth, which is the result of a high-temperature transformation process that causes pollution and consumes energy, whether on an artisanal or industrial scale. As Claude Lévi-Strauss said, there is an essential difference between the raw and the cooked, as they represent two radically opposed approaches to a single resource. Raw earth is the most humble, most ecological, and most accessible of all construction materials: it is a treasure lying beneath our feet. It is taken for granted that earth can be used to grow food but it is often forgotten that it can also be used for the equally vital task of providing shelter. Furthermore, the earth extracted for this purpose is never taken from the fertile topsoil used for growing crops but is instead drawn from the mineral undersoil beneath. This abundant natural material has enabled civilizations all over the world to construct villages and cities. From houses to public buildings, it is accessible to all social classes, from the poorest to the wealthiest. Raw earth construction has long been an unacknowledged means of democratization in architecture.

An untold story

Until now, most of this precious heritage has never been specifically showcased in a dedicated book. Nonetheless, it displays mind-boggling diversity and, in many cases, exceptional quality and design intelligence. Even the scholarly tomes, ancient and modern, that trace the global history of architecture often ignore the most striking examples of this cultural and technological legacy. As a result, this chapter in the global history of art has not yet been the subject of a complete overview. Furthermore, archaeologists have often undervalued ancient sites containing the remains of enormous temples and fortresses, luxurious palaces, and indeed entire cities built with raw earth.

Similarly, many of the leading lights of architecture, particularly those of the avant-gardes of the 1920s, have shown an arrogant disdain towards even the most masterly examples of raw earth construction. Nevertheless, the epic story of earth architecture is testament to the construction skills of people who, for a long time, were obliged to build with nothing more than the natural resources they had at hand, among which raw earth was often first and foremost. What was a constraint in times past now seems, however, to be a crucial key to our future survival. It is vital that we change the economic logic of the building industry, creating a new model that favours the use of local natural resources.

Out of obscurity

Raw earth is finally coming out of its long purgatory. Admittedly, hundreds of books on the subject have already been written, as well as thousands of scholarly articles by researchers from a range of academic backgrounds.[1] Many of these are extremely technical, however, and few are aimed at a general readership – and even fewer attempt a cultural and historical synthesis. This is the challenge that this book attempts to meet, by finding a niche among the books on art and culture aimed at an international audience. It covers 73 countries on five continents and ranges from ancient buildings to 21st-century creations, as well as illustrating many other examples that have been obliterated by war or other disasters. To give an overarching form to this wealth of material, the chosen option has been to combine a chronological and a thematic approach. This tale of architectural evolution is also punctuated by references to the use of earth in other fields, including civil and military engineering, landscaping, design, and art forms both ancient and modern, including land art, which seeks to integrate nature into the creative act.

Activism and emotional impact

Over the course of the two decades leading up to the writing of this book, the initial desire for an unprecedented visual overview of the diversity of earth architecture has been complemented by another more militant aim. The project grew on two levels, factual and emotive, resulting in around thirty

Overleaf: Boarding school for 540 students aged from 13 to 18, built from wood and earth in Formoso do Araguaia, in the state of Tocantins, Brazil, for the Bradesco Foundation (2016). Architects: Gustavo Utrabo and Pedro Duschenes (Aleph Zero), Marcelo Rosenbaum, and Adriana Benguela. In 2018, this 'Children's Village' received an Award for International Excellence from the Royal Institute of British Architects (RIBA).

interdisciplinary essays by authors renowned in their respective fields, along with more than 700 illustrations – including drawings and many previously unpublished photographs – chosen for their emotional impact. This dual approach has been adopted with the intention of stimulating debate. The showcasing of these examples of our ancestral heritage is intended to spark questions about what has led our society to marginalize, or even sometimes outlaw, the art of building with a material as natural and ecological as raw earth. This rejection is even more puzzling in an age that increasingly espouses a holistic relationship between nature, human beings, and the built environment, not to mention an ecologically responsible use of resources. The current ostracism of raw earth is even less acceptable, given that the right to build with earth has always been implicit in every culture in the world. This basic freedom must be maintained, encouraged, and facilitated, not merely in a spirit of condescension and paternalism in rural areas or emerging nations, but also in new urban neighbourhoods – such as the Domaine de la Terre, completed in France in 1985[2] – and even in major cities such as Paris.[3] Contemporary raw earth architecture has now proved its worth repeatedly and unequivocally in terms of relevance, reliability, and durability.

A basis for reflection

In order to overcome the aforementioned cultural amnesia and to shed light on the debate about our future, this book places equal emphasis on tradition and modernity. It covers four main chronological periods: the evolution of the art of raw earth architecture from ancient times to the Enlightenment; the timeless creations derived from vernacular traditions; the development of earth architecture between 1789 and 1968; and the modernization that has occurred from the 1970s to the present day. All in all, this panorama should provide a basis for potential reflection on how best to update and expand the use of earth within the context of ecological building practices.

The panoply of structures covered, from the humble to the monumental, have much to teach us, not only from a technical viewpoint but also in cultural, social, and strategic terms. We must have the foresight to see that the prevailing building practices of today are often exploitative and dangerous, forced upon us by a lobby of multinational manufacturers of industrialized materials that have come to dominate our lives. These methods lead to excess consumption of fossil fuels (petrol, gas, and coal), large-scale pollution, and greenhouse gases – in other words, the causes of the climate crisis that threatens our future. Raw earth could help us avoid these disastrous consequences, as it can be used without any major consumption of energy – it is extracted locally, is not chemically processed, and produces virtually no greenhouse gases. It is therefore vital to reappraise this abundant resource and its acknowledged ecological benefits,[4] particularly for housing but also for other buildings, large and small.

New creative insights and alternatives

In order to illustrate this potential, the chapter 'Contemporary Creativity' brings together around a hundred examples of contemporary raw earth architecture from all over the world, from countries with every type of climate and level of wealth. This diversity is testimony to a thriving alternative creativity. The public and private buildings displayed here fulfil a wide range of functions, with some even satisfying high-end luxury requirements. The examples embrace the fields of education (primary school, university campus), health (dispensary, surgical centre, regional hospital), culture (artworks, museum), tourism (guest house, hotel), sport and leisure (swimming pool, stadium), and services (office block, shopping mall). Many similar buildings have been constructed in recent years, especially in Europe, but they have received little recognition, even from the architectural profession. They nevertheless herald a dynamic new creative approach that is ecologically responsible and forward-looking, with standard bearers that range from lesser-known master builders to top architects. This profusion has the potential to overturn prejudice against raw earth architecture better than any number of lectures or articles. Some of these buildings incorporate a small proportion of cement to stabilize their structure, but many others completely forego this energy-consuming and polluting industrial ingredient – and recent

scientific research has demonstrated that cement is not essential to the stability and durability of raw earth masonry.[5]

Towards a new economy of materials

The goal of ecologically responsible architecture is not to reverse the effects of the ecological crisis, as that would mean going back to the way things were before, once the critical phase has passed. Instead, this architecture has the potential to be part of the global paradigm shift that our society urgently requires if its future survival is to be ensured.[6] This radical change, philosophical and moral as well as technological and political, is needed to free the construction sector from the grip of the technoscience that threatens to overwhelm us. The excessive use of industrialized building materials, often under the pretext of rationality, is one of the main causes of climate change. These materials are also a danger to public health, to such an extent that some manufacturers could be considered responsible for crimes against humanity: for example, those that, over the course of the 20th century, sold (and continue to sell in developing countries) products containing asbestos, which is responsible for the deaths of thousands of people all over the world; or those that refine aluminium, resulting in the byproduct of red mud, which dramatically pollutes land, water courses, and seas. Furthermore, the American economist Lester R. Brown, founder of the Worldwatch Institute in 1974 and of the Earth Policy Institute in 2001, observed in 2007 that the latter industry is heavily subsidized: 'In France, for example, the state-owned aluminum company gets electricity at the heavily subsidized rate of 1.5¢ per kilowatt-hour, while other industries pay 6¢ and residential users pay close to 12¢.'[7] These aberrant policies are proof that our society has lost its mind. It is clear that the use of natural, ecological building materials such as raw earth should be promoted, rather than those that cause the worst pollution. Going still further, some experts have called for a carbon tax on industrialized materials, including cement, in proportion to the danger they pose to the environment and the population.[8] Brown stressed the urgent need to design 'a new materials economy', while also declaring: 'We can build an eco-economy with existing technologies.' One tried-and-tested example of these technologies is raw earth architecture. Calling for equity and transparency in the marketplace, Brown also observed: 'Socialism collapsed because it did not allow prices to tell the economic truth. Capitalism may collapse because it does not allow prices to tell the ecological truth.'

Towards a 'green capitalism'?

The stakes in this debate are so high that it is vital to seek out the views of scientists and academics who have studied these issues in depth. Since traditional capitalism is now accused of trying to hide the 'inconvenient truth' (in the words of Al Gore), let us turn to Paul Hawken and Armory and Hunter Lovins, who outlined the concept of 'green capitalism' in their book *Natural Capitalism* (1999).[9] They stated: 'Capitalism, as practised, is a financially profitable, nonsustainable aberration in human development....It neglects to assign any value to the largest stocks of capital it employs – the natural resources and living systems, as well as the social and cultural systems that are the basis of human capital....In the recent past, most choices about building design and materials have been made carelessly, yielding low returns on human capital or actual losses to society.' The three economists went on to argue: 'New materials are being supplemented by rediscovered ancient ones like rammed earth, straw bales, adobe, and caliche (a dense clay) – all nontoxic, safe, durable, and versatile....Such buildings' resource and economic efficiency and their environmental sensitivity spring not merely from a desire to save money and prevent pollution but from a deeper consciousness that integrates design arts and sensibilities too long sundered from architecture and engineering....Their most extraordinary prototypes...occur when all these elements are integrated and their synergies captured.... Yet now the practices that create that magic are starting to be widely valued and appreciated. They will drive a revolution in buildings and in how we inhabit them.... Green buildings do not poison the air with fumes nor the soul with artificiality. Instead, they create delight when entered, serenity and health when occupied, and regret when departed. They grow organically in and from their place, integrating people within the rest of the natural world; do no harm to their occupants or to the earth; foster more diverse and abundant life than they give back. Achieving all this hand in hand with functionality and profitability requires a level of design integration that is not merely a technical task but an aesthetic and spiritual challenge.' It should be noted that the *Wall Street Journal* – the business Bible – called this book 'hugely important', while the *Financial Times*, another pillar of the business world, stated on 19 October 2012: 'The world's most primitive building material – earth – is being used to create some of our most advanced homes.'

Distortions and evasions

The optimism of these American pioneers of green capitalism with respect to the system's capacity to reform itself to such a radical degree is, however, open to question – as is the supposed salvation of 'sustainable development', a concept that quickly began to be distorted. This term, designed to embrace economic, social, and ecological concerns, was coined in 1987 by the UN in *Our Common Future*, the famous report by the World Commission on Environment and Development, chaired by Gro Harlem Brundtland. This document served as the basis of the Earth Summit held five years later in Rio de Janeiro and sparked debate at countless international conferences. But the promise of development that 'meets the needs of the present without compromising the ability of future generations to meet their own needs' has since been perverted by proponents of the status quo, who have become embroiled in the practice of 'greenwashing'. French pesticide manufacturers, for instance, have formed the 'Union of Plant Protection Industries', a fancifully named lobby that presents itself 'with state complicity, as...concerned about the health of soil and human beings'.[10] In France, the concrete lobby boasted in 2019 that its product is becoming 'ever more intelligent [and] will contribute to the construction of the city of the future'. It is true that reinforced concrete (a brilliant late 19th-century invention whose energy consumption and pollution levels in the manufacturing stage have recently been slightly reduced) is vital to some public works and large buildings. However, it is worth stressing that in most homes and small to medium-sized buildings, it is perfectly possible to replace it with untransformed natural materials such as raw earth. The propaganda in favour of cement and concrete has been undermined by scientists, who tend to share the opinion that 'concrete's carbon footprint works against it: it consumes a great deal of energy, and the manufacturing process for cement accounts for almost 10% of the world's CO_2 emissions.'[11]

Freeing the future – freedom to build

Several writers have expanded this debate by adding a social perspective. For example, André Gorz, a French pioneer of the philosophy of political ecology, pointed out that 'the criticism of technology, in which the domination of humanity and nature is made manifest, is one of the fundamental aspects of an ethic of liberation....Society's choices have been constantly forced upon us by the bias of technological choices, which are rarely the only ones possible. Nor are they necessarily the most efficient. Capitalism only develops technologies that follow its logic and are compatible with its continuing domination....Without the fight for different technologies, the fight for a different society is futile.'[12] This alternative approach makes construction with raw earth possible.

In his influential book *Freedom to Build*, British urbanist and sociologist John F. C. Turner, an instigator of progressive housing policies in Latin America, declared: 'When dwellers control the major decisions and are free to make their own contribution to the design, construction or management of their housing, both the process and the environment produced stimulate individual and social well-being. When people have no control over nor responsibility for key decisions in the housing process, on the other hand, dwelling environments may instead become a barrier to personal fulfilment and a burden on the economy.'[13] Turner also maintains that a building material is not interesting for what it is in itself, but for what it offers to its users and to society as a whole. This assertion is particularly pertinent as regards raw earth used in housing construction.

'Free the future!' proclaimed Ivan Illich, the Austrian philosopher and theorist of political ecology, in 1969.

Opposite: The Wa Shan Guesthouse, built with rammed earth in 2013 at the Xiangshan campus of the China Academy of Art, Hangzhou. Architects: Wang Shu (winner of the 2012 Pritzker Prize) and Lu Wenyu, co-founders of the Amateur Architecture Studio (see pp. 361, 369, and 432–433).

'We need an alternative programme, an alternative both to development and to merely political revolution,' he also declared.[14] In turn, Erich Fromm, the German-born American sociologist, noted: 'This radical questioning is possible only if one does not take the concepts of one's own society or even of an entire historical period – like Western culture since the Renaissance – for granted… it is the dawning of the awareness that the Emperor is naked, and that his splendid garments are nothing but the product of one's phantasy….Radical doubt is a process; a process of liberation from idolatrous thinking; a widening of awareness, of imaginative, creative vision of our possibilities and options.' The less-is-more ecological wisdom of raw earth construction allows us to escape slavish devotion to industrialized building materials.

The quest for a new modernity

German philosopher Hans Jonas, who in 1979 formulated the concept of the current generation's responsibility towards future generations, wrote about the overwhelming power that humanity has acquired through technology, and the resulting risk of self-destruction. He advocated the banning of any technology that represented a threat to society, and added that if a technology had several potential consequences, 'its future must be decided on the basis of the most pessimistic hypothesis.'[15] Raw earth, in contrast to conventional industrialized materials that guzzle energy and produce greenhouse gases, has been known to be harmless for centuries.

German sociologist Ulrich Beck extends this critical analysis by detailing the social changes derived from industrial and technological development and stresses the need to take accumulated risks into account if we are to safeguard our future. Beck is witheringly critical of 'the actors who are supposed to be the guarantors of security and rationality – the state, science and industry – are engaged in a highly ambivalent game…for they are urging the population to climb into an aircraft for which a landing strip has not yet been built.'[16] He deplores the ongoing process of 'detraditionalization' and loss of ancient skills, which leads to a rapid erosion of social solidarity, and calls for 'another modernity'.

The use of raw earth in construction, passed on since ancient times, is an example of this kind of alternative modernity.

French philosopher Dominique Bourg provides a fuller definition of this 'new modernity': 'Conscious of the intractability of its spiritual foundations, having renounced the myth of infinite growth, concerned about the contradictions between freedom and the market, having relativized the notion of risk, reinterpreting human rights by spurning both anthropocentrism and zealous individualism, rediscovering the speculative nature of knowledge, and seeing technology more as something that accompanies nature rather than dominating or destroying it….If "humanity is groaning, half crushed by the weight of the advances that it has made" (Henri Bergson), it may in future scream in pain at their consequences, unless it succeeds in freeing itself from the pull of the limitless "mechanization-destruction" of nature's bounty, unless it manages to once again find the simplicity of life desirable.'[17]

It is this very simplicity that favours ecological construction with raw earth. Its architectural use creates a minimalist harmony that is becoming increasingly prized, particularly in wealthier European countries. This concept has been explored at greater length by Paul Ariès[18] and in the *Manifesto for a Happy Frugality* drawn up in 2018 by a group of European architects and engineers.[19] Raw earth is a natural material that not only maintains a comfortable temperature but also helps to create a warm and sensual built environment, with living textures and vibrant colours that offer visual, tactile, and emotional pleasures far beyond the reach of any industrialized material. It allows us to build a cocoon for a new way of life, an advanced civilization that can fulfil its basic needs without falling into the excesses of materialism. This lifestyle, nurtured by minimalism, has long been exemplified by Japan, guided by Zen philosophy and the aesthetic concept of *wabi-sabi*, which gives price of place to natural materials.

The freedom to disobey

An increasing number of the voices clamouring for renewal are also putting forward rational arguments in favour of moderation. This requires the kind of

Opposite: Detail of *Stairway to Heaven* (*Himmelstreppe*, 1980–87) by German artist Hannsjörg Voth, an architectural work of art built in the desert of southern Morocco. The structure's interior is divided into two levels, the lower of which briefly served as minimalist accommodation for the artist (see pp. 292–293 and 466–467).

'insurrection of the conscience' advocated by Swiss sociologist Jean Ziegler. A similar solution has been suggested by Indian scientist and philosopher Vandana Shiva, director of the Research Foundation for Science, Technology and Ecology. As an activist influenced by Gandhi, she practices what she calls 'creative civil disobedience',[20] combining transgressiveness and ingenuity. This bold approach has been borrowed by many of the architects, teachers, engineers, and business people who have contributed to the revival of earth architecture, and whose testimonies appear in this book (see chapter 8, 'Perspectives on the Future').[21] To reach this stage, these anti-establishment rebels have had to battle – often fiercely – against the many obstacles, hindrances, and threats that contemporary society and its (often ridiculous) rules and regulations have put in their way. Needless to say, many of these constraints protect the disproportionate interests of the multinational corporations that manufacture the very same industrialized construction materials that have such a dire impact on the environment.

The remarkable results obtained by these pioneers, who were dismissed only a few decades ago as utopian cranks, have now earned the praise of one of the most eminent architects of our times, Renzo Piano: 'They are showing the way. They are the standard bearers [with] a message that is vital to contemporary architectural thinking....Building with earth: the most accessible and widespread raw material, the richest and most beautiful.'[22] The future is therefore promising, unfettered by nostalgic, romantic, or reactionary references to earlier traditions of earth architecture. Now is the time for a great leap forward that does not lose sight of reality but steers us away from our present blind rush towards the abyss.

A wake-up call from the scientific community

The British economist Sir Nicholas Stern, former Senior Vice-President of the World Bank, has stated: 'The two greatest problems of our times – overcoming poverty in the developing world and combating climate change – are inextricably linked. Failure to tackle one will undermine efforts to deal with the other.'[23] This interconnectedness has been corroborated by self-build projects using earth (initially with external guidance), in locations such as the island of Mayotte,[24] which have demonstrated that access to decent housing and facilities such as schools and health centres is crucial to any long-lasting improvement in the living conditions of poorer populations.

In 1992, 1,700 experts signed the *World Scientists' Warning to Humanity*, in which they declared that 'we are fast approaching many of the earth's limits. Current economic practices which damage the environment, in both developed and underdeveloped nations, cannot be continued without the risk that vital global systems will be damaged beyond repair....A great change in our stewardship of the earth and the life on it is required, if vast human misery is to be avoided and our global home on this planet is not to be irretrievably mutilated.' In 2017, more than 15,000 scientists signed a second warning, in which they recommended 'drastically diminishing our per capita consumption of fossil fuels, meat, and other resources'. Once again, these policies find a natural ally in the energy-saving and respectful practices of earth architecture.

Reducing CO_2 emissions by 70% in 30 years

In 1988, the UN entrusted the Intergovernmental Panel on Climate Change (IPCC) with the mission to 'provide internationally coordinated scientific assessments of the magnitude, timing and potential environmental and socio-economic impact of climate change and realistic response strategies'. In an 'Approved Summary for Policymakers' published in 2014, the IPCC concluded that CO_2 emissions are 'extremely likely to have been the dominant cause of the observed warming since the mid-20th century', but it also stated that 'Emissions scenarios leading to [lower] GHG [greenhouse gas] concentrations in 2100…are likely to maintain warming below 2°C over the 21st century relative to pre-industrial levels. These scenarios are characterized by 40% to 70% global anthropogenic GHG emissions reductions by 2050 compared to 2010.' Nevertheless, global CO_2 emissions increased by 2.7% in 2018 alone. The colossal task of reducing CO_2 emissions proposed by the IPCC requires a radical change in building policies – and in this context, raw earth has a strategic role to play.

Less is more

French economist Thomas Porcher has said: 'Everybody knows what has to be done to effectively combat global warming: 1) The massive development of renewable energies; 2) Control of energy consumption; 3) The development of local, circular economies. These ideas crop up in politicians' speeches but no government wants to put them into practice. If we are to confront the challenge of climate change, we must scrutinize our current models of production and consumption.'[25] Extensive use of raw earth in construction can contribute to these goals – in fact, it only makes sense within the confines of a local circular economy, even in an urban setting.[26]

Edgar Morin, the French sociologist and philosopher, declared that the 'seeds of a new contemporary civilization are partially present everywhere, but they remain insufficient and scattered. Our civilization trumpeted material well-being but has succumbed to a spiritual malaise. We have to rethink the very notion of "development". It creates more problems than it solves. Even "sustainable development" cannot be maintained over time. The quantitative "more, more!" needs to be replaced by the qualitative "less is more"....The instigation of new forms of solidarity is another essential aspect of the politics of civilization [that] posits an objective absent from any political programme: the need to change our lives, especially in the sense of the quality and the poetry of life.'[27] It is clear that the contemporary applications of raw earth are countless, but they are also scattered and insufficiently recognized – a state of affairs that this book seeks to remedy.

Daring to act

Progress now requires an act of daring. In fact, *Osons*[28] ('Let's Dare') was the title of a call to action published in 2015 by Nicolas Hulot (born 1955), the ecological activist who was appointed France's Minister for Ecological and Inclusive Transition in 2017; he resigned in frustration 15 months later, in order to convey his disapproval of the government's inconsistencies. In *Osons*, Hulot observes: 'Although awareness is rising, its translation into tangible effects is laughable when compared to the acceleration of the phenomena [of climate change] that we are meant to be bringing to a standstill. We are well endowed technologically but culturally deprived. ...Let's dare to finally look reality in the face: we are poisoning the Earth just as much as our own arteries....Let's dare to declare that the ecological crisis is the ultimate injustice: it strikes hardest at the most impoverished. ...Let's dare to say that the fatalism of some sparks the fanaticism of others: never forget that the cause of ecology is the cornerstone of human dignity and social justice....Let's dare to say that another

world is already possible, but what we lack is a universal spirit, a collective intelligence, vision, and will....Let's dare to say that capitalist violence has colonized every circle of power, and that we must recover our grip on industry ...which ignores the public interest: let us smash this cannibalistic order....Let's dare to achieve humility and moderation, insolence and utopia.... The definition of madness is to repeat the same action indefinitely but expect different results: let's dare not to be mad any more. Change is underway in every field; solutions do exist, but they are often too little known. Tribute must be paid to all those agents of change who are creating the world of tomorrow. Their example is worth more than all the praise heaped on brilliant exceptions. As we confront the enormous challenge of climate change, we must give these isolated initiatives the means to become the practices of tomorrow. Now is the time to radically change the paradigm and connect these social and economic innovations with the fight against climate change: [by inventing a new modernity] we build an alliance between the best of science and technology and the wisdom of the past.'

Architecture as a catalyst for change?

Cyril Dion is the co-director of the film *Demain* (*Tomorrow*), which showcases a selection of the most successful recent initiatives in applied ecology. In his book, *Petit manuel de resistance contemporaine*, Dion declares that 'throughout history, it is tales and stories that have most powerfully conveyed philosophical, ethical, and political transformations. These stories enable us to embark upon an authentic "revolution", but if they are to emerge and manifest themselves in economic and social structures, it is vital to change the architecture that determines our everyday behaviour.'[29] Our book seeks to throw light on the unknown story of raw earth architecture in order to contribute to the debate, while avoiding the naive belief that a single material can offer a miracle solution. Instead, it should be seen as just one element in a broad range of strategies.

The most enlightening description of the art of building came from Winston Churchill: 'We shape our buildings, thereafter they shape us.' Of all the spheres of art and culture, architecture is the one that influences our lives in the most lasting way, whether we are aware of it or not, and it also has a profound effect on our behaviour, mood, and health. Architecture supplies our material and psychological environment throughout our lives: we sleep, work, eat, study, and spend leisure time in buildings, for better or for worse, often without ever thinking about it. Architecture can therefore be considered a major component in our way of life, but it is almost never mentioned in debates on ecological transition – except in demands to improve buildings' thermal insulation in order to reduce their energy consumption. Although this is an important point, it is only one of the improvements that are needed in the field of construction. A truly ecological form of architecture can and must contribute to a shift in the social paradigm. The art of earth architecture will allow us a better life on Earth.

Above: Unbuilt design for a 15-storey apartment block in Paris, with a facade incorporating prefabricated rammed earth elements (2015). Architects: Joly & Loiret.

Opposite: The Ricola Herb Centre in Laufen, Switzerland, built using prefabricated rammed earth by Martin Rauch (2014). Architects: Herzog & de Meuron, winners of the 2001 Pritzker Prize.

Notes

1. See the bibliography on p. 496.
2. For more on the Domaine de la Terre, see pp. 392–395.
3. See the new neighbourhood planned for Ivry-sur-Seine, on the outskirts of Paris, pp. 472–473.
4. See the essays by Hubert Guillaud, p. 31, and Dominique Gauzin-Müller, p. 24.
5. See the essays by Hugo Houben and Henri Van Damme, pp. 36 and 38.
6. See the essay by Romain Anger, p. 22.
7. Lester R. Brown, *Eco-Economy: Building an Economy for the Earth*, New York: W.W. Norton & Co., 2001.
8. Particularly architect Anna Heringer, in Germany, and CRAterre engineer Hugo Houben, in France.
9. Paul Hawken. Amory B. Lovins, and L. Hunter Lovins, *Natural Capitalism: The Next Industrial Revolution*, New York: Little, Brown, 1999.
10. *Comment nous allons sauver le monde, manifeste pour une justice climatique*, Paris: Massot, 2019.
11. Étienne Guyon (ed.), *Du merveilleux caché dans le quotidien, la physique de l'élégance*, Paris: Flammarion, 2018.
12. Andre Gorz, 'Ecologie, politique et liberté', in *Andre Gorz, un penseur pour le XXIe siècle*, Paris: La Découverte, 2009.
13. John F. C. Turner, *Freedom to Build: Dweller Control of the Housing Process*, New York: Macmillan, 1972.
14. Ivan D. Illich, *Celebration of Awareness: A Call for Institutional Revolution*, Garden City, NY: Doubleday, 1970.
15. Hans Jonas, *The Imperative of Responsibility: In Search of an Ethics for the Technological Age* (1979), Chicago: University of Chicago Press, 1984.
16. Ulrich Beck, *Twenty Observations on a World in Turmoil*, Cambridge: Polity Press, 2012.
17. Dominique Bourg, *Une nouvelle Terre*, Paris: Desclée de Brouwer, 2018.
18. Paul Ariès, *La simplicité volontaire contre le mythe de l'abondance*, Paris: La Découverte, 2010.
19. http://www.frugalite.org/en/le-manifeste.html
20. Lionel Astruc, *Vandana Shiva: Creative Civil Disobedience*, trans. Shannon Viviès, Arles: Actes Sud, 2017.
21. See the texts by Lara K. Davis, p. 485; Dominique Gauzin-Müller, p. 486; Anna Heringer, p. 483; Sébastien Moriset, p. 484; Martin Rauch, p. 482; and S. K. Sharma, p. 480.
22. Extract from the foreword to Anger & Fontaine 2009.
23. Nicholas Stern, *A Blueprint for a Safer Planet: How to Manage Climate Change and Create a New Era of Progress and Prosperity*, London: Bodley Head, 2009.
24. See the text on the project on the island of Mayotte, p. 382.
25. Thomas Porcher, *Traité d'économie hérétique, pour en finir avec le discours dominant*, Paris: Fayard, 2018.
26. See the text by Hugo Gasnier, pp. 478–479.
27. Edgar Morin, *Mes philosophes*, Paris: Fayard, 2013.
28. Hulot 2015.
29. Cyril Dion, *Petit manuel de résistance contemporaine, récits and stratégies pour transformer le monde*, Arles: Actes Sud, 2018.

The Ecological Merits of Raw Earth Construction

Hubert Guillaud

Any consideration of the ecological benefits of earth architecture requires an assessment of the impact of building as a whole on our natural, social, economic, and cultural environments. This issue cannot be divorced from a critique of the current model of growth and its disastrous impact on our planet, on humanity, and on all living species. Any attempt to 'free the future' from the hegemonic model that is exhausting natural resources and depleting indigenous cultures will inevitably lead to one unavoidable conclusion: we must think, act, and build in a different way.

It is vital to adopt action strategies inspired by the proposals set out in a 1999 UNESCO report by the philosopher and sociologist Edgar Morin to encourage complex, multidisciplinary, and global thinking. There is an urgent need to establish conditions that will allow for creative diversity and lead to solutions that are socially and economically fair and viable, as well as compatible with global cultures and respectful of the environment. Accordingly, raw earth construction has a strong subversive potential as it possesses eco-responsible values and virtues. In contrast with the domination of industrial building materials, which require elaborate and costly manufacturing techniques, raw earth is widespread and readily available. It can be utilized in many ways: it may be rammed or compressed into bricks, or used as cob, adobe, or wattle and daub. It remains close to nature as it is barely transformed, and its use means saving rarer, nonrenewable resources, as well as reducing industrial pollution and the use of fossil fuels (it expends very little grey energy). Earth architecture therefore helps us establish a more balanced relationship with our environment.

Earth architecture also subverts the dominant economic model by giving the public, particularly those most in need, the ability to take control of their own environment. It also promotes key social values, such as self-sufficiency, cooperative and participatory organization, mutual aid, bartering, and autonomy in both production of materials and construction. Building sites are turned into a significant source of employment and can give rise to small and medium businesses and local micro-industries.

Earth architecture has many other advantages. It overturns globalized production standards by promoting a huge diversity of cultural identities. It contributes to regional development by benefiting local people. It revives the tangible and intangible values and the vernacular and scholarly legacies of societies whose architectural treasures are often classified as UNESCO World Heritage sites. It revitalizes architectural production by promoting art and crafts and rehumanizes the act of building by restoring the dignity and pride of the people involved in it. Earth architecture also preserves the human scale of architectural production. It empowers builders to embrace logic, reason, and wisdom; common sense; and ecological responsibility; and demonstrates the value of restraint in opposition to the arrogance of contemporary architecture and its worship of technique and formal innovation at any price.

In this way, the resurgence of earth architecture is playing a part in the reclamation of a primary economy based on relationships and noncommercial exchanges that stimulate the senses, the capacity to love, to cooperate, to feel, to connect with others, to live at peace with one's body and with nature. The modernization of earth architecture represents a call to establish ecologically responsible ethics for the field of construction, and helps to open up a 'path for the future of humanity'.

```
Further reading:
Houben & Guillaud 1994; Morin 1999
```

Opposite: Aerial view of a village in Mali, north of Mopti, with a central mosque (see pp. 200–213).

Earth Architecture and Changes to the Social Paradigm

Romain Anger

'It is too late to achieve sustainable development.... It is essential now to put more emphasis on raising the resilience of the system.' This was the opinion expressed by Dennis Meadows in 2012. Back in 1972, the original Meadows Report, entitled *The Limits to Growth*, the result of research commissioned from MIT by the Club of Rome, used systems dynamics and contemporary computer technology to model a 'world system' that took into account the interactions between populations, food, industry, nonrenewable resources, and pollution. The simulations predicted that, in the absence of major global political change, the economy would collapse, leading to a drop in the world's population due to a food and health crisis. Forty years ago, it was theoretically possible to slow things down and reach a balance. Now it is no longer possible. What lies ahead is likely a period of uncontrolled decline, which will bring us to some new equilibrium whose details we cannot yet know.

At the time the Meadows Report was published, 12 million copies were printed, it was translated into 27 languages, and it was read by all world leaders. It went on to influence the earliest Earth Summits, which themselves led, in 1987, to the publication of *Our Common Future*, also known as the Brundtland Report, which provided the first-ever definition of sustainable development. Now, in 2019, the 'future generations' referred to in the report have already been born. The latest IPCC report is more alarming than ever, and 2018 saw a 2.7% worldwide increase in CO_2 emissions. In the words of Edgar Morin, 'We have not yet recognized that we are moving at full tilt towards a catastrophe, like sleepwalkers.' In the Anthropocene epoch, the human race has become a geological force that is undermining the lithosphere, knocking the planet's geochemical and biological cycles out of kilter, and destroying its ecosystems. The leaders of the major economic powers are incapable of changing course, changing our future direction, or imagining the cultural change that could free us from the dogma of growth.

A transition of this kind would require a paradigm shift: a new and different representation of our world, another vision for the near future, a more coherent model for civilization. According to Carl Gustav Jung, 'Having a worldview [*Weltanschauung*] means forming an image of the world and of oneself, knowing what the world is, knowing what one is.'

We are now in the midst of the troubling decline that the analysis of the Meadows and Brundtland Reports predicted. We content ourselves with an ecology of repair, patching up our damaged planet using the same mindset that created the problems in the first place. In the field of architecture, this worldview is manifested in technological attempts to enhance a building's energy efficiency at any price, even if that enhancement endangers the harmony between humans and their environment. We must take onboard a new paradigm: an ecology of resilience. All human creations, including architecture, are reflections of a specific worldview. The main problem with today's buildings – the results of an ideology inherited a century ago by the modernist movement – is their decontextualization, their 'un-grounded' design, their detachment from their environment. They are a reflection of the people who construct them: rootless, disembodied. And as long as we fail to repair the connection that has been broken between us and the planet, we shall remain stuck in an ecology of repair. The roots that are so essential to us grow, by definition, from the earth: they are submerged in its raw material. The people of today ignore earth, water, and air, elements vital to their existence, and have an unhealthy relationship with the natural world. We have lost any awareness of ourselves as porous creatures, who are subject to these elements at all times. Instead, we view those elements as abstract entities, lumping them together under the umbrella of 'the environment'. Polluting the oceans, overheating the atmosphere, treating the earth as a garbage dump – all of these things ultimately mean contaminating our own bodies. Augustin Berque defined this worldview as follows: 'We distinguish matter, flesh, and spirit. This is like drawing distinctions between the planet, which is purely physico-chemical; the biosphere, which contains life; and the ecumene, or inhabited world, which adds human technological and symbolic systems. Again and again we find this triad: matter, flesh, and spirit.' Following Jacques Derrida, we could deconstruct the binary couples underlying this contemporary cosmology, derived from a Cartesian dualism that separates and compartmentalizes: human and nonhuman, nature and culture, spirit and matter, the humanities and the sciences, rational thought and feeling, hand and brain, etc. Some philosophers have tried to go beyond this modern paradigm – Maurice Merleau-Ponty, for example, for whom the body 'is made of the same flesh as the world'. The cosmologies of traditional societies offer alternative representations of matter and the body. David Le Breton gives an example: 'Among the Kanak people, the body borrows traits from the vegetable kingdom. A nondetached fragment of the universe that surrounds it, its existence [is] intertwined with trees, fruits, plants….*Kara* means both the skin of a person and the bark of a tree. The combination of flesh and muscles (*pie*) also means the pulp or stone of a fruit. The hard part of the body, the skeleton, is denoted by the same word as the core of wood.' This worldview gives rise to other ways of conceiving, producing, and experiencing the environment around us. These concepts are made real in striking and inventive ways by vernacular architecture built with raw earth. Of all the organic materials, earth has, by far, the most powerful symbolic and sentimental weight. The emotional charge of some of these buildings born of folk art is derived precisely from the fact that they are not cut off and separated from their surroundings. They are still contextual; rooted in the land, they are at one with the soil from which they have been built; they make us feel in the depths of our being that matter is the flesh of architecture. Matter is also the flesh of the world and the flesh of being. It is our flesh. It connects us with ourselves and with the world.

Everything that we produce as human beings, including our built environment, should generate life rather than destroy it. How can we inhabit the Earth while also contributing to biodiversity? Technological responses based entirely on a building's energy efficiency are not enough. The city of tomorrow must be resilient and autonomous, and it can therefore no longer depend on fossil fuels: it must be carbon-free. It must be a living thing, the product of a circular economy, consuming its own waste and refuse, just like any living ecosystem. Our city of the future must also be sensual and physical, by favouring the inclusion of natural materials such as stone, wood, and raw earth in urban settings. Children must be able to understand the built environment around them. Finally, all the spaces of everyday life must preserve biodiversity, encroach as little as possible on the wilderness, and re-establish harmonious relationships with the plant and animal kingdoms.

The dream of building with raw earth mixed with wood and 'biosourced' insulation in urban settings (as in Paris, where this innovative process has been underway since 2017) must become the norm. Wood provides the framework or skeleton, the load-bearing structure that makes it possible to build housing blocks of five storeys (or more). Plant fibres such as straw and hemp provide thermal insulation, while the raw earth that coats the framework forms the epidermis, the protective skin. The insulating wood and fibre turns the walls into 'carbon wells'. The earth in these walls must also be waste material, following the logic of the circular economy, in order to make use of the millions of tons of excavated earth that are regularly extracted from the urban subsoil and then stored at great expense on sites beyond the city limits. We must build with earth, with this immense but hitherto neglected resource that lies under our feet. We must build with the soil beneath our cities, realign ourselves with our environment, and become one with the natural order once again.

The Benefits and Limitations of Earth Architecture

Dominique Gauzin-Müller

The contemporary use of raw earth architecture has become increasingly frequent and diverse, reflecting an alternative form of modernity that responds to the challenges of the global ecological crisis. Given the pressing need to drastically reduce greenhouse gas emissions and slow down climate change, this abundant, energy-saving natural material has enormous potential. Its many architectural advantages have been empirically observed for thousands of years but now they have also been scientifically proven.

Environmental benefits

Renewable and abundant Soil is created via the weathering of parent rock, sometimes with the addition of river and wind deposits. Its use as a building material poses no threat to agriculture, which utilizes the uppermost layer, topsoil, which is rich in organic matter. Only the subsoil layers, primarily made up of minerals, are used in construction. This form of earth is available in a great variety of colours and textures, with different physical properties. This diversity, along with the histories and sociocultural characteristics of each region, have led to the development of a range of building techniques. The main ones are adobe, cob, wattle and daub, and rammed earth, all of which have several variant forms.

Natural and ecological Earth is easy to extract for building purposes, even with rudimentary tools. No chemical processes and very little energy are required, and it leaves no waste products. It does not pollute the air, soil, or groundwater layer, nor does it destroy the landscape. Earth is taken directly from the ground and is sometimes combined with other natural materials (straw, hemp, linen, etc.). To be considered truly eco-friendly, it should not be mixed with chemical additives, but legislation in many countries requires it to be 'stabilized' with cement or lime.

Energy-saving The 'grey' energy consumption[1] of earth architecture depends on the building techniques used, but it is usually low and can be almost negligible. Not only does the transformation of the raw material into building material require little energy, but sometimes no transport is required either: earth is often extracted on site, or close by. The reclamation of construction waste, especially from large-scale urban developments, can create eco-friendly building materials and also removes the need for costly waste-treatment processes in distant locations. Moreover, the carbon dioxide emissions resulting from the transformation of excavated soil into building material are considerably lower than those created in the production of concrete.

Technical advantages

Strong and durable Traditional architecture shows that raw earth is mechanically strong. Shibam, in Yemen, boasts seven-storey earth buildings that date back to the 16th century (see pp. 108–111), while several four- and five-storey rammed earth buildings in Lyon, France, have been occupied since the early 19th century. Earth is compatible with all climate types – even rain, when designed to provide sufficient protection from above and below. Contemporary examples are increasingly numerous and include three-storey residential buildings with supporting walls of rammed earth, found in France (see pp. 392–395) and Austria (see pp. 406–407).

Repairable and recyclable If raw earth has not been 'stabilized' with cement or lime, walls can be repaired easily and imperceptibly; retouching will leave no trace as long as the original mixture is used. Raw earth can also be recycled indefinitely. When a building reaches the end of its lifespan, its walls can be demolished and immediately returned to the soil or reused in a new construction project.

Communal and easy to handle Although some earth construction techniques require professional training, earth is well suited to collective building. It does not pose any risk of disease to workers and it causes no allergies. Nor does it irritate the eyes or skin. It is equally suited both to communal building projects and to small-scale self-builds. It can also be combined with other building materials, both traditional and contemporary, and it is particularly useful for renovation projects, as it can be readily applied over the irregularities of older walls. All in all, raw earth can meet many of the requirements of housing and community facilities in both developing and industrialized countries.

Above: Five-storey public housing block, built with rammed earth and stabilized earth blocks as part of the Domaine de la Terre project (1983–1985) in Villefontaine, France (see pp. 392–395). Architect: Jean-Vincent Berlottier.

Comfort and aesthetics

Warm and sensual Earth lends itself to a minimalist aesthetic, in keeping with the current Western trend towards creative frugality. It is a living material with a rich texture and a wide range of natural colours, from dark grey to bright yellow, with multiple shades of pink and red in between. This attractive diversity can be showcased in walls made from multiple layers of rammed earth. A comforting material with a strong emotional charge, earth has become popular with a growing number of architects and homeowners for both the beauty of its shimmering, textured surfaces and its vast colour palette.

Hygienic and comfortable Interior walls and finishes made from raw earth create a healthy living environment as they absorb smells and do not give off toxic by-products. Raw earth's granular structure, porosity, and propensity for phase changes (shifts between liquid and gaseous states) allow steam to pass through it. This creates a form of natural hygrometric regulation: excess humidity is absorbed and balance is maintained. Moreover, dense, heavy earth walls possess the property of thermal inertia,[2] meaning that heat exchanges between the exterior and interior occur very slowly: the heat that accumulates in the walls during the day is dispersed inside the building at night. Accordingly, raw earth houses stay cool in summer and warm in winter. Compact earth walls also block out sounds from outside and absorb noises made within, while their porosity prevents the reverberation of sounds inside.

Limitations The use of raw earth in construction does have some limitations, however, and as a result it must sometimes be combined with other materials. In order to prevent capillary action, earth walls are generally built on a concrete, brick, or stone base. Moreover, beyond a certain height or width, earth must be supplemented with wood, concrete, or steel. Nowadays, however, many limitations on the use of raw earth are derived from overly strict or inappropriate regulations based on a lack of knowledge about the material's capabilities. These obstacles must be overcome through informed dialogue and collaboration between decision-makers and users of raw earth: architects, engineers, artisans, property developers, official institutions, design offices, local authority departments, etc. Earth architecture can also be constrained by longstanding psychological and cultural obstacles, particularly in developing countries, where concrete breeze blocks have become a symbol of progress, despite the fact that these technologies have a major impact on greenhouse gas emissions and climate change.

1   The energy consumed over the life cycle of a material through extraction, manufacturing, transport, use, recycling, etc.
2   The capacity of a material to retain heat and gradually discharge it.

Maps

Earth architecture is found on all inhabited continents and in most countries around the world, whatever their local climate. More than seventy countries are featured in this book.
  J.D. & R.E.

Above left: Map of France. In orange: regions where rammed earth construction is predominant. In red: the southwest region where the use of raw earth bricks (adobe) is common. In yellow: regions where the use of wattle and daub is common (source: CRAterre).

Above right: Map of Great Britain. In red: regions in which various traditional techniques of earth construction were once common (source: Ruth Eaton).

Below: Map of the world. The orange areas are regions where raw earth construction is a traditional practice. The red dots indicate major examples of earth architecture that are listed as UNESCO World Heritage sites (source: CRAterre).

Opposite, above left: Map of southwest Europe (Portugal, Spain, Italy, France). The colours refer to the four main traditional techniques of raw earth construction. In yellow: rammed earth. In red: raw earth bricks (adobe). In blue: cob. In green: wattle and daub (source: Terra Incognita).

Opposite, above right: Map of China. In orange: regions where various traditional techniques of raw earth construction were in use prior to the 1960s (source: Mu Jun).

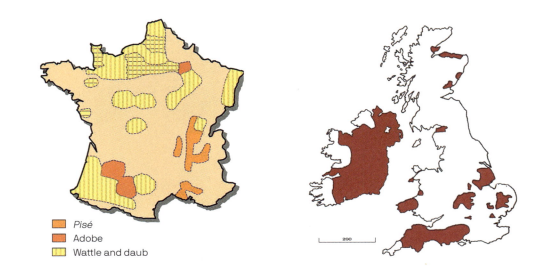

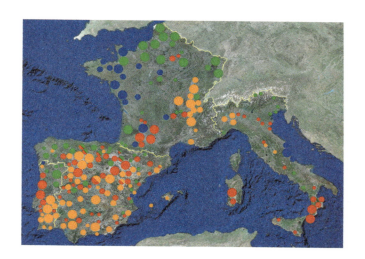
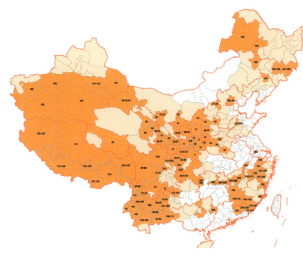
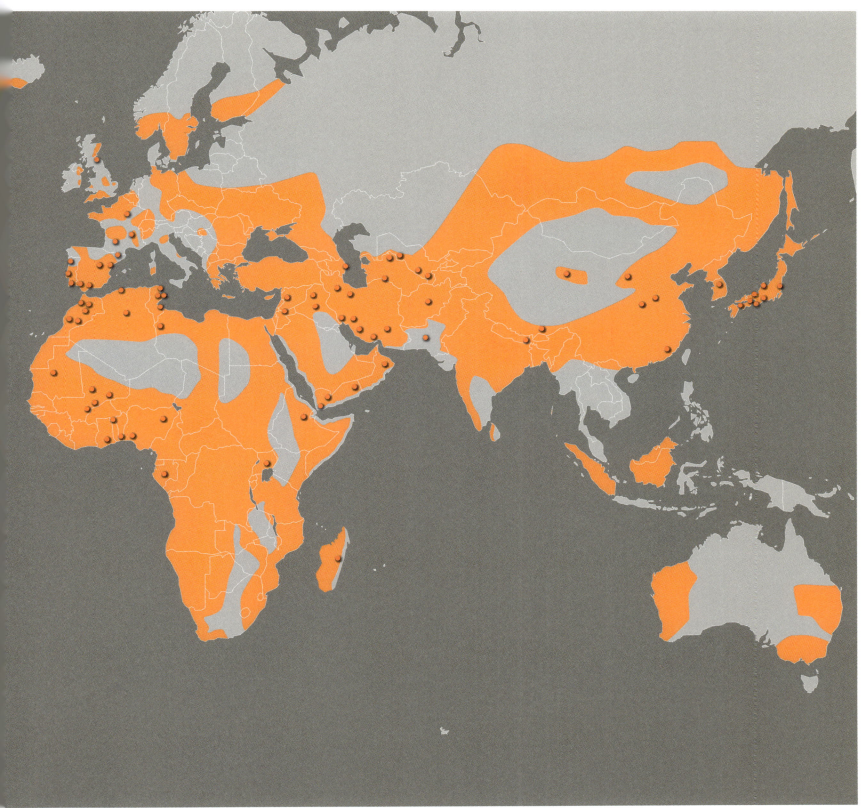

In Praise of Earth Architecture

Chapter 1

Constructional Logic

Building walls with cob (*zabour*) near the town of Sa'dah, Yemen (see pp. 48–49). See also pp. 242–245 for similar uses of this technique in Saudi Arabia

Diagram by CRAterre showing the twelve main techniques used in earth architecture, as explained opposite.

An Overview of Traditional Methods of Raw Earth Construction

Hubert Guillaud

The range of technical and architectural possibilities offered by raw earth is large and varied. The study of vernacular traditions and skills all over the world – coupled with an inventory of modern and contemporary buildings – allows us to identify a dozen different ways of using this material. Earth architecture has many potential uses in many settings – family and communal, domestic and institutional, rural and urban – and over the centuries, it has evolved into a veritable art form.

Since the Enlightenment, raw earth construction has undergone three main phases of development. In the late 18th century, the first modernization phase was initiated by François Cointeraux in France and quickly spread to other countries (see pp. 308–317). In the second half of the 20th century, major cultural, scientific, technological, and educational advances occurred, and these allowed the field to expand further. Finally, the early years of the 21st century have seen the start of a promising new phase in earth architecture's worldwide growth, most notably as an eco-friendly response to the dangers of climate change and the need for a transition to green energy.

The numbering of the paragraphs below matches the diagram shown opposite, devised by CRAterre and first published in *Treatise on Earthen Construction* (1989).

Twelve ways to use raw earth

The twelve primary raw earth building techniques can be divided into three groups. In the first, earth is used to create a preliminary load-bearing structure. In the second, it is used as a monolithic mass. In the last, it takes the form of multiple smaller masonry elements.

1: Dug-out. An architectural space is formed by digging out a hollow in the Earth's surface. This method is most closely associated with cave houses. The earth may be excavated horizontally (there are numerous examples of this in Spain, Italy, and Turkey) or vertically. Two outstanding examples of the latter technique are the underground houses of the village of Matmata, in southern Tunisia, and the *yaodongs* (house caves) that dot the so-called Loess Belt in China.

2: Earth sheltering. Earth is used to form a protective covering over a structure built from other materials (usually wood), as in flat or sloping 'sod roofs' or 'turf roofs' that are covered with grass or other plants.

3: Fill-in. Raw earth is used to fill hollow spaces in a building's framework (which may or may not be load-bearing). Several methods have been tested, including using loose earth or an earth-based agglomerate to fill hollow concrete blocks, fabric earthbags (SuperAdobe), insulating layers, interior or exterior lattices, and wooden frames with interstitial spaces.

4: Cut blocks. Blocks of turf or clay of various sizes are cut directly from the ground in regular shapes and used as masonry units. These blocks are known by different names in different parts of the world: *tepetate* in Mexico, 'caliche' in the United States, *mergel* in the Netherlands, and 'marl' in the UK.

5: Compressed earth. A range of building materials can be made by compressing earth in wooden or steel moulds or formworks, or by using a press. The first press to be used for this purpose was the portable, manually operated Cinva-Ram, invented by Raúl Ramírez in Colombia in 1952. It met with worldwide success because it allowed many sectors of society to build their own homes with easily produced compressed earth bricks (CEB) that could be stabilized with cement if required. A host of similar presses subsequently appeared on the international market, with two proving particularly effective: the Terstaram, invented in Belgium by Fernand Platbrood; and the Auram, developed by the Auroville Earth Institute in India (see pp. 384–385). Meanwhile, more sophisticated mechanical and pneumatic presses have been produced to cover the needs of large-scale building projects. The other major building technique based on the compression of raw earth is rammed earth, sometimes known by the French term *pisé*, and as *tapia* in the Spanish-speaking world. Contemporary developments in rammed earth are so numerous that the technique is discussed in greater detail later in this book.

6: Direct shaping. Earth in pliable form can be used to shape thin walls by hand. The most common method of constructing a building in this way is to use rolls of clay (like those used to make a coil pot), or braided or twisted vegetable fibres soaked in clay and layered vertically to make a wall. These ancient rural techniques can be found in Mexico but they are especially common in sub-Saharan Africa, among, for example, the Musgum people in Cameroon (see pp. 228–229), the Lobi in Burkina Faso, and the Batammariba in Togo (see pp. 226–227).

7: Stacked earth. Earth shaped into balls can be stacked in layers to form thick load-bearing walls. This type of construction is now rarely used in Europe, although there are still many cottages in Devon and elsewhere in the UK that bear witness to its traditional use (under the name of cob), while the village of Milton Abbas, dating from 1773, is a striking early example of the modernization of this method (see pp. 260–261). The same technique can be found in villages in Yemen, in the city of Najran in Saudi Arabia, in Afghanistan, and in Senegal.

8: Moulded earth. This refers to earth shaped by hand or using a mould, in order to form blocks or bricks that are usually dried in the sun before use. The material is often enriched with vegetable fibres – straw and local plants – to avoid shrinkage and improve resistance. This construction technique is often called 'adobe', a Spanish term derived from the Arabic word for 'brick', *at-tub*, and ultimately from the Egyptian words *tôôbe* or *tôbi*. In Africa, the term *banco* is widely used, while handmade pear-shaped bricks known as *tubali* can be found in some countries, such as Nigeria. In the United States, the term 'adobe' is often used more broadly to denote any type of raw earth structure.

9: Extruded earth. Derived from the industrial methods used to produce fired bricks, raw earth is mechanically extruded through a mould to create regular bricks, panels, or units. This technique has been used in the US and in Germany – the so-called Dünne 'loam loaf' technique invented in the mid-1920s (see p. 52) – and more recently experiments have been carried out at Kassel University. Research was also done in France in the 1980s, leading to the production of bricks and panels made from stabilized and extruded raw earth (under the brand name Stargil), but ultimately this line of investigation did not bear significant fruit.

10: Poured earth. Earth in a liquid state – with the consistency of sand or sometimes gravel – is poured into formworks or multipiece moulds, like thin concrete. This process is used to build monolithic walls layer by layer, and also for floors and small architectural elements. Its major drawbacks are shrinkage and cracking, but recent research has started to provide new ways of dealing with these issues.

11: Straw-clay and light clay. Earth in the form of liquid clay is mixed with straw, grass, or even heather, resulting in a material with a very fibrous appearance. In Germany, this mixture of earth and straw is generally compacted into blocks in a basic mould made from planks clamped together, then used to fill in the spaces in a timber framework; a thickness of 20 to 25 centimetres is suitable for a non-load-bearing wall, while 30 to 40 centimetres is preferred for load-bearing walls. The same mixture can also be made into flooring slabs, while its low density (600–1,200 kilograms per cubic metre) makes it good for insulation. The technique is currently in use in many European countries, as it is cheap and readily accessible.

12: Wattle and daub. Malleable earth is mixed with plant fibres and used to fill gaps in a load-bearing framework (generally made of wood), over a lattice of interwoven wood or bamboo. This process is probably one of the oldest construction techniques known to humankind. Many examples, both rural and urban, can be found in France (particularly in Normandy, Picardy, Alsace, and Champagne), Britain, Germany, Belgium, the Netherlands, and Scandinavia, as well as in Africa and Latin America.

Recent innovations

Since the dawn of the 21st century, considerable advances in traditional building practices have been made by combining basic research into raw earth and granular materials with practical experiments. This research has been driven by two primary objectives. The first of these has been combining raw earth with other materials (concrete, steel, stone, wood, and new composite materials), in order to remove its somewhat marginal status – previously, it was widely believed to be unsuitable for the new challenges of mass-produced housing and increasingly ambitious demands for structural performance. It was also an attempt to improve the image of earth architecture, which was frequently deemed obsolete. Secondly, earth was reassessed to see whether it could respond to the demands of cost-effectiveness, in terms of reduced construction time and labour costs, in keeping with an economy based on growth and profit.

Contemporary trends

Prefabricated elements were first introduced into rammed earth construction in France in the 1980s by the master builder Nicolas Meunier (who originally trained as a ceramicist). In the 21st century, this construction process has advanced in leaps and bounds, mainly thanks to the Austrian entrepreneur Martin Rauch, and it has become integrated into building practice. This crucial development has opened up new horizons for contemporary earth architecture and given it an aura of modernity that has been reflected in media coverage. For example, prefabricated earth elements play a prominent role in Salvatierra, a six-storey apartment block in Rennes, France, built in 2003 by the architect Jean-Yves Barrier (see pp. 402–403). It features cob on its facade.

Research into granular materials has also produced promising results. Mechanical resistance has been improved because particles of different sizes can be stacked more efficiently, and the relationship between the three components of matter – minerals (the particles themselves), water, and air – is now better understood. These advances have resulted in better quality control of the basic materials used in earth architecture – wattle and daub, cob, adobe, compressed earth bricks (CEB) – and matched by progress in rheology (the study of the flow of matter), which has opened up the possibility of developing 'earth concrete' that can be poured into frameworks. This promising line of research is still dependent, however, on the addition of chemical dispersants and stabilizers (such as cement or lime), but it is to be hoped that ongoing research into natural dispersants may soon make it possible to produce 'green concrete' or 'eco-concrete'.

Research into lightening earth by adding natural fibres such as hemp hurds or shives has led to the development of high-performance, hygrometric 'clay concrete' that optimizes the material's porosity. Denser mineral particles are replaced by more porous particles from plant sources. Current research is experimenting with compounds that will increase the absorption of water vapour and so help regulate environmental humidity, increasing the comfort of those living in earth buildings. Furthermore, different earthen elements can be used for different parts of a building: bricks or blocks of various sizes for load-bearing walls, panels for dividing walls, and lightweight 'hempcrete'.

Another recent line of research is based on the 3D printing of architectural elements and the use of robots that can apply layers of earth mortar quickly and precisely to build walls. It could be argued, however, that this approach demonstrates an obsession with technological innovation and a subservience to the values of our industrial society. We must not forget the greatest benefit of the art of earth architecture: it is a vital contribution towards building a sustainable future.

```
Further reading:
CRAterre 1979; Houben & Guillaud 1994; Anger & Fontaine
2009; Volhard 2015; Moevus-Dorvaux et al. 2016
```

Minaret in the village of Zinzana, Ségou region, Mali (see pp. 202–209).

Geology and Materials

Patrice Doat

The Earth's crust is more than four billion years old and it has provided scientific evidence that has furthered our understanding of the origins of our planet, which primarily consists of land, water, and air. The Earth is protected by a mineral shell but it is constantly exposed to the elements (rain, wind, snow, ice, and thaws), which wear down the rocks of mountain massifs. The resulting fragments are carried downhill by avalanches and end up in rivers and lakes. After this long journey, the splinters of mineral matter are widely dispersed and eventually spread across the world's land masses. This granular substance, known as earth, is made up of pebbles, shingle, sand, silt, and clay and is available almost everywhere. Once it is mixed with water, it can easily be turned into a building material.

From the earliest civilizations right up to the present day, human beings have used these two ingredients – earth and water – to build both rural and urban settlements on every continent, in every kind of climate. One particularly striking example is the Nile Valley in Egypt: for thousands of years, the silt swept along by the river and deposited on its banks has been the main raw material in the adobe bricks used to build the vast majority of the country's housing.

For both builders and farmers, water is the vital complement to earth. In the late 18th century, under the sway of the Enlightenment, François Cointeraux envisaged a new scientific discipline, 'agriteture', that would unite the realms of architecture and agriculture. He anticipated by two centuries today's research into 'green architecture' and 'urban agriculture'. His pioneering ideas transcended the distinction between town and country and proposed that the management of land should take into account the specific biological and geographical features of its ecosystems. Another important legacy of Cointeraux's philosophy is his emphasis on water as a fundamental component of all raw earth architecture.

How Raw Earth Buildings Stand the Test of Time

Hugo Houben and Henri Van Damme

Raw earth is made up of myriad mineral particles in a multitude of shapes and sizes. On closer examination, the numbers involved are truly mind-boggling. For example, a rammed earth wall 1 m long, 2.5 m high and 40 cm thick contains around 6,000 trillion particles. The largest of these particles – roughly spherical pebbles up to 5 cm in diameter – are 25,000 times bigger than the smallest ones, clay platelets that measure less than 0.002 mm. The only way to truly grasp this enormous quantity of particles would be to count them, but at a counting speed of 1 particle per second, the task would take 19 billion years – longer than the entire lifespan of the universe (13.8 billion years)!

Particle stacking If a wall is to be solid and resilient, it needs to be extremely dense, as any empty space represents a potential breaking point. To attain this, it's vital to control the granularity of the material, i.e. the proportion of particles of a particular diameter, as the aim is to fill any empty spaces left between large particles. Each particle must be positioned in a way that makes the mixture as homogeneous as possible. An even consistency is therefore another prerequisite. While this is easy to achieve with liquids, it is much harder with granular materials because of the natural tendency of particles to group together according to their size. A wall is not merely a pile of particles, but a sturdy configuration that can stay upright by supporting its own weight, at the very least. Two mechanisms are required to prevent the particles from rolling away from each other and causing the wall to crumble.

Friction The first of these mechanisms is friction. The surface of a soil particle is rough, like that of any material, although this roughness can often only be detected on an atomic scale. The roughness creates friction when two surfaces rub together; the harder they rub, the stronger the friction. It is this friction between particles that causes loose, dry sand to form a conical heap rather than spreading itself flat. The same friction also determines the gradient of the heap, known as the 'angle of repose'. This angle is around 35 degrees for many types of sand, but it increases if the particles are rougher and more jagged, and it remains the same no matter the height of the heap.

Cohesion The second mechanism that affects the strength of a raw earth wall is cohesion, the force that attracts particles to each other and thereby intensifies friction. The particles, like all physical matter, are subject to gravity and electrostatic forces. Gravitational attraction is intrinsically very low and between small objects like two pebbles, sand particles, or clay platelets, it is negligible. Electrostatic forces, however, can be substantial, even between very small particles. It is these forces that cause an attraction between positively and negatively charged particles.

Capillary cohesion Sand is probably the granular matter that best illustrates the cohesion that electrostatic forces can create when moisture is present. The cohesion of completely dry sand is minimal – just try building even a tiny vertical wall with it! It is virtually impossible, as an avalanche will occur as soon as the wall is more than a few grains high. Everything changes, however, in the presence of moisture. Water condenses in the narrow spaces between the particles, and is influenced by the same gravitational and electrostatic forces that keep water molecules and sand particles together. Under this influence, the water tends to spread over the surface of the sand particles. This creates surface tension and so attracts the particles to each other. These liquid 'bridges' have a curved shape and are known as 'capillary bridges', while the resulting cohesion is termed 'capillary cohesion'. The degree of cohesion depends on the relative humidity of the air or how much water has been added to the sand: an optimal equilibrium is achieved when the water is around 1% of the mixture. Constructing a vertical wall from a mixture of sand with 1% water is still a tricky task, but it is possible, even up to a considerable height. If fine sand is used, calculations and experience show that a column over 2 metres high can be built on a base 20 centimetres across. If, however, the optimal equilibrium is exceeded and the quantity of water is so high that it soaks the particles, the surface tension – and the cohesion – will vanish, and the structure will collapse. The mechanism of capillary cohesion found in sand is also present in a rammed earth wall (or an adobe brick), whether the particles are large (gravel or pebbles) or small (silt, clay, and other very fine colloidal particles, such as iron, aluminium, and manganese oxides, which

are common in tropical soils). The smaller the particles, the more capillary bridges there will be per cubic metre of earth, and the stronger the wall will be. Reducing the size of the particles by a factor of one thousand increases the resistance of a wall by a factor of ten, making it possible to build a structure ten times higher, or supporting ten times the load. In other words, a base 20 centimetres across, as mentioned above, could be used to build a column over 20 metres high if a tropical soil rich in clays and iron oxides were used. It might also be possible to make the wall even stronger, in the way described below.

Cohesion from electrostatic forces Let's take a closer look at clay soils. Unlike other granular materials, their morphology is usually described as flaky, because they are made of layers of platelets. These platelets are smooth, which considerably increases the contact surface and the potential for adhesion. If we were to build a rammed earth wall of the size described above with clay, the total surface area of the clay platelets would exceed 2 square kilometres – or 250 soccer pitches. When the atmosphere grows dry and the capillary bridges within the clay evaporate, the platelets are packed so close to each other and to the surfaces of other particles that direct electrostatic forces will hold the structure together, even without the presence of liquid to moisten them.

The strengthening of the forces of attraction that is triggered by relative humidity enables earth architecture to adapt to changing weather conditions, as long as the structure remains protected from large influxes of water. A rammed earth wall that can resist extreme humidity will become even sturdier in very dry conditions. It is therefore not surprising that many ancient buildings made from raw earth have lasted for centuries.

Above left and right: Walls of traditional rural houses near Toulouse, France, combining raw earth bricks with stone and fired brick.

Constructional Logic

Improving the Performance of Raw Earth While Retaining Its Ecological Benefits

Hugo Houben and Henri Van Damme

The upper layers of soil are made up of multiple strata (also called horizons), which are the result of a long natural process of fragmentation, migration, precipitation, cementation, and reconstruction. The topmost layer, where plants take root, is a fertile soil rich in minerals and organic matter, and so is vital to agriculture. The raw earth used for construction lies beneath this upper surface, although sometimes a mixture of two or three soil types is used to obtain the ideal granular consistency. The natural provenance of this resource is the main reason for its excellent environmental credentials as a building material. When properly selected, prepared, and applied, raw earth is a durable construction material that is completely and indefinitely recyclable and leaves only a very faint ecological footprint. Most industrial construction materials cannot match its remarkably low ecological impact because their extraction depletes natural resources or requires massive amounts of energy or because they are derived from complex manufacturing processes or chemical treatments.

Despite this, raw earth architecture faces several challenges. Under laboratory conditions, for example, it struggles to pass the tests for mechanical performance and durability (resistance to erosion, etc.) that were formulated for industrial materials and therefore do not take into account the distinctive characteristics of earth. Other challenges result from the technical requirements of earth construction, which often involves intensive reliance on qualified craftspeople. Particularly in industrialized countries, this means relatively high costs and a long construction period that is often incompatible with modern productivity targets. The old-fashioned image of earth architecture, particularly in the eyes of the indigenous populations of developing countries who are keen to embrace modernity, represents yet another obstacle.

These circumstances have given rise to two major developments. The first is the almost systematic addition, particularly in rammed earth and compressed earth bricks, of a considerable dose of industrially produced binders (cement, plaster, fly ash, blast-furnace slag). The binder is intended to correct the composition of earth that would otherwise be unsuitable for construction by increasing its mechanical resistance, reducing its sensitivity to water, and improving its ability to withstand erosion. This form of modification is known as 'stabilization'. Bearing in mind the relative solidity of earth architecture, the quantities of binder added – 3%–10% of the total mass – are substantial. The second (and more recent) development is the application of industrial techniques used in making concrete to earth construction, in order to both reduce the need for manpower and speed up the building process. Meticulous control of particle-size distribution and the use of clay dispersants have made it possible to create earth mixtures with a low water content (only 15%) that can be poured into forms in exactly the same way as concrete. The use of dispersants enhances the densification of clay once it dries and improves resistance to compression just as much as the addition of cement. Some types of earth fluidized by the latest 'superplasticizers' have even proved to be 'self-placing' or 'self-levelling'. There is no longer a need to mechanically vibrate earth enriched in this way to ensure that it spreads out to form a floor tile or fill the edges of a mould. Other mixtures, in contrast, stiffen quickly enough, once in place, for modern 3D printing techniques to be used. And the combination of these two techniques – fluidification followed by accelerated stiffening – makes it possible to pour out and unmould an earth form as quickly as a concrete one.

As far as environmental impact is concerned, these recent developments raise multiple questions. Even after stabilization, earth is still a humble construction material. Its resistance to compression is relatively low, running from a fraction of a megapascal to twenty megapascals at most, with the average being just a few megapascals (1 megapascal corresponds to 100 grams of pressure per square millimetre). This generally leads to the construction of very bulky walls, which have some advantages – particularly for users, in terms of hygrothermal comfort – but also increase a building's carbon footprint. Even the addition of small amounts of cement can have a considerable effect, and the same is true of synthetic dispersants, which generally have an even bigger carbon footprint than cement. It therefore seems appropriate to question the extent to which these new practices preserve the ecological benefits of raw earth construction.

Rammed earth, for example, has a carbon footprint of some 20 grams of carbon dioxide per kilogram of material, which is extraordinarily low, but the picture changes radically as soon as cement is added as a stabilizer. The average carbon footprint of clinker (the artificial rock left in a furnace which, after grinding, provides the basis for Portland cement) is around 830 grams of carbon dioxide per kilogram, i.e. forty times greater than that of rammed earth. So even a modest addition of cement to earth represents a significant increase in carbon footprint.

It is also necessary to consider the improvements to mechanical performance and the environmental cost of the quantities of cement used for stabilization. Relevant data has been collected for various types of raw earth (adobe, rammed earth, compressed earth bricks) and has been compared with the results obtained from over a thousand kinds of concrete, running from ordinary concrete to ultra-high-performance concrete (UHPC). The findings are thought-provoking. Five kilograms of cement must be added to every cubic metre of even a 'good' concrete (such as UHPC) to increase resistance by one megapascal, while twice that amount is required to achieve the same result with compressed earth bricks (CEB). Rammed earth needs six to eight times that sum and stabilized adobe bricks even more. The effects on the carbon footprint follow similar lines. While a cubic metre of UHPC emits less than five kilograms of carbon dioxide per megapascal of increased resistance, the emissions of stabilized adobe and rammed earth bricks for the same mechanical result are ten times greater. CEB stabilization is the best – or rather the least bad – solution, with a carbon footprint comparable to that of low-range concrete. The conclusion is obvious: the stabilization of raw earth with cement cannot be recommended in either mechanical or environmental terms as its benefits are very modest, even with the addition of large quantities of binder. A similar analysis of earth that has been fluidified and then stiffened with the help of dispersants and inorganic or organic coagulants would lead us to a similar conclusion. The carbon footprint of the compounds used can considerably diminish the ecological aspects of raw earth construction.

Does this mean that raw earth should not be considered a 'modern' material or that it is incompatible with any form of industrial rationalization? Not at all. Construction with unstabilized additive-free earth still offers durability, even if there is still room for improvement. It can adapt to climatic or environmental vicissitudes, as long as it respects the appropriate architectural logic and takes advantage of any available technical innovations. Raw earth can also be adapted to suit a range of social and economic circumstances, creating job opportunities when a large pool of workers is available or, in contrast, providing a means to reduce expenses and productivity when labour costs threaten to make a project uncompetitive. Despite its drawbacks, stabilization with hydraulic binders can be the best option when social costs or feasibility outweigh environmental concerns. Ultimately, research into additives and technologies that open up new horizons is not incompatible with the growth of earth architecture, as long as its natural frugality is not sacrificed to a headlong rush for modernity at all costs. Under these conditions, building with raw earth could become widespread in the 21st century, while preserving its soul and retaining its ecological benefits.

Further reading:
Van Damme & Houben 2018

Animal Architects

Long before humans built the earliest raw earth homes – the oldest, in Mesopotamia, date back almost 10,000 years – animals were using the same material to build shelters in a diverse range of ecosystems, sometimes with startling ingenuity. Some birds use earth to make nests of all shapes and sizes (**below right**). In Canada, beavers build dams over rivers to regulate the flow of water to meet their collective needs. Some frogs in Brazil build a ring-shaped nest of earth, using a technique similar to cob (**centre right**). In Australia, some crab species are able to rapidly build a sturdy vault over their heads with sandy earth (**above right**). Termites, however, are the animals who have taken earth architecture to the greatest heights – quite literally. In Africa, some termite mounds – made from a mixture of earth and organic secretions – reach heights of 8 metres (**opposite**). The structure of these 'towers' creates passive ventilation and an optimum temperature and humidity. This allows these remarkable structures to maintain an interior microclimate that encourages the growth of a fungus that is essential to the life of the termite colony. The interior temperature must remain stable at around 30°C, with only one degree of margin, even as the temperature outside can range from 0 to 40°C. Termite mounds can therefore hold the climate at bay in ways that 21st-century humans struggle to match.

    J.D. & R.E.

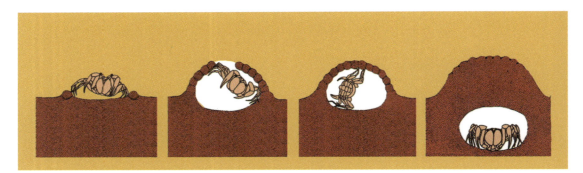

Earth Artisans

Below: The artist Silla Camara adds mural decorations to a house in the village of Djajibinni in Mauritania, *ca.* 1985 (see pp. 172–175).

Opposite: The master builder El Hadji Falké Barmou, winner of the 1986 Aga Khan Award for Architecture for the Yaama Mosque, built in 1982 in the region of Tahoua, Niger.

Imaginary Buildings

Architects sometimes use their talents to create imaginary structures that may then influence their built work. This artistic approach is particularly well illustrated by the designs of Catalan architect Josep Esteve. As a founder member of CRAterre, he took part in a pilot programme to build public housing in Rosso, Mauritania in the 1970s (see p. 388). In order to draw on local building techniques, Esteve developed ways to build arches, domes, and so-called Nubian vaults from raw earth bricks. He has always seen drawing as an essential form of expression that complements real-life construction. As well as making minutely detailed plans of structures that he intends to build (**opposite, above**), he also enjoys creating images of phantasmagorical architecture (**below and opposite, below**), which may be fanciful but nevertheless display his deep understanding of the principles of building with earth. This complex and inventive visual language imaginatively explores the formal and spatial qualities of these constructed systems,

with their functional constraints and technical demands. Esteve's watercolours conjure a fantastical architectural world with virtuoso skill, but they also throw light on the dreamlike qualities of real earth buildings. These harmonious compositions suggest an element of playfulness and poetry that is often lacking in the field of architecture.

H.G.

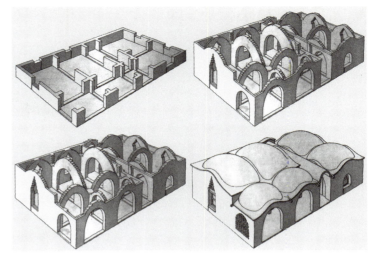

Constructional Logic

Building with Rammed Earth

Of all the techniques of raw earth construction, rammed earth is the only one that allows load-bearing walls to be built to a height of several storeys. Many ancient monuments around the world are testament to its remarkable strength. These structures were achieved by packing together, either manually or mechanically, layers of slightly damp earth, 12 to 15 centimetres deep, within a wooden or metal frame. The thickness of the walls may vary from 40 to 60 centimetres, depending on the number of storeys. This ancient technique can be found all over the planet, but Morocco, Spain, and France boast the most varied and sophisticated applications, both traditional and contemporary. The rammed earth technique was modernized by French architect François Cointeraux (beginning in around 1790) and spread around the world in the 19th century. It is still being updated in the 21st century, most notably by CRAterre and Martin Rauch in Europe, Rick Joy in the United States, and Elie Mouyal in Morocco. Hannsjörg Voth has extended the use of rammed earth into the realm of contemporary art by creating monumental pieces of land art in Morocco

(see pp. 466–467). New practices – such as the use of prefabricated blocks of rammed earth, invented in 1986 by master builder Nicolas Meunier – have cut down both the workload and the construction period. These days, automatic compression systems can make the segments of a wall in advance and, after drying, these can be put in place mechanically. If rammed earth has an optimal granular composition (e.g. gravel, sand, or clay), it does not need to be stabilized with lime or cement to improve resistance.

J.D.

```
Further reading:
Houben & Guillaud 1994; CRAterre 2018a;
CRAterre 2018b
```

Opposite and below right: Rammed earth has been a trusted building technique for centuries.

Below left: The construction of Hannsjörg Voth's artwork *City of Orion* (see p. 466).

Building with Cob

Cob is a traditional building technique that uses a mixture of clay soil, water, and either straw, grasses, or thin twigs. This mixture is often shaped into balls while it is still malleable. To form a wall, these balls are piled in horizontal layers 40 to 60 centimetres high and then adjusted and smoothed. Cob has been used strikingly to build the Royal Palace of Abomey in Benin (see pp. 284–285) and the organic shapes of Lobi and Gurunsi houses in Burkina Faso, as well as in Afghanistan (using the *pakhsa* technique), Yemen, the Najran region of Saudi Arabia (see pp. 242–245), and sub-Saharan Africa (**right and opposite**). Cob was also once common in England, particularly in the county of Devon. In France, this ancient technique was primarily used in the region near Rennes, Brittany, and the Bessin and Cotentin peninsula. More recently, cob has been used in innovative projects such as the Salvatierra building (2003; see p. 402) in Rennes, built by Jean-Yves Barrier, with its south facade made from large prefabricated blocks of cob (laid with the help of a crane) that serve to capture the sun's energy.

H.G.

Further reading:
McCann 1983; Petitjean 1995;
Scherrer 2003; Patte & Streiff 2007

Constructional Logic

Building with Raw Earth Bricks

The adobe technique was first invented in Mesopotamia in the 9th millennium BCE. It consists of bricks made from a mixture of clay, sandy earth, water, and often straw, which serves as a binder. The bricks were originally kneaded by hand into balls but were later shaped in rectangular wooden moulds. They were then left to dry in the sun (**above right**). As well as their initial use in house building, the production of adobe bricks in large quantities enabled Mesopotamia to devise the monumental architecture typical of this urban civilization (temples, palaces, and ziggurats). In the 21st century, adobe architecture is still found all over the world. Earth can now be mechanically rammed to make compressed earth blocks (CEB). This technique was invented in Colombia in 1952 by the engineer Raúl Ramírez; his Cinva-Ram was a small press that came in kit form and could be easily transported on the back of a mule. The Cinva-Ram was designed to help ordinary people build their own houses, and it went on to enjoy international success. In the 1970s, a new generation of motorized mechanical presses (**opposite, above left**) considerably boosted the use of CEB (**opposite, above right**: compressed blocks being made in India for a Satprem Maïni project). These innovations have helped to streamline the processes of raw earth construction, not only in developing nations but also elsewhere, allowing earth to be viewed positively as a modern, effective, and inexpensive material.

H.G.

Further reading:
Aurenche 1981; Houben & Guillaud 1994; Guillaud & Houben 2011

Below right: A mosque by Hassan Fathy, under construction in Abiquiú, New Mexico, in 1981.

Constructional Logic

Hybrid Techniques

Several construction techniques make use of raw earth in combination with other materials. Wattle and daub is a mixture of clay, water, and straw that is used to fill spaces in a load-bearing wooden structure (**opposite, above right, and below**). It was widely used in Europe from Roman times until the Renaissance, giving rise to the technique known as 'half-timbering'. This can still be found today in rural areas of Europe, Africa, Asia, and Latin America, as well as in public and private buildings in many old towns in Europe, particularly in France, Britain, Germany, and Scandinavia. The principle of half-timbering also evolved into 'light earth', in which raw earth is combined with straw (**opposite, above left**) or other forms of plant fibre, such as hemp and wood shavings. These materials make it possible to prefabricate construction elements such as floor slabs and insulating panels for walls and roofs. Mixtures of this type can also be applied at high pressure to a metal skeleton, as in one experiment undertaken in Chile. In Spain, bricks of compressed earth are sometimes inserted into a framework of fired bricks (**below right**). In Germany in the early 20th century, whole families would work together to make earth bricks before construction began (**centre right**), using the Dünne loam-loaf technique.

H.G.

Further reading:
Volhard 2015

Above right: Two images of a residential building designed by Herwig Van Soom in Blanden, Belgium. The load-bearing wooden framework is filled in with straw before the application of an external coat of earth mortar.

Constructional Logic

Arches and Vaults

Arches and vaults built from bricks of raw earth (**below and opposite**) have existed in Asia Minor since the 3rd millennium BCE. They also continued to be a feature of this region long after raw earth bricks had been superseded by fired bricks everywhere else. They take a wide variety of architectural forms. In Nigeria, for example, palaces and great mosques (such as the Great Mosque of Zaria) feature arches of raw earth, packed around beams of azara wood bound together with plant fibres (see pp. 220–223). Arches and vaults became less common in the modern era, but they were revived in the late 1940s by Egyptian architect Hassan Fathy in his buildings for the village of New Gourna (see the sequence of four diagrams by John Norton, **opposite above**, and pp. 334–339). Subsequently, the principle of the so-called Nubian vault, which is built outwards from a gable wall in courses of sloping bricks that do not require formworks, has been used in many housing projects in areas with little sturdy wood available, notably in projects run by the NGO Development Workshop in the Sahel region of Africa (**below** and p. 389).

Arch and vault construction is now among the theoretical and practical topics covered by professional courses in earth architecture.
    H.G.

Further reading:
Fathy 1970; Joffroy & Guillaud 1994

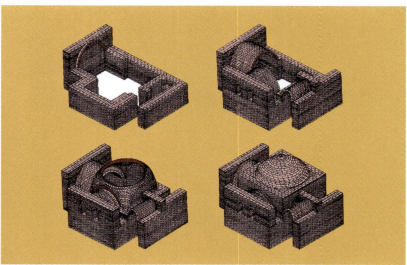

Constructional Logic

Domes

Raw earth domes may take several forms: hemispherical, segmental, pointed, or faceted. Requiring sophisticated technical knowledge to build, they are common in the Islamic architectural tradition. In southwest Iran, for example, large icehouses called *yakhchal* were covered by pointed domes built from stepped layers of earthen bricks (see p. 122). In religious buildings (chapels, churches, mosques, temples) and mausoleums, domes are often raised on a drum, but more sophisticated examples may be raised on pendentives or, in the Byzantine tradition, squinches. In Egypt, so-called Nubian vaults were built without support, using brick courses that sloped slightly inwards. This technique was modernized by the Egyptian architect Hassan Fathy in *ca.* 1948 (see pp. 336–339). Other vernacular traditions can be found elsewhere in Africa, notably in the Musgum houses of Cameroon (see pp. 228–229).

H.G.

```
Further reading:
Besenval 1984; Joffroy & Guillaud 1994
```

Right: The domes of this distinctive urban complex in Iran are notable for their sensual shapes and textures.

Textured Walls

Traditional raw earth houses in Africa often feature a panoply of decorations on their exteriors (**below and opposite**). Texturing can give walls a serene beauty and sensuality, and these qualities are further enhanced by colour, which reflects the geological properties of the ground from which the soil was taken. The overall effect imbues these buildings with a strong personality and poetic radiance (see pp. 218–219 and 224–225). In many regions, these artistic traditions remain vibrant and creative, although their existence often remains under threat in urban areas.

J.D. & R.E.

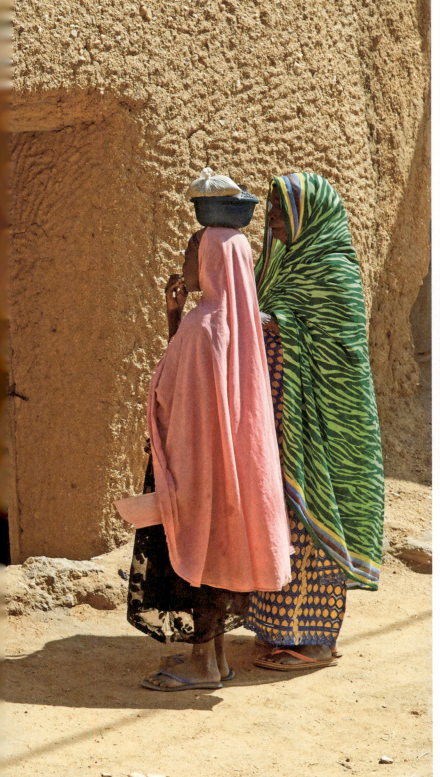

Constructional Logic

Architecture and Sculpture
A Harmonious Fusion

One of the benefits of raw earth, a natural material used when it is moist and malleable, is its ability to bring together two realms of artistic expression: architecture and sculpture. Contemporary artistic and architectural practices in richer countries have nullified this synergy, however, by establishing separate processes of creation for each discipline that are hard to reconcile. In contrast, vernacular architecture often exhibits the harmony of an intuitive and pragmatic creative process, carried out by builders who are simultaneously architects, artisans, and artists. They become the inspired creators of a *Gesamtkunstwerk*, a 'total work of art'. Two works created in Mali are fine examples of this manifestation of the vernacular spirit: the modest mosque of Nando (**right**) and the mosque of Koporo Pen, whose sculpted walls are studded with almost sensual forms (**overleaf**).

J.D. & R.E.

Right: Mosque in the village of Nando, Mali (see pp. 180–183 and 508).

Overleaf: Mosque in the village de Koporo Pen, Mali (see pp. 202–209).

Constructional Logic

Chapter 2

Archaeological Evidence

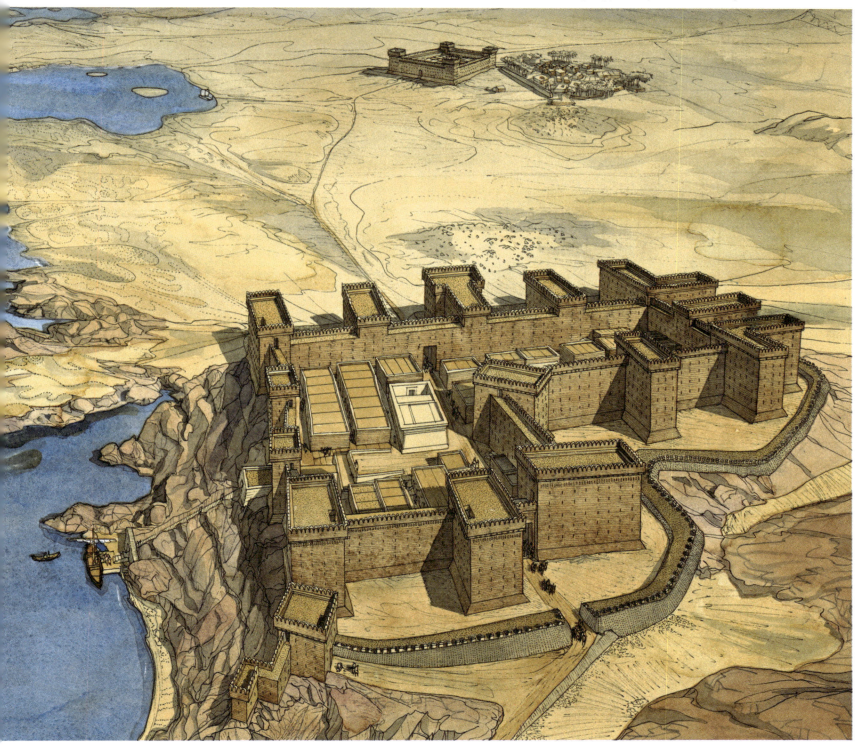

Fortresses built from earth bricks in Buhen, Egypt, during the reign of Senusret III, in the 19th century BCE. They were situated on the banks of the Nile in Nubia and served to defend the country's southern borders (see pp. 84–85). Reconstruction by Jean-Claude Golvin.

Earth Architecture in Antiquity

Hubert Guillaud

The primordial importance of raw earth in the construction of human settlements all over the world, from ancient times to the modern era, has been confirmed both by major archaeological digs exploring cultures and civilizations of the past and by the excavation of humbler dwellings. This evidence, which was long ignored or hidden, has helped to broaden the geographical and historical scope of archaeological research. Until the late 19th century, archaeological practice had been extremely Eurocentric, focusing primarily on ancient Rome and Greece, with occasional inroads into the regions formerly known as the Levant and the Near East, now considered part of western Asia.

Earth architecture was independently developed all over the globe: in Mesopotamia (on the plains of the Tigris and the Euphrates, in modern-day Iraq and Syria), in Egypt (along the Nile, from Nubia to the Delta), in Pakistan (by the banks of the Indus and the Hakra), in China (on the plateaux overlooking the Yellow River), in Peru (on the desert coastline of the Pacific Ocean, fed by watercourses flowing down from the Andes), in Central and North America (along the banks of the Mississippi) and throughout Africa, both north and south of the Sahara. The fertile soils and alluvial sand and clay that sparked the Neolithic agricultural revolution also provided humankind with its first solid and durable building material: sun-dried raw earth bricks. This material therefore became a major vector of urban development, as demonstrated by revealing studies into the mass production of these bricks in Mesopotamia. It is not possible to trace the entire extent of this epic journey through time and space here, so we shall confine ourselves to a few outstanding landmarks (readers seeking further information should consult the bibliography on p. 496).

Western Asia

The invention of raw earth bricks in Mesopotamia marked a major advance in the evolution of building practices. Originally modelled by hand (in the 9th and 8th millennia BCE) and then shaped in wooden moulds, raw earth bricks were used in domestic architecture from the 4th millennium BCE onwards, but they also made it possible to construct larger, more imposing buildings, such as temples and palaces. This is evident in the White Temple of Uruk and the Temple Oval of Khafajah (p. 75) in the Tigris Valley, which were built in the 3rd millennium BCE on top of high platforms made with raw earth bricks. Furthermore, the cultural relationships between the eastern Mediterranean basin (Jericho and Mureybet, dating from around 9000–8000 BCE), Mesopotamia, the territories of the Taurus-Zagros mountain range (in Iran and Iraq) and Anatolia (in present-day Turkey) can be gauged by the transmission of raw earth building techniques and architectural styles. In Anatolia, Çatal Hüyük (7560–5600 BCE; pp. 72–73) was a highly compact agglomeration of houses, built from wooden frameworks filled with raw earth bricks (their entrances were on the roof). During the course of the 2nd millennium BCE, temples devoted to the great Sumerian divinities (Ishtar, Ninmah, Marduk) were built with raw earth bricks and dominated the landscape of the urban civilization of Sumer, one of the oldest in the world. The famous Ishtar Gate of Babylon (p. 77) was breathtaking, with its inner mass of raw earth bricks and its exterior blue glazed cladding of fired brick. In the period 2100–2000 BCE, the Mesopotamian skyline was distinguished by towering ziggurats made with raw earth bricks, often also clad with fired bricks. Archaeologists' attempts to reconstruct these masterpieces – Etemenanki in Babylon (p. 79) and the ziggurat of Ur – have stirred up great controversy, although the partial restoration of Dur Untash, more commonly known as Chogha Zanbil (*ca.* 1250 BCE; p. 78), in Iran proved exemplary. Outside its sacred precinct (*temenos*), the palace-hypogeum contains a superb array of vaulted raw earth tombs.

The transmission of knowledge about arches, vaults, and domes is more difficult to pin down as their origins are still unclear. Various sources for these innovations have been hypothesized: Mesopotamia, Syria, Egypt, and Afghanistan (as suggested by Roland Besenval in his book *Technologie de la voûte dans l'Orient ancien*). What is certain is that Assyrian kings went on to build palaces of staggering dimensions in Mesopotamia. Dur-Sharrukin (Khorsabad), the capital of King Sargon II, took six years to build (713–707 BCE). It stood on an platform of earth, 12 metres high, and contained within its seven-gated walls not only the royal palace but also a citadel, an arsenal, a throne room, royal apartments and princely residences, a ziggurat, and a temple dedicated to Nabu, the god of wisdom and writing. Writing itself – another milestone in human history – was also invented in Mesopotamia, in the form of inscriptions made with a reed stylus on clay tablets.

The Americas

In Mexico, the Aztecs founded the city of Tenochtitlan on an island in Lake Texcoco in 1325 or 1369 CE (pp. 94–95). Their civilization did not last long, however, as the arrival of the Spanish conquistadors in 1519 triggered its downfall. Spanish chroniclers record the discovery of a splendid, gleaming white earthen city with a population of almost half a million, built on a marshy area spread over 1,000 hectares. An ordinary Aztec home was simple, with no upper storeys, a flat roof-terrace, and a blind facade leading on to a street or canal. On 13 August 1521, the 'Venice of the New World' was pillaged and destroyed by the soldiers of Hernán Cortés, who led the Spanish colonizing forces and obliterated the Aztec civilization.

In Peru, the earliest sacred buildings were erected in the 2nd millennium BCE, usually in the form of stepped pyramids, before the emergence of pre-Inca sacred sites, known as *huacas*. Northern Peru was notable for its enormous aqueduct system that transported water from the Andes to the desert regions near the coast. The Moche culture (100–700 CE), which emerged by the sea after the fall of the earlier Nazca civilization, went on to expand this great feat of civil engineering. In the valley of the river Moche, near Trujillo, large ceremonial adobe brick buildings were constructed a stone's throw away from flimsy houses made of reeds daubed with clay. The remains of the famous Huaca de la Luna (pp. 90–91) and the pyramid of El Brujo in the Chicama Valley contain magnificent coloured reliefs and friezes depicting sacred rituals. The stunning archaeological site of Chan Chan (pp. 92–93) was at its peak in the 13th century. It is spread over 20 square kilometres, with nine palace compounds bounded by cob and adobe walls of up to 500 metres in length, as well as whole neighbourhoods and the homes of the Chimú rulers. In the Tschudi Citadel (one of the best preserved), the outer walls are clad with a smooth layer of clay decorated with relief friezes adorned with repeat motifs and animal imagery.

In North America, the remains of huge mounds built in the Ohio and Mississippi Valleys between 1200 and 1730 CE testify to the use of raw earth to construct sacred sites on a monumental scale (pp. 96–97).

Central Asia

The mausoleum-fortress of Koi Krylgan Kala (p. 86), in the Khorezm region of Uzbekistan, was built in the 4th century BCE from raw and rammed earth bricks. It takes the form of a central circular citadel, 45 metres in diameter, with a concentric outer wall enclosing an inner ring some 15 metres wide. The Parthian Empire, which stretched from Mesopotamia to India, emerged in the 3rd century BCE from the ruins of the empire of Alexander the Great. Its capital, the fortified city of Nisa in Turkmenistan, contains significant traces of earth architecture. In the same country, the ancient city-oasis of Merv, which was at its peak from the 11th to the 13th centuries CE, under the Seljuks, rivalled Baghdad as the oldest capital in the Islamic world. The Great Kyz Kala, dating from the 8th century CE, is one of the largest raw earth *köshks* (suburban palaces with pavilions and gardens) still in existence. Its outer walls (p. 87) have distinctive corrugations, and it also contains fortifications (*kalas*) and a large cold-storage room built from raw earth bricks. Similar structures were built in the desert regions of Iran up to the 20th century.

Africa

In mainland Africa, archaeological research in Eritrea and Ethiopia has revealed an abundance of cultural exchange between the African continent and Arabia, starting in the 2nd millennium BCE and continuing for over 3,000 years. Little remains, however, of the Ethiopian kingdom of Meroe, which preceded that of Aksum. Both used raw earth bricks in their civil buildings, as did the Kerma in the kingdom of Kush, in present-day Sudan, as evidenced by two surviving temples (*deffufa*). From the 4th millennium BCE onwards, raw earth bricks were the primary material used in Egyptian buildings, following their introduction from Mesopotamia. The Middle Kingdom and the Second Dynasty marked the highpoints of Egyptian military power, and many fortresses were built in Nubia to defend the Empire's southern border. The fortress of Buhen (pp. 84–85), built with raw earth bricks, was one of the masterpieces of this form of defensive architecture, although unfortunately nothing of it remains today, as its well-preserved vestiges were engulfed by Lake Nasser after the completion of the Aswan High Dam. In contrast, many archaeological sites dating from the New Empire (1552–1070 BCE) still bear witness to this blossoming of earth architecture, including the artisans' village of Deir el-Medina (p. 82), the royal city of Tell el-Amarna, founded *ca.* 1350 BCE by the pharoah Akhenaten, and the granaries of the Ramesseum in Luxor (p. 83).

Europe

The spread of raw earth bricks in North Africa and western Asia was paralleled in Europe by the dissemination of wattle and daub. After the Neolithic period – the 5th–4th millennia BCE – this technique was passed on from east to west, from the Danube valley to Alsace, in present-day France. This ancient tradition laid down the basic principles of earth-and-wood construction, which, alongside the advances made in carpentry in the Renaissance, became the standard model for half-timbered civil and domestic architecture. This type of building was predominant in western, northern, and central Europe until recently. Cob seems to have emerged from indigenous European cultures; the Celts, for example, often used it for their homes. From the 5th century BCE onwards, moulded raw earth bricks were gradually introduced into Europe from the East (Asia Minor, Anatolia, the Balkans, and Greek trading posts). This humble brick is inextricably linked with the rise of urbanism. As for rammed earth, most experts agree that it was first developed by the Punic civilization of Carthage (Tunisia) and then taken up by the Romans, who imported it into Italy, Spain, and France. More recently, the Berber dynasties of the Almoravids (11th–12th centuries CE) and the Almohads (12th–13th centuries CE) contributed to the spread of rammed earth construction in Spain with their great city walls and remarkable monuments such as the Alhambra in Granada (13th–14th centuries CE; pp. 144–145).

Further reading:
Mellaart 1967; Besenval 1984; Sauvage 1998;
Aurenche et al. 2011

The walls of Itchan Kala, the inner citadel of the city of Khiva, built in the late 17th century (see p. 86). In 1991, it became Uzbekistan's first UNESCO World Heritage site.

Archaeological Evidence

What Archaeology Can Teach Us

David Gandreau

Archaeological sites attest to the use of raw earth as a construction material for at least 11,000 years. It seems to have emerged at the same time as the first semi-nomadic settlements, the oldest known examples of which are primarily situated in Asia Minor and date back to the pre-ceramic Neolithic period of the late 10th and 9th millennium BCE.

Eleven millennia of earth architecture

The cultures associated with earth construction constantly improved its techniques and extended its use across every continent. Countless archaeological sites all over the world are testament to the use of earth in walls, floors, furnishings, and even roofs.

The quality of the construction and finish often demonstrates a remarkable degree of expertise. On the east bank of the Euphrates, in present-day Syria, for example, the Neolithic village of Dja'de el-Mughara, dating from the mid-9th millennium BCE, contains some superbly preserved polychrome murals. These geometric red-and-black designs painted on a white ground on sturdy earth walls are among the oldest of their kind yet discovered.

In Armenia, the sites of Aratashen and Aknashen, on the Ararat plain, dating from the later Neolithic period (6,000–5200 BCE), confirm that builders demonstrated great skill in their choice of earth, techniques, and workmanship. Bronze Age sites also display a deep understanding of the material, in even the humblest domestic structures. For example, the town of Qatna (from the first half of the 2nd millennium BCE), to the north of Damascus in Syria, boasts raw earth brick walls constructed with extraordinary precision.

The 2nd millennium BCE saw the appearance of more complex architectural elements, such as arches and vaults built from raw earth bricks. Four thousand years ago, these features were widespread in Asia Minor, where they were used in Babylonian and Assyrian palaces, as well as in Haft-Tappeh, near Suse in the southwest of present-day Iran. Similar techniques were also known in Pharaonic Egypt, as can be seen from the famous Ramesseum, centre of the royal cult of Ramses II, situated in the Theban necropolis across the river from Luxor. With the long Nubian vaults of its granaries, built from overlapping arches of earthen brick, the site covers an area of almost 5 hectares.

The sophisticated use of arches and vaults gradually developed to support greater loads and eventually enabled the construction of domes, as found in the round hall at Nisa in Turkmenistan, the former capital of the Parthian Empire founded in the 3rd century BCE. By the Middle Ages (7th–12th centuries), buildings combining arches, vaults, and domes were common in Central Asia – the citadel in Bam, Iran, is a perfect example – and in the Sudano-Sahelian region of Africa, where mosques were built as part of the expansion of Islam after 622 CE.

Alongside high-quality building techniques, a wide variety of architectural approaches are also evident. Gaulish houses, for example, are still regularly described as rudimentary structures built with cob or wattle and daub (often nothing remains of them but the holes for supporting posts), but in fact they could be much more elaborate. The Verberie House, for example, discovered in the Oise region of France and dated to the Second Iron Age (3rd–1st century BCE), had an area of 250 square metres. It was probably covered with a thatched saddle roof to protect the walls, fashioned from packed earth around a wooden framework and demonstrating an ingenious use of local materials.

Equally noteworthy are the pre-Columbian pyramids of Mexico, and the ziggurats of Asia, such as the monumental Chogha Zanbil in present-day Iran, which soared to a height of over 50 metres and was built with millions of raw earth bricks more than 3,000 years ago. Nor should we forget the monuments that incorporated raw earth but are now better known for their stone or fired clay bricks, such as the Egyptian pyramids in Gizeh, Persepolis (Persia), Delos (Greece), Carthage (the Punic Empire), and Volubilis (the Roman Empire).

On the larger scale of cities and regions, there are plentiful examples of earth architecture. In the Bronze Age, this material co-existed with and perhaps even sparked the first urban revolution. Mesopotamian cities built of earth along the length of the Euphrates, such as Ur, Babylon, and Mari, are already well known. Others, such as Gonur Tepe in Turkmenistan and Sarazm in Tajikistan, are now providing important information about the development of early urban civilizations. Earth was also used to build many medieval cities, including Merv in Turkmenistan, believed to be one of the biggest settlements in the world in the 11th and 12th centuries. Moreover, several French cities, including Lyon, Carpentras, Narbonne, Béziers, and Perpignan, still contain buildings made from rammed earth or archaeological evidence of its use. In Lyon, for example, some of the rammed earth buildings on the Croix-Rousse are six storeys high and are inhabited to this day.

Of all these archaeological sites that include earth architecture, over eighty have been declared UNESCO World Heritage sites and at least as many have been shortlisted, awaiting classification. The architectural remains discovered by archaeologists have aroused a growing interest in the scientific community, as well as among organizations that protect cultural heritage and local populations and promote tourism. These sites have come to be seen as vectors for the development of the region in which they are located, because of their historical value and their ancient use of local resources.

Ecologically responsible contemporary architecture: what can be learned?

The archaeological heritage of earth architecture, the fruit of over 11,000 years of building experimentation, is an inexhaustible and hugely varied resource for research and learning. It demonstrates that earth architecture has always enabled societies to expand their built environment, simply by taking advantage of this local zero-carbon resource.

Within this legacy, we can see the principles of environmental sustainability to which contemporary architects and planners now aspire: the use of local and recycled materials; the integration of built space into the environment; ecological design; energy efficiency; passive heating systems; urban planning. Archaeology has unearthed countless sites that were already meeting these criteria in ancient times.

How did these ancient construction practices provide protection against natural disasters such as cyclones, earthquakes, and flooding? How were they adapted for urban growth? What were their limitations? These questions, which are not only technical but also social and cultural, can be answered by the traces of earth architecture found in archaeological sites. Many lessons can be drawn from this archaeological heritage, and these in turn will allow us to develop new forms of earth architecture that is in greater harmony with its surroundings and attuned to today's ecological challenges.

Opposite: Loaf-shaped earth brick (*ca*. 7000 BCE), moulded by hand, discovered at the archaeological site of Jericho, Palestine.

Above: Earth bricks from Mesopotamia (Iraq), dating back to the 3rd millennium BCE, from the collection of the Vorderasiatisches Museum, Berlin.

Çatal Hüyük
A Neolithic Settlement in Anatolia

This crucially important archaeological site is an example of the settlements built in various parts of the world during what is known as the Neolithic revolution. Situated in Anatolia, Turkey, it was discovered in 1961 by James Mellaart, who saw it as proof of the early presence of settled communities beyond the Fertile Crescent (Iraq and Syria). As Mellaart points out in his book *Çatal Hüyük: A Neolithic Town in Anatolia* (1967), it is one of the oldest settlements from that period. The scientific community is undecided, however, as to whether Çatal Hüyük was a large village, a small town, or a cross between the two, owing to its fluctuating population (estimated as between 3,500 and 8,000 people) and its large extent (13 hectares). In any case, the remains on this site, which was first occupied in 7560 BCE, more than 9,000 years ago, provide evidence of a human settlement built entirely of raw earth, in the form of adobe. In terms of architecture, urban planning, and art, it is without any known parallel. The houses are packed together, rather than being separated by streets: the entrances were on the roofs, whose flat terraces formed a continuous open space that could be used for communal activities (**centre right**). The highly elaborate interiors incorporate furniture and benches made out of earth (**below right**). Every home bears signs of a vibrant culture and devotional spirit, as the walls are decorated with sculpted motifs and painted murals. One of the murals is exceptional, as it depicts the ground plan of Çatal Hüyük itself (**opposite, above**), which was declared a UNESCO World Heritage site in 2012.

J.D.

Further reading:
Mellaart 1967

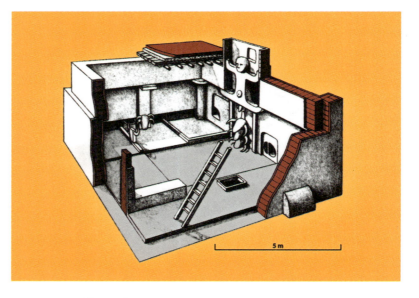

Archaeological Evidence

Mesopotamia

The civilizations that have grown up in Mesopotamia over the millennia have left behind a multitude of concepts and practices, some of which remain cornerstones of our contemporary way of life. It was in this region that, following the achievements of the Neolithic era (which began around 12,000 years ago), a series of revolutions laid the foundations for a radically new world. These innovations included sedentary housing, livestock farming, agriculture, and irrigation. Mesopotamia was home to the first villages to have a regional economy and the first cities to generate a complex, sophisticated, and diverse civilization. Mesopotamia also developed a writing system, pressed into clay tablets, that was used in the fields of commerce, law, and literature. However, the region was lacking in some natural resources, including stone and wood. This deficit was overcome by using earth for large-scale construction, a field that grew to produce an extraordinary range of both domestic and monumental architecture, which was used to express political, religious, and military ambitions. The result was an astonishing panoply of masterpieces made with raw earth: entire cities and towns, ramparts and monumental gates, palaces, and temples.

Right: The Temple of Ishtar-Kititum in Ischali in modern-day Iraq.

Opposite, above: The Royal Palace of Mari in Syria, built for King Zimri-Lim, dating from the mid-3rd millennium BCE.

Opposite, below: The Temple Oval at Khafajah in modern-day Iraq, dating from around 2400 BCE.

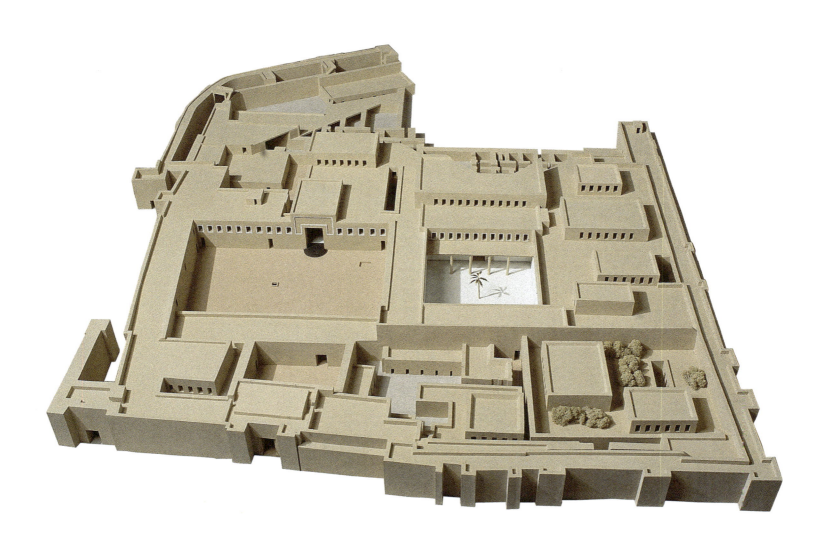
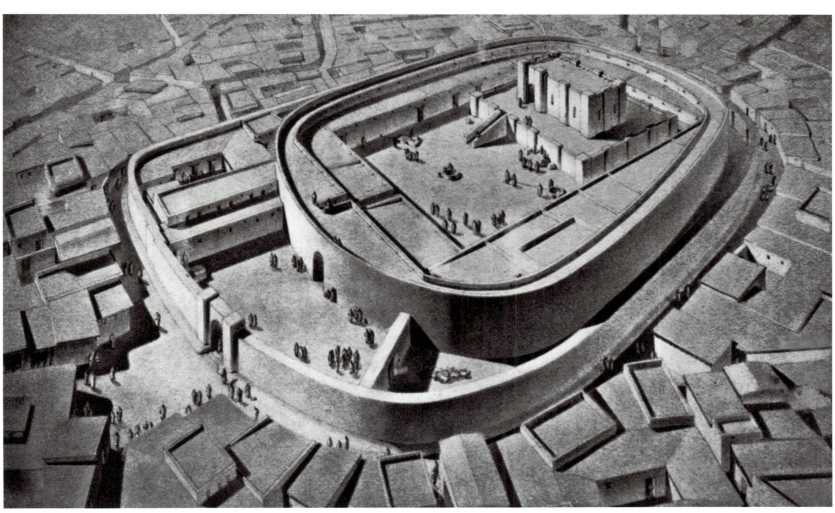

Archaeological Evidence

From the late 4th millennium BCE onwards, cities in Mesopotamia reflected a new social and economic dynamic. They became centres for the collection and distribution of food and raw materials, as well as the manufacture of saleable products. This transformation, which archaeologist Vere Gordon Childe called an urban revolution, was heavily shaped by an emerging social group: artisans who had acquired the skills to erect a wide range of domestic and monumental buildings.

Above right: Reconstruction of the temple and palace in the former Assyrian capital of Assur.

Below: The city of Al-Rawda, Syria, *ca.* 2250 BCE. Reconstruction by Corinne Castel.

Opposite: The Gate of Ishtar in Babylon, *ca.* 600 BCE. Glazed ceramic tiles cover the raw earth bricks that make up the gate's internal mass.

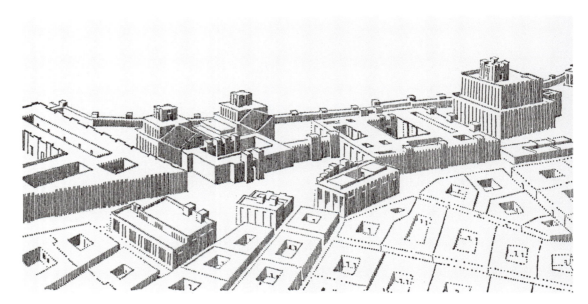

The ziggurats of Mesopotamia were religious buildings whose great height – often 50 metres or more – reflected a spiritual relationship between the earthly realm of humans and the heavenly realm of the gods. They were built on a square or rectangular base and were made of a series of terraces, with a temple on the highest one. The inner mass of the ziggurat contained millions of raw earth bricks, while its exterior was clad with fired bricks. The outer bricks were often glazed and could be seen glittering from far away, reinforcing the ziggurat's spiritual significance within the urban landscape.

J.D. & R.E.

Above right: King Nebuchadnezzar I dedicated the ziggurat of Babylon to the god Marduk.

Below: Ziggurat in Chogha Zanbil, Iran, built between 1400 and 1000 BCE.

Opposite, above: The ziggurat of Ur in modern-day Iraq, built by King Ur-Nammu, *ca.* 2100 BCE.

Opposite, below: The ziggurat of Babylon, or Etemenanki (thought to be the inspiration for the Tower of Babel), was built *ca.* 1970 BCE on a base 91 metres square. Its height is estimated to have been between 50 and 90 metres.

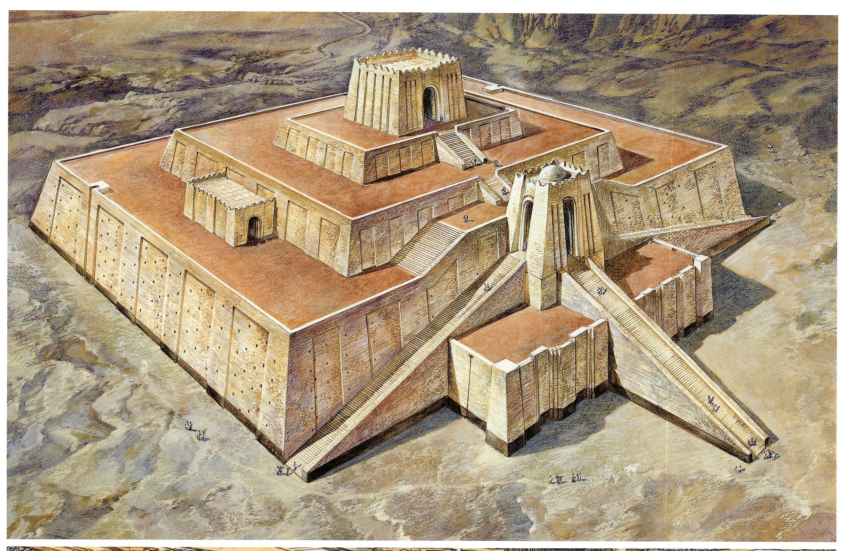
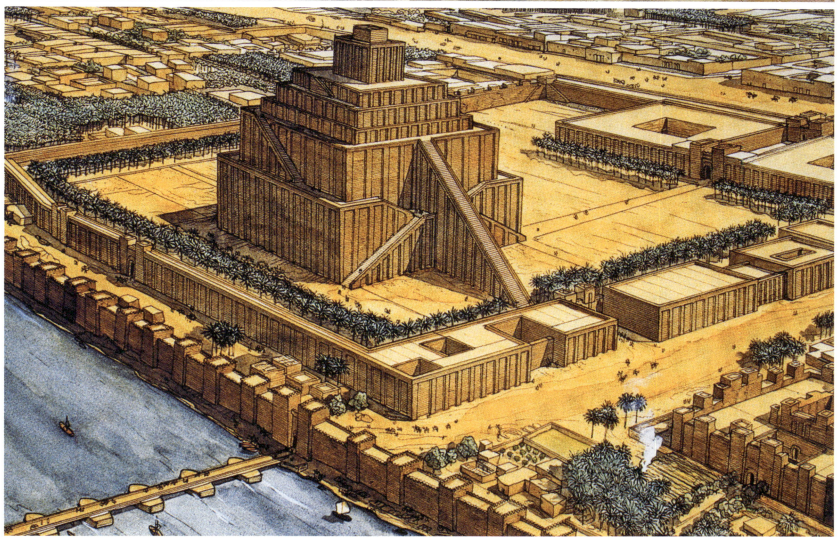

Archaeological Evidence

Egypt

Like Mesopotamia, ancient Egypt made great use of earth architecture. This choice is explained by both its geographical location and its dominant religious beliefs. The Egyptian civilization grew up alongside a major river – the Nile – that brought in huge quantities of silt every year. This provided fertile soil for farming and also ensured the availability of the nation's main construction material along the entire length of the river, from Nubia in the south to the Nile Delta in the north, which emptied into the Mediterranean. As Herodotus once said, 'Egypt is a gift of the Nile.' However, the area that benefited from this gift was limited to the two river banks. Beyond these two narrow, fertile strips lay vast expanses of desert, filled with little but sand and stone. The latter served as the other key building material in ancient Egypt, particularly for sacred sites devoted to the cult of eternal life, which was granted to the pharaohs and their families.

J.D.

Above left and centre: Mural frieze discovered in the tomb of Rekhmire, showing different stages in the manufacture of earth bricks.

Opposite, above right: A pharaoh symbolically shaping the first earth brick for a temple.

Below right: Panoramic view of the Nile Valley on the outskirts of the city of Memphis. Reconstruction by Jean-Claude Golvin.

Archaeological Evidence

The durability of stone was used in ancient Egypt to guarantee the longevity of the pyramids and the temples devoted to the cult of the most prominent deceased members of each dynasty. In contrast, earth was the material most widely utilized for domestic and utilitarian architecture for farmers and townspeople, as well as priests (lodgings and temple outbuildings) and soldiers (sturdy fortresses designed to defend Egypt's borders). This use of stone and earth for different types of architecture was not always rigid, however; some pharaohs even built pyramids from earth (see overleaf).
J.D.

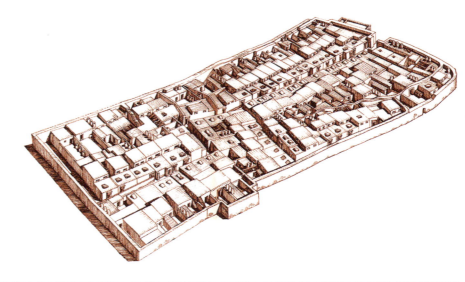

Above right: Deir el-Medina, a village built in adobe between 1295 and 1100 BCE. It comprised 68 houses for the senior artisans responsible for decorating the tombs in the Valley of the Kings.

Below right: The city of Thebes at the time of Rameses II. In the foreground is the temple of Luxor – and its earthen perimeter wall – overlooking the Avenue of the Sphinxes, which crossed the city and was lined mostly with adobe houses.

Opposite, above: The Ramesseum, the temple of Rameses II, was built between 1304 and 1213 BCE. Its inner sanctuary (centre, in white) was made of stone while its outbuildings (in ochre) were built with raw earth bricks. This archaeological site contains earthen vaults dating back over three thousand years.

Opposite, below: The Temple of Thoth, in the city of Hermopolis Magna. Its central sanctuary, devoted to religious rituals, was built from stone (in white), while earth (in ochre) was used for more utilitarian areas: the perimeter walls, granaries, and priests' lodgings. Reconstructions by Jean-Claude Golvin.

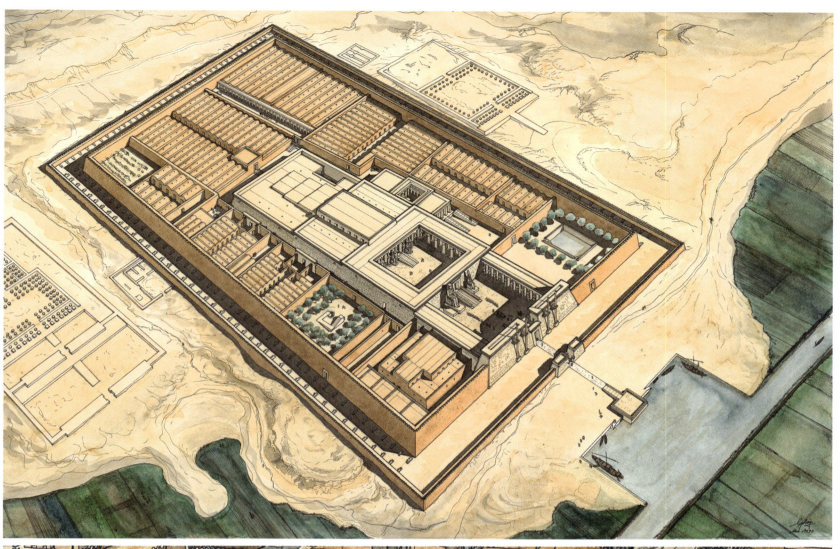
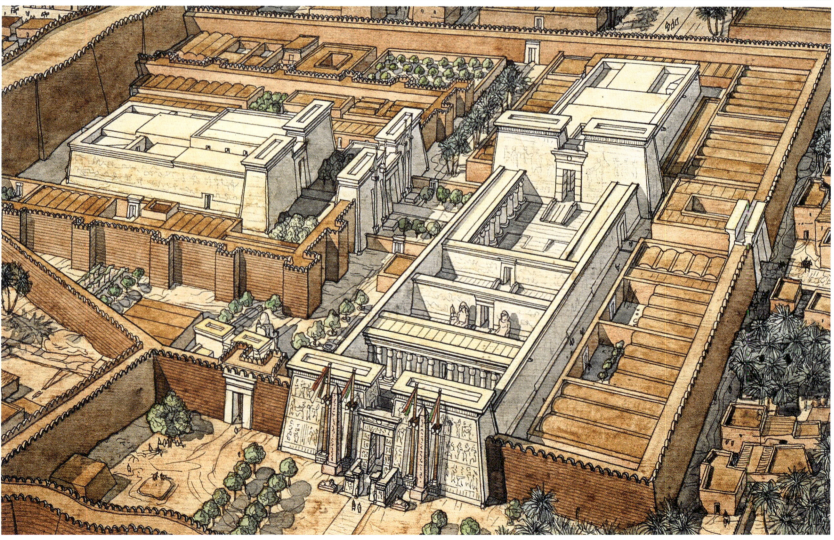

The great diversity of earth architecture in ancient Egypt bears witness to both a body of common knowledge, mainly utilized for building urban and rural houses, and to specialist building skills that were often very sophisticated. In the case of the pyramids, for example, the internal mass of adobe bricks was reinforced by a network of stone walls. Other techniques were developed to strengthen the earthen outer walls of temples by giving them a curved profile. However, this engineering ingenuity really came into its own in defensive fortifications. The resistance of these structures to the vagaries of time was so great that their majestic remains were still standing in the mid-20th century – it was only the waters of the Aswan Dam, newly created to regulate the flow of the Nile, that finally swept away these imposing examples of military architecture. It was also around this time that the Egyptian architect Hassan Fathy rediscovered a centuries-old technique that was still in use in villages in Nubia: the Nubian vault. Fathy breathed new life into this ancient form by incorporating it into his projects (see pp. 336–339).

J.D.

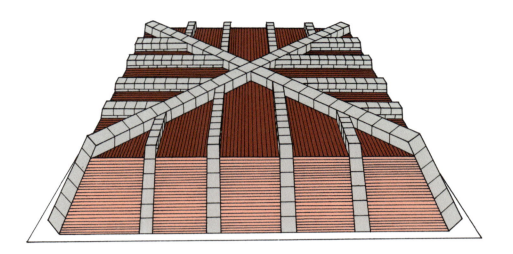

Above left: The internal structure of the pyramid of Senusret II (r. 1897–78 BCE); the mass of raw earth bricks was strengthened by a series of diagonal and parallel stone walls.

Above right: Plan of the fortress of Buhen.

Below: The fortress of Buhen, built in Nubia with earth bricks in the reign of Senusret III, in the 19th century BCE. It defended Egypt's southern borders. Reconstruction by Jean-Claude Golvin.

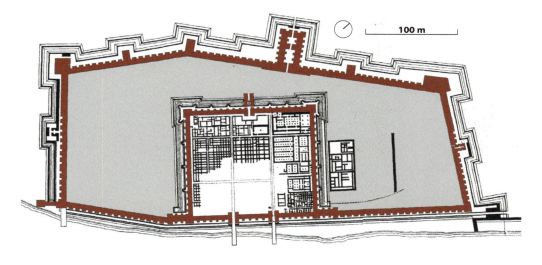

Archaeological Evidence

Pakistan, Uzbekistan, Turkmenistan

Several countries in Central Asia possess major archaeological sites that feature monumental earth architecture. In Turkmenistan, the strategic site of Merv was occupied from the 3rd millennium BCE to the 18th century CE by a series of different civilizations. From the 11th to the 13th century CE, it was one of the biggest cities in the world, with an estimated population of half a million. The State Historical and Cultural Park of Ancient Merv (listed as a UNESCO World Heritage site in 1999) contains the remains of the Great Kyz Kala (**opposite, below**), an imposing fortress built between the 6th and 8th centuries CE. A fortress in Uzbekistan is also listed by UNESCO: Itchan Kala, which protected the city of Khiva. Its undulating outer wall (**below right** and p. 69) is particularly spectacular. Another fortified building, the mausoleum of Koi Krylgan Kala, 45 metres in diameter (**above right**), was built with adobe and rammed earth in the 4th century BCE. Pakistan contains the remains of one of the oldest cities ever built: Mohenjo-Daro (**opposite, above**) in the Indus Valley, laid out in a grid pattern and dating back (like the earliest cities in Mesopotamia and Egypt) to around 2500 BCE. Its houses, as well as its enormous granary and public baths, were built with a combination of raw earth and fired clay bricks. Mohenjo-Daro was listed as a UNESCO World Heritage site in 1980.

J.D.

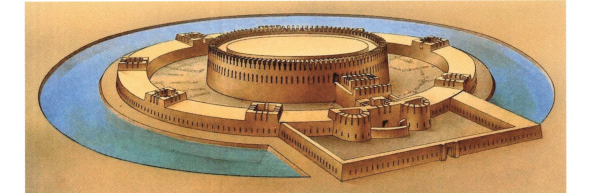

Archaeological Evidence

Peru
La Huaca del Sol

Near the city of Trujillo in northern Peru, the remains of La Huaca del Sol bear witness to the monumentality of one of the tallest buildings built in the Americas before European colonization. It was among the most spectacular accomplishments of the Moche culture, which emerged in the first century CE and disappeared around 600 years later. La Huaca del Sol (**above left and below**) is one of the architectural highlights of their capital, also known as Moche. It was the product of centuries of building, as it was made by regularly adding new layers of brick, forming a platform designed to hold the palace of an incoming sovereign. This particular *huaca* (meaning 'sacred place or object') was set on an enormous rectangular base (136 x 228 metres) and soared to a height of 41 metres. It has been calculated that 130 million adobe bricks were required to complete this gigantic building. Many of the bricks were stamped with graphic marks (**above right**) that corresponded to the specific communities that took part in the construction process.

R.E.

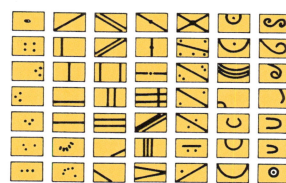

The 16th-century Spanish conquistadors who stumbled upon La Huaca del Sol did not treat the site with respect. Firstly, they were responsible for giving it its Spanish name, incorrectly suggesting that it had been associated with worship of the sun (*sol* in Spanish), and, secondly, they set about destroying much of its structure in the vain hope of finding treasure hidden within it. As well as their mastery of the art of earth architecture, the Moche people also excelled at using earth to make stunning friezes that originally covered huge areas of the walls, filling them with human, mythological, and animal figures. These artistic treasures (**right and opposite**) were first recorded by archaeologist Ricardo Morales Gamarra at the neighbouring site of La Huaca de la Luna.
J.D.

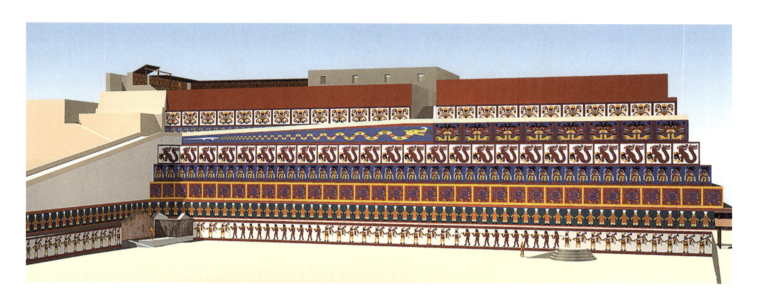

Archaeological Evidence

Peru
Chan Chan

The impressive archaeological site of Chan Chan, listed as a UNESCO World Heritage site in 1986, stands on the edge of the Pacific Ocean in present-day Peru. It bears witness to the dynamic creativity of Chimú culture, which lasted from the 9th to the 15th century CE. The remains reveal a monumental urban hub divided into nine districts (*ciudadelas*), as well as fortified palaces complete with temples (*huacas*), ceremonial halls, mortuary chambers, and living quarters. Chimú art found its supreme form of expression in adobe and cob walls covered with a layer of smooth clay that was then embellished by friezes with a wide range of anthropomorphic and zoomorphic motifs (**right and opposite**).

J.D.

Mexico
The Island City of Tenochtitlan

Founded in the 14th century CE, Tenochtitlan was the capital of the Aztec or Méxica people. Hernán Cortés, the leader of the Spanish conquistadors who arrived there in 1519, wrote in praise of its grandeur and harmony. This admiration did not prevent him from destroying it two years later in order to wipe out the Aztec civilization and make way for the capital of New Spain. This masterpiece of urban planning, one of the biggest cities ever conceived at that time – with between 200,000 and 900,000 inhabitants – was wiped off the map. The city had been built on a sacred site, Lake Texcoco. Vast amounts of earth were removed from its banks to create huge artificial islands that contained the city's four main districts, spread over almost 1,000 hectares and linked by a network of roads and canals. In order to feed Tenochtitlan's large population, the Aztecs pioneered urban agriculture by edging the city with thousands of *chinampas*, small artificial islands formed by weaving an underwater fence of reeds and twigs. Soil and vegetation would build up inside the fence, creating the appearance of a floating garden. A topsoil of very fertile silt made it possible to farm the *chinampas* intensively, with four harvests a year.

J.D. & R.E.

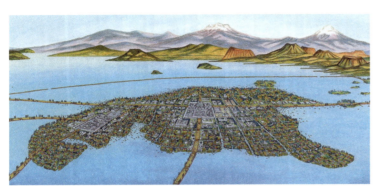
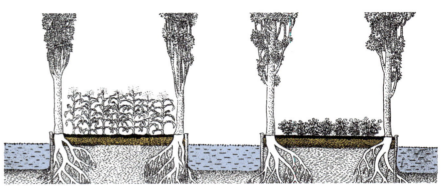

Opposite, above left: An overview of the island city of Tenochtitlan.

Opposite, above right: Cross-sections of a *chinampa*.

Opposite, below: Detail of *Tenochtitlan* (1945), a mural by Diego Rivera.

Below: Map of Tenochtitlan in 1524.

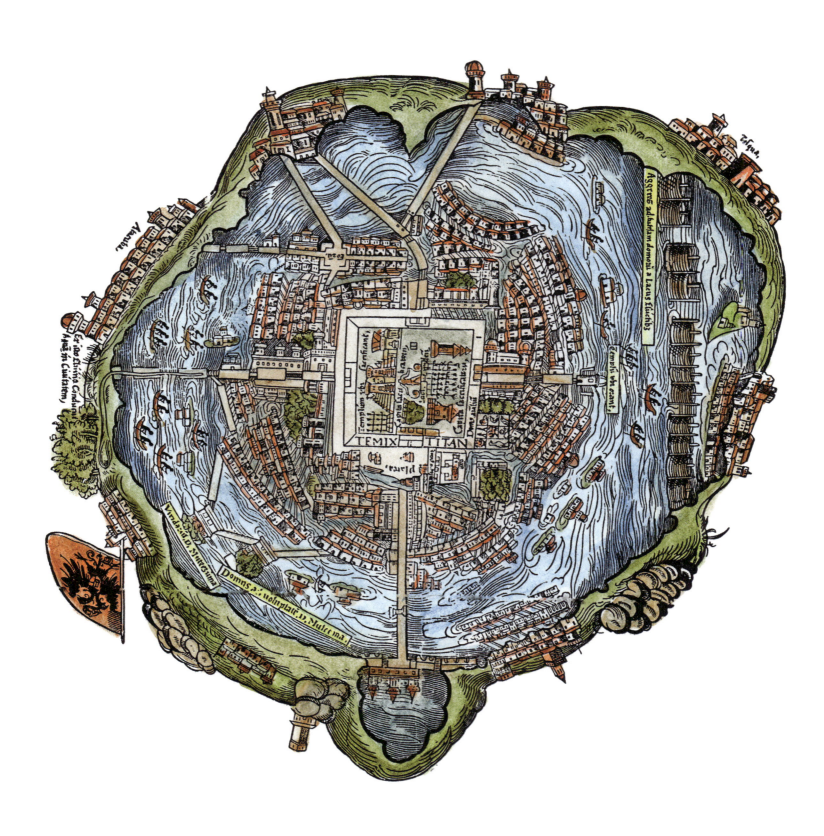

North America
The Mound Builders

Among the earliest sophisticated cultures to have emerged in North America, the culture of the Mound Builders is thought to have originated in around 3500 BCE and to have lasted for almost 5,000 years. Its archaeological remains include architectural structures that are unique in the world. Many sites include huge earthen mounds in geometric or organic shapes, which served various functions: religious, ceremonial, residential, or funerary. Despite this extensive evidence, many white Americans long refused to acknowledge these monumental configurations as the work of Native Americans and instead clung to far-fetched theories that attributed them to outsiders from Mesopotamia, Egypt, Israel, Africa, China, or Europe.

J.D. & R.E.

Above right: This oval ring of earthen mounds in Watson Brake, Louisiana, is 300 metres in diameter and is thought to have been built around 3900–3300 BCE.

Below right: The Poverty Point earthworks in Louisiana measure over one kilometre across and were created between 3,500 and 4,500 years ago.

Opposite, above: Built between 100 BCE and 500 CE, the Newark earthworks in Ohio include a circular enclosure measuring 350 metres in diameter and an octagon 460 metres across, surrounded by 2-metre-high embankments of earth.

Opposite, below: Artist's impression of a temple mound town by the Mississippi river.

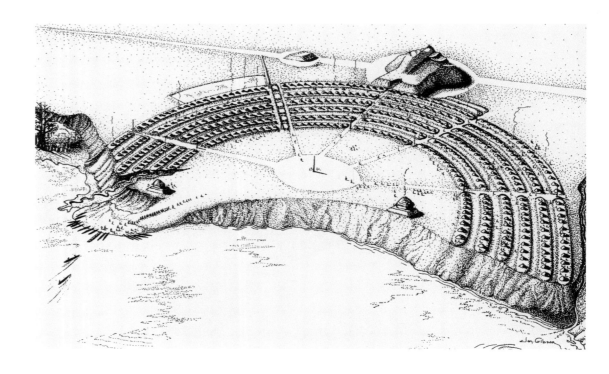

Archaeological Evidence

Europe

Early in human history, modes of living were transformed by the Neolithic revolution, which began about ten thousand years ago and ushered in agriculture and livestock rearing. This was a long process that occurred at different speeds on different continents, independently of each other, from Africa to the Americas, from China to Asia Minor. In the latter case, changes took root in the bio-geographical region of the Fertile Crescent (mainly located in present-day Iraq and Syria). Another consequence of this revolution was the establishment of permanent settlements built from earth, and in the 7th millennium BCE this new technology spread from Turkey to Eastern Europe. One of the first results was the rectangular Danubian house, which could sometimes reach 45 metres in length. As the Danube Valley had an abundance of trees, this type of house was constructed using sturdy wooden posts embedded in the ground, joined together by walls of wattle and daub. Over the next two thousand years, this construction method gradually moved westwards across Europe. In the wake of many local adaptations, the architectural archetype of a load-bearing wooden framework filled in with earth remained commonplace in Europe for centuries afterwards. It is still evident in countless rural and urban houses today.

J.D.

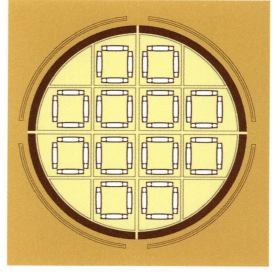

Above: A Neolithic house of the kind discovered in Romania.

Below left: Plan of the earthen ramparts of the Neolithic village of Poljanica in Bulgaria.

Below right: Plan of an 11th-century Viking fortress in Trelleborg, Sweden.

Opposite: A Neolithic house of the kind discovered in Bulgaria and Romania (above).

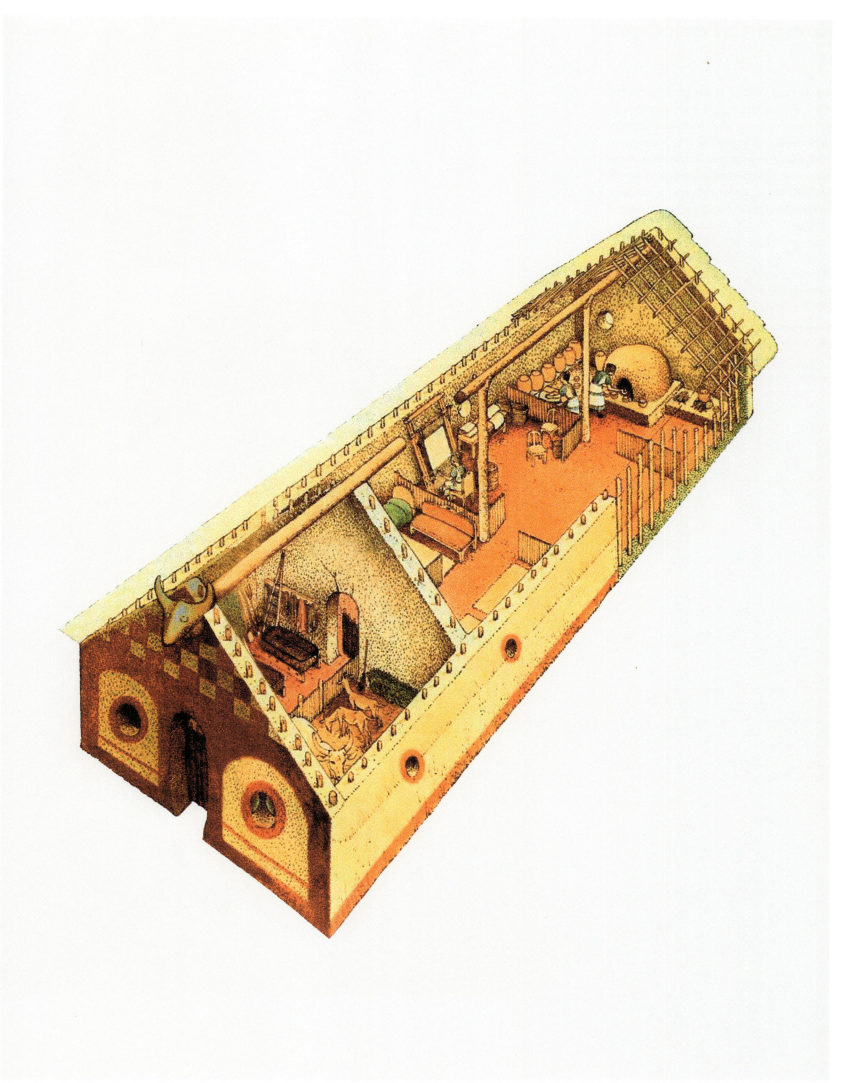

Archaeological Evidence

Raw Earth Sculptures

It was long believed that sculptures made from raw earth could not survive in the long term unless they were fired at high temperatures. In the early 21st century, however, state-of-the-art research has shown that some masterpieces from the ancient world, such as these three heads, were in fact made from unbaked earth.
    R.E.

Above right: Head of Amenhotep III, 14th century BCE, Egyptian Museum, Cairo.

Below right: Head of a bodhisattva, *ca.* 7th century, Afghanistan; Guimet Museum, Paris.

Opposite: Head of a bearded man, *ca.* 1500 BCE, Elamite civilization, Iran; Louvre, Paris.

Archaeological Evidence

Chapter 3

Historical Innovations

The ancient city of Shibam, Yemen, is a masterpiece of town planning as well as vernacular and ecological architecture. With its dense urban fabric and its tower-houses of raw earth ranging from five to seven storeys in height, it is a striking example of creative intelligence, harmony, and durability (see pp. 108–113).

Detail of the outer wall of a mosque, Mali (see pp. 202–209).

Revolutions in the Art of Earth Architecture

Jean Dethier

Several significant phases in the evolution and expansion of the art of building with raw earth occurred within the context of great revolutionary upheavals that radically changed the perspectives of the societies concerned.

Raw earth construction first emerged in ancient times – notably in Mesopotamia but also in other parts of the world – as part of the Neolithic revolution. This term refers to humankind's transition from nomadism to sedentary settlements, which triggered the need to build the first fixed dwellings and the first villages from the natural materials that were locally available. These constructions took on monumental dimensions during the urban revolution that began in the 3rd millennium BCE, which gave rise to the first large agglomerations in the Fertile Crescent in Asia Minor (Syria, Iraq), as well as their imposing fortified walls, palaces, and temples, all built with raw earth.

This building technique was refined and passed on over thousands of years in many cultures and civilizations, from the Americas to Asia and from Africa to Europe. In this way, across the world, an enormously broad range of planned architectural forms emerged one after another, influenced by the liveliness and infinite diversity of vernacular traditions.

From its origins in the 7th century, Arab-Muslim civilization developed its own art of raw earth architecture. This spread quickly as a result of Islam's territorial expansion, particularly in Morocco, where it was enriched by the remarkable expertise of the Berbers, and later in Andalusia, where it fused with Jewish and Christian traditions. The acropolis of the Alhambra in Granada, at the heart of that prosperous region, is testament to the unprecedented sophistication of this cultural synergy. Having begun to master this form of architecture, Spain then exported it to the Americas from the 15th century onwards and used it in the construction of dozens of colonial towns. This transatlantic transfer of technology came into contact, in turn, with the architectural skills already developed by the local indigenous cultures, including their own use of raw earth. These cultural transfers from Asia Minor to North Africa and Southern Europe and then the Americas occurred under the auspices of two revolutionary developments that shook the world order: the Arab conquest and modern colonial imperialism.

In the late 18th century, another crucial evolution began to take shape. It spread through Europe and beyond, triggered by the ideals of the Enlightenment and the French Revolution. It was in this context that the architect François Cointeraux took the first steps in the modernization of the ancient art of building with earth.

In the 1940s, the Egyptian architect Hassan Fathy revived this process within the dual context of the identity revolution taking place in the Muslim world and the struggle for liberation from the colonial yoke, as declared by the Bandung Conference in 1955. Both of these movements were driven by the political will of emerging countries to usher in a new world order that would guarantee them an independence that granted real autonomy.

In the 1970s, the energy revolution resulting from the two worldwide oil crises and the ongoing ecological revolution were among the major catalysts that provided a political, social, and technological context for the foundation of CRAterre in France in the late 1970s. For nearly five decades, this group has promoted an ambitious global strategy to revive the art of building with raw earth, making it the third major pioneer of this field in modern times, after Cointeraux and Fathy.

Ending the Prejudice Against Earth Architecture: What Can History Teach Us?

Ruth Eaton

'Raw earth is a poor material, for poor people and poor countries.' 'Buildings made from it are primitive and fragile, reflecting a dark and marginal past.' Negative and baseless preconceptions of this kind obscure a very different objective reality. As the history of earth architecture has long since fallen out of general knowledge, there is now a need to put the record straight.

Raw earth architecture can be found on every continent, in an extremely wide range of climates, from tropical to semi-desert to temperate, in wet and dry, in hot and cold, and on plains and in the mountains. In all of these geographical contexts, the mastery of this humble material has provided humans with durable shelter.

The adaptability of raw earth can also be seen in the two major modes of settlement adopted when humans first became sedentary: rural, where its use has often been dominant (and sometimes still is), and urban. Historians and archaeologists believe that a crucial stage in the development of civilization was the establishment of urban settlements in ancient Mesopotamia – also known as the 'urban revolution' – with the earliest towns primarily being built with raw earth. These building skills were later perfected in countless cities over the centuries, as is evident from the vibrant civilizations of ancient Egypt and other parts of Africa, as well as in China, Europe, and the Americas.

With an extraordinary diversity of buildings created all over the world, raw earth has always satisfied the needs of every social class, from the poorest to the most affluent. This has been demonstrated in multiple cultures from antiquity to the present day. Enormous palaces were built for the upper echelons of society, from ancient times (Mari in Mesopotamia) up to the early 20th century (in Morocco, Yemen, and Saudi Arabia). In Europe, the monumental Alhambra in Granada is a masterpiece of earth architecture that showcases a highly sophisticated mode of living. These accomplishments find their contemporary equivalents in luxurious villas built by wealthy families in the United States (particularly in Arizona and New Mexico) or by European jet-setters amid the palm groves of Marrakech. In Australia and Europe, similar homes have also been built for the middle classes.

Beyond the realm of housing, earth architecture has long been used to create a great variety of buildings. These include military constructions such as fortresses, such as Bam in Iran and Bahla in Oman; large-scale defensive structures built to deter invaders, such as the Great Wall of China, partially built with rammed earth; and the imposing Nubian fortress of Buhen in ancient Egypt, which protected the southern limits of Egyptian territory on both sides of the Nile. In Morocco, the rammed earth walls of the winding streets of the old towns – medinas – would measure hundreds of miles if they were laid straight. Many medinas were enlarged in the 17th century and still form part of the urban landscape today. As for civil architecture, there are countless examples, serving social, cultural, agricultural, or religious purposes; think of the thousands of remarkable mosques built in Africa, the Middle East, and even China. Since around the dawn of the 21st century, these diverse uses of raw earth have been extended into the realms of culture (museums), medicine (hospitals), tourism (hotels and guest houses), and education (schools, polytechnics, training centres, and even university and scientific buildings).

Raw earth architecture has given rise to an extremely broad repertoire of artistic forms that often exert a powerful aesthetic appeal. Cultures and civilizations worldwide have exploited this modest material with great ingenuity, using it to express their differences and reflect their own distinguishing traits. The building techniques and architectural languages display artistic spirit, often in a spectacular way. Vibrant vernacular architecture has emerged all over the world, often as a result of fruitful collaboration between local creativity and practical experience, resulting in unique and extraordinary examples of beauty and harmony.

While the majority of raw earth buildings are only one or two storeys in height, there are nevertheless many examples that prove that it is possible to far exceed this limit. In Mesopotamia, the Etemenanki – a ziggurat that once stood in the centre of Babylon and may have given rise to the Tower of Babel myth – could claim, at over 90 metres high, to be the first skyscraper in history. Its exceptional size was achieved in tribute to the gods, but civil architecture could also rise to impressive heights. The Yemeni town of Shibam was filled with tower blocks built from raw earth, closely packed together and rising to between five and seven storeys tall, creating an urban landscape that seems to prefigure Baron Haussmann's renovation of Paris under Napoleon III in the 19th century. The same quest to build vertically appeared throughout Europe in the centuries that followed, resulting in the rammed earth buildings of the Croix-Rousse district of Lyon, France, and the loam houses of Weilburg, Germany. The survival of so many raw earth buildings, particularly the hundreds of thousands of rural homes erected across Europe in the 19th century, bear witness to the solidity and durability of this type of architecture.

History shows us that raw earth architecture has been the anonymous hero of an epic global journey that began many millennia ago and has unfairly become one of the least known chapters in global art and architectural history. This rich creative field is not a mere relic of the past; it is now experiencing a resurgence all over the world. Even though this boom has been sparked by a new interest in ancient traditions, more recent examples of earth architecture can be just as inspiring.

It is notable that, of the 869 cultural, architectural, and urban sites that have been classified as UNESCO World Heritage Sites since 1978, more than 160 of these, spread across 60 countries, were built – in whole or in part – with raw earth. Their presence on this list reflects a major shift in priorities, as only a few decades ago many of these buildings were little known, or even derided.

Moreover, since the 1970s, a growing number of cultural and scientific experts – including the pioneers at CRAterre – have explored the potential of vernacular earth architecture. The intelligence and ingenuity behind it are now being applied to develop new building strategies and technical innovations as a means of creating the reliable and sustainable eco-architecture of tomorrow. In fact, it seems that the ancient techniques of earth architecture, even those on the brink of obsolescence, often enjoy a surprising upswing when a society is confronted by a serious crisis or a major collective challenge.

In Europe, the mass destruction of two world wars led Germany to implement ambitious programmes to rebuild whole neighbourhoods and villages with earth.

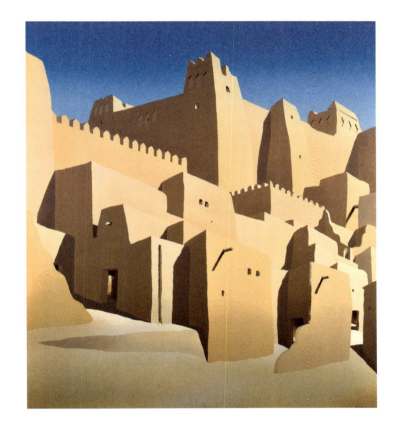

Now the eco-revolution and the challenges of climate change have resulted in an ambitious, dynamic, and promising drive to modernize earth architecture, which will hopefully continue to flourish over the course of the 21st century.

Above: Painting by Ricardo Wolfson, 1980, acrylic on canvas. Evocation of the kasbahs in Morocco's pre-Saharan valleys (see pp. 156–165). Jean Dethier collection, Paris. Commissioned for the exhibition *Des architectures de terre* at the Centre Pompidou, Paris, 1981 (see pp. 390–391).

Yemen
The City of Shibam

Shibam, in central Yemen, is one of the most remarkable illustrations of the extraordinary potential of earth architecture to be found anywhere in the world. It is not only an example of an entire city built with earth, but also a pioneering embodiment of the concept of vertical housing, built long before our industrial era. Shibam proves that a city built with adobe is perfectly capable of reconciling and integrating the demands of harmony and beauty, urbanity and density, compactness and durability, material wealth and land economy, climatic comfort and environmental efficiency. The city was founded in the 16th century and is situated between two very different rural landscapes: arid, sandy desert and lush palm groves (see overleaf). Its rectangular plan (**opposite, above**) covers less than 8 hectares (*ca.* 330 × 230 metres). This tightly knit urban fabric includes a palace, several mosques, and communal spaces, as well as almost five hundred apartment blocks

(**below and opposite**). These range from five to seven storeys in height, with two rooms on each floor. The lower levels were used to store food and other goods, while the upper ones served to house families, which often comprised ten people or more. The uppermost storey was the domain of the women, and extended outside onto flat roof areas that served as communal terraces, allowing households to interact. Nowadays, Shibam has a population of around 7,000 people.

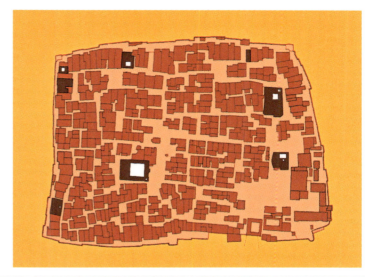

Historical Innovations

The whitewash on the upper storeys of the buildings is reapplied every year to ensure the optimal reflection of sunlight. The resulting heat protection is enhanced by the densely packed arrangement of the buildings, which keeps the load-bearing exterior walls of the houses in shade. These walls can be up to a metre thick at their base, tapering to around 30 centimetres at the top. The compact configuration of the neighbourhoods leaves no room for an inner courtyard inside the houses, unusually for the Arab-Muslim world; in Shibam, only mosques and single-storey palaces have courtyards. All of the city's buildings were constructed on stone foundations with adobe bricks (known locally as *madar*), which were manufactured and laid by skilled artisans, whose professional training was overseen by a traditional association of master builders (a pattern that can still found today in Djenné, Mali). It is virtually impossible to verify the exact date when Shibam's apartment blocks were originally constructed, as they have been repeatedly modified, extended, and restored, but it is believed that most of them were built in the 19th century, and some may be considerably older.

Above and below right: Views of the city of Shibam.

Historical Innovations

As a unique example of earth architecture and city planning, the entire city of Shibam was listed as a UNESCO World Heritage site in 1982. In 2015, however, UNESCO was obliged to place Shibam on the List of World Heritage in Danger – despite initiatives by various NGOs and the unwavering efforts of the architect Salma Samar Damluji to restore the city. Unfortunately, the unremitting violence of the war that has engulfed Yemen in recent years has undermined all projects of this kind. The very survival of a city whose supremely talented builders should serve as a beacon for earth architecture in the 21st century, particularly in urban settings, is now uncertain.

J.D.

```
Further reading:
Damluji 1992
```

Right and opposite: Views of the city of Shibam.

Below, left to right: Plans, elevations, and cross-sections of some typical Shibam tower-houses.

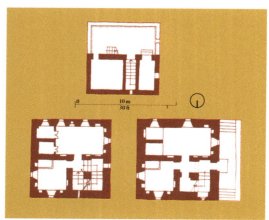

Iran
Ancient Cities

The ancient city of Yazd, situated on Iran's central plain, was known as the Pearl of the Desert for its exceptional architectural beauty. An aerial view (**centre right**) reveals a stunning array of vaults and domes made with raw earth bricks covered with a layer of earth and straw (*kahgel*), interspersed with elegant wind towers (*badgirs*). Yazd is a prime example of the ability of builders to adapt to a hostile environment by taking full advantage of the resources available. Each of its neighbourhoods was supplied with water from the surrounding mountains via a network of wells and underground channels called *qanats*. The most sophisticated residences included rooms set entirely below ground level in order to maintain a cool temperature in the scorching summer heat. Vaulted water tanks and cold stores were also kept cool by wind towers, the most striking of which adorned beautiful mansion houses such as Aghazadeh (**overleaf, below right**) and Khan-e Lari, built under the Qajar dynasty (1789–1925). The streets are punctuated by arcades roofed with earthen brick (*sabats*), providing valuable shade (**above right and opposite**). Yazd is one of the finest examples of urban planning in a desert setting, successfully achieving a balance between human needs and nature.

H.G.

Below right: An aerial view of the West Sabat House inside the citadel of Bam, Iran. Much of the citadel was destroyed by an earthquake in 2003.

Overleaf and pp. 118–119: Other towns in the region, including Ardestan and Meybod, reflect the same architectural legacy. Aerial images show the density of the urban fabric.

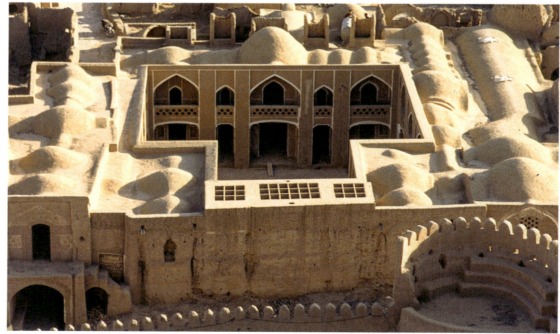

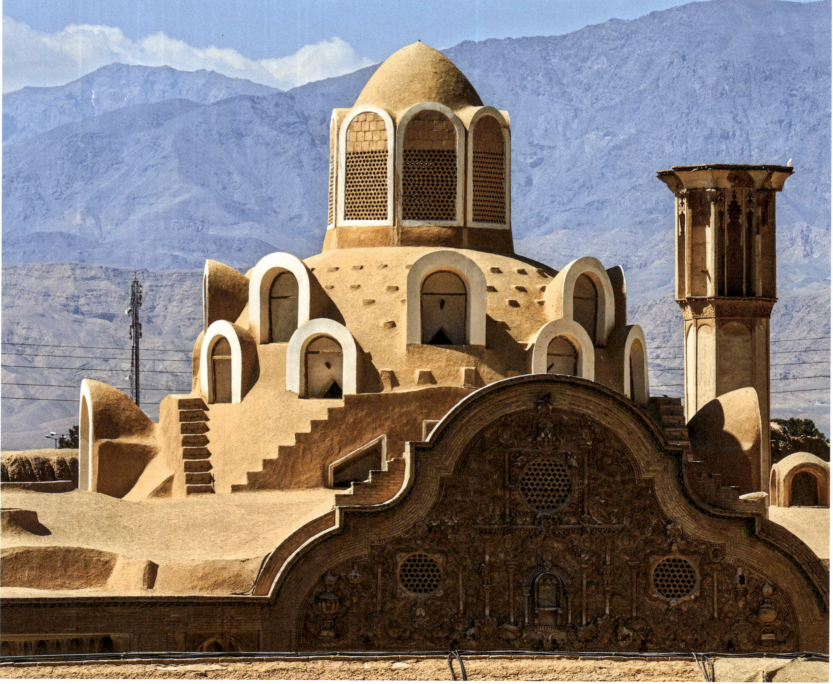

Chapter 3

Iran
The Citadel of Bam

The historic Citadel of Bam (Arg-e Bam) is situated in Iran, southeast of Kerman and north of Jiroft. It evolved during the Achaemenid, Parthian, and Sasanian periods, and its growth was closely linked to the system of *qanats*, underwater canals connected to wells that were built to irrigate the nearby oasis. The citadel was built entirely from layers of cob (*chineh*) and adobe (*khesht*). With its triple ramparts and numerous watchtowers, it is a remarkable defensive structure. The citadel included bazaars, schools, mosques, madrasas, and public baths, as well as military barracks. On 26 December 2003, both the citadel and the modern town of Bam were devastated by a massive earthquake. A year later, the citadel was added to the UNESCO List of World Heritage in Danger, and it has since been subject to a major restoration programme that is still ongoing.

H.G.

Above and below right: Views of the Citadel of Bam.

Historical Innovations

Iran
Wind Towers and Cold Rooms

As well as its countless masterpieces of earth architecture built over the centuries, the country that is now Iran is also the birthplace of remarkable technological ingenuity. Two inventions whose origins are lost in the mists of time have proved particularly effective. A *badgir* (literally 'catch-wind' in Farsi) is a traditional architectural feature used to create natural air-conditioning. It comprises a series of vertical brick tubes with slits cut into the top, designed to capture wind and convey it inside a building (**opposite, above and below**). Several of these elements were grouped into a square or octagonal tower, arranged to create a cooling downward air current and an upward rising current that eliminates warm air from the interior. The city of Yazd is popularly known as the 'City of Wind Catchers' due to its abundance of *badgirs*. A *yakhchal* (**below right**) is another structure designed to combat excessive heat, as its distinctive form serves as a natural refrigerator. Its conical, half-buried dome, with earthen walls at least two metres thick at its base, was used in summer to store ice brought down from the surrounding mountains in the winter. Some *yakhchals* had a capacity of 5,000 cubic metres. Another strategy involved combining a *yakhchal* and a *badgir*, reinforcing the cooling effect by allowing warm air to escape from an opening in the top of the dome (**above right**).

J.D.

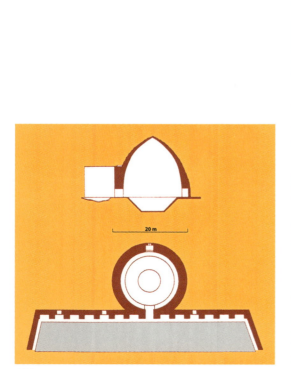

China
The Great Wall

The Great Wall of China is a huge series of military fortifications, designed to defend China's northern borders; it was built, destroyed, and rebuilt over the course of two millennia, up until the 17th century. The Great Wall is not, therefore, a single construction tracing a line from east to west but instead a conglomeration of strategically positioned walls that together form a single ensemble over 20,000 kilometres in length. On average, the wall is 6 to 7 metres high and 4 to 5 metres wide. The enormous geographical and geological diversity of the regions through which it runs resulted in the use of a variety of construction materials. In areas where stone was unavailable, for example, sections of the wall were built with rammed earth. This is particularly true of the final section in the far west, in Gansu province, which concludes in dramatic style with the Jiayuguan Fortress (**right, above and below**). In 1987, several sections of this Chinese national treasure were listed as UNESCO World Heritage sites.

J.D.

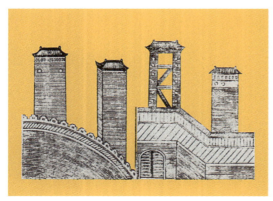

China
Tulou of the Hakka People

In the 12th century CE, in the province of Fujian in southeastern China, the havoc wreaked by bandits who had long bedeviled the Chinese countryside gave rise to a unique form of rural domestic architecture, specific to the Hakka ethnic group: the *tulou* (**below and opposite**). This ancestral tradition, which has survived to this day, has been well documented. In 2008, a set of 46 *tulou* was classified as a UNESCO World Heritage site, which has since become a tourist attraction. These enormous fortress-like complexes are often circular, with a diameter of up to 70 metres, and can be up to five storeys in height. Their imposing outer wall, built with rammed earth, can be 2 to 3 metres thick, serving a defensive function, while the solidity and density of the structure also help to regulate the temperature inside. The austere, monolithic exterior contrasts with the harmonious subtlety of the concentric space within, which encouraged the settlement's several hundred residents to live together on a communal and egalitarian

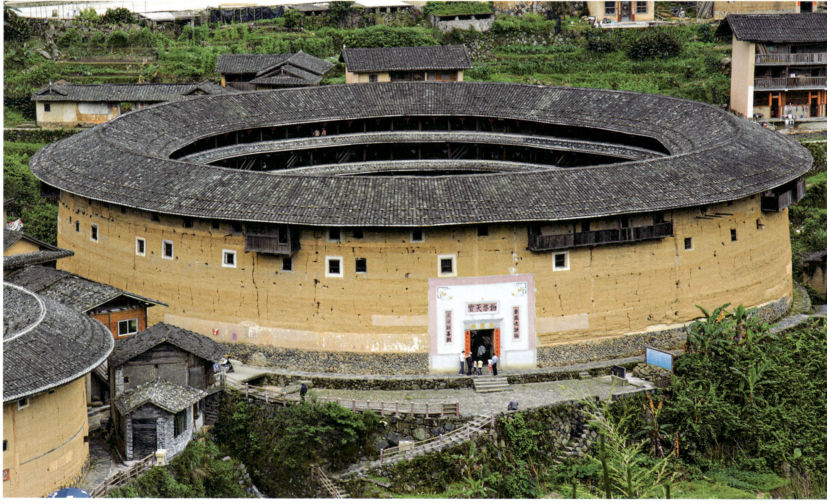

basis. The central courtyard contained the lowest-level buildings: a temple to the ancestors, kitchens, and wells. This nucleus was surrounded by a circular outer building lined with circular galleries. Each family occupied a trapezoidal section of this circular building, spread across multiple storeys: animals were confined to the ground floor, while the floor immediately above was used for storage and the upper levels served as living quarters. The oldest surviving *tulou* dates back to 1308, the most recent to 1981. For over seven centuries, this type of building has been one of the world's most sophisticated examples of the art of communal living.

J.D.

Further reading:
Dunzhen 1980; Dingcheng 2014

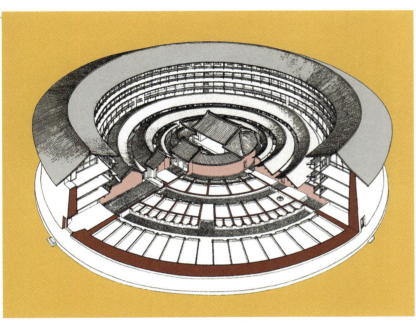

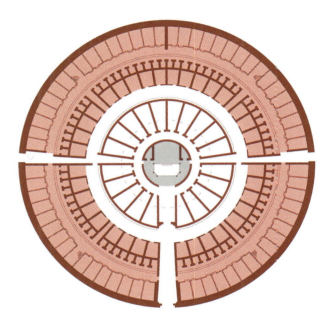

India
Monasteries in the Spiti Valley

In the state of Himachal Pradesh in the far north of India, the Spiti Valley boasts several masterpieces of earth architecture. The Buddhist monastery of Tabo (**right**) was built in the 10th century and is now classified as a national historic treasure. The Key Gompa monastery (**overleaf**) dates back to the 11th century.
    R.E.

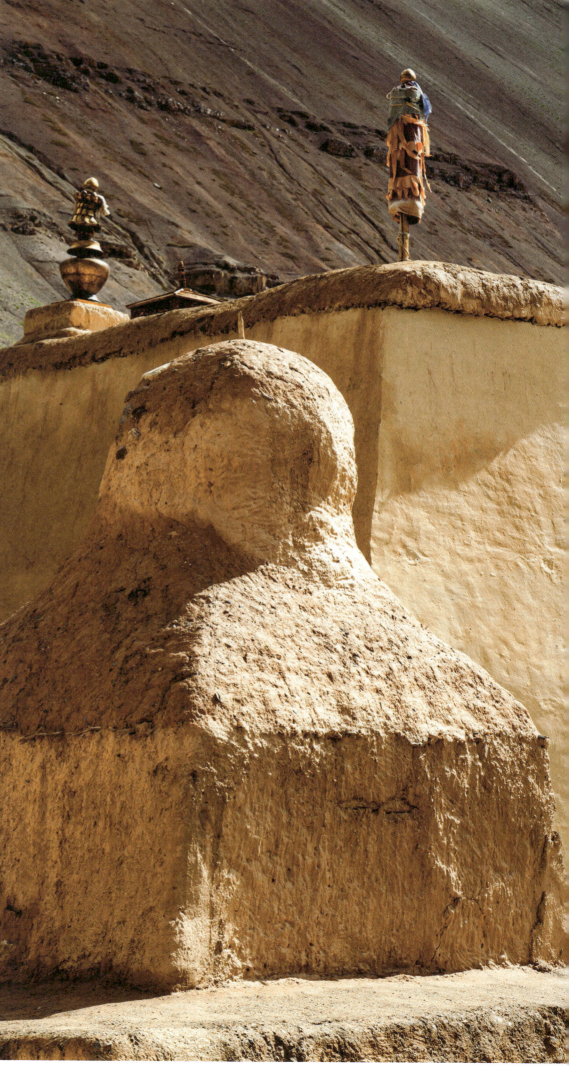

Japan
Temples, Streets, and Gardens

The architectural uses of earth in Japan illustrate the way that this humble material has been integrated into the philosophy of Zen Buddhism and the aesthetic code of *wabi-sabi*. The Zen garden of the Ryoan-ji temple in Kyoto (**below right**) exemplifies the art of *karesansui*, the making of rock gardens. This sublime composition, created in the 15th century, features fifteen rocks emerging from a layer of white gravel, bordered by a reddish outer wall of rammed earth. This haven of spirituality and meditation has been recognized by UNESCO as a World Heritage site. The walls of the Kannon-ji temple in Tokushima (**above left**) illustrate a traditional method of decorating a rammed earth wall by studding it with pieces of glazed ceramic. In the old samurai district of Nagamachi in the city of Kanazawa, the streets are lined with artfully textured earthen walls (**above right**).

R.E.

United States
The Indian Pueblos of Taos

The Indian pueblos are some of the still-inhabited communal dwellings in the southwest United States. It was the Spanish conquistadors who first gave the name to the dwellings of the Anasazi people in the 16th century, in reference to the villages (*pueblos*) in which they lived, and whose architecture was unlike anything else in the New World. Of the 25 pueblos that have survived, the best preserved is Taos, New Mexico (**below right**). It was probably founded in the 13th century and is the only community entirely constructed with adobe to have remained continuously occupied up to the present day. It was listed as a World Heritage site in 1992. Its houses are compact, tiered structures with three to five storeys. They are stacked so that the terrace of one house is positioned on the flat roof of its neighbour below (**below left**). The women were responsible for renewing the outer layer of earth in regular ceremonies (**above right**). They also built and used traditional conical bread ovens (**above left**). Not far away, in Ranchos de Taos, Spaniards built the adobe Church of Saint Francis of Assisi (**overleaf**), a century after the rebellion of 1680, which pitted the indigenous population against the missionaries who were trying to convert them to Christianity.

J.D.

Historical Innovations

United States
Spanish Colonial Churches

Prior to its incorporation into the Union in 1850, the modern state of New Mexico was inhabited by the indigenous Pueblo peoples before being colonized by the Spanish in the 16th century and declared part of the viceroyalty of New Spain. This conquest was marked by the construction of many Catholic churches from raw earth, which have since become a major feature of the cultural landscape. The Church of Saint Francis of Assisi (**below and opposite**), built in Ranchos de Taos in 1772, stands as a remarkable testimony to this historic intrusion. Its outer walls are particularly striking, as they seem to be straining to reconcile sober austerity with sculptural sensuality. This expressive power became a source of inspiration for several major artists of the 20th century, including Georgia O'Keeffe, Ansel Adams, and Paul Strand. Every year, the local community gathers together to refurbish the church's outer walls, in a ceremony similar to the one used to communally repair the walls of the Great Mosque of Djenné in Mali (see pp. 192–195).

J.D. & R.E.

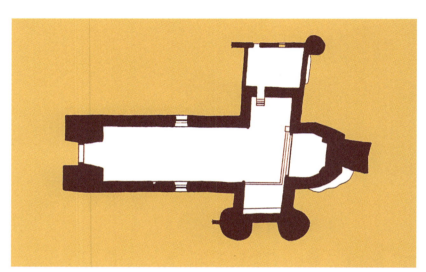

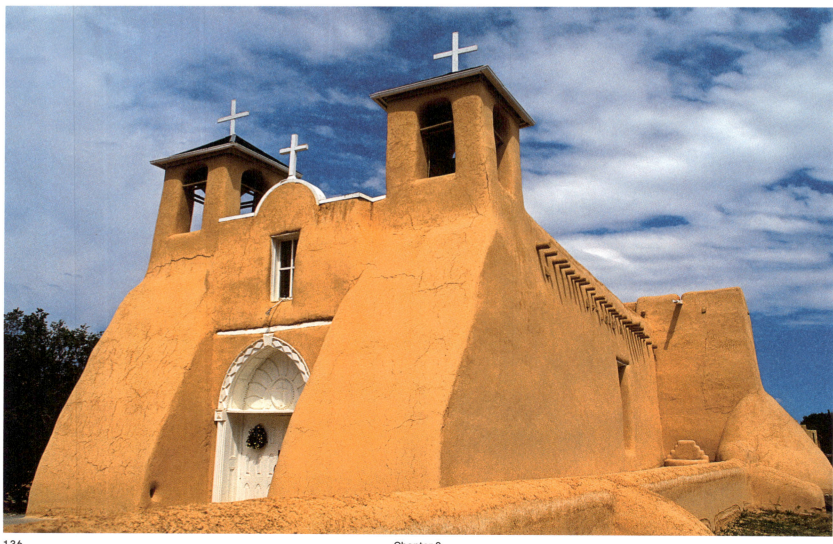

Latin America
Colonial Churches

The colonization of the Americas first by the Spanish and then the Portuguese, starting in the 16th century, resulted in the construction of countless earthen Catholic churches in both towns and rural areas.
R.E.

Above left: The Church of San Clemente in Coro, Venezuela.

Above centre and right: The elevation and ground plan of the Church of Yaguarón, Paraguay.

Below: The Jesuit Mission Church of Concepción in Chiquitanía, Bolivia. Built in 1752, it is part of a group of six Jesuit missions known collectively as the Missions of the Chiquitos, which were classified as a UNESCO World Heritage site in 1990.

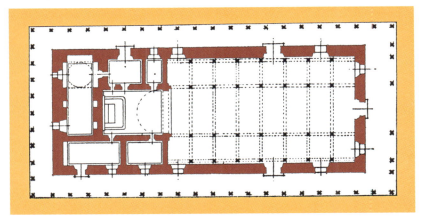

Historical Innovations

Latin America
Colonial Towns

It is estimated that, in the 16th century, the European colonization of the Americas led to the construction of over 200 new settlements. Most of these were built on a grid plan, and earth was the predominant material, either in the form of rammed earth or adobe.
R.E.

Above right: A colonial town in Colombia built on a grid plan.

Below: The town of Tiradentes, founded in 1702 in the state of Minas Gerais, Brazil.

Opposite, above left and right: Plans incorporating housing and agriculture in Uruguay (1781).

Overleaf: Historic neighbourhoods in the cities of Antigua, Guatemala (below left), Coro, Venezuela (above left), and Oaxaca, Mexico (below right).

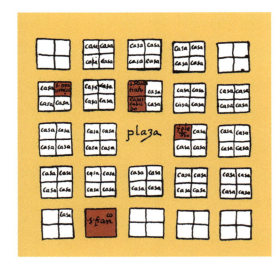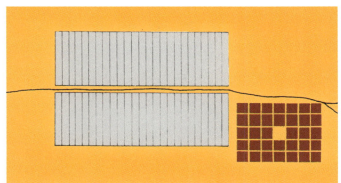

Historical Innovations

141

Historical Innovations

Spain
The Alhambra, Granada

The Alhambra, overlooking the city of Granada in the heart of Andalusia, is one of the most remarkable and majestic beacons of Islamic architecture in the world. It is the only palace complex from the civilization of Al-Andalus that has reached the 21st century in an excellent state of conservation. In 1984, it was listed as a UNESCO World Heritage site. This medieval acropolis, perched on a hill, was built in the 13th century by the Nasrid king Mohammed ben Nazar. Eight centuries later, the huge fortified rammed earth walls of its citadel, the Alcazaba (**above right and opposite**), still bear witness to the remarkable skills that the Berbers brought with them from Morocco, where this type of construction had been perfected centuries earlier. Many other examples of this ancient architectural lore can still be seen in Spain – in Baños de la Encina (**below right**), in the province of Jaén – and also in Morocco, particularly in Rabat, where the outer walls of the Chellah necropolis (**centre right**) date from the 14th century.

J.D.

Morocco
Medinas

The medina is a particular type of town invented by Arab-Islamic civilizations. This urban model is partly inherited from the earthen cities built five thousand years ago in Mesopotamia. Each medina grows organically, with almost all the buildings inward-facing, arranged around a courtyard. This layout allows houses to be built back to back, resulting in a compact configuration and a dense overall structure that provides effective protection against climatic extremes. Morocco is the country that has most successfully preserved the coherence, vitality, and harmony of its traditional medinas, since it values them as an unsurpassed treasure. The oldest and most prestigious medina of all, in the city of Fez, was founded in the 8th century and, although it was largely built with stone, rammed earth was the principal material used to build its long defensive wall, its fortified bastions (*borjs*; **above and centre right**), and the buildings around the monumental *mechouar* (plaza), which leads to the royal palace (**below right**). Three other imperial Moroccan cities also have rammed earth outer walls; the oldest of these, in Rabat, dates back to the 14th century (**opposite, above**). In Meknes, the Sultan Moulay Ismail built an enormous palace complex with rammed earth in 1672, later captured in a famous painting by Eugène Delacroix (see p. 352). As for the medina in Marrakech, built in the 10th century, its adobe courtyard houses (**opposite, below**) exude a timeless charm. All four of these medinas have been listed as UNESCO World Heritage sites, and each of them eloquently demonstrates the potential of earth architecture in an urban setting.

J.D.

Asia
Agricultural Landscapes

For thousands of years, humanity has used the resources provided by land to fulfil two basic needs: a food supply, by using the topsoil for agriculture, and shelter, by transforming the subsoil into walls and other architectural elements. Sometimes, however, there are exceptional cases in which these two different approaches come together in a creative fusion. This process has resulted in artificial agricultural landscapes with such a powerful visual impact that they can be considered veritable works of architecture. Such is the case with rice fields in Asia that extend down mountain slopes via an elaborate network of terraces, held in place by simple walls made of stone or earth (**right and opposite**). These walls are built in a slightly curved formation to resist the strong pressure to which they are subjected. The folk knowledge required to achieve such feats emerged one or two millennia ago, depending on the region in question. The countries in which this ancient agricultural art holds sway include Vietnam, Sri Lanka, Indonesia (the island of Bali), the Philippines, and China (Yunnan province). In the latter two cases, the mountainside rice terraces of Banaue in the Philippines and Hani and Honghe in Yunnan were listed as UNESCO World Heritage sites in 1995 and 2013, respectively. These masterpieces of agronomic landscaping are imbued with a timeless and breathtaking beauty that reflects a state of harmony between human endeavour and the natural world. These enduring ecosystems, created in mountainous regions by farming communities, stand as striking examples of land management and ecological balance, achieved via a meticulous knowledge of both the terrain and the water supply needed to provide continuous irrigation for thousands of rice plants.

    J.D.

Historical Innovations

Chapter 4

Vernacular Heritage

Ksar (fortified village) on the edge of a palm grove in the southern Draa Valley, Morocco (see pp. 156–161).

What Can We Learn from Vernacular Traditions?

Anne-Monique Bardagot and Nathalie Sabatier

The information about vernacular architecture that has been gathered and recorded by ethnologists, geographers, and sociologists forms part of a study of human settlements that aims to create a deeper understanding of a society or region. Themes covered by this study include environments, everyday life, customs, beliefs, and social structures, as well as the provenance and production of building materials and construction methods. And because raw earth is still widely used all over the world and has given rise to an extraordinary range of architectural styles and structures, research into this natural resource has been similarly far-reaching.

In 1964, Austrian architect Bernard Rudofsky curated the exhibition *Architecture Without Architects* at MoMA, New York. Visitors were overwhelmed by the beauty and intelligence of the vernacular architecture on display, created by communities from all over the world. In 1981, the Belgian architect Jean Dethier curated the exhibition *Des architectures de terre* at the Centre Pompidou in Paris (see pp. 390–391), showcasing architectural legacies that were often little known, ignored, or even disparaged. These two exhibitions had a global impact.

The oil crisis of the 1970s triggered an awareness of the need to build in a different way, a more environmentally friendly way, most notably by choosing local natural materials that required little or no industrial processing or transportation, in order to save energy and resources. A small group of architects thus began to undertake ethno-historical studies of vernacular architecture and research into bioclimatology. The multidisciplinary team at CRAterre (founded in 1979) was the only research group to focus specifically on techniques derived from the realm of earth architecture.

Prior to the Second World War, the art of raw earth architecture in Europe was transmitted by word of mouth, via practical experience. In the Auvergne-Rhône-Alpes region of France, for example, builders regularly used rammed earth. They possessed the right tools, an understanding of what constituted 'good earth', and time-honoured wisdom handed down from one generation to the next. Since then, however, training in all sectors of the construction industry in industrialized countries has ignored traditional natural materials such as raw earth in favour of supposedly 'modern' industrial materials such as reinforced concrete.

Traditionally, the overall cost of a raw earth building was relatively modest. Its future users would play a role in the building process, helping to fetch and prepare the earth, often with the assistance of their extended family as well as their friends and neighbours. In the early 21st century, this ancient practice has been revived as a new form of community solidarity. Participatory self-build projects of this kind, often led by public housing organizations, create mobility by allowing people to build their own homes. This form of activism is often driven by a desire to contribute to the dynamic of ecological transition in the spirit of economic solidarity by making use of biosourced or geosourced organic materials such as raw earth. The digital revolution has also amplified this call to action by providing instant access to a plethora of relevant information in the form of videos, discussion forums, and promotional appeals for community building projects.

The practices of vernacular architecture always form part of a production process that requires multiple participants. To guarantee the future of these practices, it is vital to strengthen all the elements of the 'earth sector', to engage professional competencies, and to establish a production process that can meet new needs. It is also essential to continue to collect and analyse information about every facet of this architectural field, in order to consider all possible approaches and reshape earth architecture for the modern world.

```
Further reading:
Correia et al. 2014; Mileto et al. 2018
```

An impluvium is a traditional style of house found in Senegal and Nigeria. The rooms are arranged around a circular courtyard, which contains a round basin to collect rain water.

Opposite above: An impluvium near the town of Kaduna, Nigeria.
Opposite, below: An impluvium in Casamance, Senegal.

The Vernacular Spirit and the Builders of Today

Hubert Guillaud

In 1982, Ivan Illich defined the 'vernacular' as 'a technical term that comes from Roman law [that] designates the inverse of a commodity... "Vernacular" means those things that are homemade, homespun, home-grown, not destined for the marketplace, but that are for home use only.' In architecture, however, 'vernacular' is applied to buildings with traditional local features that reflect the characteristics of a social group (its culture and lifestyle) or a specific geography and climate. It also implies the use of natural local construction materials: stone, wood, bamboo or, in many cases, raw earth. This symbiosis between multiple factors gives rise to an identity-based form of architectural expression that represents great folk artistry and a true *genius loci*. Vernacular architecture is born from the building ingenuity of the (often anonymous) local people who are involved in both its design and its construction. It is the fruit of collective forms of organization and social commitment that value solidarity, mutual aid, and the convivial sharing of knowledge and skills.

Prior to the emergence of the US counterculture of the 1960s and 1970s, very few architects took into account the resources and potential of vernacular heritage. They overlooked one obvious point: from ancient times right up to the modern era, natural local materials had always been used to construct not only homes and communal buildings but also entire villages, towns, and functional structures (dykes, fortifications, etc.). Most of these works fell into the category of 'architecture without architects', a phrase that has become commonplace since Bernard Rudofsky used it in 1964 as the title of his MoMA exhibition in New York. It is significant that this influential show was mounted in a museum renowned for its promotion of the avant-garde. It also implicitly questioned the domination of architects waving the flag for the International Style, which by definition was radically opposed to any intrusion from regional or, worse yet, vernacular idioms.

Since the 1970s, this transgressive spirit has exerted a growing influence. University degrees and professional courses that teach the theory and practice of building with natural materials have risen in popularity. This shift reflects a broader ethical commitment to create ecologically responsible architecture that finds new uses for biologically and geologically sourced materials. In the 21st century, this approach has been reflected worldwide in an enthusiasm for new buildings made with raw earth, in some cases involving the active participation of future inhabitants, in keeping with traditional social dynamics.

To reinforce this positive growth, it is vital to appreciate the lessons that a global understanding of the vernacular creative impulse can teach the builders of today. This knowledge would promote and support what could become the 'great building site of the contemporary vernacular'.

However, in many countries, architects attempting to modernize the use of natural local materials are confronted by a major obstacle: the technocratic and supposedly scientific rules and regulations that ensure the universal domination of industrial construction materials. In order to be truly creative, these architects are often obliged to engage, in the words of Patrice Doat (see pp. 476–477), in an 'act of disobedience'. Nevertheless, many talented architects are increasingly drawing on the conceptual heritage of the vernacular in their raw earth buildings. This book provides an overview of modern and contemporary work in its final two chapters.

```
Further reading:
Rudofsky 1964; Norberg-Schulz 1980; Illich 1982;
Oliver 1997; Frey 2010; Correia et al. 2014
```

Opposite: Sankore Mosque, buily in the 14th century in the Timbuktu region of Mali.

Vernacular Heritage

Morocco
Ksour of the Pre-Saharan Valleys

Morocco is one of the three countries in the world (alongside Mali and Yemen) with the most remarkable living heritage of traditional earth architecture, not only for its quality but also for its diversity and sheer quantity. This inheritance bears witness to exceptional creative intelligence. The old towns (medinas), with their rammed earth walls, are located mostly on the plains north of the High Atlas mountains (pp. 146–147), while the pre-Saharan valleys to the south of these mountains are dotted with oases full of architectural treasures. There are two main types of settlement here, both illustrating the Berbers' mastery of rammed earth and adobe: villages, called *ksour* (*ksar* in the singular), and kasbahs, the residences of the tribal chiefs. Hundreds of *ksour* are dotted across the palm groves that wind through the arid land, forming miraculous ribbons of greenery along the edge of the Sahara Desert. These villages (**right, opposite**, and pp. 158–161), which are sometimes surrounded by fortified walls, are extremely compact, thereby ensuring shade and protection against the torrid summer heat. Until the early 20th century, *ksour* were built with rammed earth in one of two ways: either according to a predetermined, almost geometric ground plan, or in a more improvised, organic fashion. In both cases, the houses were generally built with two or three storeys, topped by a roof terrace that was used to dry harvested dates.

The houses of the *ksour* are set along the edges of long, narrow, partially roofed streets. On the inside, they are designed around an inner courtyard lined with arches. To limit the effects of heat, blinding sunlight, and sandstorms, there is only one opening to the outside world, on the roof. The spatial organization of a *ksar* is often similar to that of a residential neighbourhood in a medina, which gives an unexpected urban feel to such a rural setting. A *ksar* is always situated close to an oasis, which was the only agricultural resource available to its inhabitants. Like the houses, this fragile ecosystem has three levels: cereal crops are planted around fruit trees, which themselves stand in the shade of palm trees. This clever configuration is complemented by an equally remarkable form of regional planning. The hundred or so kilometres of the inhabited part of the Draa Valley contain an almost equal number of *ksour* arranged along the banks of the river (*oued*) and across the nearby palm grove. This spatial distribution, housing around 50,000 people, recalls the avant-garde ideal of the 'linear city' popularized by 20th-century European architects, in which the inhabitants of multiple decentralized self-contained units would cooperate to create a strong collective identity. Le Corbusier, among others, was obsessed by this notion but never managed to bring it to fruition. The Berbers, however, took stock of the constraints and benefits of the Draa Valley to create a strikingly similar organization of inhabited space, built entirely from raw earth.

J.D.

Further reading:
Guillaud & Zerhouni 2001; Naji 2001

Morocco
Kasbahs of the Pre-Saharan Valleys

The oases and their hinterlands in southern Morocco were traditionally the fiefdom of tribal peoples, predominantly the Amazigh or Berber. Their chief (*caid*) lived in a *tighremt*, an Amazigh term that is analagous to the Arabic word 'kasbah'. The *tighremts* (**right and opposite**) were fortified three- or four-storey houses built on a square base. Their rammed earth facade was occasionally interrupted by small openings, and its upper section was delicately ornamented with adobe bricks. The interior (**overleaf**) was arranged around a courtyard lined with intricately carved galleries and arcades that provided warmth and conviviality – and the wealthier the *caid*, the more elaborate the arrangement of the spaces. The Amridil *tighremt* in Skoura (**opposite, above**), for example, was effectively a small, autonomous town, while those in Ouarzazate and Telouet were both constructed on a similarly grand scale in the late 19th century by the area's most powerful tribal chief, Thami El Glaoui (see pp. 268–269). Although most kasbahs were built out of reach of other settlements, some were integrated into, or attached to, a village. One example of this is the *ksar* of Tissergate, near Zagora (see pp. 282–283).

J.D.

Further reading:
Jacques-Meunié 1962

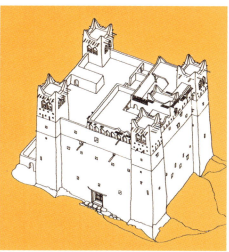

Vernacular Heritage

Vernacular Heritage

Libya
The Oasis Town of Ghadames

Ghadames is a Berber town built with raw earth in northwest Libya. It dates back to ancient times, and for centuries it was a vital port of call for caravans crossing the Sahara. It therefore combined two key functions: that of a transcontinental hub of trade and transport, and that of an oasis of regional significance. This interweaving of the global and the local, the urban and the rural, can be seen clearly in the aerial photograph (**below centre**), which also illustrates the organic nature of the town's growth. The houses, built around inner courtyards, are packed together to provide protection from the scorching heat (51°C in summer), while the streets cannot be seen from above, as they were designed as covered galleries to offer shelter from the burning sun. The walls of most rooms are pierced by vertical slits, which channel a great deal of the heat towards the roofs and courtyards. Ghadames was almost totally abandoned at the end of the 20th century, despite having been classified as a UNESCO World Heritage site since 1986. Due to further threats from the ongoing civil war in Libya, this urban masterpiece was placed on the List of World Heritage in Danger in 2016.

J.D.

Above left, below left, below right: The covered alleyways of Ghadames are designed to protect against the sun's heat.

Below centre: An aerial view of Ghadames.

Above right: The medina walls of Ghadames.

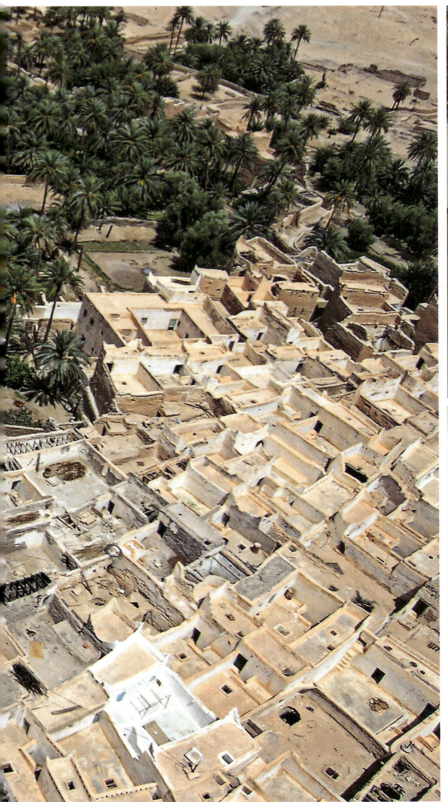

Vernacular Heritage

Egypt
Houses of Dakhla Oasis

The houses and shady streets in the village of Balat, in Dakhla Oasis in northwest Egypt, demonstrate an ancient symbiosis between architecture and sculpture (**below and opposite**). This type of domestic architecture possesses an exceptional formal and spatial fluidity, and also establishes a poetic dialogue between light and shade. The traditional villages of this oasis are among the last, barely surviving examples of the vernacular creativity of Egyptian farming communities, as they have increasingly been abandoned since the end of the 20th century.

J.D.

Further reading:
Schuiten 2014

Vernacular Heritage

Egypt
Necropolis

This enormous necropolis (**right**) was built on the outskirts of Asyut, near Aswan, in Upper Egypt. Its alleyways are lined with tombs, each one topped by a dome, all built with raw earth. Its quality and size make it a highly sophisticated example of urban planning for the world after death. Another instance of this tradition can be seen in two of the conical tombs (**below**) from the old Coptic necropolis of Bagawat, near Kharga Oasis, which is another striking example of elegant funerary architecture built from earth.

R.E.

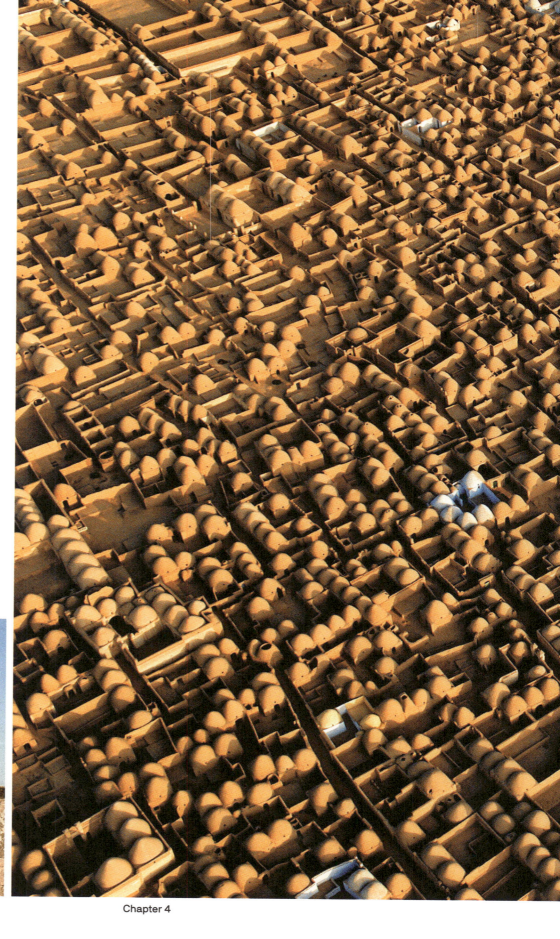

Mauritania
Oualata

In the Adrar region of Mauritania, in northwest Africa, the ancient city of Oualata has always been a remarkable showcase of creativity. Its earthen walls are embellished inside and outside with compelling decorative compositions that either feature variations on imaginative geometry or frame elements of domestic architecture, such as doors, alcoves, and stairs (**right**). The white exterior motifs (**overleaf, left and right**) contrast boldly with the reddish colour of the walls and endow each home with a strong, individual personality. As in other West African countries, these murals are created by women (see p. 42). Oualata, like Chinguetti, Tichitt, and Ouadane, was founded in the 12th century as a stopover for caravans crossing the desert. All four of these cultural treasures of the Mauritanian Sahara were listed as a UNESCO World Heritage site in 1996.
 J.D.

```
Further reading:
Courtney-Clarke 1990
```

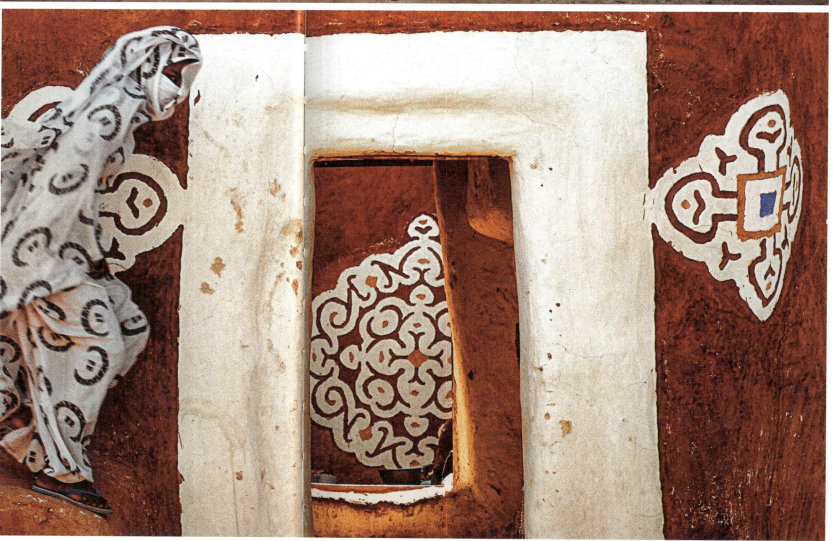

Mali
Dogon Villages

In Mali, as in Morocco and Yemen, the art of building with raw earth is an ancient tradition that is still alive and well, particularly among the Dogon, a community that has fascinated ethnologists ever since the early 20th century. Dogon art also inspired the European avant-garde artists of the early 20th century in their quest for innovation. In the 15th century, the Dogon resisted the onrush of Islam by taking refuge near the imposing cliffs of Bandiagara, which are 150 kilometres in length and reach heights of up to 500 metres. The rich cosmogony of the Dogon revolves around a single god, Amma, who created the Earth, then married her and brought forth children made of clay. The cult of ancestors is crucial to the culture of this farming people and it is largely expressed through earth, which is used for home building and venerated as a sacred natural resource (**right and opposite**). The Dogon live in compact villages grouped at the foot of the cliffs, or on the plateau above, and their domestic architecture falls into two main categories: houses and granaries. Houses are made up of rectangular rooms; the largest among them belong to the heads of each *guinna*, or extended family, and are often ornately decorated. The granaries (*goh*), which are used to store food reserves, are tucked into the cliff face or positioned between houses, where they are covered with a conical straw roof (*seko*).

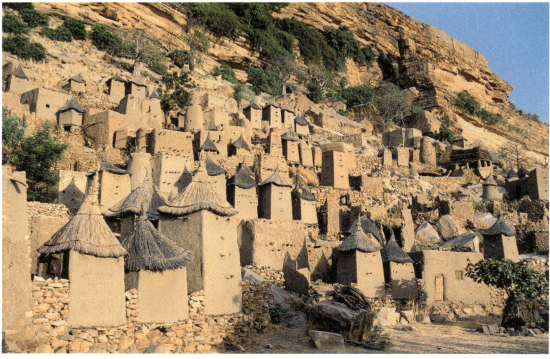

Nowadays, the religious practices of the Dogon people reflect a complex mixture of Islam and animism. Each village has a *hogon*, or spiritual leader, responsible for conducting rituals pertaining to the ancestor cult; these take place in sanctuaries (**opposite, above**) that are sometimes given anthropomorphic shapes. Each community also has its own 'house of words' (*toguna* or *shonan*; **opposite, below**), where the elders gather together to discuss important issues. Its eight earthen pillars support a heavy roof made from alternating layers of straw that shield the interior from excessive heat, while its base is adorned with motifs in relief that are again linked to Dogon cosmogony. The facades of houses (**right**) use a different formal language, without figurative elements.
    J.D. & R.E.

Further reading:
Lauber 1998

Mali
The Mosque of Nando

The mosque in the small village of Nando, in Mali's Dogon Country, is modest in size (95 square metres) and highly harmonious in design. This masterpiece (**these pages and overleaf**) demonstrates how raw earth can give rise to buildings with a great emotional impact and a surprising sense of monumentality.

    J.D.

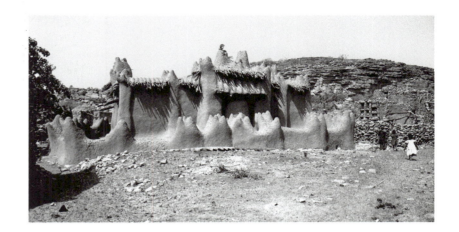

Vernacular Heritage

Mali
The City of Djenné

The city of Djenné, in central Mali, is one of the oldest – and most remarkable – in all of West Africa (**right and opposite**). The nearby archaeological site of Djenné-Djeno, first excavated in 1977, contains the remains of an earlier settlement dating back to the 3rd century BCE. This discovery had major political implications as it demonstrated the ancient heritage of the cities in sub-Saharan Africa, which had been denied by the colonial powers in an attempt to justify their supposed introduction of civilization to 'peoples without history'. Today's city of Djenné (33,000 inhabitants in 2009) was built at the end of the 9th century on a neighbouring island surrounded by the waters of the river Bani (a tributary of the Niger). In 1988, the entire city, including its imposing mosque, was listed as a UNESCO World Heritage site. This accolade, although largely symbolic, brought hope of a brighter future to Djenné's inhabitants, in the wake of the atrocities committed in the region by jihadi terrorists since 2012.

Above right: The traditional architecture of Mali provides a striking backdrop for a comic-strip adventure story.

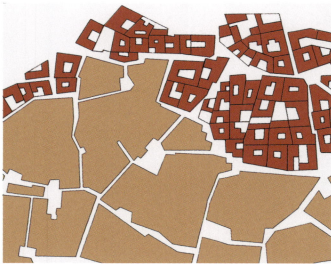

The city of Djenné (**right, opposite and overleaf**) is a labyrinth of alleyways that has grown organically and now boasts almost 2,000 houses built with raw earth. Their elaborate facades embrace a range of visual idioms and often display foreign influences. In fact, some houses are described locally as 'Moroccan', reflecting the spread of the Berber Empire to Mali in the 16th century. The residences of noble families can be distinguished by sculptural decorations that add gravitas to the front entrance, while the facades are embellished by motifs – sometimes openly erotic in nature – that reflect the status of the house's owner. Some facades in the city and the surrounding area are notable for their anthropomorphic decorations (see overleaf). The domestic space inside the houses is arranged around an inner courtyard. The city as a whole is imbued with an intense creativity that has resulted in an extraordinary urban landscape. This form of raw earth architecture has been preserved by the artisans of Djenné via an ancient guild of master builders that appears to be without parallel elsewhere in the region.

 J.D. & R.E.

Further reading:
Maas & Mommersteeg 1992; Bedaux & Van der Waals 1994

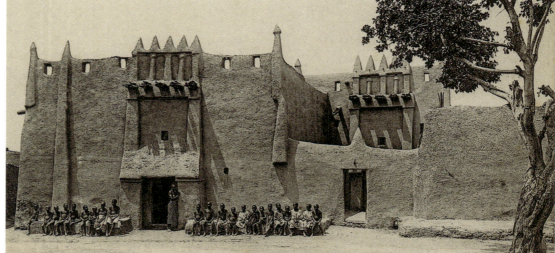

Vernacular Heritage

Mali
Urban Facades

Even the most artful photographs can sometimes strain to convey the full harmony of a facade, but architectural drawings have proved an excellent way of capturing the rhythm and textures of the earth architecture in Mali's towns and villages, and the way they blend to create a subtle and powerful built environment. These drawings (**below and opposite**) by Gérard Beaudoin were first published in the book *Soudan occidental, histoire et architecture* (1998).

J.D.

Vernacular Heritage

Mali
The Great Mosque of Djenné

The Great Mosque in the heart of the city of Djenné draws on both past and present. It was built on the ruins of an older mosque by master builder Ismaïla Traoré in 1907, at around the time that Picasso and Braque were inventing Cubism in Paris. At that time, the mosque's groundbreaking architecture (**this page and opposite**) scandalized traditionalists, but it went on to influence the design of many other buildings in Mali, both urban and rural, and has become a major symbol of the country's culture. The mosque has a trapezoidal ground plan, with sides measuring 75 metres long and a large central courtyard (**overleaf**). It was built on a raised terrace of packed earth, which serves not only to delineate the site but also to protect it from flooding. Its facade is dominated by three protruding 20-metre-high minarets that provide access to the roof terrace. The roof is supported by around one hundred massive earthen pillars that punctuate the main prayer area, which can hold a thousand worshippers. The walls were built using a spherical or conical variant of adobe brick, known as *djenné-ferey*. The Great Mosque of Djenné, like its counterpart in Mopti (built in 1935), was restored in the early 21st century by the Aga Khan Trust for Culture.

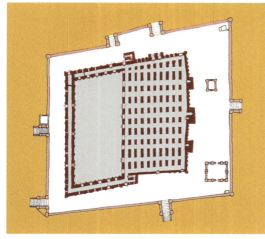

One of the most striking features of the Great Mosque is the bundles of palm wood embedded in its earthen walls (**right and previous pages**). These protruding elements cast fascinating shadows that change according to the height of the sun, but their purpose is not primarily decorative: they serve to support the temporary scaffolding that is used when repairing and maintaining the walls, which are vulnerable to the elements. The regular refurbishment of the mosque's exterior (**right and opposite**) is not regarded as a chore but rather as an elaborate festival that unites the entire community. It is a joyful ceremony involving music and song that conveys its participants' pride in playing a part in the preservation of this sacred, symbolic monument. The raising of the scaffolding and the application of earth to the walls are the responsibility of the builders' association, but the rest of the townspeople – men, women, and children – collect earth and mix it with water to prepare it for use.

J.D. & R.E.

Mali
Towns and Villages

In addition to its historic cities (Djenné, Mopti, Timbuktu, Ségou, and Gao), the vast territory of Mali boasts countless ancient villages. Despite their small size, some villages on the banks of the river Niger – such as this one (**right**) – contain a remarkable number of earthen mosques. Here, two mosques have been built side by side, tucked between houses. Even more strikingly, these religious buildings belonging to humble communities display a level of refinement rarely surpassed by their urban equivalents. The same can also be true of rural houses, which are not radically different from those in the country's cities. This impressive cultural and architectural coherence – albeit with many regional variations – is remarkable, especially given the great diversity of the ethnic groups that make up the human mosaic of Mali.

    J.D. & R.E.

Mali
Rural Mosques

West Africa began to convert to Islam in the 10th century, so mosques are ubiquitous there, and invariably built with raw earth. They play a crucial spiritual and visual role in towns and villages, displaying a religious architectural creativity unsurpassed anywhere in the world. Their spatial inventiveness is combined with craftsmanship that bears witness to the intelligence of Mali's builders, both past and present, as well as their capacity to create beauty. The unusual forms of Malian mosques are a way of paying tribute to divine power. They tend to shy away from the upward thrust of the monumental minarets found in most other Islamic countries and demonstrate their grandeur more modestly and subtly. Their artistic language fuses architecture and sculpture, becoming a hymn to harmony. Nor is this creative brilliance confined to Mali's larger settlements: it is equally evident in rural mosques, which display a vast range of architectural variations.

    J.D. & R.E.

```
Further reading:
Ago 1982; Schütyser et al. 2003
```

Right, opposite and pages 204–207: Examples of the striking creativity evident in the rural mosques of Mali.

Chapter 4

Vernacular Heritage

Mali, Ghana, and Burkina Faso
The Sacred Space of the Mosque

The unique architecture of the earthen mosques of West Africa can be more fully appreciated by studying their ground plans. Italian architect Fabrizio Ago recorded several such ground plans, which were published in his book *Moschee in adòbe* (1982).

J.D.

Right: A mosque in Larabanga, Ghana.

Below: The Sankoré Mosque in Timbuktu, Mali.

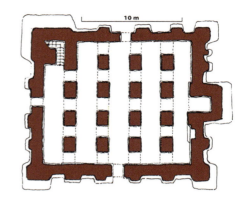

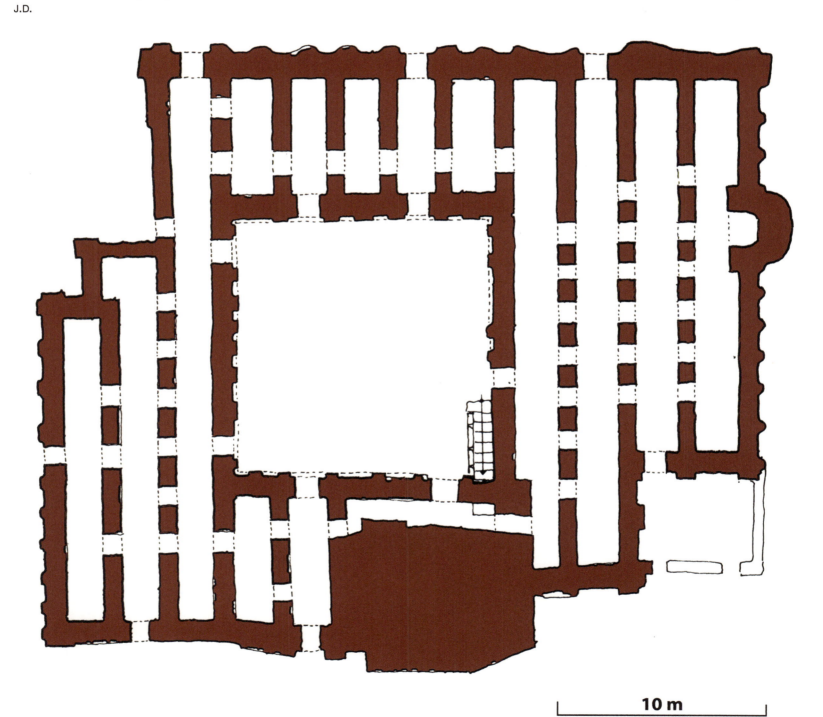

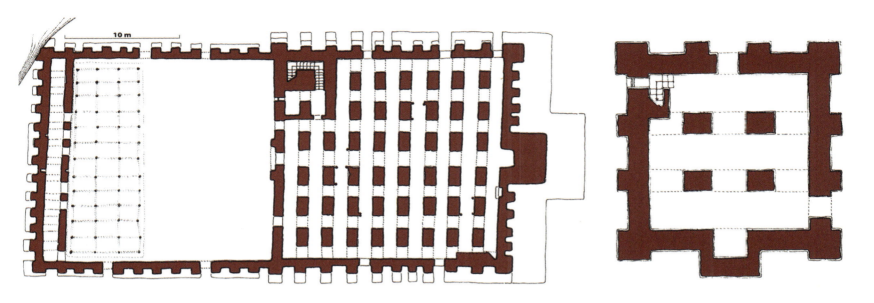
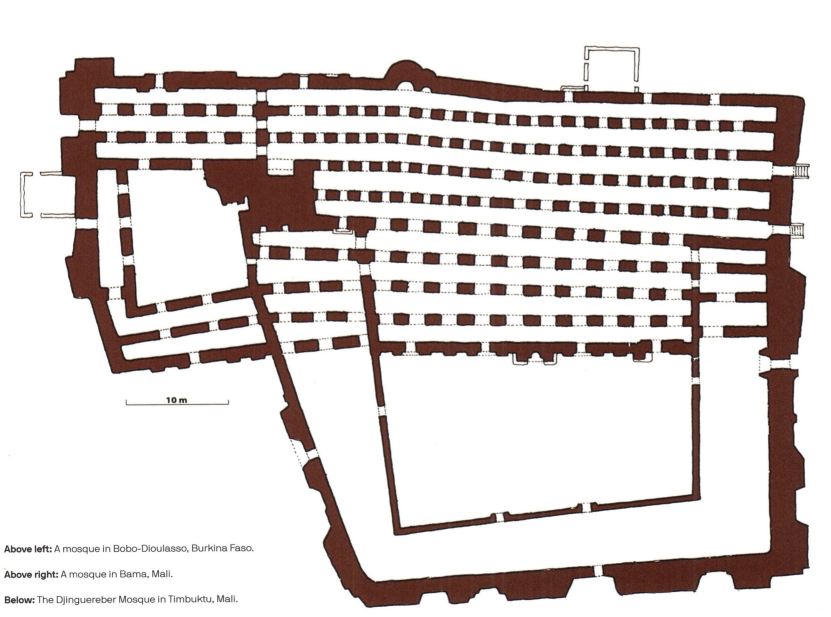

Above left: A mosque in Bobo-Dioulasso, Burkina Faso.

Above right: A mosque in Bama, Mali.

Below: The Djinguereber Mosque in Timbuktu, Mali.

Mali
Tombs and Sanctuaries

Tombs and sanctuaries in Mali are able to utilize a different architectural language than that of mosques because they are free from the constraints incumbent on places of worship. This formal freedom is expressed in idiosyncratic structures that give full rein to the artistic and expressive potential of raw earth (*banco*). The Tomb of Askia in Gao (**these pages**), built in 1495, conveys a sense of monumentality that recalls the massive ziggurats of Mesopotamia, despite its different context, relatively modest size (17 metres in height), and the array of branches piercing its surface. The Tomb of Askia was listed as a UNESCO World Heritage site in 2004, but it was also placed on the List of World Heritage in Danger in 2012, due to the destruction being wrought in the region by jihadi terrorists. In the village of Kono (**overleaf**), earth resembles waves frozen in time, as if by magic.
    J.D. & R.E.

Further reading:
CRAterre 2005

Vernacular Heritage

Mali
The Saho

The region of Mali to the north of Djenné has retained some examples of traditional earthen architecture that are remarkable for both their artistic qualities and their sociocultural role. The *saho* – literally a house (*ho*) for lying down (*sa*) – serves as a 'house of youth', a communal building for young people. These spaces are used for both initiation and socialization, allowing both boys and girls to benefit from instruction in communal and sexual mores as they progress from childhood to adulthood. The *saho* is also a place for festivities involving music, singing, and dancing. As an initiation into the moral obligation to share, young people are expected to participate in the construction of their *saho*, under the supervision of the village's master builder. Together they create a structure that bears witness to their community's creative vitality. This form of civic architecture, one of the most remarkable in Africa, combines monumentality, majesty, and communality. The size and sophistication of the *saho* contrasts with the humble rural dwellings around it, but nowadays many of them have fallen into disrepair, partly due to the encroachment of militant Islam, which has denounced the perceived depravity of these spaces for secular initiation. In the light of the risk of this heritage disappearing altogether, the Netherlands launched a programme to restore ten *sahos* in 2006, and ensured the preservation of around a hundred houses in Djenné.

J.D.

Further reading:
Gruner 1990

Right: A *saho* in Kolenze, Niger.

Mali
Erotic Architecture

In Mali, there are several mosques – urban and rural, big and small – whose perimeter walls are adorned with protuberances or cavities that recall male or female sexual organs (**right and opposite**). Any questions to local imams on this subject are invariably met with silence or protestations of ignorance – and ethnologists have scarcely been more forthcoming. Erect penises sculpted from raw earth are sometimes displayed on the roofs of urban homes, particularly in Djenné. Fertility rites are also depicted on walls in Dogon Country: one such example (**above right**) shows a woman's naked body being sprayed with white liquid.

J.D.

Vernacular Heritage

Nigeria
Emir's Palace, Zaria

The organic blending of architecture and ornament is an ancient practice shared by many cultures of West Africa. It is not merely an optional addition but an important symbol of cultural identification and belonging, on both an ethnic and a familial level. This art often takes the form of murals, and its splendour can be seen from Mauritania and Mali down to Niger and Nigeria. In the two latter countries, it has long been a standard feature in towns of the Hausa community, particularly Zinder and Zaria. Zaria is home to the palace of the Emir of Zazzau. In the 20th century, a new upper storey was added to the palace gateway (**right**), with a row of large windows in the European style. Despite this modernization, the Emir – whose role is now primarily ceremonial – has retained the building's polychrome decorations in high relief. The motifs (**above and opposite**) form a diverse and coded vocabulary that expresses a proud affiliation with the Hausa culture. In spite of this, however, the art form itself has now almost disappeared. In around 1970, Friedrich Schwerdtfeger recorded hundreds of these murals, but ten years later, most of them had vanished from the urban landscape.

    J.D. & R.E.

Further reading:
Schwerdtfeger 2007

Vernacular Heritage

Nigeria
Hausa Arches and Vaults

The master builders of the Hausa people of Nigeria are particularly adept at creating roof structures for civil and religious buildings. Their arches and vaults (**right, above and below**) are made from short sections of split palm trunk, known as azara wood, which is rot-proof and resistant to termites. These are covered with packed plant fibres and then coated with clay mortar. The technique enables the wood to span distances of 4 to 8 metres. These load-bearing structures are not visible from the outside but they come into their own inside buildings, sometimes with the help of ornamentation, as in the reception hall of the Emir of Zazzau (**opposite**). A prime example of this building technique was the Great Mosque of Zaria (**overleaf**), built in 1840 by Mallam Mikhaila Babban Gwani. This master builder was considered a genius, leading British colonizers to nickname him 'the African Michelangelo'. The mosque's enormous prayer halls were punctuated by robust earthen pillars interconnected by arches decorated with carved motifs, endowing this place of worship with solemnity and authority. Sadly, after Nigeria gained its independence, most of this masterpiece was destroyed and replaced by an unremarkable mosque made from reinforced concrete.

J.D.

```
Further reading:
Moughtin 1985; Dmochowski 1990
```

Vernacular Heritage

Nigeria
The Great Mosque of Zaria

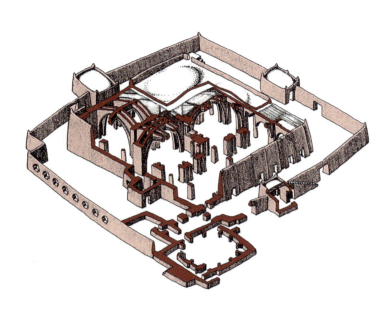

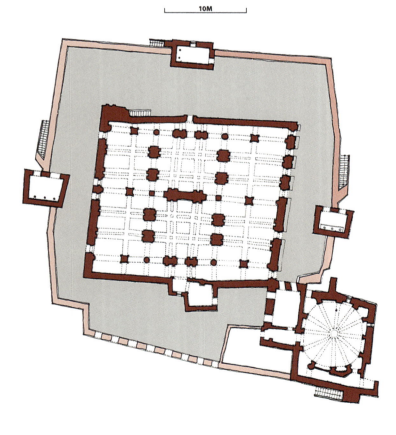

Vernacular Heritage

Niger and Nigeria
Mural Art

Spectacular murals can be found in many towns and villages in Niger and Nigeria, particularly those associated with the Hausa people. They reflect a diverse artistic vocabulary and a proud affiliation with traditional Hausa culture. These works of art are sometimes simply painted on walls (**below right**), but are often rendered in relief. The relief designs are sometimes painted in a bold range of colours (**below left** and pp. 218–219) but may also be left monochrome (**above right and opposite**), their whiteness standing out boldly against the warm red tones of the earthen walls. These variations combine to form an urban landscape of great architectural and cultural specificity.

    J.D. & R.E.

Further reading:
Schwerdtfeger 2007

Togo
Takientas of the Batammariba

In the West African country of Togo, the land of Koutammakou is home to the Batammariba, whose name means 'the people who shape earth'. The area has been listed as a UNESCO World Heritage site since 2003, and is dotted with villages famed for their *takientas* or tower-houses, traditional family homes built with cob. Each house is a variation on a basic theme: circular or oval towers arranged around a courtyard and connected by a high perimeter wall (**opposite, above and below**). The lower spaces are where animals are kept, while the upper living spaces and the granaries – each topped by a thatched conical roof – are accessed via the roof terraces. The *takienta*'s exterior wall is unbroken, apart from the doorway, which is generally flanked by a 'family' of rounded earthen fetish posts that serve as a tribute to ancestral spirits (**above and below right**). The construction of a *takienta* involves the entire community, with the men undertaking the heavy work and building up the walls with layers of earth. The women then prepare, apply, and maintain the outer coating of earth mortar. This architectural tradition is so complex that it has inspired many anthropological studies in an attempt to pin down its underlying cosmological, ontological, and metaphorical significance.

    J.D. & R.E.

Further reading:
Preston Blier 1994; CRAterre 2005

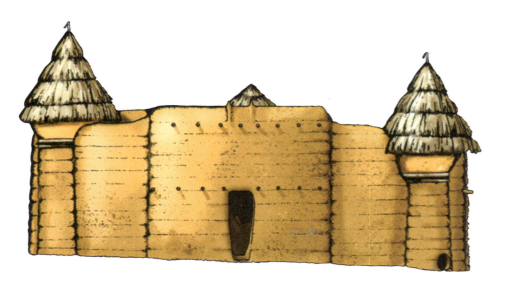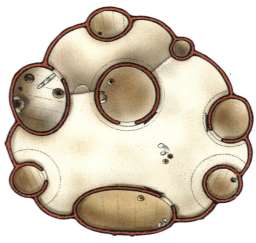

Vernacular Heritage

Cameroon
Toleks of the Musgum People

The Musgum people of Cameroon developed a distinctive form of housing: the *tolek* (**right and opposite**). It was nicknamed the *case obus* by French colonists after the term for an artillery shell, in reference to its shape. The uniqueness of this form of vernacular architecture lies in the ingenious logic of its construction. *Toleks*, which can reach heights of up to 8 metres, are fashioned like coil pots, from thick cylinders of raw earth (enriched by plant fibres) built up in circular layers that grow thinner as they rise, tapering from 35 centimetres thick at the base to 10 centimetres at the top. The end result is a load-bearing structure that uses a minimal quantity of materials to achieve maximum stability and solidity. The outer surface is decorated with a repeat motif in vertical relief (an inverted V, for example), arranged in a regular pattern. This clever addition serves at least three functions: it reinforces the load-bearing structure; it provides plenty of footholds that allow easy access to all parts of the exterior for building work or maintenance; and, finally, it proclaims the cultural identity of the village to which it belongs. Each family compound contains several *toleks* of various sizes, each with different functions. Granaries, for example, have a distinctive shape, specially adapted for storing cereals. In 1927, French novelist André Gide praised the harmony and intelligence of the Musgum structures: 'It is not so much their strangeness but rather their beauty that moves me. No ornamentation, no overload. Their pure curved line, which runs uninterrupted from their base to their summit, seems to have been achieved mathematically. The exact strength of the material appears to have been intuitively calculated. This house is made by hand like a vase, it is the work not of a builder but of a potter.'

J.D.

Further reading:
Seignobos & Jamin 2003

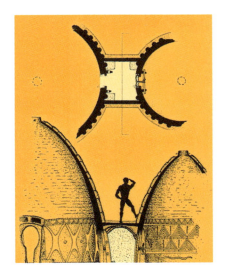

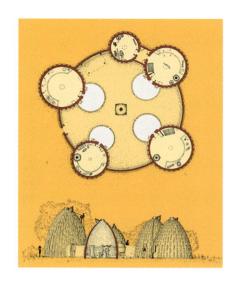

Burkina Faso
The Village of Tiébélé

The village of Tiébélé in Burkina Faso has become internationally renowned in recent years. It consists of a compact group of earthen houses in the land of the Kassena people. Every year, the women carry out a ritual refurbishment of the outer layer of their houses, repairing damage from the elements and also renewing their striking decoration of stylized red and black geometric motifs (**below and opposite**) or figures from the animal kingdom. This communal task has functional, cultural, and symbolic significance, and it gives the women a means to pass on to their daughters the values and traditions of their people. The annual festival transforms each house into an inhabited sculpture, and the village as a whole into an all-encompassing work of art.
J.D. & R.E.

```
Further reading:
CRAterre 2008
```

Niger, Mali, Algeria, and Cameroon
Interior Architecture

As well as exterior murals, the African creative spirit also finds its expression in the interior of traditional houses. This rural home in Kabylie, Algeria (**opposite, below**), brings together highly decorated architectural elements (walls, niches, and pillars) in an attractive fusion of art and functionality. Similarly, in the House of Sidi Kâ, also known as 'the baker's house', built in 1917 in Agadez, Niger (**opposite, above**), the volumetric inventiveness gives the space a sculptural quality. In the early 20th century, Leo Frobenius became the first European ethnologist to research this domestic vernacular language, and the drawings that he made of Malian houses capture their overall cohesion and striking integration of spaces (**above and centre right**). Similar features can be seen in the homes of the Masa people of Cameroon (**below right**).

J.D. & R.E.

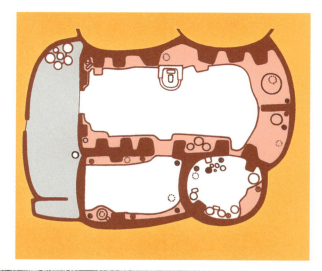

West Africa
Family Granaries

In the High Atlas mountains of Morocco, the collective granaries used to store food reserves for all the families in a village are monumental and fortified, but in West Africa, granaries are smaller family affairs, situated on the edge of a village or even within its houses. They display a great formal variety, depending on the ethnic group to which they belong. Their decoration is also extremely diverse, as each granary reflects the identity of a particular village or family.

R.E.

Below left and right: Granaries in a Dogon village in Mali.

Opposite, above from left to right: Granaries in Niger, Burkina Faso, and Ghana.

Vernacular Heritage

Yemen
The Hadhramaut Valley

Yemen is a country where the creative spirit of its artisans has long been expressed with the utmost talent and diversity through vernacular earth architecture. This tradition notably blossomed in the ancient city of Shibam (see pp. 108–109) and, in more recent times, in the palatial homes built for the upper classes in the 1920s and 1930s (see pp. 272–273). Apart from these specific examples, however, the Hadhramaut Valley as a whole boasts an exceptional heritage, with striking houses, mosques, and even entire towns that demonstrate the expertise of local master builders. For several decades now, the architect Salma Samar Damluji has been extolling this collective masterpiece in publications and restoration programmes undertaken *in situ*. She convincingly argues that the intelligence and harmony of this region's architecture deserves to be recognized as a universal model.
    J.D.

```
Further reading:
Damluji 1992; Damluji 2007
```

Right: The city of Seiyun, Yemen.

Above right, below left, and opposite above: Houses in Wadi Dawan.

Below right: The town of Al-Khuraybah, in Wadi Dawan, Yemen.

Overleaf, above left: A 16th-century Ottoman miniature that may depict the construction of the first earthen mosque.

Overleaf, below left: The minaret of the Al-Mihdhar Mosque in Tarim, built in adobe in 1914 by the master builder Awad Salman Afif al-Tirmi, soars to a height of 53 metres. It is reputed to be one of the tallest earthen structures in the world.

Overleaf, right: The holy city of Qabr Hud, the site of an annual pilgrimage.

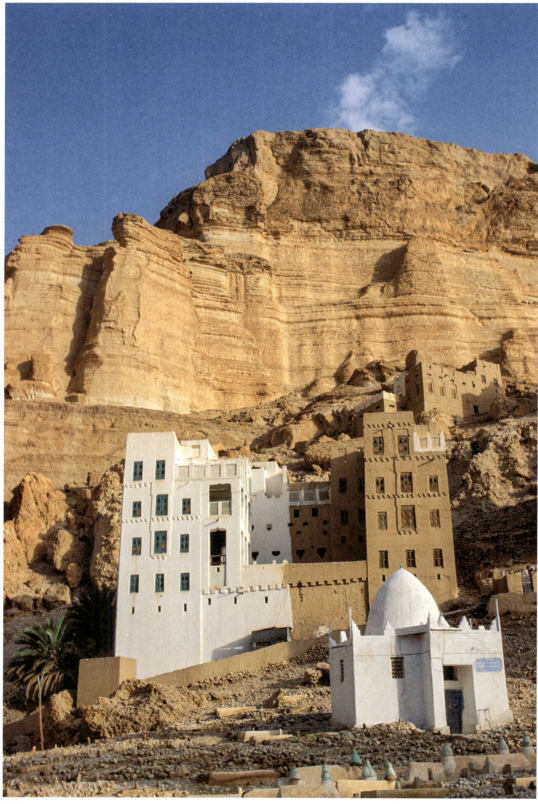

Vernacular Heritage

Vernacular Heritage

Saudi Arabia
Palaces and Houses of the Najran Region

The Najran region, in the southwest of Saudi Arabia, is notable for its mountains and huge desert, broken only by a string of oases. The latter have given rise to a form of vernacular earth architecture that expresses a strong cultural identity. Cob is the favoured technique here for buildings of all kinds, from small houses to defensive fortresses (**below and opposite**) and even palaces, with walls in which the layers of applied earth remain visible. Some homes also include rows of large flat stones protruding from the surface of their walls (**overleaf, below left**).

This simple trick serves three important functions: it creates shade, it drains off rain water, and it protects the facade from water erosion. Nowadays, both the facades (**overleaf, above left**) and the interiors (**overleaf, right**) of these houses are often given a coat of industrial paint, apparently to make them look more modern.

J.D. & R.E.

Further reading:
Mauger 2002

Vernacular Heritage

Syria
Conical Houses

In the raw earth villages of northwest Syria, tradition dictates that every room in a house is topped with a conical dome (**right and opposite**). The standard design of these structures has many potential formal variations, reflecting the strong cultural identity of each village. The base of the houses is circular; layers of raw earth bricks are then added to create a spiral that gradually tapers inwards as it approaches the top. The walls are sufficiently strong to allow a builder to climb up them as the dome is being built. Sadly, this vernacular tradition, which was already threatened by migration to cities, has been almost entirely obliterated by the war that engulfed Syria in the early 21st century.

J.D. & R.E.

Further reading:
CRAterre 2008; Kassatly & Puett 2011

India
Rural Houses in Rajasthan

Rajasthan, in northwest India, has an international reputation for its monumental buildings, including countless forts and ancient palaces. The richness and diversity of this region's cultural heritage extend even to its villages, particularly those close to Jaisalmer in the Thar Desert. Here, the practice of building houses with earth remains a tradition that is very much alive, and it is further enriched by geometric paintings (*mandana*), which local women apply to the walls (*bhitti chitra*; **below right**) and the floors (*bhumi chitra*; **above right and opposite, above**), often featuring an abundance of geometric motifs. The women also use earth to sculpt animal figures and floral relief elements that are added to walls (**opposite, below**).

R.E.

China
Rural Houses

Rural China contains a great diversity of houses built with raw earth in various techniques. They provide shelter to both peasant families and the elite. Mao Zedong, for example, was born in an earthen house in Shaoshan (**opposite, above**) that was built by his father, who came from a well-off family. The house has now become an obligatory stop on the 'red tourist' route devoted to the father of Chinese Communism. In the village of Shaxi, in Yunnan province (**below right**), the combined use of cob and adobe has given rise to a sophisticated architecture with a monumental feel. Since the late 20th century, China has become the world's largest consumer of cement, as a result of its booming urbanization. This has clearly led to a fall in the practice of raw earth construction. However, two phenomena seem to point towards a renaissance in this field, albeit still small-scale. One is the building of new rural homes by wealthy families, such as the rammed earth house built in around 2015 near Zhongdian, in Yunnan province (**above right**). The other is a small group of activist architects who are keen to devote their talents to this revival. Among them are Wang Shu and Lu Wenyu (see pp. 361, 369, 413, and 432–433), and Mu Jun (see p. 423).

J.D. & R.E.

Further reading:
Dunzhen 1980

China
Uyghur Architecture in Turpan

The oasis town of Turpan in northwest China was an important stopover on the Silk Road. It was founded by Buddhists but the arrival of the Uyghur people in the 14th century brought Islam to this desert region. The newcomers also developed agricultural practices that suited the harsh climate, creating an extensive network of underground irrigation channels (*karez*), as well as many oases and vineyards. Uyghur towns benefited from an efficient system of climate protection, with streets lined with trees, pergolas covered with shady vines (**opposite, above left**), and channels of flowing water. Raw earth was the dominant construction material, and it was used with consummate skill by the Uyghur, as is evident not only from their homes but also their *chunche* or grape drying houses (**above right**), which are studded with holes to allow the wind to pass through. The monumental Emin Mosque (**below right and opposite, above right**) was built in 1778 with adobe, with the exception of its fired brick minaret. Recently restored to its former glory, it lives up to its reputation as one of the most striking mosques in Asia.

J.D. & R.E.

Further reading:
Loubes 1988

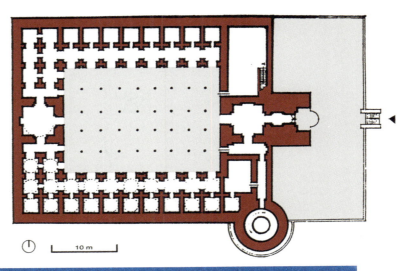

Vernacular Heritage

253

Bhutan
Rural Houses

The small Kingdom of Bhutan is nestled in the Himalayas between India and China. As a Buddhist country, Bhutan has always sought to maintain its own cultural identity and protect it from change. This is reflected in the evolution of earth architecture within the country. Bhutanese monasteries – such as Gangtey Goemba, dating from the 17th century – testify to this ancient heritage, but the vernacular tradition still thrives in villages, as evident from these harmonious houses recently built with rammed earth (**opposite, above and below**). Young women can sometimes be seen taking part in the construction work (**below**). Bhutan is now seeking to develop a small-scale tourist industry that is closely controlled, and to this end it has encouraged the construction of small hotels that offer minimalist luxury and make the most of local materials. Australian architect Kerry Hill succeeded in balancing these demands in 2005 when he used rammed earth to build five village guest lodges in Bhutan.

J.D. & R.E.

Vernacular Heritage

France
Rural Houses

France is one of the few countries in which all four major techniques of earth architecture can be found (see map on p. 26). Although many examples can be found in cities, including Lyon, Rennes, Troyes, Perpignan, and Albi, the majority are rural houses and farm buildings. Western France – including Brittany, the Rennes area, Cotentin, and Ille-et-Vilaine – has the highest concentration of cob, while wattle and daub was once popular in the north, from Normandy to Picardy and from Champagne to Alsace. Adobe bricks were particularly common in the southwest, especially in the Albi region. Rammed earth, known as *pisé*, was widespread in Bresse and especially in the huge Auvergne-Rhône-Alpes region, particularly on the Mâcon-Lyon-Grenoble axis. This area is home to the largest number of rammed earth buildings in Europe.

    J.D. & R.E.

```
Further reading:
Casel et al. 2000; Patte & Streiff 2007;
Bardel & Maillard 2009
```

Above right: A *pisé* house in Saint-Rambert-d'Albon, Isère.

Centre right: A *pisé* house in Petit-Bilieu, Isère.

Below right: A *pisé* farm building in Bresse, Ain.

Opposite, above: A 17th-century house in Juilles, in the region of Gers.

Opposite, below: A *pisé* farmhouse in Bilieu, Isère.

France
Urban and Rural Middle-Class Houses

The wealthier sectors of French society built many homes with raw earth from ancient times to the Renaissance, particularly in Lyon, which (as Lugdunum) was one of the regional capitals of the Roman Empire. In the lower Rhone Valley in southeast France, fortified towns were built with raw earth between the 10th and 14th centuries. The oldest earthen chateau, the Bâtie d'Urfé in Auvergne, was constructed in the 16th century with rammed earth (**opposite, above**). The rammed earth hall in the Notre-Dame Deanery in Montbrison is even older, as it dates back to the 13th century (see plan and elevations, **above right**). The historic centre of Rouen (**right**), like numerous other towns in Normandy and Alsace, still boasts many excellent examples of houses built with a wooden structure filled with wattle and daub. Further examples of this technique can be seen in several of the outbuildings of the medieval chateau of Crèvecoeur (**opposite, below**). In the 19th century, some bourgeois residences, such as the chateau in Vern-sur-Seiche in Ille-et-Vilaine (**opposite, centre**), were inspired by the work of François Cointeraux, the pioneer of *nouveau pisé*.

J.D. & R.E.

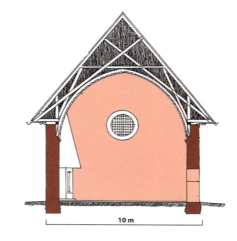
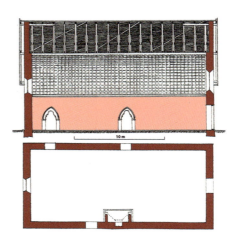

Great Britain
Cob Houses

Raw earth architecture in the British Isles dates back thousands of years. For example, much of the Emperor Hadrian's famous Roman Wall, built in 122 CE to keep out the Picts from the North, was built from turf. By the Middle Ages, this practice had diversified to give rise to a host of techniques including wychert, clay lump, rammed earth, and most of all, cob – particularly in Devon. Here, cob was widely used by all social classes, from the wealthiest to the poorest (**above right**: a modest 15th-century cottage in Cockington). One of Elizabeth I's most famous courtiers, Sir Walter Raleigh, grew up in a manor house in Hayes Barton that was built with cob in 1484. It remains a jewel in Devon's architectural crown (**opposite, above left**). In 1773, another aristocrat, Joseph Damer, later Lord Milton, commissioned the architect Sir William Chambers and the landscape gardener Capability Brown to build an entire village – Milton Abbas – in cob (**below right and map**), in order to house the 72 peasant families that worked on his land. This was the second modern village in the world to be planned and built from scratch with earth; the first was Charleval, built in 1741 in Provence, France, by César de Cadenet. Since the late 20th century, the cottages of Milton Abbas have become popular holiday homes.

J.D. & R.E.

Further reading:
McCann 1983; Terra 2000

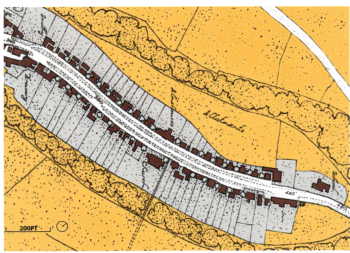

Germany
Rural and Urban Houses

Germany is blessed with an abundance of ancient sites incorporating earth architecture. Apart from the archaeological remains of Neolithic settlements, many traditional villages are still dotted with wattle-and-daub houses, built from a load-bearing wooden framework filled in with a mixture of earth and straw. Well before the industrial era, however, regional authorities – mindful of the destruction of woodland that would result from widespread use of this construction technique – sometimes encouraged locals to turn to other materials, particularly earth bricks. While vernacular practices were the norm in the countryside, cities were more open to new developments, such as the *nouveau pisé* developed in France in 1790 by the architect François Cointeraux. In the 1820s, one of Cointeraux's disciples, Wilhelm Jacob Wimpf (see p. 314), built what was then the highest rammed earth dwelling (at seven storeys) in Germany, in the centre of the city of Weilburg, Hesse. It is still standing today, a remarkable testament to its durability. In the aftermath of both world wars, Germany was the only nation in Europe to adopt an ambitious reconstruction strategy centred around earth (see pp. 299–300). Since the 1970s, a new generation of architects and engineers has updated the traditional techniques of earth architecture and even come up with new techniques of their own.

J.D.

Right: The village of Schieder-Schwalenberg in the district of Lippe, North Rhine-Westphalia.

Africa and Oceania
Sacred Art

The use of raw earth is not limited to architecture. It has also provided the raw material for other art forms, particularly in the field that has become known as the primal arts. Many examples can be found in the sacred grove of Osun-Osogbo, dedicated to the Yoruba goddess of fertility, in Nigeria (**below**). This was listed as a UNESCO World Heritage site in 2005. On the Pacific island of Malakula in Vanuatu, the ancient practice of *rambaramp* involves making funeral effigies of the honoured dead. The figures are often life size and their heads are ceremonially modelled using a mixture of earth and plant materials (**opposite, below right**). In West Africa, *bolis* (**opposite, above right**) are objects modelled out of raw earth that are attributed with magical powers, representing people or animals that are considered sacred by the Bamana people.

J.D. & R.E.

Vernacular Heritage

The Revival of Vernacular Traditions

Jean Dethier

It is often believed that the techniques of vernacular earth architecture are fixed in time and cannot be adapted to suit the demands of the modern era. However, many examples throughout the world demonstrate that this is not the case. The artisans who possess this knowledge are highly capable of coming up with new ways to utilize their skills, given the opportunity. It is not so much traditions that evolve, but rather what have come to be known as 'building cultures'. These have displayed a remarkable ability to digest, integrate, and reinvent vernacular forms.

This chapter devoted to vernacular traditions has therefore been extended to include examples of this revival, demonstrating their continuing relevance. In some locations, this architectural renaissance can be traced back to the late 19th century (e.g. Morocco) or, more frequently, to the early 20th century (e.g. Yemen, Saudi Arabia, Egypt), but it has also occurred in the present century, particularly in Mali and Niger. This trend does not manifest itself solely in housing, palaces, religious buildings, and cultural centres but also, on occasions, in urban planning; for example, in Shibam (Yemen) or Mopti (Mali), where residential neighbourhoods have recently been built with earth in a way that takes into account the demands of modern life, including the use of motor vehicles.

The chapter that follows also includes restoration projects for entire villages (the *ksar* of Tissergate in Morocco), palaces (Abomey in Benin), temples (Ghana), and 19th-century forts (Oman and Abu Dhabi). These projects bear witness to the ongoing revitalization of sites that are representative of specific vernacular traditions, and their regeneration also provides their inhabitants – and the generations to come – with new hope for the future. Many of these works have been listed as UNESCO World Heritage sites. Significantly, out of more than eight hundred architectural, urban, and archaeological sites from all over the world featured on UNESCO's list, more than 160 were built, either wholly or partially, with that most basic, most ecological, and most abundant of natural building materials: earth.

```
Further reading:
Frey 2010
```

Opposite: Interior of the Sanam Mosque, Niger.

Below: Ndomo Bogolan textile workshop in Ségou, Mali.

Morocco
The Modernization of Rammed Earth and Adobe

Morocco set about modernizing its traditional techniques of raw earth construction during the reign of Hassan I (1873–94), who instigated the construction of the new town of Tiznit and the world's first factory built from rammed earth, the Makina, in the medina in Fez. Moreover, one of the country's most powerful families, the El Glaoui, rebuilt and enlarged the monumental kasbahs that served as their rural residences in Telouet (**above right**), in the High Atlas mountains, and in Ouarzazate. These large houses were the first rammed earth and adobe buildings in Morocco to incorporate modern amenities such as heating and running water. The artistic influences of the modern city can also be seen on their interior walls and their ceilings covered with *zellige* (colourful tiled mosaics), as well as their delicately carved or painted plaster and woodwork (**opposite**). The kasbah in Ouarzazate (**centre and below right**) has recently been restored and is now a popular tourist destination.

J.D.

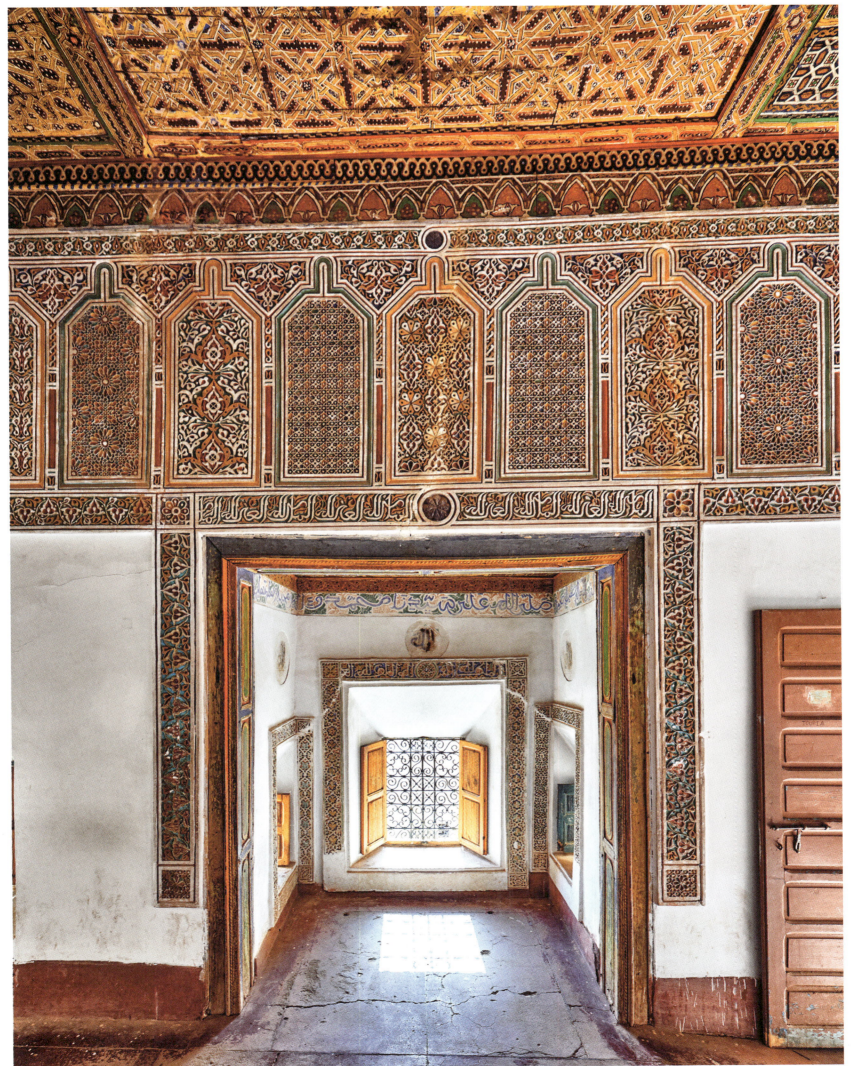

Saudi Arabia
20th-Century Palaces

The history of the Arabian Peninsula in the first half of the 20th century was marked by two decisive events. First, in 1932, Ibn Saud founded the kingdom of Saudi Arabia; then, in 1938, the first oil deposits were discovered, with American help, leading to spectacular wealth and a radical transformation of the country. In these early years, the ruling class spurned Western styles of architecture (although these would later be embraced and taken to extreme lengths) and instead remained faithful to the traditions of earth architecture, particularly when it came to building new palaces in Riyadh and elsewhere. This commitment gave rise to a modern, albeit brief, rekindling of ancient skills that had almost died out, particularly in the Najran region (see pp. 242–245).

J.D.

Below: A typical Najdi courtyard in one of the al-Badi'ah Palaces, 1937.

Right: Exterior view of the Murabba Palace, Riyadh.

Yemen
20th-Century Palaces

The revival of traditional techniques of earth architecture that occurred in Morocco and Saudi Arabia was also seen in Yemen. In the early 20th century, some of the elites in the Hadhramaut Valley acquired new wealth, largely as a result of profitable investments in Asia, and several of the region's most prominent families decided to build themselves new palaces. These buildings served three main social and cultural purposes: to demonstrate the power of their owner, dazzling onlookers with their unprecedented dimensions; to create an atmosphere of comfort and refinement, aided by modern conveniences imported from Europe; and to remain faithful to the local tradition of building with adobe, with interior spaces that are expansive and filled with light, while pushing towards the construction of ever higher and ever bigger structures. The region's master builders rose admirably to these technical challenges, enthusiastically adapting their time-honoured methods to meet the demands of a new era.

J.D. & R.E.

Above right: Palace in the city of Tarim, Yemen.

Below right: The palace of the Al Buqshan family in Khaylah, which was built in the 1950s and partially converted into a hotel in 2006.

Opposite, above left and right: The palace of Sultan Al Kathiri, built in the 1920s in Seiyun, 12 kilometres east of Shibam.

Yemen and Mali
Urban Fabrics, Old and New

Two aerial photographs provide a comparison between the layout of the old town of Shibam (**opposite, below**) in the Hadhramaut Valley, Yemen, and that of a neighbourhood built in the same town in the late 20th century (**opposite, above**). Both are built from raw earth, but the first is very compact and has grown organically over the years, while the second follows a grid pattern with streets wide enough to allow the flow of traffic. This sharp contrast shows how the same building material is capable of adapting to the prevailing needs of the times. In Mali, the modern city of Mopti was also built on a grid plan (**below**). Raw earth has also proved to be ideal for constructing less compact suburban neighbourhoods, such as La Luz, New Mexico (see pp. 346–347), built in the 1960s.

J.D. & R.E.

Vernacular Heritage

Egypt and Iran
Pigeon Towers

In many rural areas, pigeons are bred both for food (their meat is often highly prized) and for their droppings, which are used as fertilizer. Many ingenious earthen structures have been created to house them, particularly in Iran (**opposite, above left**) and Egypt (**opposite, above right**). Over the course of the 20th century, this tradition was revived in the Nile Delta (**below**), giving rise to some stunning examples of architectural invention.
R.E.

Mali and Niger
An Architectural Revival

Mali is perhaps the African country with the most diverse and inventive legacy of earth architecture. Its vernacular creativity is far from running dry in the 21st century – on the contrary, its talented artisans are positively bursting with ideas. This energy can be seen in contemporary mosques, such as the one in the Dogon village of Kani-Kombole, built in 1988 (**opposite, below**). In the city of Ségou, the thriving craft of *bogolan* (textiles dyed with earth) has led to the building of earthen workshops that experiment with new architectural idioms (**this page** and p. 267). This effervescence is also evident in Niger. In 1986, the Yaama Mosque (**opposite, above**) earned the master builder El Hadji Falké Barmou the prestigious Aga Khan Award, which is usually reserved for architects. The interior of the mosque completed in Sanam, Niger, in 2001 displays a similarly striking architectural intelligence (**overleaf**).

In the early years of the 21st century, Niger has also seen its own earth architecture revival, thanks to the campaigning of several young architects. Among them are two talented women, Mariam Kamara and Yasaman Esmaili (see pp. 487 and 490–491).
   J.D.

Vernacular Heritage

Interior of a mosque in the village of Sanam, Niger.

Morocco
Restoring the *Ksar* of Tissergate

The array of earthen villages, or *ksour* (*ksar* in the singular), in the valleys of southern Morocco are an exceptional architectural legacy (see pp. 156–161). From the 1950s onwards, however, they fell into disrepair as the neighbouring palm groves began to shrink, leading to rising poverty and large-scale emigration to urban areas. In 1967, the government announced measures to reverse this trend by launching a programme to restore around one hundred *ksour* – however, subsequent political events led to its cancellation, and in the end only Tissergate, the village chosen to kick off this ambitious project, benefited from a refurbishment. Situated in the southern part of the Draa Valley, 7 kilometres north of Zagora, Tissergate underwent a complete restoration in 1968, under the supervision of Jean Dethier and Jean Hensens, who were then working as architects in the Moroccan Ministry of Housing. Almost sixty men from the village committed themselves to the work for a whole year, in return for a modest wage and food rations supplied by a UN agency; they were instructed by local master builders who were still well versed in traditional techniques of construction with rammed earth. This communal effort made it possible to restore the mosque and *hammam* (public baths) and build a new school and dispensary, as well as to renovate houses, streets, and the village's perimeter walls. Over half a century later, the benefits of this intervention – the first of its kind to embrace an entire African village – can still be seen (**right and opposite**): the *ksar* of Tissergate is an eloquent testimony to a living architectural heritage that had previously been neglected in the pre-Saharan valleys.

R.E.

Benin
Restoring the Royal Palace of Abomey

The Royal Palace of Abomey, Benin, is a monumental complex that makes spectacular use of raw earth for both sculptural and architectural purposes. The site became the seat of power for the Kingdom of Dahomey in the 17th century. Each king had a duty to enlarge both his kingdom's territory and the palace complex itself. Its largest buildings, known as *ajalala*, were ceremonial halls. From the late 18th century onwards, these prestigious buildings and their many entrances were decorated with polychrome bas-reliefs (**below and opposite**). The motifs depicted important events in the history of the ruling dynasty and symbols associated with the sovereigns. After being classified as a UNESCO World Heritage site in 1985, the complex has benefited from a series of conservation and restoration works, including reconstruction. This ambitious project has revived the glory of an exceptional example of African royal architecture.

R.E.

Vernacular Heritage

Ghana
Restoring the Ashanti Shrines

The ancient Ashanti (or Asante) culture of Ghana once ruled a powerful empire, founded in the 17th century. It produced an enormous range of striking artworks that are now on display in some of the world's greatest museums, including the British Museum in London. This creative fertility was also evident in architecture, as recognized by the inclusion of ten Ashanti buildings on the UNESCO World Heritage List. In the 1990s, several organizations embarked on projects to restore some of the Ashanti shrines, which were made up of four separate buildings grouped around a courtyard. Their walls are adorned with devotional scenes featuring a combination of human and animal figures and geometric motifs.

R.E.

Further reading:
CRAterre 2009

Above and below left, and opposite, above: Details of the Yaw Tano Shrine at Ejisu-Besease, Ghana, restored in 1998.

Below right: Relief sculptures at the Atuo Kosua Shrine, Adwinase, Ghana.

Vernacular Heritage 287

Oman and Abu Dhabi
Restoring the 19th-Century Fortresses

Opposite, above left and right: The fortress of Al-Jahili in Al-Ain, Abu Dhabi, restored and converted into a cultural centre by German architects Roswag & Jankowski in 2008.

Below, left and right: In the Sultanate of Oman, the fortresses of Jabrin and Bahla have been restored by the Italian architects Giuseppe Biancifiori and Enrico d'Errico.

After decades of neglecting their architectural heritage, some countries in the Persian Gulf have begun restoration of the old defensive fortresses dotted along their borders. These buildings are being brought back to life to honour the artisans who built them from adobe in the late 19th century.

R.E.

Earth Architecture in Africa: Development and Potential

Sébastien Moriset

Africa is an inexhaustible repository of knowledge about raw earth architecture and of ways in which it has evolved, and it is home to some of the world's best preserved and most vibrant traditions in the field. Raw earth is ubiquitous there and has been put to many uses, from the construction of an enormous variety of homes to the building of entire towns. The continent is a showcase for earth architecture from its most modest to its most monumental. A spectacular panoply of mosques, palaces, tombs, granaries, and villages bears witness to the preeminence of raw earth as a versatile medium for human creativity. Africa also boasts a huge range of houses that display the creative autonomy of local communities through their simplicity, harmony, and adaptation to local resources. What a joy not to depend on outside resources to build and maintain one's own home! Raw earth collected *in situ* is not only cheap and appropriate, it is also immune to fluctuations in market value. No other construction material is more convenient or easier to master.

Across the length and breadth of Africa, many cultural landscapes have produced raw earth buildings that imaginatively mirror the surrounding environment. More than any other continent, Africa displays a host of architectural idioms that are immediately recognizable by their typology, volumes, colours, ornamentation, and textures. A strong sense of social solidarity has made it possible to engage the human resources needed to build these structures collectively, and to maintain them after every rainy season. In Mali, the lively annual festivals at which mosques are repaired and maintained are proof of an extraordinary capacity to mobilize volunteers for the good of the community, to a level that would be unthinkable in a pure market economy. When you watch these projects in action, you notice a striking contrast between the onerousness of the work and the enjoyment of those undertaking it. The communal tasks of tamping floors, moulding bricks, and painting murals are often accompanied by singing and dancing. Raw earth becomes a conduit for reviving and exalting a community's intangible heritage. These gatherings of builders serve as tools to maintain peace and strengthen social cohesion.

The nature of a hot climate creates a unique relationship between the human body and damp earth, giving rise to architectural wonders unimaginable at other latitudes or in less closely bound societies. The fact that the material is worked by hand, as it is in pottery, leaves plenty of scope for improvisation, allowing for the addition of haut-reliefs and bas-reliefs on walls and decorative motifs both inside and outside a house. Centuries of creativity have enabled communities to refine their techniques, tools, and formal language for transforming earth into an infinite diversity of architectures, each one distinct and unique.

As on other continents, however, there is a huge contrast between rural areas where ancient skills have survived, and so-called 'developed' urban areas where industrial materials now hold sway. Vernacular expertise is being lost and architectural creativity is clearly in decline. The traditional channels for passing on knowledge, which ensured that young people would be trained in the art of earth architecture, are now disappearing. The sovereignty of African communities in terms of their choices for how to plan and build their own environments is being eaten away. Local building cultures, often arrogantly termed 'informal' by experts, are viewed with derision and hamstrung by absurd administrative and technical regulations, sometimes to such an extent that communities are forced to accept standardized school buildings made out of concrete. Nowadays, earth is often used for construction only if other materials are unavailable, and rarely out of ecological conviction or pride in a cultural identity. Because of this, the forms of solidarity that once brought together volunteers to work on communal building projects are also disappearing. It is becoming increasingly difficult to build with earth for free, even though the material itself is still readily available.

Nevertheless, the advantages of raw earth are now widely recognized. One third of the African cultural treasures classified as UNESCO World Heritage Sites are exceptional examples of earth architecture. Several African countries have now introduced strategies to raise awareness of these national resources and promote cultural tourism. Many villagers are aware of this rich architectural heritage and view it as a source of pride. Nonetheless, a true appreciation of this inheritance also means passing on traditional knowledge and skills. Building regulations and training must include and value natural local materials. Meanwhile, architects and governments must set an example by demonstrating that raw earth can be used to create comfortable,

hygienic, light-filled, and socially uplifting buildings. It is the scandalous dumping of concrete schools in raw earth villages by bureaucrats and industrialists that should be outlawed and disparaged. Vernacular architecture must evolve in order to respond to a dynamic of regional revitalization. The architect Francis Kéré is at the forefront of the revival in raw earth construction currently underway in his home country of Burkina Faso. Pilot projects have also been launched in other nations, often by teams seeking to unite the best of a local building culture with elements of modernity. These pioneers of a contemporary raw earth architecture that is firmly rooted in its environment display a dual cultural sensibility, both vernacular and industrial, that allows them to skilfully choose the optimal resources while avoiding waste and the placement of economic burden on the populations involved. It is to be hoped that the emerging community of African architects will be attuned to the virtues and potential of raw earth and will use it to create an art of building specific to local identities, means, and needs.

Further reading:
Frey 2010; Lepik & Beygo 2016

Above: The village of Tiébélé, in Burkina Faso (see pp. 230–231).

New Ways to Restore the Legacy of Earth Architecture

Patrice Doat

Earth and water: at first sight, these two elements seem to be opposites, and combining them produces nothing but mud. These two components, however, have been used in all climates and in all historical eras to create the remarkable architectural diversity presented in this book. To produce such results, the world's cultures have each developed their own bodies of building knowledge regarding how best to combine earth and water and in which proportions. Recent scientific research into soil cohesion and the physics of granular material have confirmed that these two elements are vital when building or restoring raw earth buildings.

These scientific advances also demonstrate that water is not the enemy of earth; in truth, it is a formidable ally, playing a crucial role in transforming the latter into a building material. Water boosts the cohesion of clay by increasing the interaction between its particles. It is the forces of capillary action that allow the water to 'stick' soil particles together. The same forces allow a child to build a sandcastle and are responsible for creating surface tension, which allows some insects (such as water boatmen) to 'walk' on water. The cohesion of a raw earth wall is created by these forces, acting via the film of water that surrounds the clay particles. The presence of the correct amount of water is therefore essential – although water does become a threat when this quantity is exceeded.

The practical application of this knowledge, which allows water to serve as a binder for earth, makes it possible to repair a damaged facade and seal cracks by using a carefully measured combination of earth and water. The process makes it possible to preserve a building's architectural identity and authenticity. For this reason, the restoration of raw earth structures requires professionals with exceptional practical skills, based on an understanding of the material and the way it interacts with water. The use of water and earth draws on a shared knowledge of the past but also gives it new value for the builders of tomorrow.

Left: Detail of the rammed earth towers built in southern Morocco by the German artist Hannsjörg Voth for his artwork *City of Orion* (see pp. 466–467).

Modernizing Building Cultures to Stimulate Local Development

Hubert Guillaud

The term 'building culture' is used to refer to architecture within the contexts of anthropology and technology. It embraces both the tangible and intangible aspects of dwellings and the built environment. Building cultures, in the plural, pose questions about the symbolism, codes, and perceptions of a society. They are the memory bank of construction skills and knowledge passed on from one generation to the next, derived from a long period of experimentation, culminating in a genuine and flourishing heritage: the art of building. These building cultures also attest to human beings' shifting relationships with their environment as they conceive, construct, and manage their living spaces on scales ranging from house to village, from city to region.

As well as adapting to specific site conditions, the act of building is shaped not only by cultural, social, and economic factors but also by ethical concerns. Vernacular housing, in particular, established an optimal relationship between nature and culture, at least until the Industrial Revolution, which brought in its wake the plundering of resources and the destruction of the environment. As a reaction to this damage, vernacular wisdom has been re-examined, in both its traditional and modern hybridized forms, by new ecologically responsible building practices. The art of habitation has taken on a whole new dimension in the light of the challenges posed by sustainable development, changing ecological and energy concerns, and global conservation. These challenges also increasingly throw up issues such as the struggle against poverty and precarious living conditions endured by a large proportion of humanity, and the resilience of the built environment in the face of natural disasters precipitated by climate change (earthquakes, flooding, fires).

Most rebuilding undertaken after catastrophes of this kind takes little account of the accumulated wisdom of local building cultures. External interventions often impose quantitative objectives, to the detriment of quality, and rely on imported designs and standardized responses that are often inappropriate, overly expensive, and reproducible only with technical help from outside. The beneficiaries are also excluded from the decision-making processes. By undermining the authority of traditional artisans, this type of brutal external intervention leads to the discrediting and disruption of the local network of building professionals. These specialists are subordinated to the hegemonic power of highly qualified technicians who destabilize a workforce reduced to the level of jacks-of-all-trades, working in conditions of near-slavery and performing tasks stripped of meaning. The methodological and technological arrogance of these interventions reflects an extreme negation of cultural diversity and contempt for indigenous populations.

If a development project truly seeks to reconcile humanity, culture, and nature, it is not just advantageous but absolutely vital to realign it with local building culture and its accumulated wisdom. This approach should guarantee the autonomy of the people involved, enabling them to adopt collective and participatory practices. Social cohesion is best consolidated when people make their own materials and construct and complete their own habitats. In order to achieve this goal, one essential prerequisite of any construction or reconstruction project is to identify local building skills and knowledge, whether this means organizational practices, distribution of labour, or techniques used, and to integrate them into any new work undertaken. It is also vital to assess the project's feasibility and financial accessibility for the majority of its proposed beneficiaries. Any pilot studies must meticulously examine the potential social, economic, and environmental consequences. In order to guarantee a medium- or long-term impact, it is important to reinforce local expertise with professional training, making it possible to integrate building cultures that have been rediscovered and regenerated. This is a complex process but it can lead to a revitalization of building cultures that benefits local development and strengthens communities.

Further reading:
CRAterre 2006; CRAterre 2015

Opposite, above: Master builders from Mali working on a mosque in South Korea.

Opposite, below: Women tamping an earthen floor in the village of Gando, Burkina Faso.

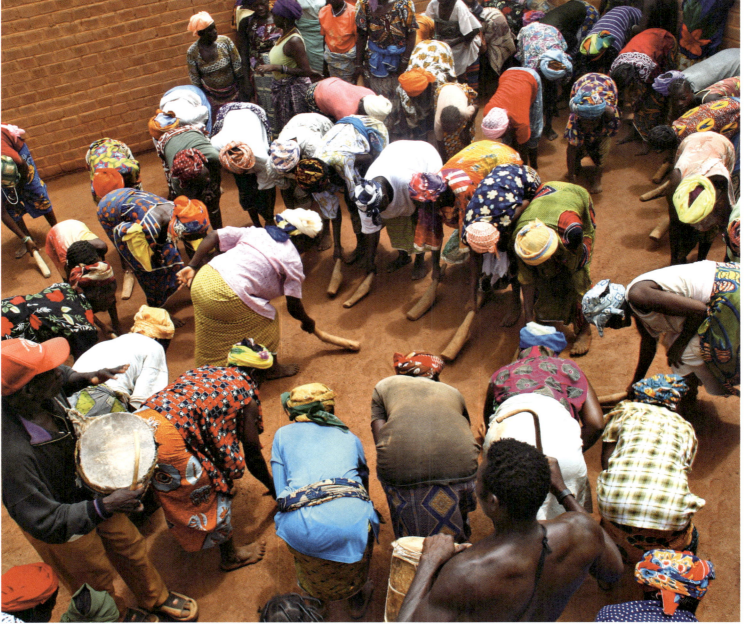

Vernacular Heritage

Chapter 5

Alternative Forms of the Modern:
1789–1968

By taking inspiration from the building traditions of his native Egypt, Hassan Fathy became one of the great modernizers of earth architecture (see pp. 334–341).

Above: Drawing by Hassan Fathy.

Below: The central square in the village of New Gourna in its original state.

The Quest for an Alternative Form of Modern Architecture: 1789–1968

Jean Dethier

The first phase of the modernization of earth architecture was bookended by two major sociopolitical upheavals: the French Revolution in 1789, which had a global impact, and the protests that took place in Europe and the United States in 1968 against a way of life that many young people considered outmoded. In the 180 years inbetween, two outstanding architects made huge contributions to this revival: François Cointeraux (see pp. 308–311), active in France from 1790 onwards, and Hassan Fathy (see pp. 334–341), working in Egypt from 1947. Many evolutionary steps punctuated this long transitional period between ancient vernacular practices and the emergence of a new kind of raw earth architecture starting in the 1970s. Before examining these, however, it is vital to take stock of a phenomenon that has radically affected public architecture, and indeed the entire construction sector: the invention of industrialized building materials. This development has led to the flagrant exploitation of nonrenewable resources, the destruction and pollution of natural environments, and a massive rise in greenhouse gases and CO_2 emissions, which are responsible for the current threat of climate change.

The dominance of industrialized materials

For thousands of years, almost all houses and settlements were built with natural materials that were gathered locally (mainly stone, wood, and earth). The 19th century saw the emergence of industrialization, initially in Europe, and as a result, construction materials quickly began to change. The manufacture of cement (invented between 1810 and 1824) and then of steel (between 1850 and 1880) triggered the revolutionary invention of reinforced concrete. Industrial aluminium also appeared around 1860. Soon, industrial materials began to be combined with natural resources: wood, for example, was transformed into plywood and laminated timber through the use of additives, and in around 1950, chemical research into oil derivatives led to the appearance of 'synthetic' building materials. All of these new materials involve long-distance transportation and industrial transformation processes that guzzle energy and create pollution.

Many other materials have been invented in the name of progress or, worse still, in the name of profit within an irresponsible capitalist system. At the start of the 20th century, for instance, cement was mixed with highly toxic asbestos to produce asbestos cement. Its widespread use in many countries has caused millions of deaths and incurable diseases, and its use in construction was not prohibited in Europe until 1997. Yet, despite its noxious effects, asbestos cement is still being sold today in many parts of the world – in other words, the building industry, driven by global expansionism and encouraged by powerful lobbies, has displayed minimal concern for social, sanitary, and environmental well-being.

These unscrupulous practices have gone unchecked in Asia, where cement manufacturers are complicit with organized crime gangs who have taken over the trade in sand, which is vital for building with reinforced concrete but has become a rare resource. The cement industry is solely responsible for at least 6% of the world's emissions of CO_2, one of the main causes of climate change (many experts put the figure as being closer to 10%). The heavily industrialized and energy-consuming manufacturing processes used to make standard building materials require tremendous quantities of essential resources – in Great Britain, for example, they account for up to 50% of the country's energy consumption.

Raw earth is well positioned to respond to the cynicism of the multinational corporations. In principle, there is no need to buy it if land is available, ready to be extracted and built upon, making it an 'a-capitalist' material. It is one of the most healthy and ecological materials imaginable. It can also be enriched or stabilized with cement, as explained elsewhere in this book (see pp. 36–39). Faced with the dominance of industrialized materials, it seems opportune to recall the morals of two of La Fontaine's fables. The first is: 'Every profession esteems itself, and calls the others ignorant and vile.' Raw earth has long suffered from this kind of disdain, without being able to defend itself, as it has no powerful lobby behind it. The second is: 'Patience and time achieve more than strength and rage.' This patience has been displayed by many builders, working in isolation, who slowly brought raw earth architecture into the 20th century, proving its viability in technological, cultural, and ecological terms. The use of raw earth as an alternative material has become particularly relevant in situations where the two most dominant modern building materials, cement and steel, are not available.

In the following sections, instead of taking a chronological approach, these developments will be grouped thematically, in order to place them in their political, social, and even military contexts.

Post-war promise

In the wake of both world wars, many European countries emerged battered and were immediately confronted with the need to rebuild countless homes, neighbourhoods, and even entire towns. Many factories producing construction materials had been destroyed, and those that survived proved unable to meet demand, so earth provided an alternative. By the end of the First World War, France had already had a century of experience with modernized earth construction, while in 1919, Clough Williams-Ellis urged Britain to bring its own practices in this field up to date – but no significant post-war progress was achieved by either country. Germany, however, heavily promoted raw earth architecture by using it to create 20,000 new housing units between 1919 and 1924. The US magazine *Engineering News-Record* praised this strategy in an article entitled 'Germany Returns to Adobe Building'. In a similar way, Adolf Loos, one of the pioneers of modernism in Austria, exhorted architects to take up the challenge: 'Do not be afraid to be considered out of fashion. Changes in traditional building methods only make sense if they guarantee their users effective improvements. It is important to give credence to traditions that have survived the test of time. Even if they are ancient, their truths have a much greater significance than some more recent false promises.'

The German reconstruction programme led to the establishment of regional centres to provide training in the various aspects of earth architecture. European institutional initiatives gave rise to early scientific research, with a special focus on the development of *Leichtlehm* or 'light clay', a blend of earth and straw (1933), and the semi-industrial production of compressed earth blocks ('Tonadur' bricks, 1949). These policies were accompanied by a string of books for both specialist and general readers and a series of educational films. Under the auspices of Albert Speer (1905–81), an architect and influential member of the Nazi party, the use of raw earth was regulated (for the first time in the world) in 1944, leading to the instigation of regulation DIN No. 189/51 in 1951. Speer was close to Hitler and in 1942 was appointed Minister of Armaments and War Production. Speer forced millions of civilian prisoners of war captured throughout Europe to work as slave labour, and he also decreed that cement and steel should be prioritized for military use and that the use of raw earth should therefore be encouraged for civilian purposes.

In 1952, not long after the war, two German engineers, Pollack and Richter, issued an impassioned appeal to future generations of builders. On the basis of their own experience, they declared: 'We must go beyond the idea that earth architecture is merely a provisional solution to the current housing crisis. This technology must now receive the same consideration as other techniques and we must promote its mechanization and industrialization. The key to the success of the future growth of the earth building sector lies, as in other fields of construction, in systematic rationalization. The absolute priority faced by the leaders of our economy …must be strategies that implement the prudent use of natural resources. More specifically, the optimal use *in situ* of raw earth to create a responsible housing policy constitutes an example of the political and institutional prudence that is necessary.' Germany thus became one of the first champions of the principles of ecological responsibility, and put those principles into action. In 1974, for example, the architect Gernot Minke (see pp. 386–387) launched the first degree course in raw earth construction in Kassel, which he supplemented with field research in Asia and Latin America.

The globalization of raw earth

From 1949 to 1990, Germany was divided into two, with the Federal Republic of Germany (West), initially under the military control of the victorious European and American countries, and the German Democratic Republic (East), occupied by the USSR. Ironically, the construction policies espoused by the far-right Nazi regime were embraced once again in Communist East Germany. A construction programme was drawn up to create 200,000 housing units, with 40% due to be built with natural materials available *in situ*. In 1952 it was calculated that the construction of 17,000 housing units with earth over two years saved the use of 100,000 tons of coal (the only energy source then available), 200 million fired bricks (which take a great deal of energy to manufacture), and 75,000 tons of transport capacity. This building expertise was exported to Communist allies: the USSR and China to the east and sub-Saharan Africa to the south. Moscow sought to demonstrate 'friendship between peoples' to newly independent African countries by providing 'technical and cultural assistance' to alleviate their severe housing crisis. As a result, Tanzania, for example, found itself a player on the strategic stage of the Cold War waged by the superpowers from 1947 to 1989.

One American reaction to Communist intervention in developing countries was the formation of the Peace Corps, under the presidency of John F. Kennedy. Its 200,000 recently graduated civilians – including many architects and engineers – were sent to around 100 countries considered to be 'underdeveloped' and vulnerable to Soviet political expansionism. Like the USSR, the United States encouraged public housing programmes and the construction of public buildings using raw earth, and the USAID agency distributed earth construction guides in multiple languages all over the world. Consequently, and perhaps paradoxically, the fate of a form of technology that would soon be termed alternative, intermediate, or soft was often tied up in the fierce political battles played out in the developing world by the forces of capitalism and communism.

From 1965 onwards, several European countries obliged young graduates to choose between doing military service or serving as a civilian aid worker, with the aim of building a global 'North–South dialogue'. All too often, however, young architects and engineers dispatched abroad in this way proved too inexperienced to 'aid' developing countries. Nevertheless, some of them did discover the beauty, intelligence, and benefits of vernacular earth architecture – and in the 1970s they started to bring this knowledge back home where they helped to modernize it. This was particularly visible in France, through teams such as CRAterre (see pp. 382–383) and public housing programmes such as the Domaine de la Terre project (see pp. 392–395). Once again, paradoxically, construction with raw earth, a material that is quintessentially local, benefited from the globalization triggered by the geopolitical strategies of the second half of the 20th century. The many uses to which earth was put reflected all the shades of the political spectrum, from the far right to the far left.

The good (but unbuilt) intentions of two master architects

During World War Two and its immediate aftermath, two of the 20th century's most influential architects designed projects that incorporated raw earth: Frank Lloyd Wright in the United States and Le Corbusier in France. In 1942, Wright expressed his idealism and social commitment by designing the Cooperative Homesteads (p. 327, above), a garden city for a car workers' cooperative outside Detroit, on a 65-hectare farm site that was intended to be self-sufficient. The future occupants of the project's 76 homes would build their own houses, partly underground, using earth excavated with a small bulldozer. An earthen embankment would be wrapped around the exterior of each home to provide insulation. The plans show that conventional load-bearing walls would be forsaken in favour of solid structures of rammed earth, grouped around large fireplaces, articulating the domestic space and giving it a warm intimacy. Although a prototype was built, the project was abandoned when the cooperative's members were enlisted into the war effort. In that same year, Wright also drew up plans for the Pottery House, which was to have been built with adobe in Texas for a wealthy client (p. 327, below). However, this project was not built until 1985 in New Mexico – using reinforced concrete.

In 1942, Le Corbusier published a book that stands out from the rest of his written work. In *Les constructions 'Murondins'*, he explained and illustrated the basic principles of construction with rammed earth and adobe, and suggested using it to build collective housing, schools, and small public buildings for refugees and casualties of the war. There is no evidence, however, that these ideas were ever put into practice. In 1946, Le Corbusier dreamed up a project to represent the new post-war spirit, entailing praise for the virtues of a natural material in terms that were both rousing and unexpected. Although known as the master of reinforced concrete, he now proclaimed that '*pisé* provides a basic architecture of precision and grandeur, all on a human scale. It makes it possible to achieve the greatest and most noble lines, free of emphasis but charged with grandeur. Life inside this *pisé* can attain a complete dignity and restore the sense of fundamental human and natural resources to the men of the machinist civilization.' Twenty kilometres to the northeast of Marseille (the site of his future Cité Radieuse), Le Corbusier wanted to build 'a haven of meditation…in the heart of the splendid landscape of Sainte-Baume' that would allow visitors to bask in the atmosphere of Provence. This pilgrimage complex, comprising a hundred two-storey units, was conceived to fit harmoniously within the landscape, but the project was criticized for harming the area's natural beauty and was never completed. Nonetheless, Le Corbusier declared himself satisfied for having attempted the enterprise in the first place.

Between 1940 and 1960, it seemed that nobody in either Europe or America proved capable of drawing any lessons from these two masters' aborted projects, or even from the highly positive results achieved in Germany in 1919 and 1946. It would take the combative environment of the US counterculture and May '68 in France to finally ignite a raw earth revival. Before that, however, Africa became a global stage for raw earth innovations.

In the throes of colonialism

From 1920 to 1940, some exciting architectural innovations emerged in the vast expanses of Africa that had been colonized by various European countries, but these were mostly atypical and sporadic, taking place within a context of deculturation and massive importation of Western models. In 1942, a lack of industrialized materials in Algeria led Franco-Belgian architect Michel Luyckx (a student of Auguste Perret) to build the world's first raw earth hospital in Adrar in the Sahara (see p. 328, above). Given the standards of hygiene and modernity required for an institution of this kind, the building was an historic breakthrough. Elsewhere, financial constraints, geographical isolation, and the experimental drive of unsung pioneers gave rise to other architectural programmes that took advantage of this local material. For example, also in the Sahara, the charming new town of Timimoun and a luxury hotel, the Oasis Rouge, were built from scratch to accommodate wealthy tourists crossing the desert. The buildings' warm, reddish tones were highlighted by relief motifs inspired by local Berber jewelry, cut from the earth while it was still damp (see p. 329). In Ghana in the 1920s, missionaries built the cathedral of Navrongo (see p. 328, centre) in a modernized style.

However, the earliest examples of the modernization of earth architecture in Africa by Europeans date back a decade earlier still. They occurred in Egypt, which was then under a British mandate. Britain had already been the breeding ground for the progressive, interdisciplinary Arts and Crafts movement, which sought a symbiosis between tradition and modernity. In architecture, it focused on reviving vernacular housing, often built with cob. The research undertaken by Leïla El-Wakil at the University of Geneva, and published in 2013 by Nicholas Warner, has revealed that two English architects inspired by these ideas, George Somers Clarke and William John Palmer-Jones, were responsible for transplanting them to the banks of the Nile in the first decade of the 20th century. Somers Clarke and Palmer-Jones drew on rural vernacular traditions of earth architecture to build sumptuous villas; Palmer-Jones also designed a dig house for the Metropolitan Museum of Art's Egyptian expeditions. (see pp. 320–321). These buildings anticipated the work of Hassan Fathy in Egypt by three decades.

In sharp contrast to these advances on African shores, huge colonial exhibitions in Europe enthralled hundreds of millions of visitors from the late 19th century to the 1930s. The colonial powers staged demonstrations of the supposed benefits of colonization in grand temporary pavilions, embellished with an array of exotic references to the heritage of the invaded countries. A whole series of monuments were reduced to kitsch as a result; the earth architecture of Malian mosques and Moroccan kasbahs was reproduced in plaster or even concrete, turning them into objects of political propaganda (see pp. 330–331). Even worse, in the 1870s, 'human zoo' exhibits were created in Europe to display indigenous people, posing alongside their supposedly reconstructed 'mud huts', as examples of a primitive Africa that the colonial powers were allegedly changing for the better through the European values of civilization and enlightenment.

Opposite: The arches, vaults, and domes of an adobe villa built in around 1980 by architect Olivier Sednaoui in Luxor, Egypt (see p. 340).

A cultural idyll in the Sun Belt

In the 1910s and 1920s, a subset of wealthy Americans became attracted to the notion of living in modern homes built from raw earth. The metropolitan elites of the East Coast were on the lookout for new vacation getaways, and descended on the Sun Belt, in the southwest of the United States. A new wave of earth architecture grew up in New Mexico around two ancient cultural hubs: the indigenous settlement of Taos, founded in the 13th century (see pp. 134–135), and the small town of Santa Fe, built in 1607 by Spanish colonizers. Despite their radically different histories, these sites had one feature in common: they were built with adobe, which gave them formal sensuality and chromatic subtlety. These qualities attracted many writers, artists, and intellectuals, who were soon followed by more affluent families. This influx triggered a property bubble fed by a desire to revel in the local colour (red and yellow ochre) of vernacular architecture. The less fastidious newcomers saw no harm in commissioning property developers to erect villas, shops, hotels, and museums that were industrially built to resemble 'handmade' earthen structures. These fake adobe buildings were the first example of Pueblo Revival, a kitsch commercial style that exploited a profitable line in regionalist exoticism. (This neo-colonialist approach would later be roundly condemned by Patrick Perez in his writings.)

More discerning clients asked their architects to create contemporary buildings with 'real' raw earth, following local vernacular traditions. Buildings influenced by this trend first saw light in 1919 with a villa designed by the Austrian architect Rudolf Schindler (see p. 326). Before successfully establishing himself in California, Schindler made a 'cultural stopover' in Santa Fe, where he discovered the traditional heritage of earth architecture that inspired his villa, but which was unfortunately sidelined in his later work. Other pioneers of this trend included two remarkable women – the art patron Mabel Dodge Luhan, in Taos (see p. 325, above), and the artist Georgia O'Keeffe, in Abiquiú – who commissioned adobe homes and brought in their wake a throng of admirers who went on to do the same. Other patrons financed the first modern public buildings to be constructed with earth in the United States, including the Cristo Rey Church in Santa Fe, which was completed in 1940, using a grand total of 180,000 adobe bricks. Works of this scale necessitated the creation of local businesses to produce raw earth bricks: the factory opened in California in 1936 by the German émigré Hans Sumpf was reputedly the largest of its type in the world. The rationalized and semi-industrial production of adobe further stimulated the expansion of earth architecture in the United States.

From the American boom of the 1920s to the military programme of 1941

Another boom was also underway in the United States in the 1920s, as public institutions and universities began to sponsor in-depth research into potential new uses of raw earth, as evidenced by a flurry of experiments and publications. Engineers collaborated with architects on military and civil fronts. The US Army and US Air Force tested barracks, roads, and landing strips made from stabilized earth. The underlying intention was to develop construction methods that could be deployed quickly overseas, in combat areas, to avoid dependence on an unpredictable supply of industrialized materials and fuels. In December 1941, the military defeat at Pearl Harbor not only precipitated the entrance of the United States into the Second World War but also led to the construction of raw earth defence systems along the coast of California, where the government feared another Japanese attack.

Meanwhile, civil engineers were building raw earth dams. Some of these were pilot projects for the New Deal, the ambitious public works programme implemented by President Franklin D. Roosevelt after his election in 1935, in response to the financial crisis sparked by the Wall Street Crash of 1929. The US government also encouraged self-building as a means to provide long-term employment for the maximum number of people. The most striking project of this type was steered by the architect Thomas Hibben, who planned to build 75 rammed earth houses in the Gardendale Homestead neighbourhood of Mount Olive, Alabama, in 1933, for people left destitute by the Great Depression. This strategy was, however, deemed by the private construction lobby to be an inappropriate distraction that went against standard capitalist practices. Hibben's pioneering programme was therefore halted and eventually cancelled. Nevertheless, a survey 60 years later of those houses that were completed showed that they were in a perfect state of conservation – and they are still occupied today.

The emergence of the counterculture and eco-activism in the United States

In the 1950s and 1960s many young people of the United States dismissed the ideals of the 'American way' as repressive, materialistic, consumerist, and individualistic, and they protested against nuclear weapons and the war in Vietnam (1955–75). The pacifist offensive of the counterculture was launched, largely inspired by the rallying call of two American philosophers: Herbert Marcuse and, above all, Henry David Thoreau (1817–62). This Harvard-educated essayist, artisan, and poet with a Franco-Scottish background was rediscovered and revered. His civic and antimilitarist activism – which would go on to inspire Gandhi in India – served as a touchstone for the movement. In his book *Walden* (1854), Thoreau advocated a 'happy frugality' closely connected to nature, and he was deeply impressed by the culture and ancestral wisdom of the Native Americans. Thoreau became his own architect by building a cabin retreat in the woods. Thoreau's admirers in the Beat Generation sought a radical overhaul of society that would pave the way for a brighter future. Young followers of the counterculture left the cities to build rural communes and improvised houses made with recycled or natural materials, such as wood and raw earth. They often drew inspiration from the vernacular legacy of the developing world, as disseminated by popular magazines of the day such as *Shelter* and *The Whole Earth Catalog*.

This creativity resulted in a range of playful buildings of all shapes and sizes, of which the premises of the Lama Foundation (see pp. 342–343), built in Taos in 1968 by Steve Baer for a community devoted to meditation and organic farming, is a particularly eloquent example. The innovative and provocative ideas driving the builders of the counterculture broke new ground and they have continued to stimulate future generations by giving form to young people's hunger for new ethical, social, spiritual, and cultural values, embodied in, among other concepts, downsizing, social solidarity, and ecological activism. Half a century on, Greenpeace and Friends of the Earth, founded on the West Coast in 1971 and 1969, respectively, remain thriving offspring of the counterculture and have spread its philosophy all over the world. Many of the leitmotifs of the American youth movement that tried to 'reinvent the future' in thought and deed are still relevant today: living better with less; finding creative ways to be self-sufficient; avoiding waste; promoting recycling, remaking, and restoration; reviving craft skills; encouraging do-it-yourself; promoting intuition and pragmatism; and exploring the art of simplicity. The counterculture sought to make its aspirations into reality in a spirit of joy and pleasure, via a vast communal laboratory that would give rise to a new, freer, and more convivial art of living, in harmony with nature.

The countercultural spirit lives on

Nevertheless, the most important innovations derived from the open-minded use of raw earth appeared just after the fizzling out of the US counterculture. For example, Santa Fe, the capital of New Mexico, attracted a new wave of moneyed young people in the 1970s who built comfortable adobe villas that were cutting-edge but well adapted to the local climate and cultural needs (see pp. 344–345). Houses built by young architects Steve Baer and David Wright are good examples of this trend. They were also responsible for early attempts to harness solar energy for domestic purposes, primarily by adopting the principle of the 'Trombe wall', devised in 1962 by the French physicist Felix Trombe and utilizing his discovery of passive solar energy. This invention combines the greenhouse effect created by glass windows with the thermal inertia of a thick wall of raw earth set behind them, according to the principles of bioclimatic architecture. This system substantially reduces the energy required to heat and cool a house. This hybrid technology is resolutely low-tech and so stood in opposition to the high-tech ethos that held sway in the architecture of the time. It is known as 'solar adobe', a term that celebrates the combining of the resources of the sun and the earth.

In the field of urban planning, architect Antoine Predock set about building the residential neighbourhood of La Luz, Albuquerque, with adobe in

1967 (see pp. 346–347). The resulting close-knit ensemble of 60 homes offered a new type of middle-class housing that tore up the staid, outmoded blueprint for American suburbs, which were relentlessly peddled by property developers in the 1940s and 1950s. New Mexico therefore became the world's first experimental laboratory for producing convincing models of contemporary raw earth housing for the middle and upper classes. Adobe proved to be more than a passing fad, as this unprecedented adventure continued – albeit more discreetly – into the 21st century in the neighbouring state of Arizona, via a new generation of architects including Rick Joy (see pp. 396–397).

Ethical and technological alternatives

It is often said that American society has a particular gift for assimilating its most challenging anti-establishment ideas, and the country's most important cultural institution, the Museum of Modern Art (MoMA) in New York, illustrated this trend in 1964. While the counterculture was proclaiming its rejection of the received wisdom of contemporary architecture and turning to cultures of the developing world for inspiration, MoMA asked Austrian architect Bernard Rudofsky to curate the exhibition *Architecture Without Architects*. For the first time, a major institution acknowledged the contribution of vernacular housing from other continents, much of it built with earth. This recognition had considerable and lasting repercussions all over the world, as is evident in Pierre Frey's book *Learning from Vernacular* (2010).

Although this now legendary exhibition did not mark a radical change in the cultural approach to architecture, it did reflect the wider context of a search for new ethical parameters that was then underway in Europe and North America. The issue attracted the attention of brilliant thinkers like Ivan Illich, Amory Lovins, André Gorz, E. F. Schumacher, Edgar Morin, and Aurelio Peccei, co-founder of the Club of Rome, which gathered together economists and business leaders from 52 countries and would go on to publish the Meadows Report (1972), which dared to ask whether there should be limits to growth. These cautionary warnings had little effect on domestic architecture but they were particularly inspiring to supporters of a revival in raw earth construction. More broadly, there was a drive to realize the social and ecological aspirations of the times through techniques that were dubbed intermediary, communal, participatory, local, or low tech, in keeping with the precept 'small is beautiful'.

The blossoming of this new philosophy was sometimes preceded by the invention of new soft technologies for earth construction, particularly in three developing countries. In Egypt, architect Hassan Fathy started to update the practices of building with adobe. In Iran, in around 1970, architect Nader Khalili invented Superadobe, a technique that involved filling hessian sacks with earth to build walls and domes; although this procedure was exported to California, it failed to take root there. In contrast, the Cinva-Ram, invented in 1952 by engineer Raúl Ramírez, was hugely successful in Colombia. Light and easy to handle, dismantle, and transport, it allowed individuals and collectives to produce their own compressed earth bricks manually, anywhere. The ram led to many technical improvements and alternative, mass-produced tools, such as the Terstaram press from Belgium and the Auram from India, designed, respectively, by Fernand Platbrood and Satprem Maïni. These tools allow the kind of communal and self-sufficient production espoused by philosopher Ivan Illich and encourage low-cost self-build housing.

The Moroccan impetus

Morocco has also witnessed ambitious innovations. From the 1870s onwards, King Hassan I demonstrated great perspicacity as regards the modernization of rammed earth (or *pisé*) for urban construction. Two particularly striking projects resulted from this policy. Hassan commissioned Italian engineers to build the first ever modern factory constructed with rammed earth – the Makina – in Fez, the country's oldest city. Meanwhile, in southwest Morocco, he also had the new town of Tiznit built with rammed earth. After the country's independence in 1956, in the reign of Mohammed V, the finance minister wanted to reduce imports of building materials, particularly steel and cement, so French engineer Alain Masson suggested updating the country's ancient methods of earth construction. Masson took advantage of the government's eagerness to find jobs for rural immigrants to the cities and in 1962, he used this inexhaustible, unqualified workforce (supervised by professional builders) to build a public housing project in Marrakech: Daoudiate, which included 3,200 small homes built from compressed earth blocks (see pp. 348–349). This was the largest earthen housing programme ever undertaken. The results were so positive that Masson undertook another project in 1965 in Ouarzazate, in collaboration with Belgian architect Jean Hensens. They drew up a prototype for an extremely cheap house, with walls and low vaulted ceilings created by packing metal formworks with rammed earth. Unfortunately, this project for 200 homes was modified beyond recognition when it was put into practice.

In the 1980s, Morocco became the preferred North African destination for European tourists. To satisfy the demands of visiting jet-setters, Moroccan architect Elie Mouyal built thirty sumptuous villas in rammed earth and adobe in the palm groves of Marrakech (see pp. 404–405). These buildings demonstrated that earth, so often unjustly associated with low-cost housing, is in fact perfectly compatible with the lifestyles of both rich and poor. Other modern earthen neighbourhoods in Europe demonstrate the same point: for example, the middle-class homes built in 1826 around the train station in Weilburg, Germany; the garden city built in 1870 in Oslo by the banker F. H. Frølich for his employees; and the workers' housing of Heuberg-Siedlung, built in 1923 in Vienna by avant-garde architect Adolf Loos. Along with other more modest earth buildings, Elie Mouyal's luxury homes in Marrakech contributed to the city's international reputation as the capital of raw earth architecture (a title later disputed by both Grenoble and Lyon in France) and raised it to the status previously enjoyed by Santa Fe in the 1920s.

Artistic and scientific curiosity

In the 19th century, Morocco provided the inspiration for another major artistic trend: Orientalism. When Eugène Delacroix visited the country in 1832, he sketched his impressions in watercolours (now preserved in the Louvre in Paris). In 1845, these works would serve as the basis for one of his most famous paintings (see p. 352), depicting the Sultan Moulay Abd al-Rahman on horseback in front of the city walls of Meknes. This regal figure is overshadowed, however, by the ochre colours and monolithic solidity of the 18th-century rammed earth ramparts behind him. Among the many other artists inspired by Morocco was Jacques Majorelle. Working in the 1920s, at the height of his powers, he recorded the architectural splendour and vivid colours of Berber villages in the High Atlas mountains (see pp. 354–355). In contrast, Jean Dubuffet (p. 353, below), a major figure in French contemporary art, travelled to Algeria, where he was enthralled by the texture and colours of the earth in the Sahara. In the 1950s this fascination was reflected in the series of paintings he called *Texturologies*, which were designed to reflect 'the exemplary life of the soil'.

This fruitful creative synergy between raw earth and art was echoed in several fields of science, including the new discipline of ethno-archaeology, which has fomented a constructive dialogue between archaeologists, ethnologists, and architects. In the early 20th century, Leo Frobenius (1873–1938), a German pioneer of ethnology and of the reassessment of African civilizations, was the first European to praise the brilliance of *banco* architecture in Mali. This proselytism was continued by the institute at the University of Frankfurt that was named after him: in 1990, one of the institute's professors, Dorothee Gruner, published a survey of West African earthen mosques. Meanwhile, archaeology, increasingly recognized as a science over the course of the 20th century, has been responsible for the discovery of a growing number of ancient earth buildings. The German Robert Koldewey excavated the remains of Babylon and the foundations of the Etemenanki ziggurat in present-day Iraq in 1899; Frenchmen André Parrot and Jean-Claude Margueron discovered and publicized the royal city of Mari in Syria; the Englishman James Mellaart discovered the Çatal Hüyük complex in Turkey in 1961; and two decades later the Americans Susan and Roderick McIntosh discovered Djenné-Djeno in Mali. In the 1970s, major discoveries were also made in Europe. In 1983, an international conference was held in Lyon to evaluate the archaeological research into 'earth architecture…, its precedents since proto-history and its contemporary continuations'. The conference concluded with a visit to the Domaine de la Terre project, which was then under construction.

European academics were not alone, however, in exploring the symbiosis between past and present. Since the early 20th century, accomplished artisans have been bringing the ancient expertise of their own regions up to date in order to construct modern earth buildings – including luxurious palaces – in Morocco, Yemen, and Saudi Arabia. Finally, as further evidence of the globalization of earth architecture, Australia and New Zealand have embraced it, despite lacking an historical tradition of this technique, ever since texts by French pioneer François Cointeraux were published in the *Sydney Gazette* in 1823, kickstarting large-scale projects involving earth construction.

These developments over five continents from 1789 to 1968 allowed raw earth architecture to blossom into a host of eco-friendly forms. This bodes well for a future in which humanity faces the most serious environmental crisis of all time.

Below: Detail of a building covered in red earth mortar, typical of the modern architecture of the Algerian Sahara.

Overleaf: Facade design for the School of Rural Architecture, founded by François Cointeraux (early 19th century).

François Cointeraux: First Great Pioneer of Modern Earth Architecture

Jean Dethier

To best understand the ideas, ambitions, and contributions of this French architect and master builder, it is necessary to place them in the context of the major upheavals that occurred during his lifetime. In 1789, after the radical breakthroughs of the Enlightenment, the French Revolution introduced a new model for society, enshrined in the motto 'Liberty, Equality, Fraternity' and in the Declaration of the Rights of Man. This radical change in political and social life was followed by further changes initiated by the physiocrats, whose social and economic strategy promoted the 'great work of agriculture' and the 'government of nature'. It was within this maelstrom, at the height of the revolutionary period, that Cointeraux began to write and work. His ambition was to modernize the ancient building technique of rammed earth, which had been used in the villages of his native region, between Lyon and Grenoble: he renamed it *nouveau pisé*. The term refers to monolithic masonry created by compressing successive layers of raw earth inside a wooden frame measuring between 40 and 60 centimetres wide, depending on the height of the wall being built. It was a fast, cheap technique that met the needs of rural democratization as well as the expectations of a new form of society, particularly the emerging class of farmer-labourers who worked the lands expropriated from aristocrats after the Revolution. As well as the various housing designs that he produced for both the affluent and the poor, Cointeraux also proposed constructing other utilitarian buildings with rammed earth, including enormous four-storey factories. Initially focused on the countryside, his plans were subsequently extended to cities, especially Lyon and its suburbs where, under his influence, housing blocks of five to seven storeys were built with rammed earth in the early 19th century.

The activism of François Cointeraux was also apparent in his methods of communication. As a self-declared 'professor of rural architecture', he founded schools in Paris, Lyon, and Grenoble to disseminate his teachings. From 1790 onwards, he published around sixty booklets and pamphlets, some of which have been translated into as many as eight languages, a remarkable feat for a humble rural worker with great ambitions to reform society. Cointeraux emerged, above all, as the first modern promoter of autonomous housing construction. His verve and passion went beyond architecture into the spheres of politics and even social critique. It was in this sometimes provocative spirit of symbiosis that he declared in 1797: 'Architecture has always been discussed in isolation. Agriculture has always been considered separately. That is a mistake: these two arts can only be furthered by fusing their principles in a single crucible of the mind. The end result is a new science, which I call agritecture.' The pioneering works of Cointeraux were known and admired from the early 19th century onwards. In 1807, the emperor Napoleon I drew on them for the construction, using rammed earth, of a new military town intended to accommodate 15,000 people: Napoléonville, in western France. Ten years later, Cointeraux achieved professional recognition when his innovations were incorporated by Jean-Baptiste Rondelet into his famous and highly influential *Theoretical and Practical Treatise on the Art of Building* (1802–17), which was much reprinted and translated. In France, the influence of Cointeraux was apparent for almost a century. It was evident in the wide range of architecture made with *nouveau pisé*, particularly in the Lyon region with its castles and middle-class housing, model farms and wine cellars, workers' housing, as well as a town hall and a school, completed in around 1910 in Dolomieu, Isère.

Cointeraux's influence beyond France
The persuasive powers of this modest but tenacious theorist and practitioner seemed to have no limits. By the end of the 18th century he had won over an array of prestigious European architects to his cause. These included David Gilly, architect to the court of King Frederick II in Germany. In 1793, Gilly opened the *Bauschule*, a school of building, in Berlin, basing it on the French schools founded by Cointeraux. Five years later, Gilly built the Palace Kleinmachnow near Berlin with rammed earth, and he also sponsored a translation of Cointeraux's writings. These, in their turn, impressed impresario Wilhelm Jacob Wimpf, who in 1826 erected a block of middle-class apartments in Weilburg which – at seven storeys – was the tallest rammed earth building in Germany and rivalled its French counterparts in Lyon.

In Russia, Nikolai L'vov, an architect favoured by Tsar Paul I, was a devoted reader of Cointeraux and had his work translated into Russian in 1796. L'vov put the

Frenchman's ideas into practice in his early residential buildings, including his own house in Torjok. After L'vov had sung the praises of rammed earth in court, the Tsar commissioned him to build some barracks, followed by the prestigious Priory Palace in Gatchina (now recently restored). Thrilled by the results, the Tsar helped L'vov to found two schools that would train hundreds of Russians to work with *nouveau pisé* according to the tenets of Cointeraux.

In England, Henry Holland, a neoclassical architect popular with the aristocracy, translated the work of Cointeraux into English and thus sparked the spread of his ideas in Great Britain for more than forty years and in North America for even longer. In Denmark, the architect Klaus Seidelin translated Cointeraux in 1796; in 1870, more than four thousand Danish homes were built from earth. In the same year, the banker Fritz Frølich commissioned the construction in earth of the garden city Frølichbyen in Oslo, Norway. A similar enthusiasm was evident among the Swedish middle classes in Stockholm. In Italy, the writings of Cointeraux were translated as early as 1793, thanks to the efforts of Giuseppe Del Rosso, while the proximity of Switzerland to Lyon meant that it became the first foreign country where the modernized rammed earth technique was used, in schools and a village built by Alfred Zschokke. The strategies formulated by Cointeraux therefore met with great success throughout Europe, particularly among the educated elite.

In the United States, Thomas Jefferson declared that architecture must become a tool to improve the lives of citizens, both in towns and in the country. In 1792, after visiting one of the rammed earth houses built by Cointeraux near Lyon, Jefferson wrote to President George Washington to report on the *pisé de terre* buildings he had seen in France and the potential advantages of this technique for the new villages being built by the pioneers opening up the West. In 1806, S. W. Johnson published his treaty *Rural Economy: Containing a Treatise on Pisé Building*; it freely plagiarized the works of Cointeraux, who thus unwittingly contributed to the success of the book. Several buildings attest to this influence. In 1821, William Wallace Anderson had an elegant Neo-Palladian residence in Stateburg, South Carolina, built with rammed earth. In 1972 it was declared a place of historic interest, as it was judged to be 'the largest complex in the United States of *pisé de terre* (rammed earth) buildings'. In 1851, Anderson insisted that Stateburg's church should also be built with rammed earth, and this was also later classified as a national monument, after surviving an earthquake in 1886 and a hurricane in 1898. Further examples of raw earth construction in the United States include the Ursuline Academy in San Antonio, Texas, built in 1851 by masons brought over from France, and several villas completed between 1830 and 1860 in the towns of Geneva, Bath, and Oswego in the north of New York State.

Cointeraux also had followers in New Zealand, where French architect Louis Perret built the Pompallier House in the town of Russell in 1842 (now a national monument). Australia, meanwhile, discovered *pisé* in 1817 via *The Farmer's Dictionary*, written by Abraham Rees, and in 1823 the *Sydney Gazette* began to publish the works of Cointeraux in serial form.

From oblivion to rediscovery

Influenced by the Enlightenment and the French Revolution, François Cointeraux was the first architect to develop a coherent theory and devise a basic principle for modernizing raw earth construction. By the early 20th century, however, his work had mostly been forgotten. Now he has been re-evaluated and is considered one of three great pioneers of the field, alongside Hassan Fathy in Egypt and CRAterre in France. Within CRAterre, it was Patrice Doat who rediscovered the writings of Cointeraux, and Hubert Guillaud who published the first detailed analysis of them. They both have a great appreciation for 'everything that his ideas can still teach us' and have expressed a shared desire to 'continue and expand the work he started'. Other contemporary scholars are also studying this exceptional inventor. Jean-Philippe Garric, professor of art history at the Sorbonne, Paris, has even declared that 'Cointeraux seems like a one-man avant-garde'.

```
Further reading:
Guillaud 1997; Baridon, Garric, & Richaud 2016
```

François Cointeraux
Pioneer of Modern Earth Architecture

After the upheavals of the French Revolution, François Cointeraux emerged as an extremely important figure: he was the first architect in history to study, teach, and practise a modernized form of earth architecture. **Opposite, above:** Cointeraux's most famous illustration demonstrates one of his most passionate beliefs: that in the new egalitarian society born from the French Revolution, housing built with earth could meet the needs of all social classes. Hence his depiction of a house for poorer citizens that would allow them to escape destitution, and another similar but less austere house for the better-off. In fact, the only difference between the two is the ornamentation on the latter's facade. **Opposite, below:** Cointeraux also recommended rammed earth as a building material to meet the needs of an increasingly industrialized society, as in this design for a four-storey textile factory produced by Cointeraux in 1790. **Centre and below right:** Cointeraux's work met with the immediate approval of France's most famous and influential architectural theorist, Jean-Baptiste Rondelet, owing to its practicality and accessibility, as well as its aesthetic qualities. These drawings of a rammed earth house and its construction process illustrate Cointeraux's approach. They were published in Rondelet's seven-volume *Theoretical and Practical Treatise on the Art of Building* (1802–17) which went on to have an enormous influence as a result of its sixteen editions and numerous translations.

R.E. & J.D.

Above right: Title pages of two major works by Cointeraux, one dedicated to the people of France and the other to 'all peoples'.

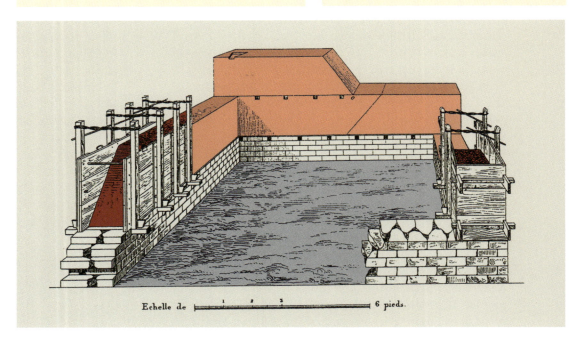

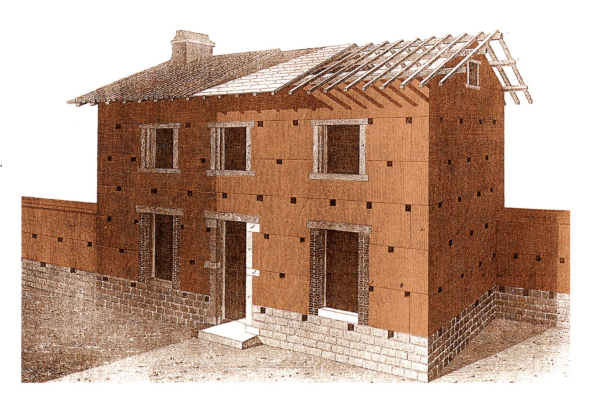

310   Chapter 5

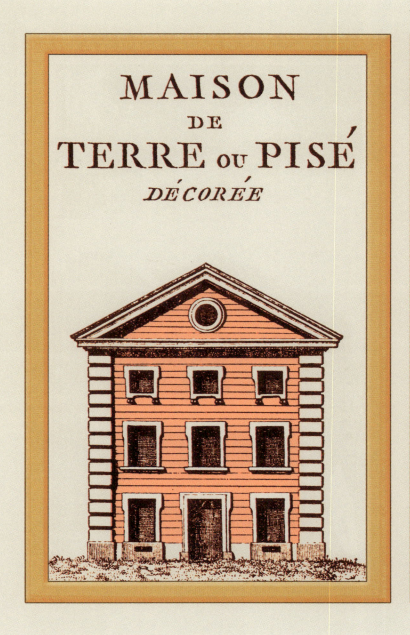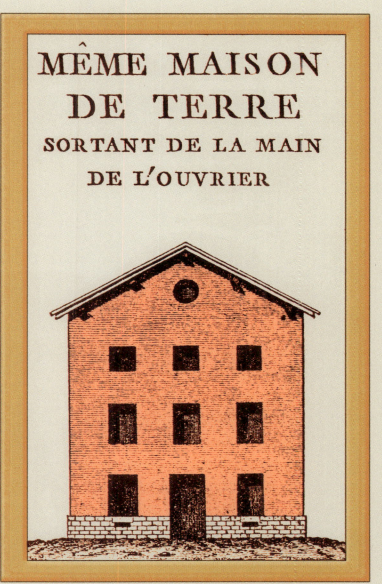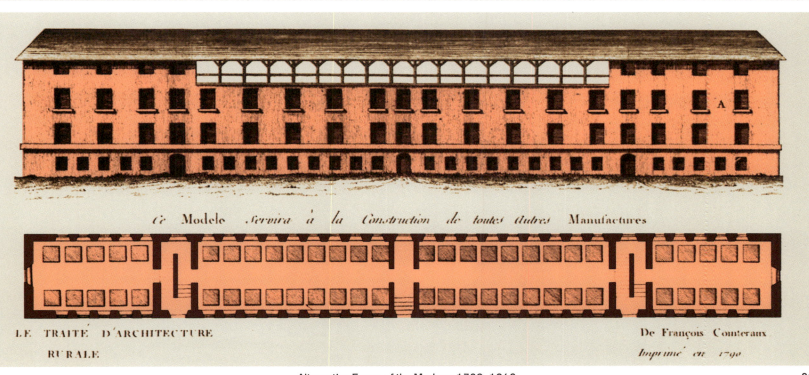

François Cointeraux
His Influence in France

The theories expounded by Cointeraux, and his projects inspired by them, influenced builders in many countries, but most of all in France. **Right, above and below, and opposite, below:** Three large 19th-century middle-class homes built with rammed earth in the Saône Valley, France, Cointeraux's own birthplace. Some of these houses have sophisticated interiors that reflect the social status of their owners. **Opposite, above:** Workers' housing built with rammed earth in 1882 in Saint-Simeon-de-Bressieux, Isère. **Opposite, centre:** The town hall and primary school in Dolomieu, Isère, which occupy the same rammed earth complex, constructed in 1910.
  R.E.

Alternative Forms of the Modern: 1789–1968

François Cointeraux
His Influence in Europe

The influence of Cointeraux can be seen throughout Europe, from Scandinavia to Italy, from Britain to Germany and even Russia. **Above right:** Four housing blocks, ranging from four to seven storeys in height, built with rammed earth in the centre of Weilburg, Germany, in 1820–40 by Wilhelm Jacob Wimpf. **Below right:** The Priory Palace in Gatchina, Russia, built with rammed earth by architect Nikolai L'vov in 1798. **Opposite, above left:** An aristocratic residence in Germany. **Opposite, above right:** A rammed earth primary school built in Thundorf, Switzerland, in 1843.

R.E.

Alternative Forms of the Modern: 1789–1968

François Cointeraux
His Influence in North America and Australasia

Over the course of the 19th century, the influence of Cointeraux stretched far beyond his native France, across Europe, and into North America and Australasia. Two of the most famous rammed earth buildings in the United States can be found in Stateburg, South Carolina. They are listed in the National Register of Historic Places and have been officially recognized as National Historic Landmarks. They were commissioned by William Wallace Anderson, the owner of a large plantation, who became fascinated with rammed earth architecture and decided to use it to build his own neoclassical home, the Borough House (**above**) and its annexes. He subsequently continued to champion the technique and in 1850 it was used for the Church of the Holy Cross by architect Edward C. Jones (**opposite**). **Below:** The Pompallier House in Russell, New Zealand, was built with rammed earth in 1841 to house a Catholic mission. The mission's headquarters were in Lyon, France, which was also the hometown of its architect, Louis Perret, a disciple of Cointeraux.

J.D. & R.E.

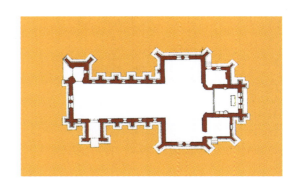

Alternative Forms of the Modern: 1789–1968

Peru
Urban Architecture

For almost two thousand years, Peru has been the setting for remarkable developments in the field of monumental earth architecture. This is still evident today in the sites of La Huaca del Sol (see pp. 88–89) and Chan Chan (see pp. 92–93). Some of the skills required to build these monuments were passed on and diversified over the centuries, mostly via the oral transmission methods common to folk cultures and vernacular architecture. Building practices were gradually adapted to suit a new urban context, both in the cities built by Spanish colonizers in the 16th century and in the neighbourhoods created after the independence of Peru in 1821.
R.E.

Above and below right: Late 19th-century houses in central Trujillo.

Opposite, above: The Archbishop's Palace in Trujillo.

Opposite, below: The cloisters of the Convent of La Merced in Lima, founded in the 16th century.

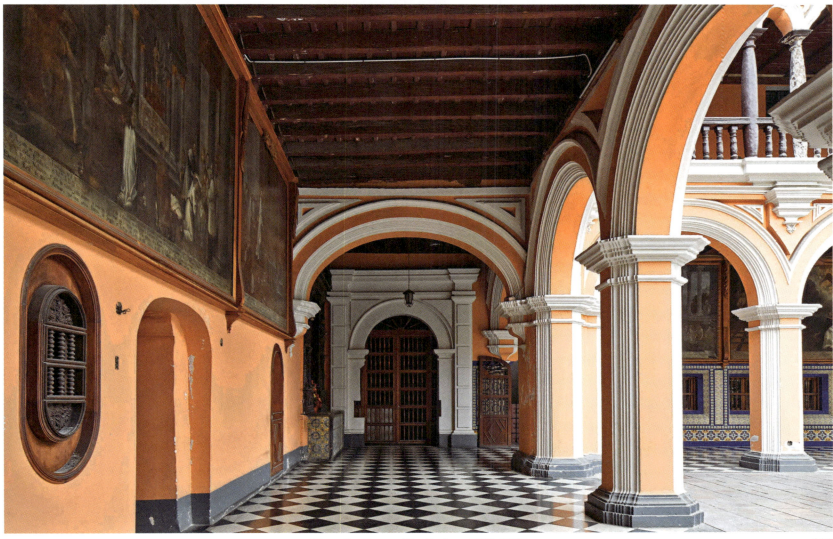

Alternative Forms of the Modern: 1789–1968

Egypt
Influence of the Arts and Crafts Movement

The first examples of modernized raw earth architecture in Africa were built in the early 20th century in Egypt, when it was still under British rule. By then, Britain itself had seen the rise of the interdisciplinary Arts and Crafts movement, which sought to reconcile tradition and modernity. This quest had, however, failed to embrace any renewal of vernacular housing in general, or earth architecture in particular, despite the long tradition of cob in England, most notably in Devon. Nevertheless, two English architects, George Somers Clarke and William John Palmer-Jones, took the principles of the Arts and Crafts movement with them to Egypt in the 1910s, and recent research by Leïla El-Wakil and Nicholas Warner has revealed that they were the first to create modernized adobe buildings there. They drew on rural vernacular traditions – particularly those of Nubia – to create sumptuous villas. Palmer-Jones also designed a dig house for use by the Metropolitan Museum of Art's Egyptian expeditions (**opposite, below**). The buildings created by Somers Clarke and Palmer-Jones anticipated the work of local architect Hassan Fathy by three decades.

J.D. & R.E.

Further reading:
El-Wakil 2018

Right and opposite, above: Plan, elevation, and views of Bayt Clarke, the home Somers Clarke built for himself at Elkab, on the river Nile.

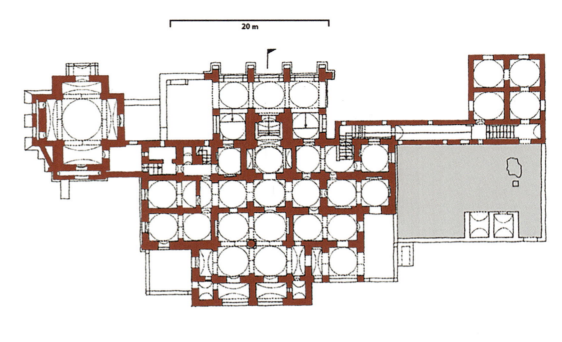

France and Germany
During and After the Two World Wars

The two world wars (1914–18 and 1939–45) had enormous consequences on both military and civilian life in Europe. The earlier conflict was marked by the massive use of industrially produced weapons (tanks, submarines, machine guns, poison gas, etc.) created as a result of technological innovations. However, military strategists turned to a centuries-old technique to shore up the improvised front lines: tens of millions of hessian sacks filled with earth were used to stabilize the trenches (**above right**). In France, similar sandbags also served to protect masterpieces of civil and religious architecture, including the facades and interiors of Gothic buildings such as Amiens Cathedral (**below right**). After both wars, Germany was the only country in Europe to develop a national reconstruction programme based around earth, and tens of thousands of rural and urban homes were built as a result (**opposite, above**).

J.D.

Alternative Forms of the Modern: 1789–1968

United States
Neo-Regionalism in New Mexico

In the 1910s, a privileged section of American society started to invest in the construction of vacation homes with raw earth, particularly in New Mexico. Two historic settlements built with adobe provided a fulcrum for these ventures: the Indian pueblo of Taos and the city of Santa Fe, founded in 1607 by Spanish colonists. These highpoints of regional culture also attracted numerous writers, artists, and intellectuals, mostly drawn from New York and Boston, and many of them set up home in the area. Prominent among these newcomers were two exceptional women: the art patron Mabel Dodge Luhan, who moved to Taos, and the artist Georgia O'Keeffe, who put down roots in Abiquiú. They both built residences in adobe that acted as beacons in the new community, leading to an 'adobe revival' style that was quickly embraced for other houses, as well as cultural buildings (museums and art galleries), hotels, and shops.

J.D. & R.E.

Above and below right, and opposite below: A selection of buildings in the pueblo style in New Mexico.

Centre right: Old Martina's Restaurant, Taos.

Opposite, above: The Mabel Dodge Luhan House, Taos.

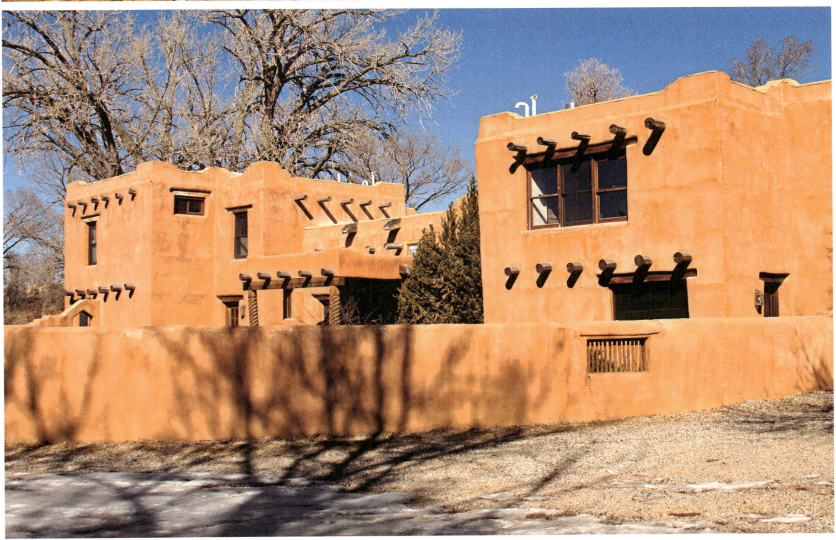

Alternative Forms of the Modern: 1789–1968

United States
Designs by Frank Lloyd Wright and Rudolph Schindler

In the first half of the 20th century, two great pioneers of modern architecture both drew up plans for raw earth houses in the United States; two of these projects were commissioned by wealthy clients and a third was intended for workers, but unfortunately none of them came to fruition. Rudolph Schindler, recently arrived from Austria, spent some time in New Mexico, where in 1918 he designed a grand adobe villa for a site in Taos (**right, above and below**). In his turn, Frank Lloyd Wright planned a garden city called the Cooperative Homesteads (**opposite, above and centre**) in 1942 for a cooperative of car workers from Detroit whose militant idealism inspired him. The project's 76 houses of rammed earth were designed to be built by the workers themselves. An earthen embankment would be partially wrapped around each home, ensuring optimal insulation in a region where winters are extremely cold. Although a prototype house was built, the pilot scheme was soon abandoned as the workers were called up to join the war effort. Also in 1942, Wright designed the curving forms of the Pottery House (**opposite, below**) – ideally suited to adobe – for a rich client from Texas.

J.D.

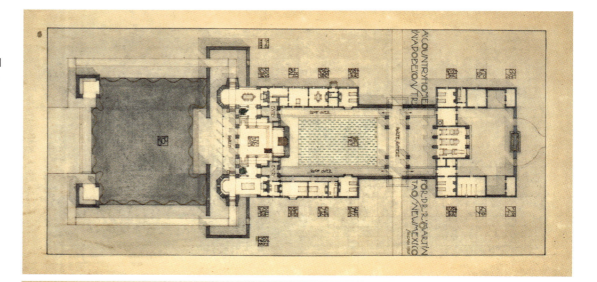

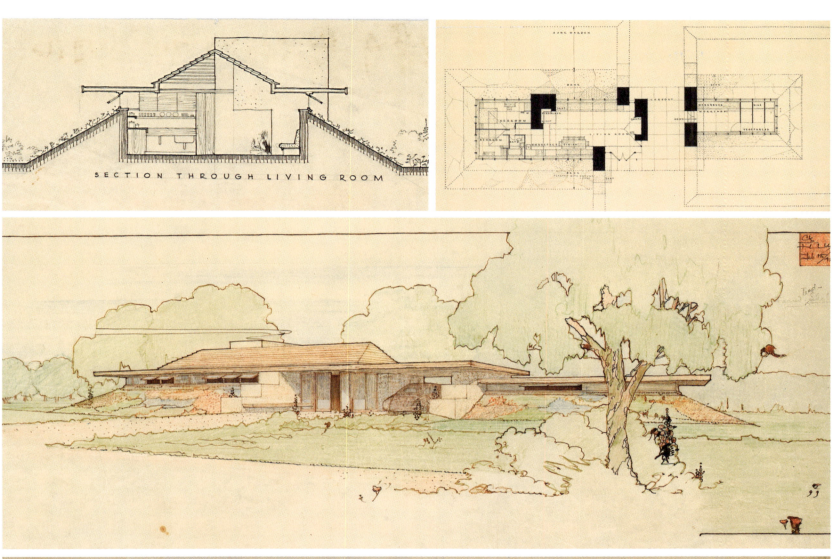
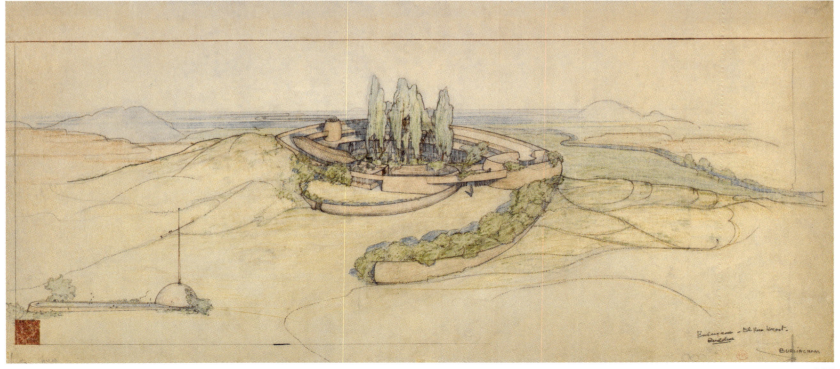

Alternative Forms of the Modern: 1789–1968

327

Africa
Colonial Innovations

In the first half of the 20th century, large expanses of Africa were still under the rule of European colonizers. Nevertheless, some architectural innovations did emerge, despite a context in which imported Western models were dominant. In 1942, a shortage of industrialized materials in Algeria led Franco-Belgian architect Michel Luyckx, a disciple of Auguste Perret, to build the world's first large-scale raw earth hospital in Adrar, in the Sahara Desert. The levels of hygiene and functionality required for such a facility made this building's design particularly groundbreaking (**above right**). The same combination of limited means, geographical isolation, and a desire to experiment gave rise to other architectural projects that sought to adapt earth to suit the demands of modernity. A new neighbourhood was built in Timimoun, Algeria, along with the Oasis Rouge (**opposite, below**), the first luxury hotel aimed at tourists crossing the desert. Here, the warm, reddish walls are enhanced by decorative friezes (**opposite, above**), based around motifs inspired by Berber jewelry; the reliefs were carved out of the earth while it was still moist. In Ghana, French and Canadian missionaries demonstrated similar aspirations towards modernity in Navrongo Catholic Cathedral (**centre right**), built in the 1920s.

J.D.

Below: A French colonial building in Mali, built in the early 20th century to echo the traditional local style.

Alternative Forms of the Modern: 1789–1968

France
Architectural Kitsch in Colonial Exhibitions

In parallel with the advances made in earth architecture in Africa in the early 20th century, spectacular colonial exhibitions in Europe attracted millions of curious visitors in the 1920s and 1930s. These events allowed the colonizing nations to display the alleged benefits of colonization in enormous temporary pavilions, replete with exotic references to the architecture of the regions under their rule. This array of fake monuments used plaster or even concrete to reproduce the earthen mosques of Mali or the kasbahs of Morocco, thereby reducing them to tools of political propaganda.

J.D.

Above right: The Equatorial East Africa and Madagascar Pavilion at the International Exhibition of Modern Decorative and Industrial Arts, Paris, 1925.

Below right: 'Mosque' built for the French West African exhibit, Colonial Exhibition, Paris, 1931.

Opposite: Views of the French West African pavilion, Colonial Exhibition, Paris, 1931.

France
Designs by Le Corbusier

In 1942, Le Corbusier published his most unusual book: *Les constructions 'Murondins'*. In it, he explained the underlying principles of construction with adobe and *pisé* (rammed earth) and suggested that apartment blocks, schools, and other community facilities should be built for refugees and people wounded in the ongoing Second World War, using materials found *in situ*. In 1946, he came up with a grand scheme to use earth as a building material for a residential complex for pilgrims to Sainte-Baume in the south of France, an unexpected passion project. The great prophet of reinforced concrete now proclaimed that '*pisé* provides a basic architecture of precision and grandeur, all on a human scale. It makes it possible to achieve the greatest and most noble lines, free of emphasis but charged with grandeur. Life inside this *pisé* can attain a complete dignity and restore the sense of fundamental human and natural resources to the men of the machinist civilization.' He planned to use *pisé* to build 'a haven of meditation...in the heart of the splendid landscape of Sainte-Baume', near Marseille, a place where the natural magic of Provence could be fully appreciated. Inspired by Le Corbusier's 'new spirit' (*Esprit Nouveau*), this complex comprised a hundred two-storey units and was conceived 'in total deference to the landscape and in a passionately desired harmony. It has been designed with the humblest technology in existence: that of *pisé*.' The project (**right and opposite**) was vilified, however, for potentially spoiling the landscape and it was eventually abandoned. Le Corbusier would declare himself 'satisfied for having attempted an enterprise destined to profoundly touch the bottom of the human heart, in this period in which everyone is working only for utilitarian and pecuniary ends'.

J.D.

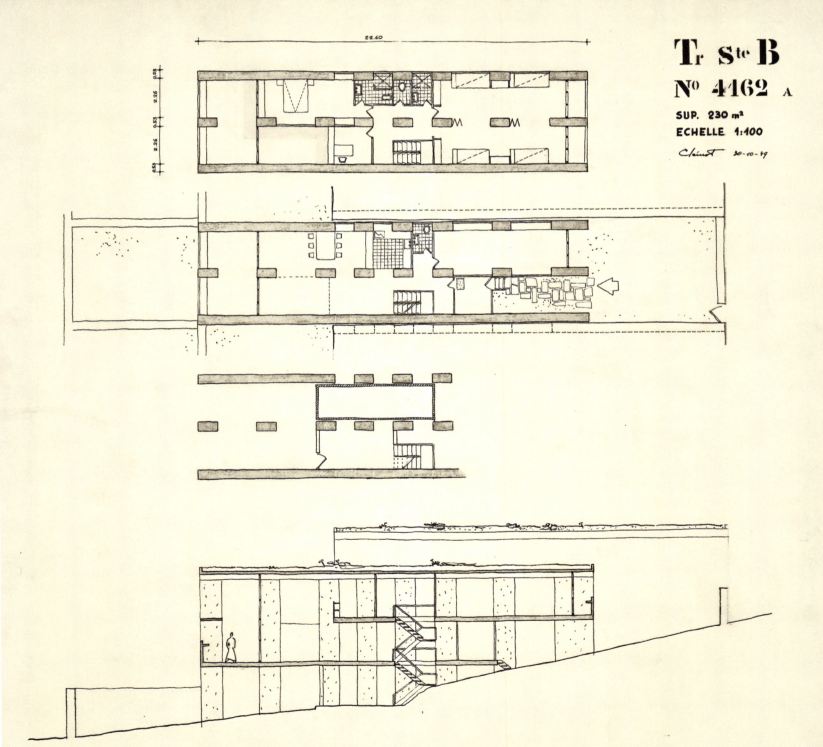

Hassan Fathy: Second Great Pioneer of Modern Earth Architecture

Jean Dethier

From the 1790s onwards, the French master builder François Cointeraux pioneered the modernization of the art of building with raw earth. A hundred and fifty years later, between 1940 and 1970, the Egyptian Hassan Fathy made his own significant contribution to this cultural, social, and technological renaissance. Despite their similarities, the two men came from very different backgrounds. While Cointeraux was an autodidact from rural, working-class stock, Fathy came from a family of rich landowners and acquired a cosmopolitan (and musical) education typical of the Arab middle classes. He went on to study architecture at Cairo Polytechnic School, which offered training modelled on contemporary European practice. By the time he left, he was immersed in the ideas of the modernist architecture movement that held sway in the West. Nevertheless, the careers of both Cointeraux and Fathy were distinguished by their fervent support of a very specific form of modernization: building with raw earth.

Both were convinced that the way forward involved passing on their knowledge to other building professionals. Cointeraux established rural schools that trained builders in *nouveau pisé*, while Fathy founded a dedicated technological institute. Furthermore, they both spread their ideas through their writings. Fathy published two books that are now recognized as classics. The first, *Building with the People, the Story of a Village in Egypt: Gourna* was published in French in 1970. This literary account told of Fathy's struggles to convince his patrons and clients of the validity of his decision to design and build this new settlement with raw earth. Fathy's second book, *Natural Energy and Vernacular Architecture* (1986), was a more academic work. It was a well-considered tribute to the folk architecture of Egypt and the wider Arab world as an efficient model of ecological construction and optimal climate protection for its inhabitants. Fathy, like Cointeraux before him, admired the intelligence and harmony of the traditional rural housing that inspired his attempt to rationalize these ancient building techniques. The final years of both men's long lives were marked by honours bestowed on them for their exceptional creativity. In 1817, at the age of 77, Cointeraux received the endorsement of Jean-Baptiste Rondelet in his *Theoretical and Practical Treatise on the Art of Building* (1802–17) for the invention of *nouveau pisé*. In his turn, Fathy, at the age of 80, won the prestigious Aga Khan Award for Architecture, which rewards contemporary work that promotes the cultural identity of the Muslim world. In his acceptance speech, Fathy focused on a question that particularly preoccupied him: 'How can we move from the current concept of the architect-builder to the self-sufficient practice of the self-builder? A single man cannot build a house but ten men can easily join forces to build ten, or even a hundred. We must adapt building techniques to fit the constraints and demands of the economics of the poor.' Cointeraux and Fathy both favoured self-building and considered raw earth – *pisé* for the former and adobe bricks for the latter – the optimal material to give builders the self-sufficiency they need and deserve. Both men wanted to find practical solutions that would guarantee accessible rural housing for all. The keen activism of Cointeraux (born in 1740 in Lyon) was born from the upheavals of the Enlightenment and the French Revolution, while that of Fathy (born in 1900 in Alexandria) developed within the context of two other major historical shifts.

In 1922, Egypt ceased to be a British protectorate and became a nominally independent kingdom, though the British maintained a strong military presence. This underlying dependency led to the foundation, in 1928, of the Muslim Brotherhood, whose declared aim was 'nonviolent struggle against Western control and blind imitation of the European model' in the Islamic countries. Fathy was in his twenties when these cultural forces began to assert themselves and he himself adopted a militant standpoint that would encounter vehement opposition and even aggression from his detractors. Nevertheless, Fathy had a rare ability to bring together two apparently irreconcilable positions. In the 1940s, his community projects broke new ground at the same time that they inspired a form of forward-looking social and cultural transformation from the historical and folk traditions of his country. His doctrine chimed with the declarations made at the 20th century's most important gathering of the political leaders of the so-called Third World: the Bandung Conference. This first summit meeting of the countries often dubbed 'developing' by the West took place in Indonesia in 1955, and it involved twenty-nine countries from Asia and Africa, including Egypt. These young nations were striving to affirm their identity in the face of two great geopolitical

forces – capitalism and communism – from which they wanted to separate themselves. These dissidents sought a 'third way' as an alternative to these two dominant models, hence the name 'Third World'. The participants of the summit took their lead from India, drawing on the spirituality and strategy of Gandhi, who had undermined the British Empire and led his country to independence in 1947, before his assassination the following year. One of Gandhi's key tenets was collective solidarity: 'To fight against the bases of the colonial or neocolonial economy and its perverse effects, we must boycott industrial products imported from European countries and value all our own local natural resources and those of our artisans. In this way we shall be able to short-circuit the business deals of the industrial powers by favouring autonomous production in every field.'

In Egypt as elsewhere, this vision of the future involved a re-evaluation of vernacular culture and a will to depend as little as possible on foreign models and European imports. Although cement and steel, the components of reinforced concrete, had often been viewed in Egypt as markers of progress, they now became symbols of heavy technological and economic dependence. This drive towards autonomy had repercussions on the practice of architecture and encouraged the use of building materials that were available or produced locally. Fathy therefore began to explore the use of raw earth extracted *in situ*. His pioneering approach responded to two different, but sometimes convergent, political demands: the first one formulated in 1928 after a groundswell of protest against the established order, and a second, more recent demand for the practical application of the principles of self-sufficiency. While Fathy had begun his career as an architect in the 1930s creating reinforced concrete buildings in the style of neo-Western formalism, in the following decade he championed the rediscovery of earth as a construction material, making it the heart of his philosophy.

Having freed himself of the shackles of Western ideology early on, Fathy personified the intellectual who achieved cultural and technical nonalignment and was, moreover, the first to apply it to architectural strategy and practice. He drew inspiration from the age-old vernacular heritage of the master builders in Nubia in southern Egypt, saying admiringly that 'the peasants never speak of art or architecture; they simply create it simply and efficiently, with remarkable talent.' Fathy adopted their ancestral techniques for construction with adobe, which was still being used to build walls, domes, and vaults, including the famed 'Nubian vault', which he admired. He updated these sophisticated methods to design houses, mosques, theatres, schools, markets, and community buildings. Communal facilities of this kind were planned for two new villages that Fathy planned down to the last detail: New Gourna, near Luxor, in Nubia, and New Baris, in northwest Egypt.

These two projects were landmark in concept but both fell victim to circumstances for which neither Fathy nor his decision to build with earth could be blamed. New Gourna suffered the consequences of the Egyptian government's forced resettlement of the inhabitants of the original village of Gourna, a great distance away. The displaced population chose to boycott what they saw as a repressive concentration camp and even tried to destroy it by flooding. New Baris, which had been making promising progress, was undermined in 1967 by the Six-Day War, which prompted the eventual abandonment of the site. Although these two failures have sometimes been used to discredit both Fathy's work and his use of adobe, the importance of his cultural and strategic insights can be better appreciated in retrospect, along with the worldwide impact of his proselytism on behalf of raw earth. The French newspaper *Le Monde* described Fathy after his death in 1980 as 'modernity drawn from the wellsprings of tradition', and said 'By rejecting the Western canons that he considered unsuitable for developing countries, the Egyptian architect built a sophisticated body of work inspired by vernacular models.'

Further reading:
Richards et al. 1985; Steele 1997; Hamid 2010; El-Wakil 2018; Damluji & Bertini 2018

Above: Hassan Fathy (left) with his American followers, *ca.* 1980, on the site of the mosque that he built in Abiquiú, New Mexico (see pp. 308 and 342–345).

Hassan Fathy
Pioneering Projects, 1947 Onwards

The work of Egyptian architect Hassan Fathy is multifaceted. His training in Cairo followed the prevailing European precepts and he became an adept of formalism in the International Style, as propagated by the Bauhaus. This influence is evident in the villa of Umm Kalthum, built by Fathy from reinforced concrete in 1939 (**opposite, above left**). Over the course of the 1940s, however, he abandoned industrialized materials and promoted the modernization of his country's earth architecture traditions.

Below, opposite centre, and opposite below: Adobe public buildings in the village of New Baris, whose construction began in 1963 in the Kharga Oasis. This pilot project was abandoned in 1967, after the Six-Day War, but the first elements of what should have been Fathy's rural masterpiece still stand in the silence of the desert, resisting the passage of time. **Opposite, above right:** Adobe primary school in the village of New Gourna (*ca.* 1948).

J.D.

Right: The market and other public buildings in New Baris, built in 1965.

Opposite, above: Hassan Fathy's plans for the village of New Gourna in the south (left) and New Baris, in Kharga Oasis, north of Egypt (right).

Opposite, below: The construction technique used to build the so-called Nubian vaults can be clearly seen in the market of New Baris. Adobe bricks are laid at an oblique angle, using a traditional technique that Fathy revived and updated.

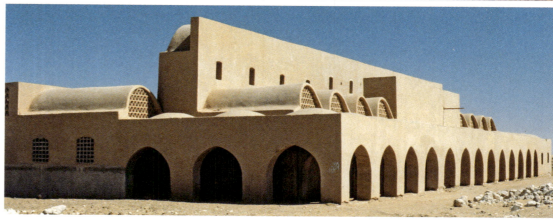

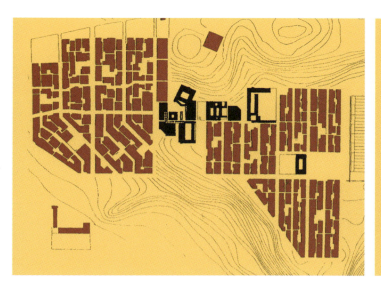
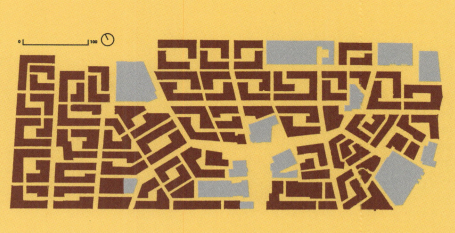

Alternative Forms of the Modern: 1789–1968

Hassan Fathy
His Influence in Egypt and Elsewhere

The enduring influence of Hassan Fathy has reached many parts of the world. His most prominent followers in Egypt were Abel Famy (**above right**) and Ramses Wissa Wassef. Wissa Wassef's legacy includes an arts centre for children, completed in 1951 (**opposite, centre**), and, like Fathy, he won the prestigious Aga Khan Award. In 1979, the brothers Hany and Abdel Rahman El-Miniawy, also from Egypt, built the experimental village of Maader, Algeria (**opposite, below**), which was at the forefront of the agrarian revolution. Still in Egypt, French architect Olivier Sednaoui built a delightful adobe villa with large domes in Luxor (**centre right**). The organization Development Workshop, founded in 1973, started off by working alongside Fathy himself. Headed by John Norton, it has gone on to develop housing projects for the rural poor in Africa and Asia. This work has been recognized twice by the UN's World Habitat Awards. Some of the other architects most strongly influenced by Hassan Fathy are discussed in more detail elsewhere in this book: Elie Mouyal (see p. 404) and Denis Coquard (p. 455) in Morocco; Francis Kéré (pp. 386 and 418–419) in Burkina Faso; Anna Heringer (pp. 420–421); CRAterre (pp. 370–383); and Thomas Granier (pp. 388–389). Granier is a master builder who founded the association La Voûte Nubienne (AVN) in 2000, whose name is derived from the traditional style of vault that Fathy revived in the 1940s.

J.D.

Below right: Centre for the French Archaeological Mission, Egypt.

Alternative Forms of the Modern: 1789–1968

United States
The Counterculture of the 1960s and 1970s

During the 1950s and 1960s, a subsection of young Americans began to question the American way of life, deeming it overly restrictive, materialistic, and individualistic. This dissatisfaction would go on to fuel protests against the Vietnam War (1955–75) and nuclear weapons. This pacifist movement drew particular inspiration from the writings of the philosopher Henry David Thoreau (1817–62). This Harvard-educated essayist, craftsman, and poet of Franco-Scottish extraction had been rediscovered and his civic, antimilitarist stance was seen as a guiding light. In his book *Walden* (1854), Thoreau advocated a simple lifestyle, rooted in nature and the ancient culture and wisdom of the Native Americans. Many young people embraced these ideas, dropped out of city life, and headed to rural areas to experiment with communal living. This trend gave rise to playful earthen buildings that explored cultural, poetic, and anarchic concepts, such as the Lama Foundation (**right**) in Taos, New Mexico, built in adobe in 1968 by Steve Baer for a community devoted to meditation and living in harmony with the land.

J.D. & R.E.

GREENPEACE

United States
Solar Adobe

The revival of earth architecture in the United States truly began in earnest in the 1970s, when the counterculture had begun to wane. Members of the moneyed class built themselves stylish, comfortable villas in the area around Santa Fe, New Mexico. Some of the most innovative examples of this trend were designed by Steve Baer and David Wright, two young pioneers of an ecological approach to architecture. They modernized the use of adobe and they also promoted the use of passive solar energy for domestic purposes. Thus was born the term 'solar adobe', which celebrated the union of the natural resources of earth and sun.

J.D.

Right and below: The Karen Terry House near Santa Fe, designed by architect David Wright.

Opposite, above: The Balcomb House (also known as Unit One) in Santa Fe, designed by William Lumpkins.

Opposite, below: A semi-subterranean house built in 1980 near Santa Fe, by architects Georgina and John MacGowan.

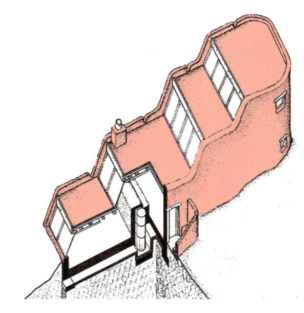
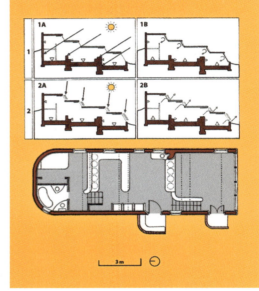

United States
La Luz, New Mexico

The rise of the counterculture helped to develop a new sense of civic and ecological responsibility in some progressive circles in the United States, an awareness that sometimes found its way into urban planning. With these precepts in mind, the architect Antoine Predock set about building the residential neighbourhood of La Luz in the suburbs of Albuquerque, the largest city in New Mexico, in 1967. His sixty harmoniously grouped homes laid down the ground rules for a new type of housing aimed at a wealthy clientele. La Luz (**right and opposite**) presented a bright and intelligent alternative to the outmoded, antisocial model of American suburbia that begun to spread across the United States in the 1940s. La Luz was a convincing example of community housing built with earth for the upper-middle classes, with a contemporary spirit free of regionalist nostalgia. In 1979, Belgian architect Jean Dethier visited this inspiring project and wanted to create something similar for a less privileged sector of the population. The result was the Domaine de la Terre (see pp. 392–395), a pilot neighbourhood of 65 public housing units built with rammed earth and adobe, that opened in Villefontaine, France, in 1985. This innovative project, with technical assistance from CRAterre, received considerable attention from the international media and played a major role in the renaissance of earth architecture in Europe.

R.E.

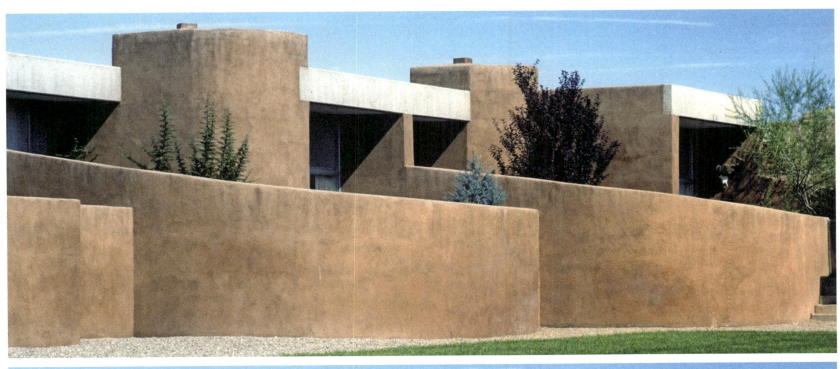

Morocco
Experiments in Public Housing in Marrakech and Ouarzazate

After Morocco gained independence in 1956, the country's cities were overwhelmed by an influx of rural migrants looking for work. In Marrakech, the newcomers constructed an entire improvised neighbourhood of courtyard houses that combined the rural tradition of adobe with the highly compact organic layout of a medina (**opposite above and below**). However, the new government subsequently declared this 'spontaneous housing' to be illegal and decided to demolish it and rehouse its occupants in an outlying suburb. This project was entrusted to the French engineer Alain Masson, who took advantage of the government's Rural Promotion programme (later renamed National Promotion), set up to provide employment for migrants from the country. In 1962, Masson used this almost unlimited supply of unskilled labour, working under the supervision of professional builders, to create the Daoudiate development, which consisted of 2,700 houses made from blocks of compressed earth (**centre right and below right**). Although this project proved overly rigid in its rationality, its completion was nevertheless considered a social and political achievement. Its success led to a similar project in Ouarzazate that provided a prototype for extremely cheap housing, built with large metal formworks (**above right**) that marked out the houses' walls and low vaulted roofs and were then packed with rammed earth.

J.D.

Alternative Forms of the Modern: 1789–1968

349

Africa
Vernacular Heritage

In July 1969, at around the time that man first walked on the moon, thousands of people converged on Algiers to take part in the first Pan-African Cultural Festival. This massive event was designed to celebrate the diversity of artistic creation throughout the continent of Africa, but the organizers 'forgot' to invite any African architects. This oversight was discovered four months before the start of the festival by architect Jean Dethier, then working for Morocco's Ministry of Housing. He persuaded the Moroccan authorities to take last-minute measures to make up for this omission. As a result, every evening, an open-air audiovisual presentation highlighting traditional and modern African earth architecture was shown in a continuous loop. To make this overview of architectural heritage of some twenty countries more lively and memorable, Dethier commissioned a series of striking watercolours (**below and opposite**) by illustrator Jean-Marie Louis. The resulting exhibition was hugely

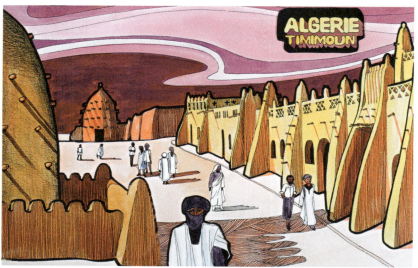
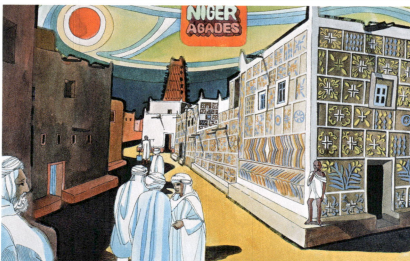
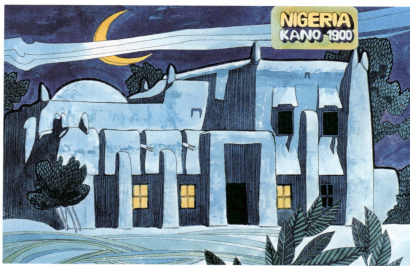

successful. It also established Morocco as the only country in Africa that both treasured its remarkable ancient villages, the *ksour*, built with rammed earth and adobe in the pre-Saharan valleys (see p. 282–283), and promoted the contemporary urban use of these natural materials to build public housing, particularly in Marrakech (see previous pages).

R.E.

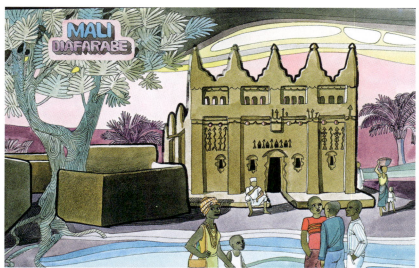

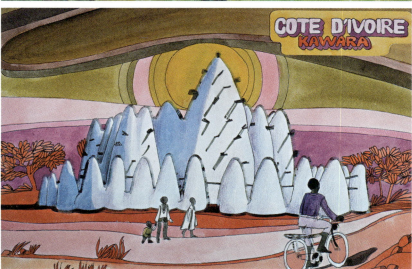
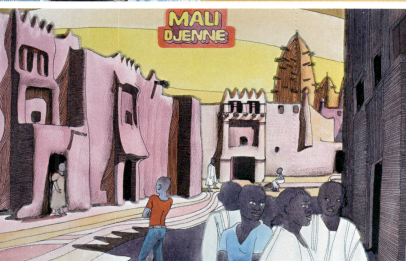

Alternative Forms of the Modern: 1789–1968

Orientalism and Modern Art
Eugène Delacroix
Frida Kahlo
Jean Dubuffet

Architecture is not the only art form to be inspired by raw earth; it has also fascinated many painters. After a stay in Morocco, Eugène Delacroix painted *The Sultan of Morocco and His Entourage* (1845; **below**), an image that kickstarted the Orientalist movement. It depicts the 18th-century Sultan Moulay Abd al-Rahman on horseback but his figure is overshadowed by the rammed earth city walls of Meknes in the background. Frida Kahlo's *Self-Portrait on the Border between Mexico and the United States of America* (1932; **opposite, above**) uses metaphor to confront the crucial ethical dilemma facing civilization: what is more important, culture or material wellbeing? Kahlo herself is seen standing in the centre. To the left, Mexico's ancient heritage is symbolized by its architectural treasures and, in the foreground, flowers with visible roots; to the right, America's industrial might is represented by its factories and, in the foreground, symbols of domestic convenience. In the late 1940s, Jean Dubuffet discovered the powerful textures and colours of the earth in the Sahara, and went on to produce many works inspired the time he spent there, including *Blond Landscape* (1952; **opposite, below**).

J.D.

Colonial Art
Jacques Majorelle in Morocco

Orientalist art, invented in Europe but inspired by the Islamic world, emerged in the 1840s as a result of Delacroix's formative period in Morocco (see p. 352). For a hundred years, the genre veered between grandiose and poignant, kitsch and sublime. In the 1920s, a new trend emerged, however, via the work of the French painter Jacques Majorelle, who also drew inspiration from direct contact with Morocco. He unveiled a little-known aspect of the country to the outside world: the beauty and harmony of the rural life of the Berbers, who for centuries had been living in the High Atlas mountains and the oases of the pre-Saharan valleys, where the landscapes are artfully shaped by the local peasants and all the buildings are made of earth. Of the many Western artists inspired by Morocco, Majorelle was the only one to pay homage to the visual splendour of these remote regions, which were not annexed by French forces until 1934. Majorelle was fascinated by the Berbers' architectural traditions and commissioned some builders from southern Morocco to build an earthen tower-observatory in the grounds of his modern Bauhaus-style villa in Marrakech. This idyllic house and garden, which provided the setting for much of Majorelle's work, would later be saved from ruin and expertly restored by Yves Saint Laurent and Pierre Bergé.

J.D.

Right: Jacques Majorelle, *Kasbah in the Atlas Mountains*, ca. 1939, gouache on paper.

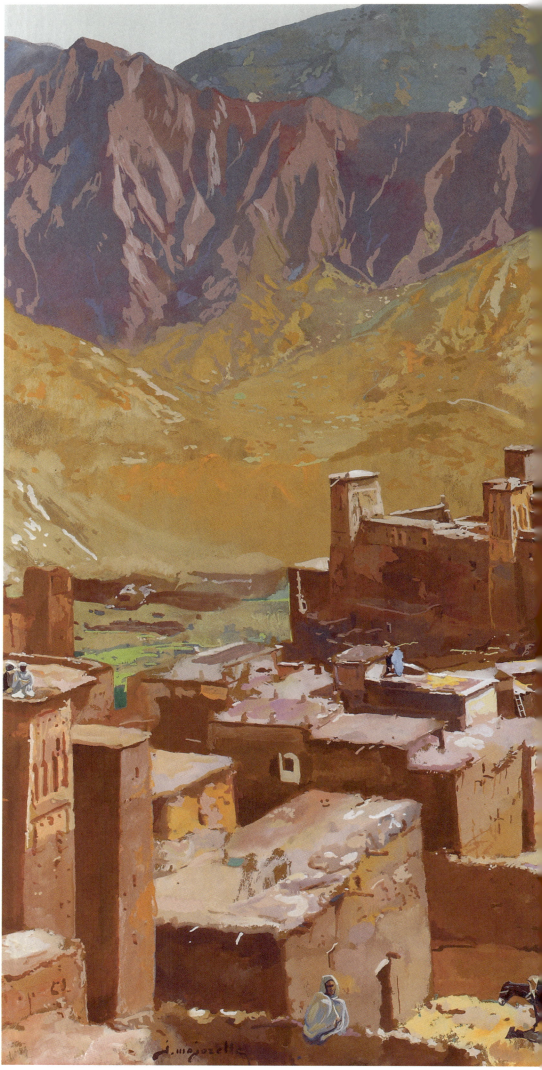

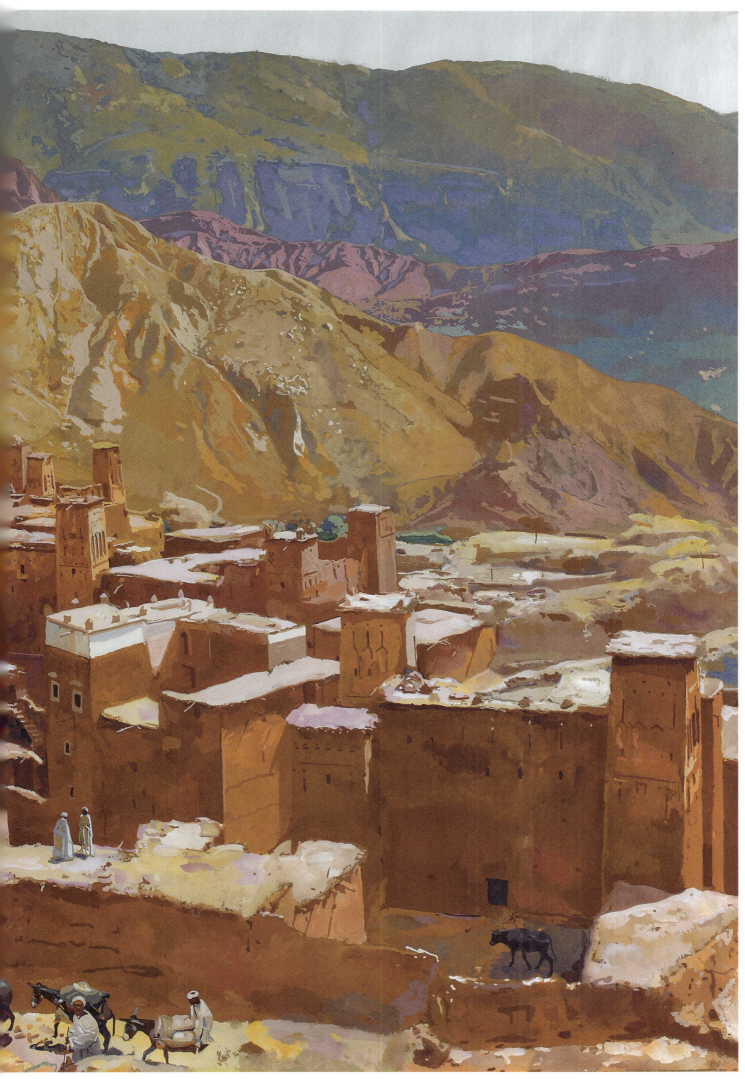

Chapter 6

Contemporary Creativity:
1970 to the Present Day

One of the rammed earth buildings designed by a team led by Marci Webster-Mannison and completed in 2005 on the campus of Charles Sturt University in Thurgoona, New South Wales, Australia (see p. 430).

Half a Century of Evolution: 1970–2020

Ariane Wilson

In the last fifty years, the creed of eco-architecture has evolved from a minority interest to a prevailing discourse, first beneath the banner of sustainable development and now that of ecological transition. The growing awareness and actions of political institutions, the building industry, the world of mainstream architecture, and earth architects themselves have advanced at different speeds but are now converging, shaking up alliances and ethical standards within the realm of earth architecture to no small degree.

Enduring concepts

The notion of sustainability has always been present, in various guises, in arguments in favour of earth architecture. Since the treatises of the 18th century, authors have stressed the potential to improve traditional practices in order to extend the lifespan of earth buildings. The same concept of increased durability can also be found in the repeated emphasis on the solidity and incombustibility of these structures. The concept of sustainability, referring to the notion of the conservation of resources, first emerged in treatises published in periods that were marked by shortages of wood, coal, and oil. According to these historic texts, building with earth means following the immutable laws according to which the Earth itself was built.

In the mid-20th century, two new philosophies of earth architecture began to look towards other aspects of sustainability. The first viewed tradition as a 'reactivation of knowledge'. Hassan Fathy, for example, considered earth architecture as a tried and tested means of building and living that continues to offer viable principles of economic and social organization in a contemporary context. The second philosophy was propagated by architects who, like Bernard Rudofsky in his 1964 exhibition at MoMA in New York, expressed an admiration for the 'architecture without architects' of vernacular cultures, as the expression of a close bond with a location that harmonized with 'the eternal validity of the principles of nature'.

The notion of sustainability has, therefore, always been implicit in earth architecture but it was first explicitly articulated by decision-makers at precisely the time when this 'eternal validity' appeared to be under threat. The Club of Rome's 1972 report *The Limits to Growth* was already calling for a new world order: it had become clear that the Western model of unfettered industrial growth could not be emulated or embraced by the so-called developing countries. In view of this fact, architects were encouraged to shoulder a moral responsibility for the conservation of nature through their building practices. The architectural profession was not, however, heavily involved in this raising of awareness. Soft architecture, solar architecture, bioclimatic architecture: all of these initiatives remained marginal. But the small niche occupied by earth architecture was well placed to respond to new priorities.

It was not until the 1980s, in the wake of oil crises and the first international summits on ecology, that handbooks of earth architecture were published – by the founders of CRAterre in France (pp. 370–75) and by Franz Volhard and Gernot Minke in Germany (pp. 386–387) – and they still stand as key works today. These texts reiterate the arguments of their forerunners: the idea that earth architecture stands in opposition to the dehumanized architecture that emanated from the modernist movement and that it can play a role in improving living conditions for those in poverty; a wish to see it recognized as true architecture; and a desire to develop and improve traditional techniques. Some new elements also emerged in these handbooks. The advantages of earth architecture were reformulated in more explicitly ecological terms. The natural origins and nontoxicity of earth were key to the field of 'building biology' or *Baubiologie* (the science of relationships between the built environment and its inhabitants). Questions were asked about the role of earth in the age of composite materials. In addition, a renewed interest in architectural heritage and the fear of seeing its underlying body of skills disappear sparked a drive to catalogue forms of earth architecture, not only from a technical perspective but also as 'cultural resources' that are both universal and locally distinct.

This global approach, reflected by the exhibition *Des architectures de terre*, curated by Jean Dethier at the Centre Pompidou in Paris in 1981 (see pp. 390–391), also touchedon postcolonial concerns about technological and cultural independence and quality of life in the countries that were then grouped together under the name of the Third World. Earth architecture could enhance

The Etosha Pavilion at Basel Zoo, Switzerland, built from rammed earth in 1999 by Martin Rauch (see p. 482). Architect: Peter Steiner.

autonomy in the field of building and encourage growth that was sensitive to local needs rather than merely to the financial profits of powerful outside players. The introduction of social issues such as housing, employment, training, and equal opportunities into the promotion of earth architecture prefigured the ecology–economy–society triangle of 'sustainable development', a term coined in 1987 by the Brundtland Report.

The opening in 1985 of a pilot raw earth neighbourhood in Villefontaine, France (see pp. 392–393), strengthened the links between activism and institutions; national and regional bodies that were open to experimentation began to embrace ideas propounded by movements opposed to the ideology of industrialization. Working in conjunction with scientists, engineers, and builders, young architects devised an avant-garde vernacular by modernizing a range of techniques (rammed earth without added cement, CEBs, clay-straw), in order to demonstrate that raw earth, long considered anachronistic, was able to meet the energy needs and economic challenges of contemporary housing. Earth architecture thus became part of an ideological debate about development by means of 'intermediate' or 'appropriate' technology.

The promotion of raw earth construction has therefore followed an oscillating path between clinging to tradition and demanding its modernization. Even now, this to-and-fro movement can still be seen in the political aims of arguments for and against earth as a construction material and still shapes its relationship with the ongoing normalization of the concept of sustainable development.

The ten years between 1985 and 1995 were marked by a series of high-profile ecological disasters (Bhopal, Chernobyl, the *Exxon Valdez*), the creation of the IPCC (Intergovernmental Panel on Climate Change), the Brundtland Report, the first Earth Summit in Rio de Janeiro (followed by the Kyoto Protocol), the introduction of energy regulations and labelling, and a string of publications that opened a philosophical debate about ecology and humanity's effect on the world. The subject of the environment was gradually incorporated into political and social discourse until, by the eve of the 21st century, a consensus had been reached. Nevertheless, ecology was not yet at the centre of architectural discourse; only a few of the participating figures embraced activist agendas such as the integration of life into urban spaces, architecture as an environment in itself, bioclimatic building design, or a return to natural materials.

It was not until the first decade of this century that the field of architecture made sustainable development a watchword, at the same time as political, media, and financial circles were rallying around a concept of a new, greener form of capitalism. Sustainable development gave architects a shared aim and a shared vocabulary. By the 2010s, the powers-that-be were finally ready to embrace architectural alternatives proposed by young collectives, such as reusing and recycling building materials, and little by little, the use of earth as a building material.

In a disjointed form of convergence, the concerns of earth architecture, which has had ecological arguments in its favour for centuries, began to overlap with the environmental concerns of politicians first formalized in the 1980s, but it took another twenty years for it to be embraced by the field of architecture, which could ignore ecological arguments no longer. Over this period of evolution, has the radicalism of earth construction been drowned out by greenwashing? Does it retain its ideological impact, now that the cause it promotes is more widely accepted?

Opposite: The Wa Shan Guesthouse, built from rammed earth in 2013 on the Xiangshan campus of China Academy of Art, Hangzhou. Architects: Wang Shu and Lu Wenyu, co-founders of the Amateur Architecture Studio, with technical support from two French architects from CRAterre, Juliette Goudy and Marc Auzet (see pp. 432–433).

The consolidation of earth

Resistance to earth architecture persists in many countries, even in places where it has played a significant role in the past and where raw earth vernacular homes are still very much part of the landscape. A desire for the greater material comfort offered by orthodox modernity often leads to a rejection of local techniques, which are seen as tarnished by their connotations of poverty. In industrialized and service-oriented countries, however, earth architecture has managed to shake off the prejudices against it and overcome the obstacles to its use.

Its first victory was an aesthetic one. Moving beyond the formal beauty of traditional structures, the intrinsic appearance of earth has come to be admired for its own sake. Its rawness has become beautiful, desirable, honest, pure – qualities that would, paradoxically, have found favour alongside the essentialism of the modern movement. Earth architecture now rejoices in its raw material and architectural magazines publish close-ups of its sensual colours and textures.

Raw earth has come to prominence via recent interest from some of today's most celebrated architects. It echoes the trend towards 'green' design and organic wellness. Additionally, the TERRA Award (an international prize for contemporary raw earth architecture, launched in France in 2016) has demonstrated that earth can still be highly attractive while remaining sensitive to local realities. The winning buildings are clearly contemporary but they testify to a quest for dialogue with their cultural, social, and geographical context. Furthermore, the wide range of techniques and briefs on display guarantees a great variety of forms of architectural expression.

Now that the war of aesthetics and quality has been won, battle continues on the technological and production fronts. Rather than promoting it as a resource that is of interest primarily because it challenges received opinion, there is a tendency to treat earth as one material among many and to demonstrate its potential to industrialized, urban countries. It is now becoming (relatively) commonplace. Germany has drawn up national legislation allowing building with earth that puts it on par with other materials. Earth panels that can be used as dividing walls and ceilings, powdered clay, raw earth bricks, and prefabricated *pisé* modules are now manufactured industrially in small quantities.

To boost its position on the market, the field of earth architecture is now striving to strengthen the natural material of earth, speeding up and industrializing its manufacturing process, making it easier to work with, and thereby reducing production costs. Although earth's environmental benefits are now widely acknowledged, the myth that it is fragile and ephemeral still persists. Some researchers see the modernization of earth architecture primarily as a quest for ways to make it more durable. The techniques involved are very diverse, however, and the differences between them reflect political and economic circumstances.

In some places, attempts are being made to improve earth's physical performance by studying the architectural forms that are best suited to its inherent characteristics, such as buildings in Peru that have survived centuries of earthquakes. Elsewhere, however, earth is being reinforced with additives at an early stage in the production process. Some experiments are focused on stabilizing earth with materials of plant or animal origin, while others investigate the latest natural admixtures, such as nano-compounds inspired by clay polymers.

These days, however, raw earth is also often stabilized with synthetic additives such as lime or cement. Perhaps because of a lack of understanding of earth's capabilities or alternative nonpolluting additives, or perhaps because they are trying to comply with legislation designed around other materials, some architects profess a love for raw earth yet do not hesitate to add cement to it – sometimes up to 15% in the United States and Australia. Whatever the reason for it, this practice undermines one of earth's most attractive qualities – its recyclability – and it has thus come under heavy criticism: the architect Anna Heringer, for example, has campaigned for the use of pure earth under the slogan 'Let's embrace vulnerability!' (see p. 483).

The controversy over stabilization also applies to technological developments designed to speed up the construction process. While the Austrian entrepreneur Martin Rauch mass-produces prefabricated rammed earth walls without altering the material (see p. 482), other builders have experimented with techniques pioneered by the cement industry, such as granularity

control and rapid coagulation, as well as applied dispersants and super-plastics. Early attempts at poured, self-spreading 'environmental clay concrete' used cement to speed up drying, but research is currently underway to replace cement with silicate and magnesium oxide or to use a flocculation-deflocculation process. Others are experimenting with natural substances such as tannins and alginates to enhance dispersion. Poured earth without added mineral binders could eventually replace conventional concrete in some building types and thus transform perceptions of the industrial potential of earth-based construction.

The most significant scientific endorsement of earth in recent years has come from research into the physics of granular materials. A thorough understanding of the components of soil, their cohesion mechanisms and, above all, the binding role played by water (more friend than foe) has allowed common preconceptions to be overturned and has offered the potential for improving the material from the inside (see pp. 36–39). It is now known that extremely small soil particles – known as 'fines' – are more vital to cohesion than clay. This discovery has led to the use of soil from major excavations for large infrastructure projects as fines, as well as the creation of major new product lines made from reused earth.

Finally, some labs are researching ways to combine digital techniques with raw earth, such as design parametrization, in order to experiment with forms never previously created with this material, or the 3D printing of structures using extrusion, layer by layer, in order to speed up the construction process.

Maintaining a rebellious spirit

The last half-century has seen a remarkable renaissance of earth architecture, which had long been viewed with disdain. This resurgence is obviously a cause for celebration but it also entails a degree of risk, in view of some of the widespread beliefs about earth as a building material.

One of these risks is the inclusion of raw earth within commercial strategies that could damage its cultural and social benefits under an eco-friendly disguise. The world's biggest cement manufacturer, LafargeHolcim Ltd, and the British financial institution CDC have, for example, launched a joint venture selling compressed earth blocks stabilized with 5–7% cement. This supposedly 'innovative green building solution' is aimed at the market for thousands of standardized housing units in sub-Saharan Africa. Stabilization of earth with small amounts of cement may well be a lesser evil than pure cement, with its massively high levels of CO_2 emissions. However, products marketed by multinational corporations are by necessity far removed from the dominant argument in favour of earth over the last fifty years: that earth can help the inhabitants of poorer areas to free themselves from financial and cultural dependence.

A second risk stems from the introduction of raw earth to the property market: is the urge to erect commercially desirable buildings – higher, faster, and as profitably as possible – compatible with the quality of habitability that has always been lauded by advocates of raw earth? If major industrial groups respond to the interest in some types of earth architecture by investing in research programmes, will the labs involved be obliged to focus on the most profitable results? Will the powerful institutions that provide accreditation for construction materials be able to match their valuable knowledge of industrialized materials with an understanding of raw earth that takes its unique characteristics into account? Should we be wary of technological enthusiasm that pays no attention to the cultural richness of earth architecture? Is it not ironic that state-of-the-art robots are being used to build earth architecture in regions that cannot afford to pay for such luxuries themselves? As with ecology in general, will high-tech always overshadow low-tech? Is earth architecture merely being dragged along by the current trend towards sustainable development and energy transition that is being trumpeted by new deals between political authorities, the property sector, and industry, which do not always have public interests at heart?

Since the 1970s, the pioneers of the earth architecture revival have remained at the cutting edge. As advocates of raw earth, they have promoted its benefits through a carefully constructed argument that embraces science, education, politics, and land management and thus have largely defined the terms in which earth architecture is understood. Within this context, however, earth architecture has been included in a range of different

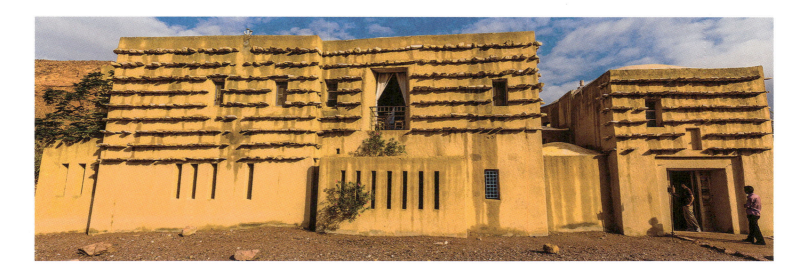

Eco-lodge in Jordan, built *ca*. 2005. The treatment of the walls is inspired by the architectural traditions of the Najran region of Saudi Arabia, where rows of flat stones are often inserted into walls (see p. 244).

strategies, each with its own cultural or political basis. This diversity makes it difficult to generalize about the directions in which earth architecture is heading, but until recently there was always a common thread: the commitment to humanism that has underpinned the rediscovery of this material over the last half-century. Now, however, this shared ethic has become more fragile. Earth architecture has reached a pivotal moment, and it may yet fall victim to its own pioneering success and lose its integrity and ecological benefits. The greed of big construction companies, the industrialization of earth concrete, and the co-opting of earth into the ambivalent politics of energy transition could lead to widespread and watered-down uses, driven by commercial interests, paying no attention to local conditions, and causing the loss of traditional community skills.

As we have seen, earth architecture predates the ecology movement and has always gone hand in hand with it. Nonetheless, it must be wary of buying into the dominant ideology and the falsehoods being peddled alongside it. Although there is a risk that the art of raw earth architecture may sell its soul to the system it was fighting against, a multiplicity of uses and approaches clearly can coexist, providing they can be distinguished from one another. Very often, building with earth is advertised as a straightforward patent remedy. But earth and its implementation come in many forms. Choices of composition, building technique, and construction location always have political and economic implications, and may even alienate earth architecture from the Earth itself. It is therefore important not to confuse prestige and modest success, earth as a trend and earth as a movement, earth with strings attached and earth as altruism – in each case, the former must never be allowed to obscure the latter. Purists can remain faithful to self-building without industrial intervention whenever earth is available locally, even at the same time as robots are 3D printing raw earth houses in the name of energy efficiency; advocates of downsizing can embrace earth as the ideal of 'creative frugality' at the same time as other builders endorse sustainable development as a vector of economic growth.

Raw earth will continue to act as a counterweight, serving as an architectural expression of unique local features, a source of beauty in buildings, and a means of constructing eco-friendly, low-cost, and high-quality environments. Earth architecture must remain subversive, disobedient, and idealistic. It can only achieve this by being realistic, pragmatic, and empathetic towards society and the state of the world.

```
Further reading:
CRAterre 1979; Dethier 1983; Volhard 1983; Anger & Fontaine
2009; Wilson 2014; Fissabre & Wilson 2016; Joffroy,
Guillaud, & Sadozai 2018
```

Overview of Contemporary Architectural Practices

Hubert Guillaud

Since 1979, the renaissance of earth architecture has been driven by extremely positive results from scientific research undertaken in universities and architectural and engineering schools. PhD theses have been published on a broad range of subjects, providing many important new insights. There has also been an upsurge in graduate and postgraduate courses, as well as an increase in professional training workshops, leading to the emergence of new earth architecture professionals. Specialist networks have sprung up all over the world: some on an international scale, such as the UNESCO Chair on Earthen Architecture, spearheaded by CRAterre, and ICOMOS-ISCEAH, the International Scientific Committee on the Conservation of Earthen Architectural Heritage; others on a national level (Dachverband Lehm in Germany, ArquiTierra in Spain, AsTerre in France, Ebuki in the United Kingdom and Ireland, the Earth Building Association of Australia), or on a regional level, with organizations such as the Latin American network Proterra. All of these initiatives have led to a rise in earth architecture projects both locally and globally. The European Pirate project has also been a great advance as it has integrated training in earth building into a broader educational strategy (the ECVET vocational training scheme). Earth architecture is gradually becoming normalized, although this is less to do with the material itself than with the building practices utilized and whether they meet the needs of the professionals involved (property developers, architects, builders, insurance companies, banks, etc.). Initial resistance often needs to be overcome before work on new projects can be started.

The revival of earth architecture has also been boosted by the rise in organizations and individuals sharing their knowledge online. A PC or smartphone can now be a gateway to a wealth of information, from research, university or professional training, self-builds and do-it-yourself home kits to data on the most advanced methods of raw earth construction. This endless source of inspiration is supplemented by a multitude of 3D images and photographs of recent projects.

Dominant trends in the earth architecture revival

The dominant trends in contemporary raw earth architecture have emerged from a context of technological rediscoveries and innovations. Adobe and raw earth bricks are still used in many countries and are often chosen for self-build projects. A new market was created in Germany in 1984 by Claytec, a company founded by Peter Breidenbach, which mass-produces raw earth bricks and poured-clay panels with a reed mat backing (for ceilings and interior insulation), and also sells clay plaster by the sack. Similar businesses have emerged elsewhere in Europe, marketing clay products mainly in the form of surface finishes or natural paints for decoration: for example, Akterre (founded in France by Andreas Krewet), Tierrafino, Alliance 4, and Argilus. In Germany in 1980, Franz Volhard began to sell 'light clay' or *Leichtlehm*, which includes straw fibres to create a modern variation of wattle and daub; it subsequently became popular in Europe thanks to its insulation and humidity regulation properties. Across the Atlantic, sod dwellings have returned to favour in Uruguay and Argentina, countries with a long history of using this technique. Cob is still used in its traditional forms, but it has also become the subject of experiments that aim to introduce prefabricated elements and mechanized processes. Meanwhile,

rammed earth has found great favour with architects, particularly in the United States, Australia, Latin America, and Europe (France, Germany, Switzerland, Austria). This popularity may be partly due to its visual and conceptual similarities with concrete, the apparent weight of the material perhaps creating a reassuring feel.

Recent innovations include the prefabrication of rammed earth blocks, either on site or nearby, which can then be assembled like a gigantic Lego set. The Austrian entrepreneur Martin Rauch has become a leader in this field. Compressed earth bricks (CEB), stabilized with cement, are most commonly found in Africa, India, and Latin America, where they have given an ancient material a sheen of modernity. Progress has also been made in 3D printing with clay stabilized and poured *in situ*, although for the moment this is still confined to basic experimental structures. However, advances in rheology – the study of the flow of matter – will surely open up new horizons in the future, with the use of natural polymers as additives to raw earth being one potential line of research. Finally, earthen surfaces are becoming increasingly popular in interiors due to their natural colours and attractive textures, as well as their lack of chemical pollutants.

Raw earth buildings have now become almost as varied as those built using other materials and techniques. It is only on a structural level that they face greater limitations, when there is a need to use raw earth to support weight – although even this drawback can be overcome by packing earth around a load-bearing framework made of wood, steel, or other materials. Nevertheless, earth is now used to construct not only individual houses and small-scale communal homes but also a wide range of buildings serving many different functions. This is a very recent phenomenon that was unthinkable as recently as the late 20th century. Earth architecture can be found in the fields of education (kindergartens, schools, training centres, university campuses), culture (museums, concert halls, libraries), health (medical practices and even hospitals), leisure (community centres, restaurants), tourism (hotels, guest houses), religion (churches, mosques), administration (individual or shared office spaces), sport (swimming pools), shopping (department stores, covered markets), science (research centres), industry (warehouses, factories), military construction (defensive fortifications), and civil engineering (dams and reservoirs). All of these recent creations are extensively illustrated in this chapter.

New urban architecture with earth

In the early 21st century, this vibrant creativity can be found all over the world, in a wide range of climates and cultures, even in countries without a longstanding tradition of earth architecture, such as Australia and Austria. Although earth architecture is often wrongly perceived as a rural phenomenon, this blinkered view has no historical basis, as demonstrated by, among

Previous pages, left and right: Professional training centre built with cob in the village of Rudrapur, Bangladesh (see p. 429). Architect: Anna Heringer.

Opposite: Project in West Africa supported by the association La Voûte Nubienne (see pp. 388–389).

others, the ancient civilization of Mesopotamia. In the centuries since, many towns and neighbourhoods have been built with raw earth: in Yemen, Morocco, Mali, Peru, Chile, Brazil, Ecuador, the United States, China, Spain (Granada), France (Lyon), and Germany (Weilburg). In many cases, they are now listed by UNESCO as World Heritage sites. Some of the most striking examples of contemporary earth architecture are located in Berlin, Marrakech, Basel, Orléans, and Hangzhou (all of which are featured in chapters 3 to 6). Raw earth has sometimes even been used to construct entire urban communities from scratch. Examples include the district of Villefontaine in the French town of L'Isle-d'Abeau, between Lyon and Grenoble, which in 1985 became home to the Domaine de la Terre, Europe's first public housing complex to be built with raw earth (see pp. 392–395).

If a new circular economy is to be established (see pp. 478–479), many more architectural schemes of this type will be needed, in both urban and suburban settings. Furthermore, studies undertaken in France since 2016 have provided scientific proof of the viability of using raw earth extracted during large urban infrastructure projects (such as underground rail lines) for subsequent building schemes, rather than shipping earth at great expense to distant locations. In 2017, it was decided to put this idea into practice: one notable project is the construction of an entire neighbourhood with housing and community facilities in Ivry-sur-Seine, on the outskirts of Paris, planned for completion in the 2020s (see pp. 472–473).

Ambitions and potential for growth

Worldwide, earth architecture since the year 2000 has demonstrated enormous creativity and improvements in quality. It is widely admired not only for its visual and tactile appeal but also for its low carbon footprint and thermal properties.

Meanwhile, since the 1980s, more than a hundred earth architecture sites in some sixty countries have been added to UNESCO's prestigious World Heritage List. This has given a considerable cultural boost to the ancient architectural treasures of African countries, which had often previously been neglected. Furthermore, the boom in earth architecture in other parts of the world is also greatly indebted to this recognition. It is clear that the future of earth architecture is ultimately dependent on a dynamic relationship between tradition and modernity, between conservation of heritage and contemporary creativity.

Between these two poles, the cultural and technical expressiveness of new raw earth architecture is constantly evolving and growing increasingly diverse. The early 21st century has also seen a rise in the involvement of influential winners of major architectural honours such as the Pritzker Prize, the Aga Khan Award, and the TERRA Award. Architects of the stature of Renzo Piano, Wang Shu, Herzog & de Meuron, and the Snøhetta agency have all helped to revitalize the image of earth architecture, in the face of continuing resistance and pressure from industrial lobbies.

```
Further reading:
Bardou & Arzoumanian 1978; CRAterre 1979; Dethier 1983;
Houben & Guillaud 1994; Gauzin-Müller 2016
```

Portraits of Three Pioneers

Hubert Guillaud

Francis Kéré

Francis Kéré, born in Burkina Faso in 1965, won well-deserved international acclaim with his very first completed project, in 2001: a primary school (see p. 418) in his birthplace, the village of Gando, which he left at the age of seven, with the support of his community, in order to receive schooling elsewhere. After completing his secondary education and training as a carpenter in the capital, Ouagadougou, he headed to Germany, to study at the Technical University of Berlin. He graduated as a qualified architect in 2004. His first project, undertaken while he was still a student in Europe, was clearly a gesture of recognition of the inhabitants of his native village. It was an act of solidarity, of militancy, the paying of an outstanding debt to the children of Gando, who would otherwise be deprived of access to education. The programme for his school reflected a need to economize – to do more with less – and a willingness to adapt to the physical, climatic, and social constraints of the setting. The importance of these precepts, which constituted a true architectural manifesto, was endorsed by the school's teaching staff. The building's architecture is 'radically simple' – which was also the title of an exhibition on Kéré's work curated by the architectural historian and theorist Andres Lepik in 2016, at the Pinakothek der Moderne in Munich.

The Gando school uses innovative architectural language to symbolize and give form to the ancient wisdom underlying a local folk proverb: 'If you want your earth house to withstand time and weather, give it good boots and a big hat'. Its walls are made from compressed earth blocks (CEB) and stand on a stone foundation reinforced by a concrete floor, while the roof, with its substantial overhang, rests on a light structure made of low-cost steel that is raised well above the walls in order to guarantee the comfortable temperature required by teachers and pupils alike. The building of the school involved the active participation of the villagers and therefore also provided training for future builders. In fact, the project as a whole represents progress towards the future and shows that architecture cannot confine itself to strictly utilitarian ends but must reflect social and humanist concerns.

In the two decades since then, Kéré has built a wide range of communal buildings in the same spirit, using earth extracted *in situ*, first in his native village and then elsewhere in Burkina Faso: primary and secondary schools, colleges, public libraries, women's centres, dispensaries, clinics, and cultural facilities. Kéré knows how to convince these communities to accept earth as a building material, even though they often initially reject it as being poor, outmoded, and even anti-modern. He is a pioneer who has paved the way for a form of ecological architecture that is resolutely contemporary and specifically African. He seeks to revive local traditions and reinterpret ancient vernacular knowledge without falling into nostalgia or clinging to the past; instead, he approaches this heritage with a sense of freedom and creative panache. Kéré has emerged as a key figure in the worldwide revival of earth architecture by orienting it towards the future in cultural, social, ethical, ecological, and technological terms, during both the construction and the use phases.

```
Further reading:
Lepik & Beygo 2016
```

Wang Shu and Lu Wenyu

The work of the architect Wang Shu, professor and director of the architecture department of the prestigious China Academy of Art (CAA) in Hangzhou, was recognized in 2007 by the Global Award for Sustainable Architecture and in 2012 by the renowned Pritzker Prize. The career of Wang Shu (born 1963) places him in the vanguard of a 'critical revitalization' of the architectural cultures of China, a land where the art of building with raw earth dates back thousands of years but is now under threat from unchecked urbanization and the dominance of industrial building practices, even in rural regions. Along with his wife Lu Wenyu (born 1966), Wang Shu defied this trend by founding the Amateur Architecture Studio in Hangzhou in 1997. Here, these activist architects display intense creativity and showcase the unique features of Chinese regional cultures by boldly reimagining them. They campaign in favour of the revival of craft techniques and the recycling of materials salvaged from the widescale demolition of older buildings.

With his awareness of the challenges associated with the ecological revolution, it was inevitable that Wang Shu would develop an interest in the work of CRAterre. His fruitful encounters with its members in Grenoble from 2009 onwards have strengthened his interest in modernized forms of rammed earth architecture. Subsequently, two young architects trained by CRAterre[1] were sent to Hangzhou to set up a specialized research laboratory to train technicians, artisans, and instructors in contemporary uses of raw earth. This Franco-Chinese cooperative project resulted in the construction, on the CAA campus, of the Wa Shan Guesthouse, designed to house teachers and researchers (see pp. 432–433). This masterful building, opened in 2013, displays an intelligent and harmonious combination of high parallel walls of rammed red earth, concrete supporting structures, and a huge wave-shaped roof of pinewood. The building's beauty and calculated complexity have inspired a remarkable documentary.[2] Wang Shu and Lu Wenyu are pioneers of a new humanist ecological architecture steeped in Chinese tradition but resolutely focused on the future. The couple also create art installations – most notably at the 2006 Venice Architecture Biennale – which add further support to their radical arguments against global cultural uniformity, of which early 21st-century China has become one of the major victims.

```
Further reading:
Wang Shu 2013; Holm, Kjeldsen, & Kallehauge 2017
```

1 Marc Auzet and Juliette Goudy.
2 *Wa Shan, la maison d'hôtes* (26 mins.), directed by Juliette Garcias and produced in France in 2015 by Les Films d'Ici for Arte.

CRAterre:
Pioneers of Modern Earth Architecture since 1979

Jean Dethier

Over the last two centuries, the modernization of the art of earth architecture has had three guiding lights: French master builder and entrepreneur François Cointeraux, from the 1790s onwards (see pp. 308–309); Egyptian architect Hassan Fathy, from 1947 onwards (see pp. 334–341); and CRAterre, the International Centre for Earth Construction, founded in France in 1979. The French architects Patrice Doat and Hubert Guillaud and the Belgian engineer Hugo Houben form the nucleus of the CRAterre group,[1] which brings together complementary social, scientific, cultural, and educational aspirations. The three founders have now been joined by some sixty others of many nationalities, trained in different fields but united by their shared convictions and desire for action. This nonprofit association has become increasingly dynamic since the seventies and eighties, calling into question our current social models and confronting new environmental, economic, and technological challenges. The multidisciplinary vocations of its members give CRAterre the coherence and strength needed to push forward a large-scale project of unprecedented ambition: that of creating an international strategy to regenerate, modernize, and promote the art of building with raw earth.

In 2009, thirty years after the group's founding, Renzo Piano, one of today's most eminent architects, spoke in praise of the 'seriousness and expertise' of CRAterre: 'Patrice Doat and his team have painstakingly gone back to sources and fundamentals without being lured away by the desires and temptations, the vanities and traps that architecture offers on a daily basis. This long journey has turned out to be a giant leap forward. Today, in these times…of sustainable development, they are showing the way. They are the standard bearers. Through the extraordinary lessons of observing vernacular architecture, they have managed to extract the essentials and understand them via methodical, scientific analysis, as well as to convey a message of modesty in the face of material reality. It is an example of a life's work that commands respect and has now justifiably earned universal recognition. Building with earth: the most accessible and widespread raw material of all, the most varied and colourful, the richest and most beautiful. Through the Grenoble School of Architecture, the Grands Ateliers, and CRAterre, a school of living architecture has established a place in the sun that is not only well deserved but also vital to contemporary architectural thinking.'[2]

How has this small group, initially outside the mainstream and lacking in financial means, managed to earn such high praise? Here follows an attempt to explicate CRAterre's 'seven pillars of wisdom' underlying the strategy that has won such recognition.

1. Creating an innovative, dynamic, and attractive way of teaching

For thousands of years, the highly specific skills of raw earth construction have been passed on empirically by generations of self-builders and artisans. Although the professions of architect and engineer first emerged in Europe during the Renaissance, no formal training in the field of earth architecture had ever been aimed at them. CRAterre set out to fill this void in 1979, embarking on a crucial mission to keep this ancient knowledge alive. This battle has now been won, thanks to the wide range of initiatives that CRAterre has implemented. The fundamentals of earth architecture are now studied by all first-year students at the Grenoble School of Architecture, which has also offered, since 1984, a 'professional postgraduate qualification', now under the auspices of the UNESCO Chair on Earthen Architecture, Building Cultures and Sustainable Development. This was followed in 2000 by the introduction of a specialized master's degree, in which the uses of earth are taught alongside those of stone, wood, steel, concrete, and polymers. This approach represented a huge advance, as for the first time it placed all of these materials on the same level. This course anticipated the foundation, in 2001, of a complementary learning hub, the Grands Ateliers in Villefontaine, which is unparalleled in the breadth of

---

1   The other founding members of CRAterre were architect François Vitoux, ethnologists Nathalie Sabatier and Anne-Monique Bardagot, and geologist Michel Dayre, along with two other architects who have since chosen to pursue other interests (mainly in Peru), Alain Hays and Sylvia Matuk. In addition, CRAterre Belgium was founded in Brussels in 1985 (and dissolved in 1999); its founding members were Hugo Houben, Dirk Belmans, Titane Galer, and Jacques Evrard.
2   Extract from the foreword to the book *Bâtir en terre, du grain de sable à l'architecture* (Anger & Fontaine 2009).

Below: A student project run by CRAterre in Grenoble; it involved constructing a house within 24 hours (see pp. 380–381).

its teaching. Its interdisciplinary approach enables future architects, engineers, and artists to build life-size prototypes using a host of traditional and modern materials, including raw earth. Practical experiments allow theory and practice to be combined, giving equal weight to 'thinking' and 'doing'. This playful teaching method exposes students to the creative stimulation and the joy of working in a group setting. In this way, they gain vital practical skills and discover for themselves the concepts of space, structure, and form, which conventional courses only tackle on a theoretical level. In 2012, the Grands Ateliers also became the headquarters of CRAterre's sister organization, Amàco, which is devoted to research, training, and experimentation with raw materials, including earth, as well as biosourced and geosourced materials. Lastly, since 2002, the Grands Ateliers has hosted the Grains d'Isère, an annual week-long international festival of earth architecture. Both celebratory and creative, the Grains d'Isère gives everyone involved in this sector a unique chance to come together: researchers, teachers, students, and professionals of all kinds (including artisans and artists), as well the general public. Activities are also organized for children and teenagers to introduce them to the joys of building with earth and teach them about its future potential. Taken as a whole, all of these educational schemes form a single organic, indivisible whole with a progressive outlook that attracts participants from all over the world.

2. Ensuring long-lasting integration with established institutions

The educational objectives that are so crucial to future developments can only thrive within the right context. Because of this, since its creation in 1979, CRAterre has been based at the Grenoble School of Architecture (ENSAG), which is now part of Grenoble Alpes University. This dynamic and highly prestigious school also happens to be situated in the Auvergne-Rhône-Alpes region, which boasts the most abundant and diverse heritage of ancient, modern, and contemporary rammed earth architecture in Europe. A partnership has also been established with UNESCO, the UN institution responsible for promoting culture, science, and education, which are the three driving forces behind CRAterre. In 1998, this humble establishment managed to convince UNESCO to establish a Chair on Earthen Architecture, Building Cultures and Sustainable Development. Developed and driven by CRAterre, the Chair places Grenoble at the centre of a global network with more than 40 partners from 24 countries which, in their turn, disseminate information on a regional level. In this way, a triangular relationship has been built between the university, a UN agency, and CRAterre, a bold step that has ensured a long life for this pioneering project. Furthermore, the enduring relationship between CRAterre and UNESCO has led to fruitful collaborative projects, designed to study, conserve, restore, and evaluate more than a hundred priceless examples of earth architecture that appear on UNESCO's World Heritage List.

3. Tackling the problem of low-income housing

It is widely agreed that the two greatest challenges of the 21st century are climate change and global poverty, but the latter cannot be resolved without also tackling the worldwide problem of inadequate housing for low-income people. This affects not only the poorer countries of Africa, Asia, and Latin America, but also countries that are considered rich but nevertheless have huge numbers of disadvantaged people, many struggling to survive without a home. CRAterre has participated in several innovative public housing programmes, both in France, in the form of the Domaine de la Terre, launched in 1985 (see pp. 392–395), and, since 1982, in Africa, with some 30,000 housing units built by their own inhabitants or by cooperatives or small local firms. Since 2010, this line of work has expanded to include Haiti. These initiatives are made possible by CRAterre's basic threefold strategy of combining training, research, and practical experience. Training and research are heavily project-based, with members of CRAterre working *in situ* on pilot schemes in conjunction with their future users. These sites also serve as training grounds for local artisans.

4. Establishing a synergy between culture and science

CRAterre is an interdisciplinary team that embraces multiple cultural and scientific approaches. Any effective contribution to the future of earth architecture must be based on basic and applied research as much as on technical innovations. Accordingly, since 2000, CRAterre has carried out studies on the components and physical properties of granular materials, including raw earth. This cutting-edge research has led to specific applications with ecological benefits: poured earth concrete (PEC), mixtures of raw earth and plant fibres, prefabricated rammed earth construction elements, 3D printing, etc. In 2009, the pioneering work of CRAterre was promoted by a touring exhibition curated by the Cité des Sciences et de l'Industrie in Paris, which attracted over a million visitors.

5. Understanding vernacular skills in order to update them

As part of the drive to study and appreciate global vernacular housing traditions that first emerged in the 1960s and 1970s, CRAterre decided to encourage this interest by incorporating it into the group's broader strategies, using a three-part approach. The first phase is to acquire a detailed understanding of the cultural and technological traits of each population's domestic architecture, a process aided by the unique grasp of local building cultures that derives from CRAterre's interdisciplinary approach. Using this knowledge as a basis, the second phase involves coming up with ways to protect and restore existing masterpieces of earth architecture, allowing future generations to draw on ancient knowledge and find inspiration to fight against global housing uniformity. As a result of these studies, some sites have been added to UNESCO's World Heritage List. The third and final phase is the cultural recognition of these hidden treasures, which can lead – sometimes alongside tourism, if carefully managed – to their survival and adaptation to contemporary needs. There is no intent to move towards a romanticized, sentimentalized, or commercialized form of the 'neo-vernacular'. Instead, the aim is to creatively reinterpret, from a contemporary perspective, the building techniques passed down by traditions that value wisdom, harmony, and skill, and that are often by their very nature rooted in ecological practices.

6. Promoting the ecological uses of earth

The fight against climate change calls for the use of natural building materials that require no industrial transformation and that can be prepared and utilized without guzzling energy or generating greenhouse gases. These materials should be gathered and used locally, benefiting the regional economy and avoiding the need for long-distance transportation. Raw earth, the quintessential recyclable material, ticks all these boxes and it has many other qualities besides, such as heat regulation (see pp. 21 and 24–25). However, the architectural use of raw earth also requires skills, skills that CRAterre has explored from every angle by refining, teaching, and applying them over the last forty years. The worldwide dissemination of these techniques is inextricably linked with the recent boom in earth architecture. Moreover, CRAterre's research has proved scientifically that the use of industrial additives to stabilize or reinforce raw earth is not essential to ensure strength and durability (see pp. 38–39). This recent breakthrough makes it possible to avoid the damaging use of cement, an industrial product that is high in greenhouse gas emissions.

7. Spreading knowledge and passing on skills

The body of knowledge collected by CRAterre is passed on in various ways. As well as the resources available via its website (www.craterre.org), CRAterre has a prolific publishing programme. The most notable of its hundred or so publications are the encyclopaedic *Earth Construction: A Comprehensive Guide*,[3] and *Bâtir en terre*,[4] which seeks to reconcile science and culture. Amàco has furthered this democratization of knowledge by producing a variety of films and videos and holding seminars to teach technical skills. The founders of CRAterre have also gathered together an almost exhaustive library of more than 25,000 items from all over the world, although due to a lack of finances, access to this unique treasure trove is restricted and difficult, even for researchers. The same is true of CRAterre's wide-ranging photographic archive. Despite these drawbacks, however, CRAterre's message has become, in the words of Renzo Piano, 'vital to contemporary architectural thinking'.

The relevance and realism of this sevenfold proactive approach – together with the close-knit nature of the group – have played a key role in CRAterre's longevity and international impact. Its continued existence is all the more remarkable when we remember that many of the groups founded in the same period, sometimes with similar aims, have long since disappeared without trace. However, other teams (many trained by CRAterre) have followed in its footsteps in different parts of the world, giving rise to a more structured and diversified form of activism.

In Japan, artists with the rare talent of reconciling the lessons of history, the demands of modernity, and the challenges of the future are honoured with the prestigious title of 'living national treasures'. This description fits the pioneering work of CRAterre, but it could also apply to earth itself, as a living natural material that is part of our homes and landscapes. It is a primary resource that has been too long despised, overlooked, or neglected by the promoters of industrial modernity. Now that it has been recognized as an ecological construction material with a crucial role to play in the future, raw earth is more alive than ever.

Three quotations sum up CRAterre's pioneering holistic and global approach over the last forty years:

'Act as if it were impossible to fail.'
Dorothea Brande

'The great movements of transformation always start in a marginal, deviant, modest, or invisible way.'
Edgar Morin

'First they ignore you, then they laugh at you, then they fight you, then you win.'
Mahatma Gandhi

---

3   Houben & Guillaud 1994.
4   Anger & Fontaine 2009.

A Note from the Founders of CRAterre

Patrice Doat, Hubert Guillaud, and Hugo Houben

In the early 1970s, the teaching of architecture in France broke away from the academic model of the École des Beaux-Arts in Paris, which no longer met the needs of a changing society, particularly after the cultural, social, and political upheavals of May 1968. The industrial production of housing was called into question by the oil crisis of 1973, which gave rise to calls for ecological responsibility and energy conservation. Since then, architectural training has opened to the real world, absorbing the teachings of the humanities. The search for new sources of inspiration has also sparked an interest in vernacular architecture.

Dissent

As students at the Grenoble School of Architecture, we were well aware of the social role of architects, but highly critical of the overly conformist and outmoded teaching of the art of building. Our combative stance turned into political disobedience: we claimed our autonomy, our freedom of both thought and action. We argued in favour of an ecological approach, and this led to our interest in natural building materials, particularly raw earth, and primarily *pisé* or rammed earth. This was the main material used in the vernacular rural housing of our region of Rhône-Alpes, which we were cataloguing alongside ethnologists. From 1973 onwards, these field studies spurred us to promote the merits of earth construction: simplicity of workmanship, solidity, low cost, durability, pollution-free production process, ecological benefits, and potential for self-builds. We founded CRAterre[1] in Grenoble in 1979 and published our first book, *Building with Earth*, in which we declared: 'For us, building with earth means giving disadvantaged populations the means to improve their habitat...by giving users control over their environments.'

This militant attitude cleared the ground for our first practical projects in 1975, both in France and in Africa (Algeria, Cameroon, Mauritania, and Burkina Faso). Our research laboratory, CRAterre-ENSAG, earned the support of government institutions, which gave us several contracts. In 1982, the French Ministry of Housing and Urban Planning asked us to define 'research pathways for [the revival of construction with] earth'. We put forward a series of measures designed to encourage basic and operational scientific research, university and professional training, and international programmes for documentation and dissemination. We were invited to contribute to a two-pronged cultural event that would trigger a wide-ranging public debate on the ecological benefits of earth construction. On one hand, there was the 1981 exhibition at the Centre Pompidou, *Des architectures de terre* (see pp. 390–391), curated by Jean Dethier. This was coupled with an experimental project designed to demonstrate the architectural and economic potential of raw earth construction, which led in 1985 to the pilot neighbourhood of Domaine de la Terre in Villefontaine, Isère, consisting of 64 social housing units (see pp. 393–395. These two initiatives had an enormous international impact.

During the same period, we were commissioned to create a large-scale social housing programme on Mayotte (see pp. 382–383), an archipelago off southeast Africa with an area of 374 square kilometres. Nineteen artisanal brick factories were set up as cooperatives, in order to produce the millions of compressed earth blocks required for this project. This operation made it possible to put an end to the spoliation of the sand in the local lagoon, which was then being used to make concrete. We followed the process closely between 1980 and 2000,[2] and during that period, over 20,000 low-cost housing units and several public buildings were completed. This huge and pioneering project continued into the 21st century and now stands as the biggest of its kind in the world. These results were not achieved without struggle, however, as this use of the earth's resources was often challenged by industrial lobbies perturbed by the shrinking of the cement market. However, the need for local, community-based development finally won the day, both for environmental reasons (lessening the risk of exhausting the island's mineral resources) and social and economic reasons (the creation of many jobs in the field of raw earth construction).

Strategy

'A material is not interesting for what it is, but for what it can do for society.' This statement by the English architect John F. C. Turner serves as the basis for our holistic approach to a better understanding of the issues surrounding social and affordable housing in different parts of the world. As part of the Grenoble School of Architecture and its work in the fields of research, training, practical application, and dissemination, the CRAterre teaching team prepares its students to respond to the challenges of our time by passing on the theoretical and practical tools of an architect who serves the needs of society. Our work was honoured in 1986 when CRAterre was granted the status of a national research laboratory by the French Ministry of Culture. Our team – which at that time comprised thirty people from six professions and ten nationalities – confirmed its commitment by creating a specialist higher education course aimed at a general public from all walks of life, the CEAA Terre, recognized by a diploma, the DSA Terre.[3] This innovative training brings together 'the head and the hand': theory and practice, knowledge and experimentation on the ground. This course has come to set standards for the training of architects, and has enabled them to 'think globally and act locally'. Our next step was the creation of the Grands Ateliers, a hub of radical innovation that seeks to merge the teaching of architecture, building, art, and science. It opened in 2001 in Villefontaine in southeastern France, the home of the Domaine de la Terre project.

The ongoing need to substantially increase the number of specialists skilled in the use of raw earth was reflected in 1998 by the creation of the UNESCO Chair on Earthen Architecture, Building Cultures and Sustainable Development. This was formulated and implemented by CRAterre in collaboration with UNESCO, with the aim of establishing a global network of university graduates and professionals with DSA Terre diplomas. During the same period, the CRAterre team collaborated with ICCROM (the International Centre for the Study of the Preservation and Restoration of Cultural Property, based in Rome) and the Getty Conservation Institute in Los Angeles to develop the Gaia and Terra projects, which strengthened the inextricable connection between local development and the conservation of raw earth architectural heritage all over the world. Our team were also recruited by UNESCO in 1998 to coordinate its World Heritage Programme for Earth Architecture. In 2011 the French government presented a dual award to CRAterre – along with the Grenoble School of Architecture and the Grands Ateliers – for excellence as a research laboratory (LabEx)[4] and as a centre for innovative training (IDEFI),[5] providing some measure of the ground covered by CRAterre in the last five decades.

Future

Our continuing commitment – furthered by successive generations of students from the Grenoble School of Architecture – has resulted in initiatives whose success has been widely recognized. We have always had three basic prerequisites: the inalienable right to build with earth; the need to fight against the interests of the lobbies, technocrats, and bureaucrats who misguidedly reign over the construction sector and the regulation of materials; and the obligation to plan for actual or foreseeable environmental, social, and economic disasters. This three-part strategy converges into one crucial and pressing objective.

Raw earth construction has now become widely accepted and recognized; its usefulness is no longer disputed. Its 21st-century revival will help bring about a new and necessary social paradigm that will make it possible to move beyond an obsolete system. The eco-friendly art of building with raw earth, and the legacy of an ancient tradition that has been endlessly regenerated for thousands of years, will provide innovations that allow us to live hand in hand with our planet. This knowledge is vital, as it allows not only autonomy but also mutual aid, which has become more subversive than ever. Moreover, it guarantees a vast number of the world's citizens access to adequate, sanitary housing. It represents the ethical bedrock of the 'disobedience of the architect' in the face of standardization, the damaging overuse of industrial materials, and, above all, the reign of 'concrete for all'. We must trust in the new generation, who are benefiting from a growing range of university and professional courses that will enable them to tackle the huge challenge of social and affordable housing with the best means at their disposal. Nevertheless, there is still a need to encourage more institutions to participate, in order to fulfil the dream of scientist and Nobel Prize winner Pierre-Gilles de Gennes, the dream of passing on the virtues of simplicity that natural construction materials possess. In this lies the path to thinking, acting – and building – differently.

Further reading:
CRAterre 1979; Houben & Guillaud 1994

---

1 The Centre for Earth Research and Application, which was later renamed the International Centre for Construction with Earth, while retaining the acronym CRAterre.
2 In conjunction with the architect Vincent Liétar at the Société Immobilière de Mayotte, and the craftspeople of the association Art.terre Mayotte.
3 A specialist diploma in earth architecture awarded by the Grenoble School of Architecture.
4 Laboratory of Excellence 2011–19, for the research unit for Architecture, the Environment and Building Cultures.
5 Initiative of Excellence in Innovative Teaching, 2012–19, Building Matters workshop, created in conjunction with the Grands Ateliers.

The Work of CRAterre
Educational Innovations

If the future of earth architecture is to be guaranteed, it is vital to allow new generations of architects, engineers, and other workers in the building industry to access specialized training in the properties, benefits, methods, and potential of this material. This is the educational mission that has driven CRAterre ever since its foundation in 1979, under the auspices of the Grenoble School of Architecture in Isère, France, as well as, from 2001 onwards, at the Grands Ateliers, its experimental centre in Villefontaine. Within this crucible of teaching innovation, the following quotation by André Gide is put into practice on a daily basis: 'Many ideas and strategies seem impossible as long as nobody deploys the creative intelligence needed to test them.' Great emphasis is placed on the 'intelligence of the hand', which leads to an understanding of how the hand speaks to the brain and how the brain can also speak back to establish a dialogue. In a dynamic environment that combines self-discovery, community spirit, and playful exploration, students of many disciplines turn thought into action by building, often at life size, all the traditional archetypal forms used in raw earth architecture – walls, arches, vaults, domes – as well as prototypes that allow them to come up with new uses for earth (**right and opposite**).

J.D. & R.E.

The Work of CRAterre
More Educational Innovations

In the 1980s, Patrice Doat, one of the co-founders of CRAterre, launched an innovative teaching programme for architecture students in Grenoble. Two decades later, this approach was taken further in the Grands Ateliers, which opened in Villefontaine in 2001. Here, Doat founded the Grains d'Isère, an annual international festival devoted to the many possible uses of earth. This celebratory event brings together students, teachers, researchers, architects, and engineers, as well as artists, both young and old. Furthermore, local children and teenagers are also invited to take part in this collective endeavour. The end result is a multidisciplinary creative hub that uses earth to create dance, performances, video, architecture, and sculpture. These creative fusions have given rise to a wide range of temporary artworks.

J.D.

Above right: Collective work by primary school children.

Centre right: An introduction to the various forms and textures of earth, devised for teenagers by architecture students.

Below right: Japanese architect Kinya Maruyama works on a bamboo structure covered with earth.

Opposite: A tall cylinder built from wattle and daub by Daniel Duchert, containing 'a sound installation that echoes the motion of the granular material of which all earth is comprised'.

The Work of CRAterre
Public Housing Prototypes

Since its founding in 1979, CRAterre's innovative training programmes have been combined with a strategy that brings together a range of collaborators – builders, scientists, teachers, and students – in order to conceive and construct life-size prototypes of raw earth public housing. The challenge is always to combine technical skill and innovation in the shortest time possible. Three of these many experiments are shown here.
    J.D. & R.E.

Below right: Grenoble, 1987: a 24-hour project (split into three 8-hour sessions) to build a 50-square-metre modular house designed by Josep Esteve. This project sought to demonstrate that earth architecture can be fast and efficient if it is carefully planned. The six diagrams (**opposite, above**) trace the evolution of the project.

Above and centre right: Paris, 1988: a five-day project to build an 80-square-metre House of the Future, designed by the architects Lipsky & Rollet. Its three earthen modules are protected by a lightweight metal framework covered with a composite fabric. This project demonstrates the potential of elegantly combining raw earth with industrialized materials.

Opposite, below: 2016: Terra Nostra is a prototype for cheap, ecologically responsible housing. The modules were prefabricated over a period of four months at the Grands Ateliers, before being transported to Lyon and assembled in three weeks. This project, coordinated by Maxime Bonnevie, has since been further developed in Grenoble as part of a public housing programme.

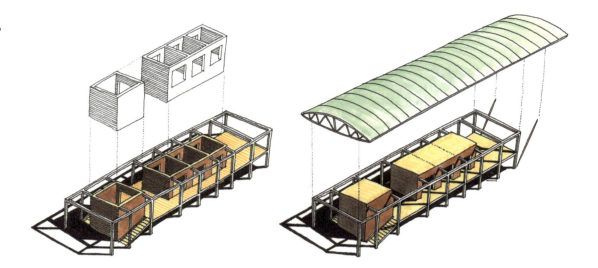

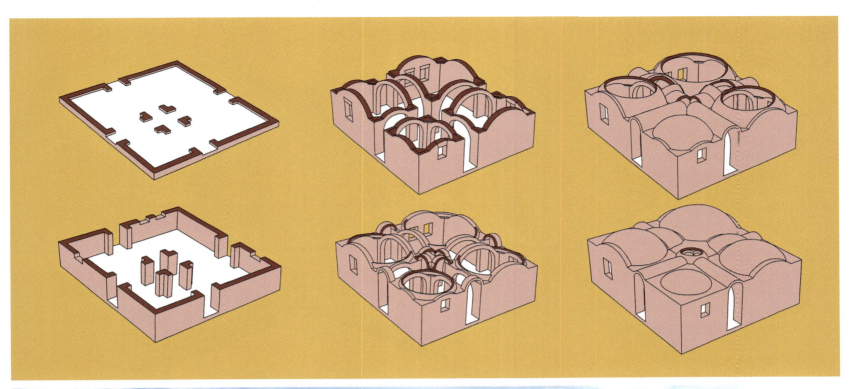

Contemporary Creativity: 1970 to the Present Day

The Work of CRAterre
A Public Housing Scheme in Africa

Mayotte is an island situated off the southeast coast of Africa. In 1976, its population voted in a referendum to remain part of the French Republic, and subsequently a major housing programme was launched for this 374-square-kilometre territory. There were two main challenges: the fragility of traditional local houses, largely made of plant materials and vulnerable to hurricanes and other weather phenomena, and the widespread use of concrete, which was threatening the delicate ecological balance of the lagoon by encouraging the extraction of sand from its banks. Research was carried out into regional traditions in order to devise a public housing programme based on local materials such as laterite earth and pozzolana (a volcanic rock). A local property company, the Société Immobilière de Mayotte (SIM), was responsible for running the programme, and commissioned a feasibility study from CRAterre. Nineteen brick-making workshops were put into operation and a group of students from the Grenoble School of Architecture (CRAterre's mother organization) set about building an initial group of eight housing units using compressed earth bricks (**opposite, above**). These prototypes were approved and the programme was expanded across the island, with the objective of creating jobs and building experience through on-the-job training. More than 20,000 homes were built (**opposite, below**), along with several public buildings, including schools (**right**). The pilot project proved that raw earth could be an excellent choice for large-scale housing schemes and it remains unique, not only for its scope and efficiency but also for its social, cultural, technological, and economic benefits to the local community.

H.G.

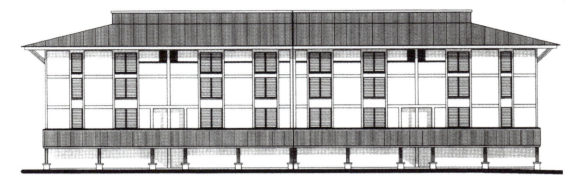

Contemporary Creativity: 1970 to the Present Day

The Raw Earth Revival
Auroville Earth Institute, India

In 1988, Serge Maïni, better known as Satprem, became one of the first people to complete CRAterre's training course at Grenoble School of Architecture. He went on to instigate several initiatives to train students in earth architecture, including a team in India. The latter project led to his decision to set up a personal project in the country. Inspired by the Indian government's creation of the Housing and Urban Development Corporation (HUDCO), Maïni founded the Auroville Earth Institute in 2004. With the help of a young Indian colleague, T. Ayyappan, he developed a wide range of innovative techniques using stabilized earth, particularly for vaults and domes. These adventurous prototypes have since been utilized in various public buildings and low-cost housing programmes both in India and elsewhere, with the aim of encouraging self-building. These projects also promoted the use of compressed earth bricks (CEB), made with a series of manual and mechanized block presses (the Auram) invented by Maïni himself. He currently works in partnership with architect Lara K. Davis (see p. 485), who studied at MIT.

H.G.

Opposite, above left: Serge Maïni's own house.

Opposite, below left: The vault of the conference hall at the Sharanam Centre for Rural Development (2017), which reaches 15 metres at its highest point.

Centre: Al-Medy Mosque in Riad, Saudi Arabia, which took a mere seven weeks to build.

Above right: Single-storey dormitories at the Sharanam Centre for Rural Development in Pondicherry (2016).

Below right: Vikas housing block in Auroville (1998).

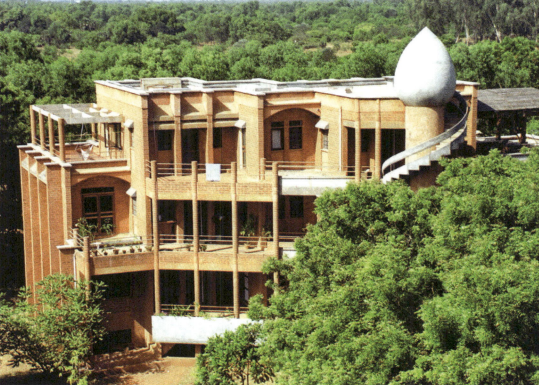

The Raw Earth Revival
Gernot Minke in Germany

For three decades, starting in the 1970s, architect and engineer Gernot Minke was a major figure in the revival of earth architecture in Germany. Based at Kassel University, he developed the first teaching and research programme on the subject in the entire country, in addition to writing reference books that have been widely translated into other languages. Minke offered his students solid practical and theoretical training, and also organized hands-on building projects in developing countries. In Guatemala in 1978, he experimented with a system for building extremely cheap homes by stacking long sacks filled with earth (**below right**). Their roofs were planted with protective vegetation that would have a cooling effect on the interior (**centre right**). In the village of Sorsum, Germany, Minke designed a 600-square-metre kindergarten in 1996, following the principles of Steiner-Waldorf education, which places great emphasis on the use of natural materials (**opposite below, and left plan**). Minke was also responsible for the construction of earthen buildings in a dozen other countries, including a research laboratory in New Delhi, India (**opposite, above and right plan**).

J.D. & R.E.

```
Further reading:
Minke 2000; Minke 2006
```

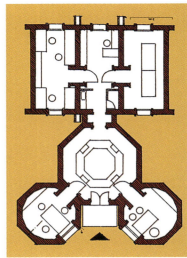

Contemporary Creativity: 1970 to the Present Day

The Raw Earth Revival
Africa and Latin America

The Association for the Development of Traditional African Urbanism and Architecture (ADAUA) was set up in 1975 and oversaw the use of earth for the headquarters of the Pan African Institute for Development in Burkina Faso, and a pilot housing scheme in Rosso, Mauritania (**above right**). In Chile, Marcelo Cortés built a prototype house in 2005 that updated the tradition of using a load-bearing structure made of wood (replaced by metal in this case), which was then filled in with earth (**below right**). This ancient technique has proved remarkably resistant to earthquakes.

Opposite: The association La Voûte Nubienne (AVN) was founded in 2000 by the French master builder Thomas Granier. Following the pioneering work of Egyptian architect Hassan Fathy, which was continued in the 1980s by the Development Workshop, the AVN seeks to bring the benefits of Nubian vaults to housing for the poor. This style of earth architecture dates back to ancient Nubia, in upper Egypt, and because it does not require formwork (see p. 54), it offers a means to make roofs in areas where wood is scarce. AVN now has 15 regional teams operating in six countries in West Africa, where it trains local workers and builds rural and urban houses, as well as schools and dispensaries. These initiatives have won many awards.

    J.D.

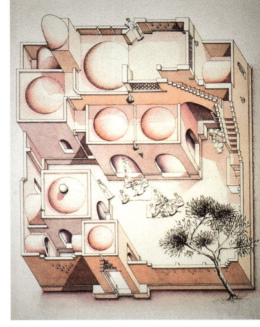

Contemporary Creativity: 1970 to the Present Day

Exhibition
Centre Pompidou, Paris

In the 1970s, earth architecture was virtually unknown to the general public, and even to many architects. It began to gain attention, however, with the onset of the oil crisis, which deprived the world of some of its major sources of energy, leading to severe restrictions in Europe, particularly in the energy-guzzling building sector. Jean Dethier, then a curator of architecture exhibitions at the Centre Pompidou, Paris, decided to take advantage of this situation by throwing a spotlight on building with earth, which has the advantage of not requiring fossil fuels. In 1981, he curated a huge exhibition, *Des architectures de terre*, which presented for the first time an overview of the vernacular traditions, contemporary uses, and ecological future of earth architecture. Dethier saw the show as a manifesto, and its spectacular design took the form of an imaginary town made up of fifteen gigantic model buildings, showcasing the architecture of various countries. The exhibition's overwhelming success led to its extension into a sixteen-year tour that took it to 24 cities on four continents. In total, it welcomed three million visitors (a record for a museum show). The pioneering nature of this now legendary exhibition was made even more evident by the fact that it strategically coincided with the construction of the Domaine de la Terre, a demonstration of contemporary French earth architecture that was completed in 1985 (**overleaf**).
    R.E.

```
Further reading:
Dethier 1983
```

Above right: Poster for the exhibition *Des architectures de terre* at the Centre Pompidou, Paris, 28 October 1981–1 February 1982.

Below right and opposite: Views of the exhibition.

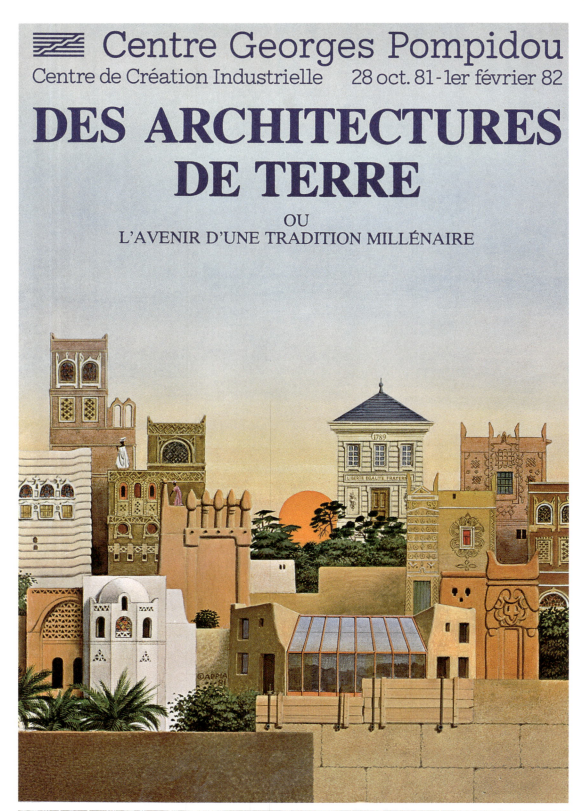

Contemporary Creativity: 1970 to the Present Day

Public Housing
The Domaine de la Terre, France

When Belgian architect Jean Dethier curated the exhibition *Des architectures de terre* at the Centre Pompidou in 1981 (see previous pages), he wanted it to be accompanied by a practical demonstration of the contemporary relevance of this kind of ecological architecture. His points of reference for this idea included the construction of pilot public housing projects (*Siedlungen*) in Germany in the 1920s. Dethier was determined to promote a building scheme on a similarly ambitious scale in France, despite criticisms of his perceived utopianism from some quarters. The project was eventually launched with the collaboration of various public institutions. Dethier initially considered siting the project in Paris but he eventually opted for the Rhône-Alpes region, between Lyon and Grenoble, where there is an historical tradition of earth architecture. The chosen site was the new town of L'Isle-d'Abeau, which was conceived as a launchpad for the housing of the future. After the local authorities had been persuaded to support the project, a national architecture competition was held to design an urban neighbourhood containing 65 public housing units. It was eventually decided not to choose one outright winner but instead to commission ten teams to each come up with a prototype involving one of the following techniques of earth construction: rammed earth, compressed earth blocks (CEB), or a mixture of earth and straw.

R.E.

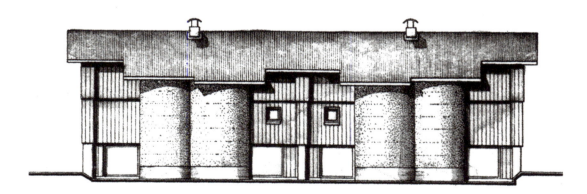

Right and opposite: Photographs and ground plan of the Domaine de la Terre, and details of rammed earth houses by Odile Perreau Hamburger (opposite, centre) and Jourda & Perraudin (opposite, below).

Contemporary Creativity: 1970 to the Present Day

Below left and right: Housing blocks designed by François Confino (left) and Jean-Vincent Berlottier (right).

Opposite: Housing blocks designed by architects Jourda & Perraudin.

The supervision of this experimental scheme was carried out by CRAterre, and in 1985 the leafy neighbourhood of the Domaine de la Terre was finally unveiled in Villefontaine, Isère. It received enormous coverage from the mass media and specialist publications alike, and for many years it was a place of pilgrimage for academics and other interested parties. It was visited by experts from the UN-Habitat agency, who declared: 'This ambitious and innovative operation confirms the advantages of modernizing earth architecture: the advances achieved in France should benefit from wide-ranging international exposure.' In 2008, the neighbourhood was classified as 'an exemplary legacy of sustainable development'. In 2015, a research team analysing developments in earth architecture in Europe over the previous thirty years concluded that the Domaine de la Terre had played an important role in its resurgence. In 2001, Villefontaine also became the home of the Grands Ateliers, an educational centre that aimed to revitalize the teaching of architecture. Since then, the Grands Ateliers have been carrying out experiments (in conjunction with CRAterre and – more recently – Amàco) that point to the way forward for earth architecture.

R.E.

```
Further reading:
Dethier 1985
```

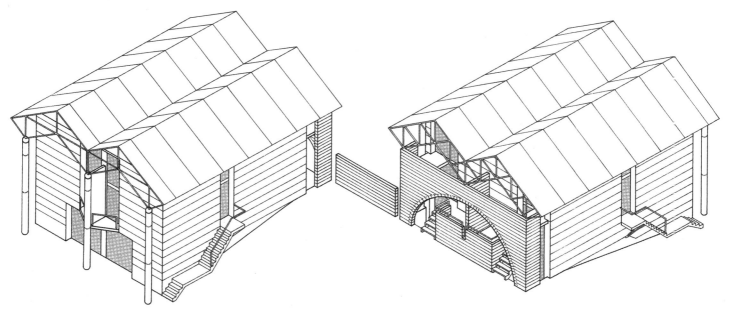

Contemporary Creativity: 1970 to the Present Day 395

Houses
United States

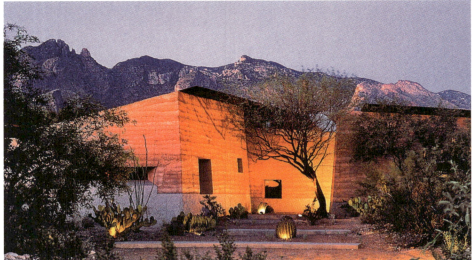

The houses built with rammed earth in Tucson, Arizona, by Rick Joy are splendid examples of the revival of domestic raw earth architecture in the United States in the early 21st century. Before becoming an architect in 1990, at the age of 32, Joy worked as a musician, sculptor, and carpenter. His dual education in artistry and craftsmanship explains his distinctive sensibility and technique. While advocating conceptual and material minimalism, he nevertheless imbues his buildings with sensual warmth and serene beauty. His houses also have a poetic relationship with their natural surroundings and the properties of the soil. He skilfully gives his ecological architecture a voluptuousness derived directly from the spirit, texture, and luminosity of rammed earth. Using this raw material, extracted *in situ*, Joy creates walls with a radiant harmony that is as elegant as it is powerful. He even establishes a dialogue between raw earth and industrial materials such as Corten steel, achieving a beauty that blends cutting-edge modernity and vernacular traditions. Rick Joy is the only American architect to have built his own studio from raw earth, in 1999 (see pp. 448–449). This inviting workspace exemplifies the sophistication that characterizes his earth architecture.

J.D.

```
Further reading:
Joy 2002
```

Above left and right: The Catalina House (1998).

Above centre and below: The Tucson Mountain House (2001).

Houses
United States

Modern earth architecture first appeared in a domestic context in the United States in New Mexico in the 1960s (see pp. 342–347), but since then it has gradually spread westwards. David Easton was among the first architects to embrace it; he founded Rammed Earth Works in California in 1976 and built an impressive and varied portfolio. In the 1990s, however, the creative centre shifted to Arizona, with the emphasis once again on rammed earth. The key figure there was Rick Joy (see previous pages). More recently, other architects with a similar interest in ecological responsibility have come to the fore. Examples of this trend include the luxury villas built by Eddie Jones (**opposite, above and below**) and the work of Paul Weiner with his company DesignBuild Collaborative (**below**). Weiner is unusual in that he combines the roles of architect and property developer, which allows him to ensure an impeccable level of workmanship in his high-end residences.

J.D.

Houses
Australia

In 2014, in the Pilbara region of Western Australia, architect Luigi Rosselli built a compact group of twelve small lodges (**this page and opposite**), covering an area of 575 square metres and intended to provide accommodation for shepherds. A 230-metre-long load-bearing wall was built on this formerly virgin landscape, using rammed earth. Its undulations help to individualize the houses. A similar structural concept could also be transposed to an urban setting, where its compact nature would be even more valuable. The houses' flat roofs are covered with a thick layer of soil planted with vegetation, in order to provide thermal protection from the subtropical climate. In 2017, this design won a TERRA Award, an international prize founded in France in 2000, and given to the most creative earth architecture projects of the year.

R.E. & J.D.

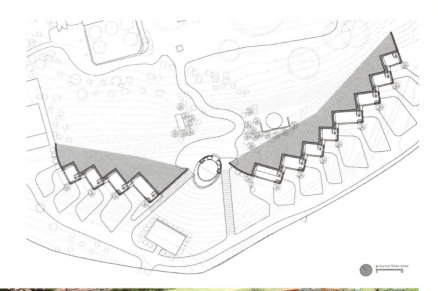

Houses
France
Colombia

The bioclimatic Salvatierra project in Rennes, France (**below right**), which contains 43 public housing units with a total surface area of 3,600 square metres spread across six storeys, is distinguished by its south-facing facade, built from prefabricated cob elements, 50 centimetres thick. The thermal inertia of this natural ecological material regulates the building's interior temperature. This pioneering project, built between 2000 and 2003 by architect Jean-Yves Barrier, showcases the potential of cob, once widely used in the countryside in this part of Brittany but later fallen from fashion.

In Colombia, architect Dario Angulo, who was trained by CRAterre in France, set up the firm TierraTEC in 1994, becoming a pioneer in the semi-industrial production of compressed earth blocks (stabilized with 5%–7% cement). Over the next 25 years, TierraTEC went on to produce eight million of these blocks, and in the process transformed the Colombian construction industry's perception of earth, which had previously been overlooked or even disdained. As a result, more than a thousand homes have been built for well-off members of the country's middle classes, mainly in newly created suburbs in Bogotá. **Above right, centre right, and opposite above:** Residential blocks designed by architects J. P. Urbina and M. Sánchez. Angulo has now branched out into teaching programmes that go hand in hand with his commitment to public housing.

J.D.

Houses
Morocco

In the 1980s, Morocco emerged as a popular African destination for European tourists, with Marrakech as its cultural capital. Wealthy foreigners began to build large vacation homes in the idyllic setting of its palm groves. Architect Elie Mouyal was one of the few who responded to this demand, constructing luxurious villas with rammed earth and adobe that intelligently reinterpreted the traditional spirit of Morocco. These houses confirmed that the natural material of earth – formerly dismissed as a material for the poor – has in fact always been, and always will be, a suitable material for homes for every social class. These elegant houses also showcase two special characteristics of Mouyal's creative approach. After completing his studies in France, he catalogued – and, most importantly, assimilated into his work – a huge range of architectural archetypes from the ancient cultures of the Mediterranean basin, including Morocco. This provided him with a dazzling repertoire of vaults, domes, and other elements, while his ability to sensitively combine these different structures established a new architectural idiom that avoided the trap of historicism. His other great gift was his dexterous fusion of the two creative roles

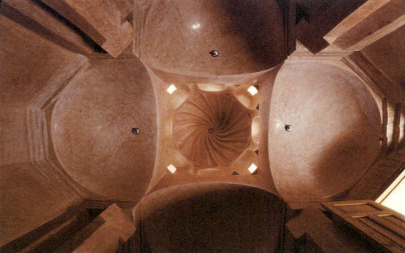

of architect and property developer. This rare symbiosis between two complementary professions added a bedrock of realism and efficiency to his virtuoso deployment of the countless potential uses of earth architecture.

J.D.

Above right: The Villa Benkirane.

Centre, from left to right: A covered courtyard; surfaces finished with *tadelakt* plaster; a series of eight arches around a central pillar; an arch made from compressed earth bricks.

Below: The Bab Atlas Residence (left) and the Villa Assaraf (right), built with rammed earth.

Houses
Austria
Switzerland

Martin Rauch has earned an international reputation as a creator of rammed earth buildings, constructed to the most exacting technical standards and displaying some of the greatest creativity in the field. He originally trained as a ceramicist, and this discipline brought him into contact with fired clay, but since 1999 he has focused his attention on raw earth, via the construction company Lehm Ton Erde ('Loam Clay Earth'), which he founded in his home town of Schlins, Austria. His work has attracted top architects, such as Herzog & de Meuron (the Ricola Herb Centre in Basel, Switzerland, 2014; see p. 19) and the Norwegian Snøhetta agency (the King Abdulaziz Center for World Culture in Dhahran, Saudi Arabia, financed by the oil company Aramco, 2018). In striking contrast to his high-flying clients, Rauch is distinguished by a modest discretion that reflects his rural background and is evident in the house (**above right and opposite**) and workshop (**below right**) that he built for himself in Schlins. The meticulous professionalism and minimalist refinement of his work are similarly rooted in three complementary aspects of his personality: his rural roots; his identification with a region marked by strict Protestantism; and his rationalist education, following the principles of the Ulm School and the Bauhaus. Apart from his exceptional skills as a builder, Rauch is notable for his unswerving commitment to raw earth and his refusal to contemplate adulterating it with industrial additives, including cement. **Opposite, below:** Refurbished interior of a rural house in Almens, Switzerland (architects: Gujan & Pally, 2013).

J.D.

```
Further reading:
Kapfinger 2001; Kapfinger & Sauer 2015;
Heringer, Blair Howe, & Rauch 2019
```

Houses
Ecuador

This century has witnessed an increasing number of countries making a commitment to the revival of earth architecture. One of the driving forces in South America has been Ecuador, where Rama Estudio built this holiday home (**right and opposite**) in Lasso, Cotopaxi province, in 2018. The architects drew inspiration from local traditions and took full advantage of the natural materials at hand (including earth), in the process expanding the vocabulary of what has come to be known as the 'contemporary vernacular'. This house exudes luxury, tranquillity, and sensuality, largely as a result of the copious use of rammed earth, known locally as *tapia*. The ground plan for this 350-square-metre house could hardly be simpler, as it – like the life of the family living there – is organized around four strong parallel lines. The alluring backdrop of rammed earth establishes a dialogue with the wooden floor and the prominent exposed framework that sets off this masterpiece of domestic architecture.

J.D. & R.E.

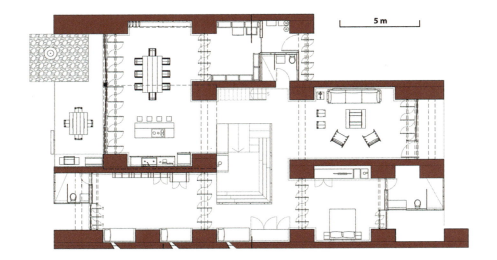

Houses
Germany
France
Senegal
Thailand

In recent years, a wide variety of earth buildings have been constructed for a range of clients all over the world. **Above right:** This 120-square-metre house in Darmstadt, Germany, was designed by architect Franz Volhard. Its wooden structure is filled in with light clay (*Leichtlehm*), a material with which Volhard is extremely experienced, having written a reference book about it (see Volhard 2015). **Centre and below right:** A bioclimatic house in southwest France, designed by Alain Klein. **Opposite, above:** The Al Hamra residence in Senegal, built by French architect Richard Rowland. **Opposite, centre and below:** Villas built from bamboo and earth in Thailand by Chiangmai Life Architects.

R.E.

```
Further reading:
Volhard 2015
```

Contemporary Creativity: 1970 to the Present Day

Houses
Africa
United States
Asia
Europe

In the 21st century, new approaches to rural housing can be seen all over the world. In China, Wang Shu and Lu Wenyu have contributed to the renaissance of the village of Wencun, which was suffering from migration to urban areas, by building a new residential building from rammed earth (**opposite, below**). In the United States, the Design Build Bluff programme at the University of Utah took inspiration from the ideas of Auburn University's Rural Studio to build a low-cost house and workshop (**opposite, above**) in the Utah desert for a Navajo craftswoman; completed in 2004, it is energy self-sufficient, incorporating solar panels. In Morocco, French landscape gardeners Ossart and Maurières have built several houses in the Taroudant region that respect local tradition while including modern touches (**above right**). In Africa, the Finnish firm Heikkinen-Komonen built a minimalist house (**centre right**) for one of their compatriots in Guinea, in keeping with the canons of Scandinavian design. In France, this structure (**below right**), built on farmland near Grenoble by Thomas Jay-Allemand (Caracol Architectures), serves as both seasonal accommodation and a storage shed.

J.D. & R.E.

Contemporary Creativity: 1970 to the Present Day   413

Chapel
Germany

Despite its modest size (108 square metres), this chapel (**below and opposite**) is not only extremely striking, it is also an act of defiance. It is Berlin's only contemporary building to have been constructed with load-bearing earth. The local authorities initially did their best to stymie the project because they found its technological innovations too radical, but the Chapel of Reconciliation, designed by the architects Rudolf Reitermann and Peter Sassenroth, was eventually completed in 2000. It is oval in shape, with two outer walls: the facade of lightweight wooden louvres on the outside is echoed inside by a 7-metre-high wall of rammed earth that surrounds the area devoted to religious services. This wall's horizontal layers create a subtle and natural interplay of colours, further evidence of the talents of the Austrian builder Martin Rauch. The harmonious textures of the 250 tonnes of earth used to build the wall give the space a serenity that encourages contemplation and meditation in believers and nonbelievers alike.

J.D.

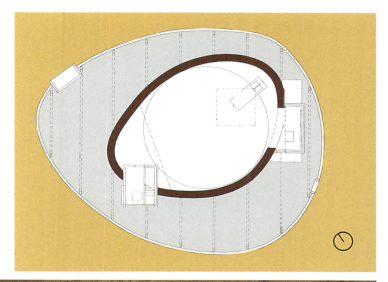

Contemporary Creativity: 1970 to the Present Day

Meditation Centres
France
Czech Republic

The anxiety, stress, and depression that afflict so many people in today's supposedly 'developed' societies have led to a boom in meditation centres. These oases of self-discovery are intended to be soothing cocoons imbued with harmony and serenity. Raw earth has proved well suited to these projects as it encourages a close, sensual relationship with the living forces of nature. In the Czech Republic, David Maštálka (from the studio A1 Architects) and the artist Vojtech Bilisic designed a meditation centre outside Prague (**below**), inspired by traditional Japanese tea houses. An elegant earthen wall combining voluptuous curves and a tactile granular surface rises from a floor covered with woven reed mats to support a translucent dome, a 'sky' that encourages waking dreams. This architectural and spiritual flair are intended to reflect ancient wisdom and bring it into the modern world. In France, a rammed earth meditation centre (**above**) in Espoey, in the Pyrenees, designed by architects Richard Rowland and Marie Nicolazzi, is scheduled to open in 2020.

   J.D. & R.E.

Primary School
Burkina Faso

The primary school (**below and opposite**) built in 2001 by architect Francis Kéré in his birthplace, the village of Gando in Burkina Faso, immediately acquired an international reputation and was considered an architectural manifesto. The innovations of this pilot project are so striking that they are discussed in more detail on page 368. The architect subsequently went on to play an influential role in the earth architecture revival.

J.D.

Further reading:
Lepik & Beygo 2016

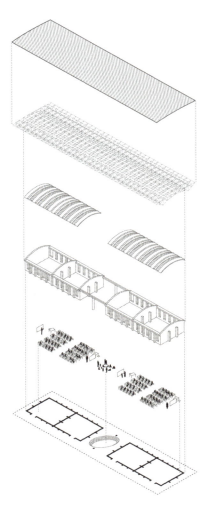

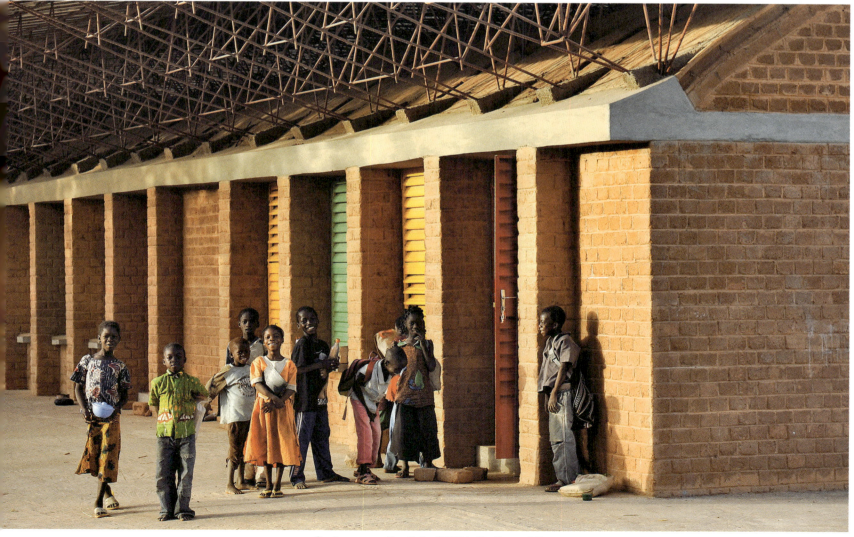

Contemporary Creativity: 1970 to the Present Day

Primary School
Bangladesh

Like the primary school built in Burkina Faso by Francis Kéré (see previous pages), Anna Heringer's variation on this theme, completed in 2006, has won international acclaim. This work reflects new practices and ways of thinking that are now emerging in contemporary architecture. Rather than undertaking a theoretical degree project – as is usual in architecture schools – Heringer decided to create an experimental building in one of the poorest countries in the world, Bangladesh, that would embody her social and ecological convictions. To make the project a reality, Heringer assembled a team of volunteers in Europe, with technical backup from architect Eike Roswag. The village of Rudrapur had no school, so the scheme was to build one by making use of two local resources: earth (in the form of cob) for the walls, and bamboo for the roof structure. These traditional elements were deployed with such skill and verve that the results were fresh and innovative. The village's inhabitants were involved in the construction work, which was used as a way of training future artisans. The school (**right and opposite**) was designed in close collaboration with METI (Modern Education and Training Institute), which aims to provide a progressive education based on joyful self-discovery. The architecture contributes to this mission by providing a serene and harmonious setting. In the three classrooms, the conventional hierarchy of rows of desks is replaced by an egalitarian circular arrangement, with the children sitting on mats on the floor. The children can also use the specially made niches in the walls of each classroom (**opposite, above**), which are designed to be womblike spaces of warm and sensual intimacy.

J.D.

```
Further reading:
Heringer, Blair Howe, & Rauch 2019
```

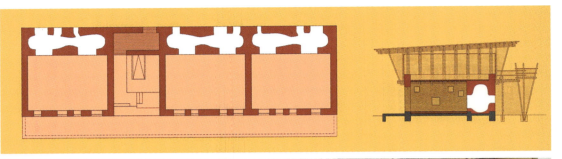

Contemporary Creativity: 1970 to the Present Day

Primary Schools
France
Thailand
China
Madagascar

Alongside the pioneering primary schools by Francis Kéré in Burkina Faso and Anna Heringer in Bangladesh (see previous pages), other projects in Asia and Europe have shown that earth architecture can be adapted to suit to a host of educational, social, and cultural environments and climates.

J.D.

Above right: A primary school in Besely, Madagascar, designed by architect Jean-Paul Viguier.

Centre right: The Floating in the Sky School for orphans, built in Thailand by Japanese architect Kikuma Watanabe. Its conical structures, or 'islets', (some open to nature, others more enclosed) were built from layers of sandbags covered in earth mortar. The complex is crowned by a thatched roof with a substantial overhang.

Below: Designed by Design & Architecture (Milena Stefanova and Bruno Marielle) and Vincent Rigassi, this school opened in 2009 in Veyrins-Thuellin, France.

Opposite, above: A prototype ecological school in Maosi, Gansu province, China, designed by Mu Jun and Edward Ng (2007).

Opposite, below: Panyaden International School in northern Thailand, built in 2010–2011 by Chiangmai Life Architects, is a complex of earth structures made of adobe, wattle and daub, and load-bearing rammed earth, protected by a roof with a large overhang, supported by a bamboo framework.

Contemporary Creativity: 1970 to the Present Day

423

High School
Burkina Faso

After making his name internationally with a primary school in Burkina Faso (see pp. 418–419), Berlin-based architect Francis Kéré continued to enhance his home region by building a school for students aged 15 to 18. Once again, Kéré topped the school with a suspended roof (**right**) that allows for transversal ventilation, while its generous overhang protects the walls from direct sunlight. These features enable the three classrooms to enjoy a comfortable temperature without any need to resort to expensive artificial air conditioning. Unlike the primary school, however, this building has walls that are made with laterite blocks rather than compressed earth bricks. Laterite is soil with a specific chemical composition that allows it to harden once it is extracted from the ground and exposed to air. The school, covering 510 square metres, was completed in 2007, and it consolidated Kéré's ethical commitment to 'do more with less' by recognizing the value of local materials, using his projects to train artisans, and promoting an ecologically responsible approach to architecture. Kéré now works on large-scale projects on other continents but continues to design a range of raw earth buildings in his native country, including educational, medical, and cultural facilities.

J.D.

Further reading:
Lepik & Beygo 2016

Secondary Schools
Africa
Australasia

France is one of the few countries in the world in which earth buildings are used for all levels of education, from primary school to university. The two examples presented here are located in former colonies that have remained under French government, one in Australasia and the other in Africa. On the island of New Caledonia, the Païamboué Middle School in Koné (**right**) was built by architects André Berthier, Joseph Frassanito, and Espaces Libres in 2015, using rammed earth stabilized with 2%–6% cement. Raw earth was chosen as the building material for this 5,800-square-metre complex by representatives of the Kanak people.

In Longoni, on the island of Mayotte, the construction of a vocational school specializing in the building trades (**opposite**), covering 3,000 square metres, is scheduled for completion in 2022. Its architects, from the firm of Encore Heureux & Co-Architectes, have given pride of place to locally available organic materials such as wood and earth, particularly in the form of compressed earth blocks (CEB).

J.D.

wood structure + wood walls
metal structure + CEB walls
wood structure + CEB walls
CEB structure + CEB walls
concrete structure + CEB walls

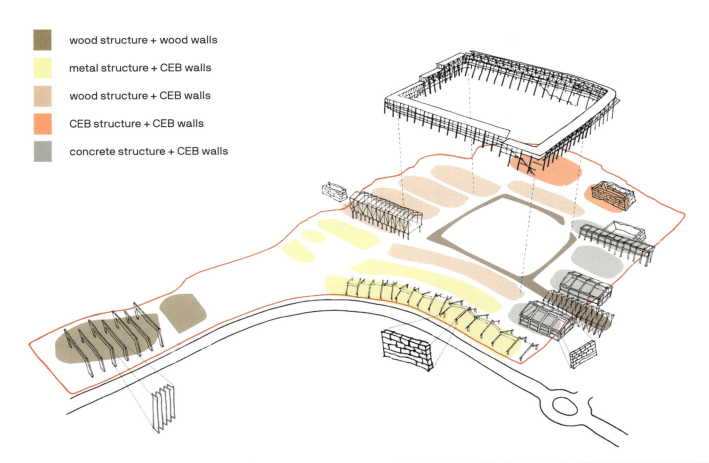

Contemporary Creativity: 1970 to the Present Day

Education and Professional Training
Europe
Africa
Asia

Throughout the world, earth has been used as a building material for educational institutions ranging from primary schools to university campuses, as well as professional training centres that play a key role in creating employment. The oldest shown here, a centre for training craftspeople (**centre right**), was built in 1969 in Errachidia, Morocco, by Jean-Paul Ichter, a pioneer of the revival of rammed earth.

In the UK, the Wales Institute for Sustainable Education (WISE) in Machynlleth (**above right**) is noted for its circular lecture hall built with rammed earth by Pat Borer and David Lea in 2010.

In Burkina Faso, Riccardo Vannucci built a centre for women's welfare in Ouagadougou (**below right**).

In Bangladesh, Anna Heringer used cob for the walls and bamboo for the framework of the DESI Training Centre, completed in 2008 (**opposite, below**); she had previously used this formula successfully in a primary school in the same village, Rudrapur (see pp. 420–421).

In 2013, Odile Vandermeeren used adobe to build three workshops at a sewing school in Niamey, Niger (**opposite, above and centre**). The project won her a TERRA Award in 2017.

J.D. & R.E.

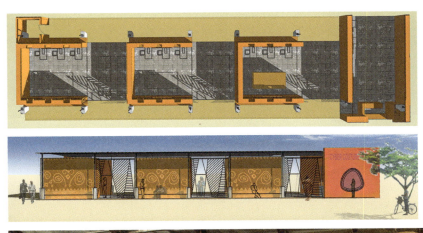

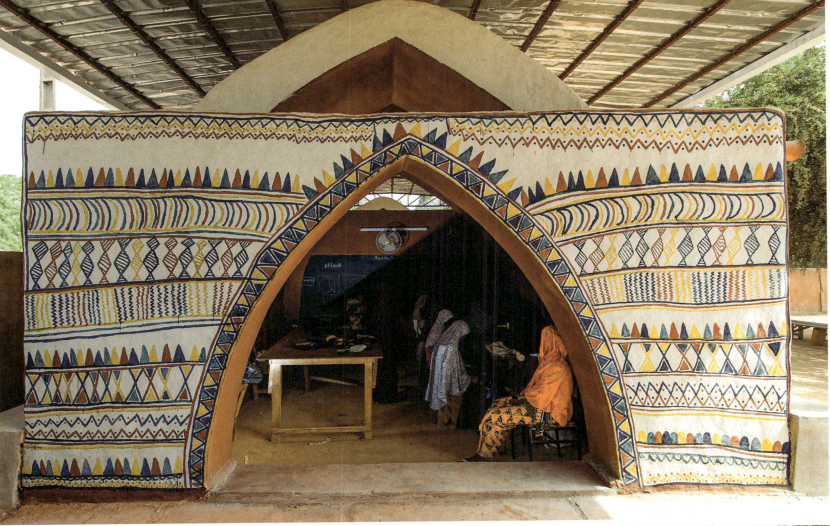

University Campuses
Australia
Mexico
France

In recent years there has been a striking rise in the use of raw earth for university campuses. In Australia, architect Marci Webster-Mannison designed several rammed earth buildings (lecture halls, laboratories, student residences) in 2003 for Charles Sturt University in Thurgoona, near Albury, New South Wales (**right** and pp. 356–357). The university's functional but sophisticated architecture adroitly expresses its connections with the country's unique culture, while also reflecting its progressive, ecologically responsible reputation and exemplifying the prowess that Australia has acquired in earth architecture over the last few decades. In Mexico, the School of Visual Arts at UABJO University in Oaxaca (**opposite, below**) was built with rammed earth in 2008 by architect Mauricio Rocha, who was also responsible for a centre for the blind in Mexico City (see p. 436). His buildings establish a dialogue between earth and concrete. In France, two buildings designed by architect Yves-Marie Maurer for the University of Rennes in the 2010s (**opposite, above**) used cob to create Trombe walls set behind an enormous south-facing pane of glass. This configuration creates efficient heat and moisture regulation, while also echoing the cob farmhouses traditionally built in this part of Brittany.

    J.D. & R.E.

Contemporary Creativity: 1970 to the Present Day

University Campus
China

The Xiangshan campus, on the outskirts of the Chinese city of Hangzhou, is a sophisticated complex without precedent in the world of academia, designed by Wang Shu, winner of the 2012 Pritzker Prize, and his wife Lu Wenyu. It was built from scratch, starting at the beginning of this century, and it now boasts a total of 22 buildings that cater to the needs of the 9,000 students who attend the China Academy of Art. An additional building known as the Wa Shan Guesthouse was added to the centre of the campus to receive distinguished guests (**below**). The campus's total built area of 67,000 square metres includes accommodation, workshops, study areas, a library, social spaces, and a meditation room. The buildings (**opposite, above**) are two or three storeys in height and are arranged within a deliberately labyrinthine architectural landscape, spatially unified by a large roof whose wooden framework seems to float dramatically above the buildings, protecting their high parallel walls. The sensual textures and warm colours of these walls immediately proclaim that they were built with rammed earth. This natural material has long been used in Chinese

vernacular architecture, whose concepts Wang Shu and Lu Wenyu are now sensitively updating in a quest to reappropriate and transform these precious ancient traditions. Unfortunately, however, the technical skills required for earth building have largely been lost in China, so Wang Shu and Lu Wenyu called on the expertise of CRAterre. This groundbreaking Franco-Chinese collaboration resulted in a true masterpiece of contemporary earth architecture.

J.D.

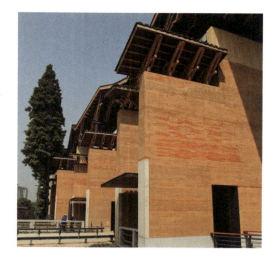

Contemporary Creativity: 1970 to the Present Day

University Campus
France

It is a measure of the advances made in earth architecture since the dawn of the 21st century that it has come to be utilized in new and sometimes unexpected areas such as scientific research facilities, which need to comply with extremely exacting technical specifications. One example of this trend is the new building for the French National Institute of Agricultural Research (INRA), which forms part of the campus of the University of Orléans. While commissioning an architectural showcase for its fragile collection of agricultural earth samples collected from all over Europe, the institute had the inspired idea of creating a building that would itself be made of raw earth; this approach ensures the hygrothermal and climatic protection necessary for the treasures contained inside. This stronghold, which also contains laboratories, was designed by architects Bruno Marielle and Milena Stefanova from the studio Design & Architecture, along with Arnaud Misse, Jean-Marie Le Tiec, and Sébastien Freitas of NAMA Architecture, a team trained by CRAterre at the Grenoble School of Architecture. All of the building's 60-centimetre-thick rammed earth walls are load-bearing (those on the exterior are stabilized with 5% lime, but the others are unadulterated). The 1,400-square-metre facility (**right**), which opened in 2014, displays an outstanding symbiosis between state-of-the-art technology, architectural excellence, and the calm ambience that is required for serious scientific research.
    J.D. & R.E.

Contemporary Creativity: 1970 to the Present Day

Hospitals and Medical Centres
Africa
Latin America
Europe

Earth was long deemed unsuitable for the construction of medical facilities as it was wrongly believed to be incompatible with stringent hygiene standards. Although architect Michel Luyckx built a hospital with rammed earth in 1942 in Adrar, Algeria (see p. 328), it remained one of a kind for decades. In fact, it was not until 1974, and the construction of a dispensary in Mopti, Mali, by André Ravereau and Philippe Lauwers that this type of earth building was revived (**above right**). In 2012, Francis Kéré built a maternity clinic and surgical centre spanning 1,900 square metres in Léo, Burkina Faso (**opposite**). In 2001, Mauricio Rocha used earth (*tepetate* and *caliche*) to build a 14,000-square-metre complex for the Centre for the Blind and Visually Impaired in Mexico City (**below right**). In France, new health centres are currently being built in small towns to stem the exodus of doctors from the countryside. This one (**centre right**) in Marsac-en-Livradois, in the Auvergne region, was built by Boris Bouchet with rammed earth.

J.D.

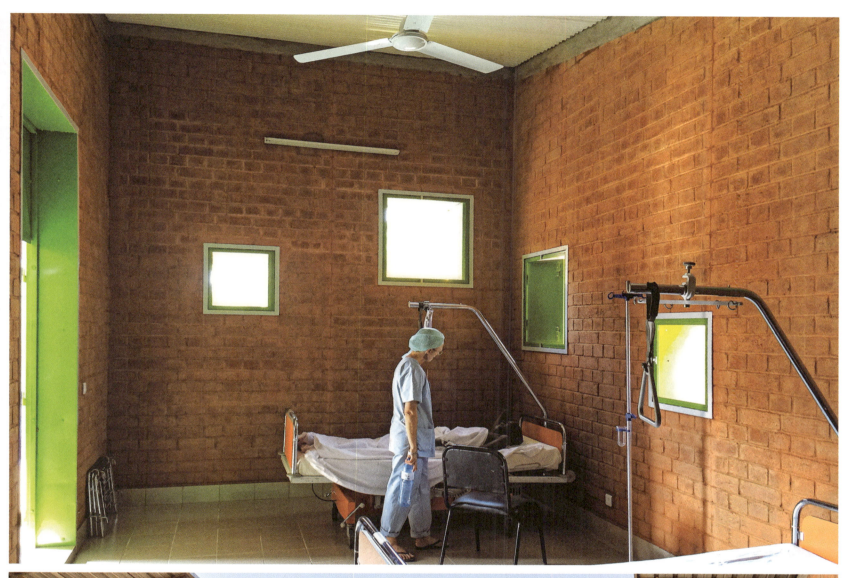

Children's Surgery Centre
Uganda

The year 2019 saw the completion in Entebbe, Uganda, of the Emergency Children's Surgery centre (**above and opposite**), the most ambitious raw earth hospital facility to date (120,000 square metres). Its gleaming rammed earth walls are red in colour, reflecting the soil on the shores of Lake Victoria. This groundbreaking project was designed by architect Renzo Piano.
J.D.

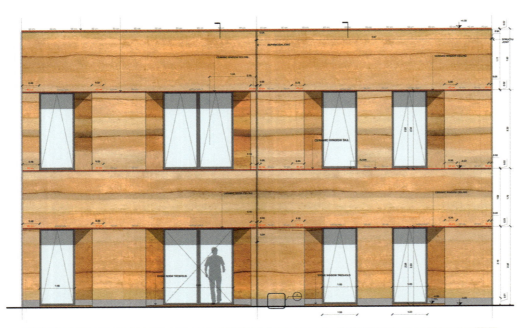

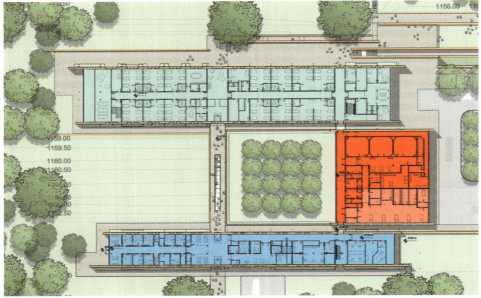

Cultural Centres
Australia

The re-evaluation of Australia's Aboriginal cultures is a relatively recent phenomenon in the country's history, and this long overdue attention has given rise to various buildings that reflect the trend. The most remarkable of these is the Uluru-Kata Tjuta Cultural Centre (**below and opposite**), which opened in 1995. Its organic form, devised by the architect Gregory Burgess, is based around two confronted shapes, symbolizing the two legendary snakes that were responsible for the creation of the sacred site of Uluru. This highly distinctive building rises up from vividly coloured soil – the same soil that was used for the centre's adobe walls and the decorative murals created by artists from the Mutitjulu community, which punctuate the galleries. This dual use of earth bestows visual and textural coherence on the architecture and the museum design. On completion of this exemplary haven of spirituality, Gregory Burgess declared:

'With enthusiasm and humility we need to learn from the nature-integrated wisdom of what is left of the world's indigenous cultures (especially the Australian Aborigines).' This conviction and respect were also evident in his design for the Brambuk Living Cultural Centre. In a similar spirit, architect Glenn Murcutt and the Troppo studio built the rammed earth Bowali Visitors' Centre in Kakadu National Park in 1994.

J.D.

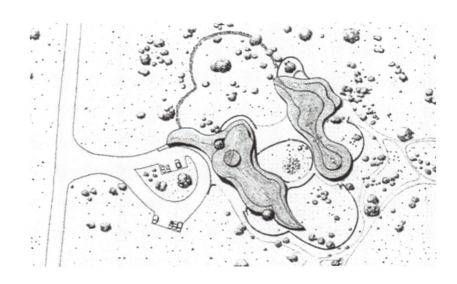

Contemporary Creativity: 1970 to the Present Day

Museums
Mali
Canada
France

The world's first museum built from raw earth was opened in Mali in the late 1970s, starting a trend that would be continued in Australia (see previous pages), North America, and Europe. **Opposite, below:** The National Museum of Mali was completed in 1981 by architect Jean-Loup Pivin. **Opposite, above:** The Nk'Mip Desert Cultural Centre, which opened in 2006 in Osoyoos, Canada, was built by the firm of DIALOG. **Right:** The MuRéNa archaeological museum in Narbonne, France, due to open in 2020, was built with rammed earth by Canadian firm Sirewall (architects: Norman Foster & Partners).

J.D.

Contemporary Creativity: 1970 to the Present Day

Public Libraries
Africa
Asia

Public libraries have played a key role in providing resources to poor and isolated rural settings, especially in developing countries. In Sri Lanka, Milinda Pathiraja and Ganga Ratnayake, from the Robust Architecture Workshop, built an attractive 1,400-square-metre library and training centre in 2015, incorporating load-bearing walls of rammed earth (**below right**). Situated on the Ambepussa military base, it is designed to help retrain veterans of the civil war that devastated Sri Lanka until 2009. In Niger, architects Mariam Kamara and Yasaman Esmaili, from Atelier Masomi, skilfully converted the magnificent old mosque in the village of Dandaji into a public library (**above right**). In Ghana, French architects Rachel Méau and Maude Cannat built a rural literacy and reading centre with rammed earth (**opposite, above**).

J.D. & R.E.

Overleaf: In 2012, Belgian firm BC Architects built this rural library in Muyinga, Burundi, using compressed earth bricks (CEB). The building was born from a combination of research into local architectural traditions and innovations borrowed from elsewhere, such as the installation of hammocks as relaxing and enticing places to read.

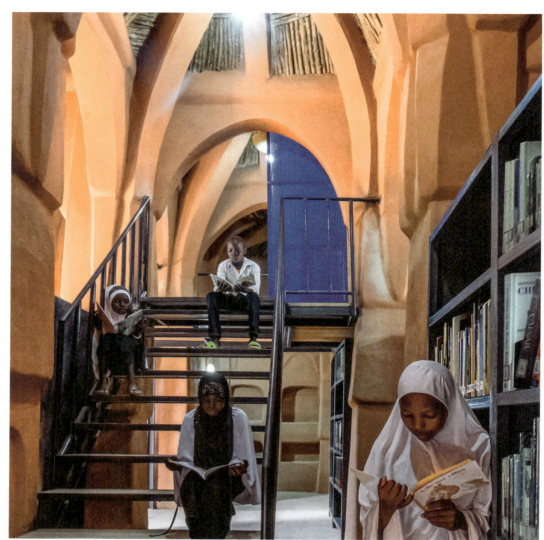

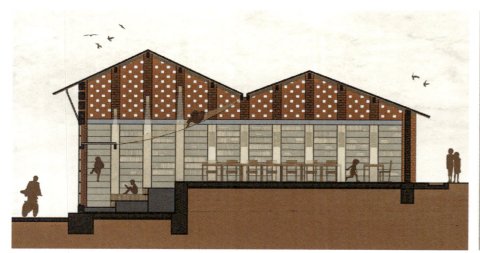
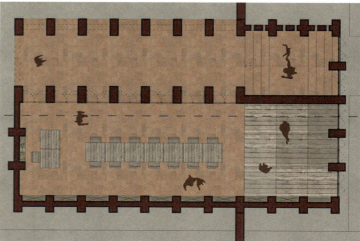

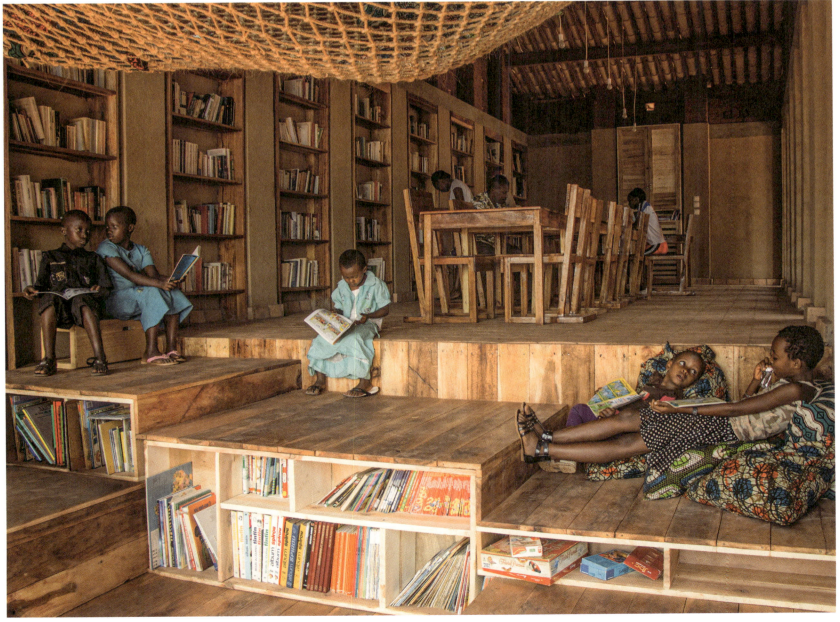

Contemporary Creativity: 1970 to the Present Day

Offices
United States
Austria

In recent years, earth has been used to serve a wide range of functions inside buildings. It has become increasingly popular, for example, in offices designed for the liberal professions or businesses, in both Europe and the United States. **Opposite, above:** The administrative offices of the Gugler printing plant in Pielach, Austria. This 600-square-metre building was constructed with load-bearing rammed earth by Martin Rauch in 1999 (architects: Ablinger, Vedral & Partner). **Below and opposite, below:** The studio that architect Rick Joy built for himself in Tucson, Arizona. Parallel interior and exterior walls of rammed earth mark the office and courtyard, creating a sense of serenity and harmony that suits a space devoted to reflection and creativity. Rick Joy was one of five architects named as a pioneer of earth architecture by the jury of the TERRA Awards in 2016.

J.D.

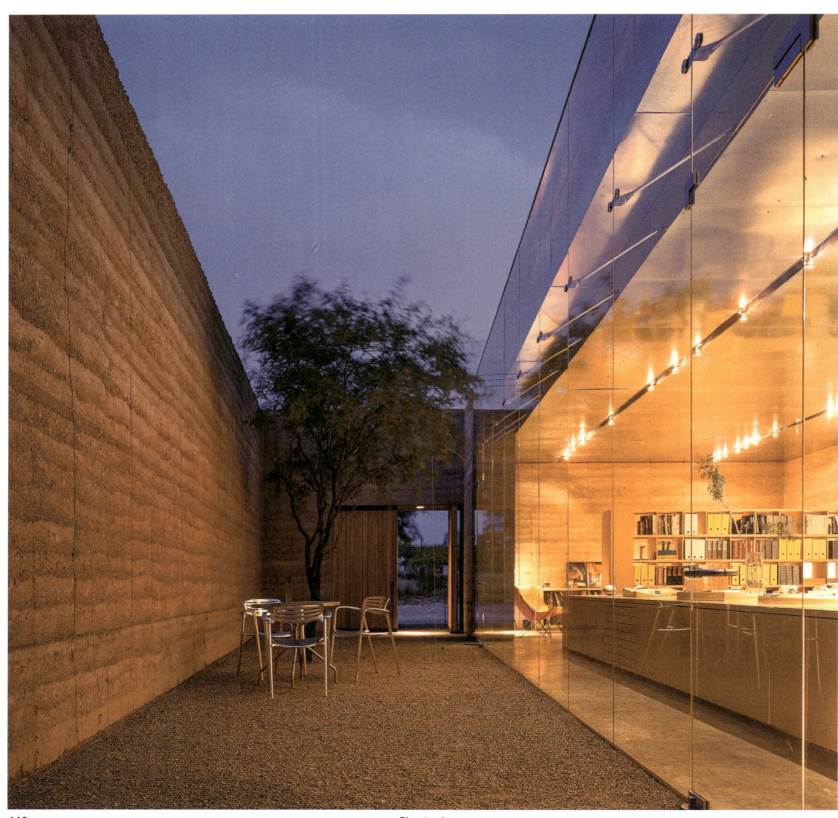

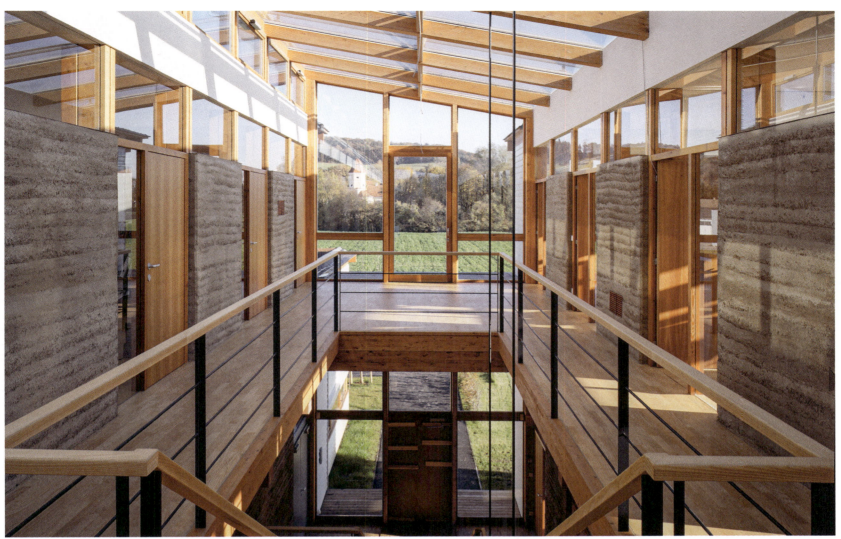

Shopping Malls
Europe
Africa

Earth architecture has recently been adapted to create shopping facilities. **Opposite and plan:** The enormous 29,000-square-metre public market built with stabilized earth bricks in the centre of Koudougou, Burkina Faso, by Swiss architects Laurent Séchaud and Pierre Jequier, winners of the Aga Khan Award in 2007. **Below right:** Construction of the Alnatura shopping mall in Darmstadt, Germany, was completed in 2018 (architects: Haas Cook Zemmrich). Its high walls of prefabricated rammed earth were designed and built by Austrian specialist Martin Rauch. The revival of earth architecture has also extended to the field of commercial air transport. **Centre right:** The terminal at the small airport of Arlit, Niger, built by Belgian architect Odile Vandermeeren.

J.D.

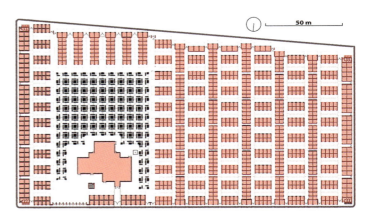

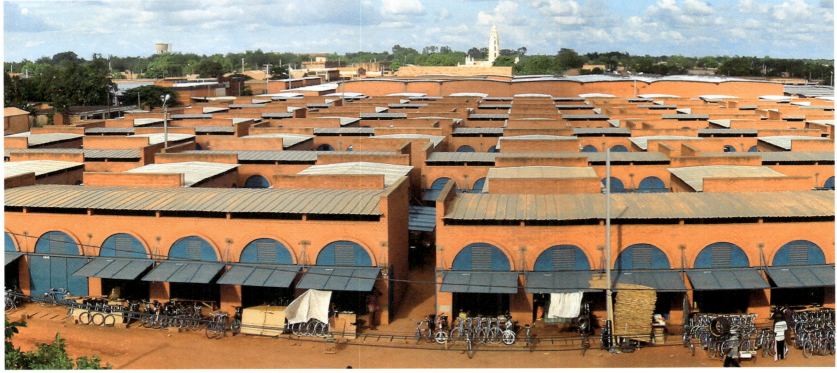

Public Swimming Pool
Spain

The worldwide revival of earth architecture also includes sports and leisure facilities, as demonstrated by this striking municipal swimming pool in Toro, in the Spanish province of Zamora. Designed by the studio Vier Arquitectos, it opened in 2010. The building's exterior (**opposite**) subtly evokes the traditionally austere earth fortresses of the Castile region, but its interior (**below**), with a surface area of 2,450 square metres, displays a thoroughly modern sensibility. Here, the *tapia* (rammed earth) is stabilized with 4% white cement and 2% lime, and the load-bearing walls are protected by coats of fungicidal and water-resistant adjuvants. The building establishes a sophisticated interplay between horizontal layers of ochre rammed earth, oblique rays of sunlight passing through the roof, and reflections on water. It is hard to imagine a more dramatic setting for a swimming pool and raw earth plays an important symbolic role. The project pushes the boundaries of earth, while combining it with another basic component of our natural environment: water.

J.D. & R.E.

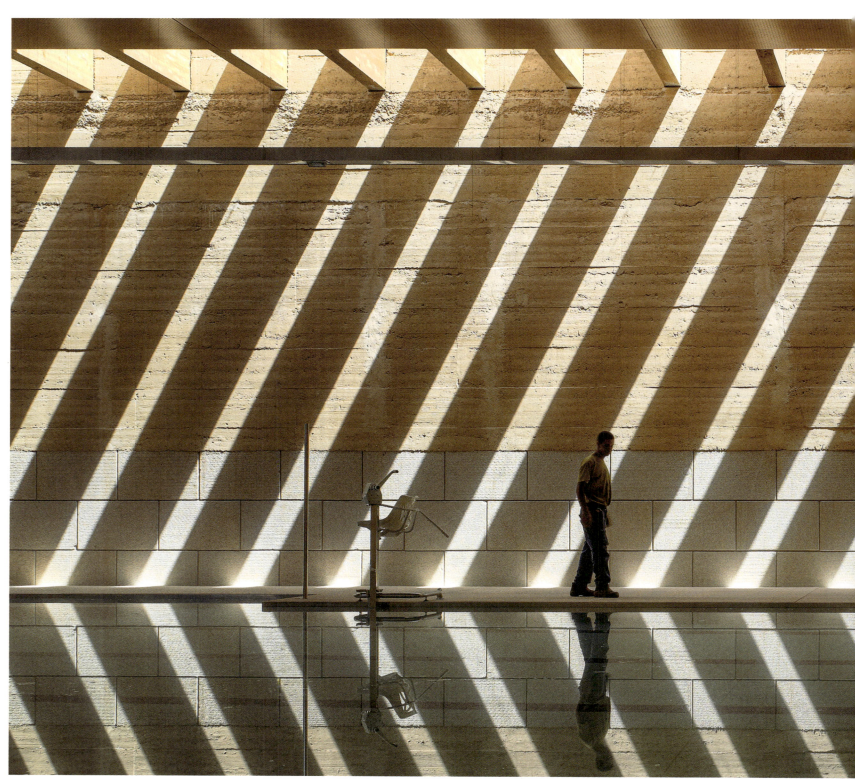

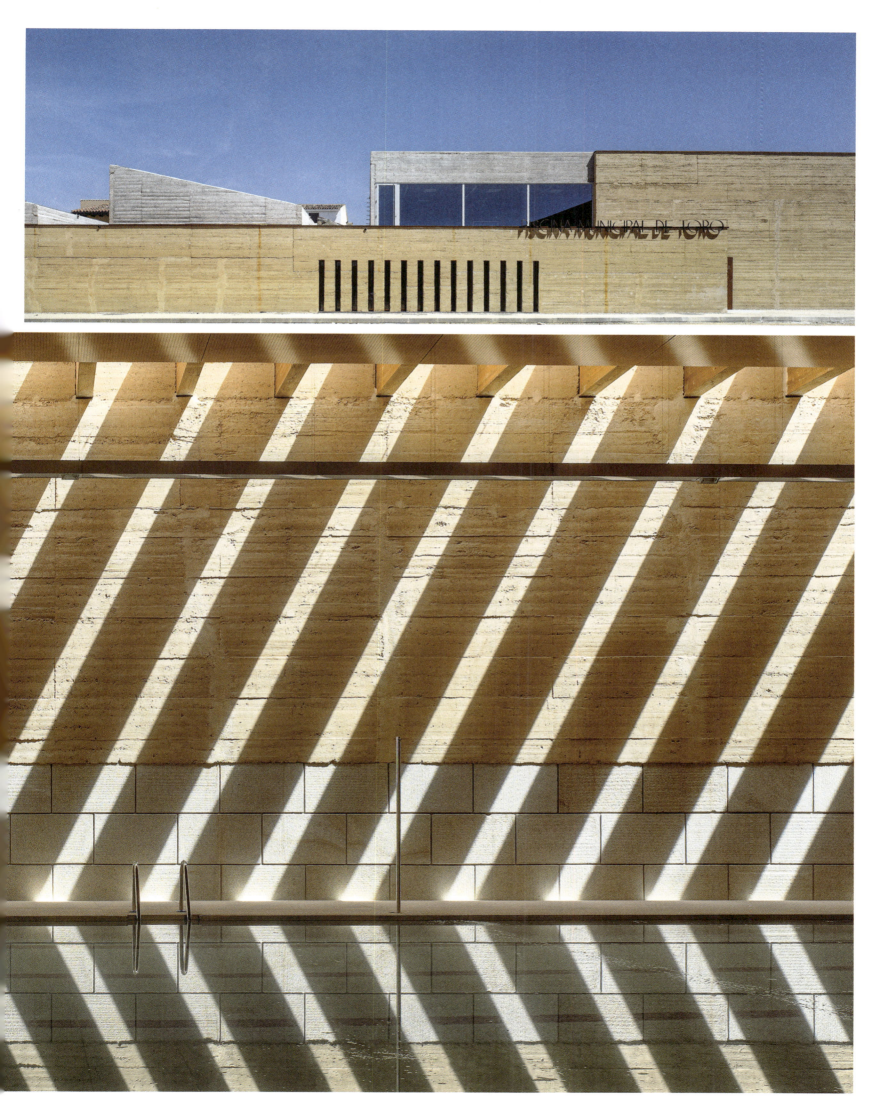

Hotels and Guest Houses
Morocco
Australia

Many hotels have taken advantage of earth as a building material in order to provide their guests with a distinctive, inviting environment. **Opposite, above and centre:** In 2010, the French architect Denis Coquard began construction on the Villa Janna, in a palm grove in Marrakech, Morocco. This ecologically focused project, with a total surface area of 4,700 square metres, was centred around a communal hub, surrounded by a cluster of houses complete with a courtyard. This layout evoked the spirit of a medina, albeit in a natural setting. Raw earth adobe bricks were used for the buildings, which also include vaults and domes inspired by the work of Hassan Fathy. The Villa Janna serves as an artists' residence and a venue for cultural events, and also includes a training centre dedicated to building with adobe and rammed earth. This unique combination was recognized in 2016 by a TERRA Award. **Opposite, below:** This ancient rammed earth kasbah near Skoura in the Dadès Valley, in the heart of one of the lushest oases in southern Morocco, was sensitively converted into the luxury Dar Ahlam Hotel at the turn of the 21st century. **Centre and below right:** The Kooralbyn resort in Queensland, Australia, designed by architect David Oliver (from the Greenway studio) in 1996, demonstrated that earth can also be used for large-scale luxury hotels. **Above right:** The Moorooduc winery estate in Australia, designed by architect Gregory Burgess, offers guest rooms that exude charm, largely thanks to the sophisticated treatment of the rammed earth walls.

J.D.

Contemporary Creativity: 1970 to the Present Day

455

Civil and Military Engineering
France
Luxembourg
Afghanistan
China

The use of raw earth for military fortifications and infrastructure dates back to ancient times. The Serre-Ponçon dam in France (**above left and below**) was completed in 1960, and it is still one of the biggest dams containing a raw earth core, with a height of 124 metres, a length of 650 metres, and a capacity of 14 million cubic metres. In Luxembourg, meanwhile, the waters of the Vianden reservoir (**above right**) sit within strong clay embankments. In the 19th century, the British built earthen forts in China during the Opium Wars (**opposite, below**), while in the 21st century, the main military use of earth comes from a modernization of traditional practices by the British company Hesco (**opposite, above**). Military camps have long been defended by bastions of earth, but now Hesco uses bulldozers to dig up soil and fill easily transportable folding units made from wire mesh with a strong fabric liner. These units can be piled on top of each other to form defensive barriers up to 10 metres high.

J.D.

Contemporary Creativity: 1970 to the Present Day

457

From Walls to Objects
Europe
Canada
Africa
Asia

Opposite: These two rammed earth walls feature a striking range of textures and colours, further evidence of the artistic talent and technical prowess of Martin Rauch. **Above:** Rauch built this 180-metre wall in 1993 alongside the entrance walkway of a hospital in Feldkirch, Austria. **Below:** A wall in one of the cemeteries that Rauch has built in Austria.

Right: A very different approach was used for this spectacular rammed earth wall at the Nk'Mip Desert Cultural Centre in Osoyoos, Canada, which exudes monumental grandeur. Built in 2006 by the firm of Sirewall for the architecture studio DIALOG, it attracted great attention internationally for its multicoloured horizontal layers. It also created fierce controversy, however, on cultural, ethical, and technical grounds, because its innovative aesthetic effects were created with the aid of industrial additives: the earth used for the wall was heavily stabilized with cement, and its colours were achieved by adding artificial pigments. These choices led to a conceptual clash between two conflicting schools of thought. One, based in German-speaking Europe and spearheaded by Martin Rauch and Anna Heringer, argued in favour of ecological responsibility and could not countenance the adulteration of a natural material under any circumstances. The other side of the argument was put forward by equally talented builders who considered the debate a waste of energy in comparison to the overriding need to gain recognition for earth architecture and safeguard its future.
    J.D.

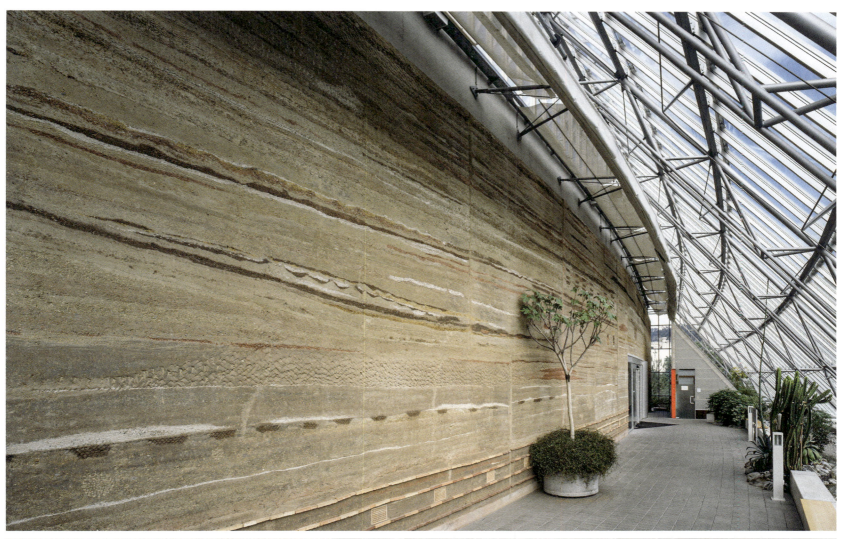

Right: Detail of the multicoloured rammed earth columns built in 2008 by Steven Jimel for the Villa Janna, Marrakech.

Centre: Entrance pavilion at the Eden Project, Cornwall, UK, built with wattle and daub in 2001 by the studio Abey Smallcombe.

Below left: The dome of the refectory in the Koutaba Monastery in Cameroon, 10 metres across, built in 2004 by architect Alain Klein and engineer André Accetta.

Below right: A column of stacking drawers, 120 centimetres high, made from rammed earth by Mathilde and Nicolas Béguin of the Atelier Alba, France.

Opposite, above: Two earthen triptychs created in the Grands Ateliers run by CRAterre in Villefontaine, France, designed by Gisèle Taxil (left) and Daniel Duchert (right).

Opposite, below: Japanese master builder Naoki Kusumi gave a sense of refinement and harmony to the large earthen wall in the foyer of the Capitaland Tower, built in Singapore in 2004.

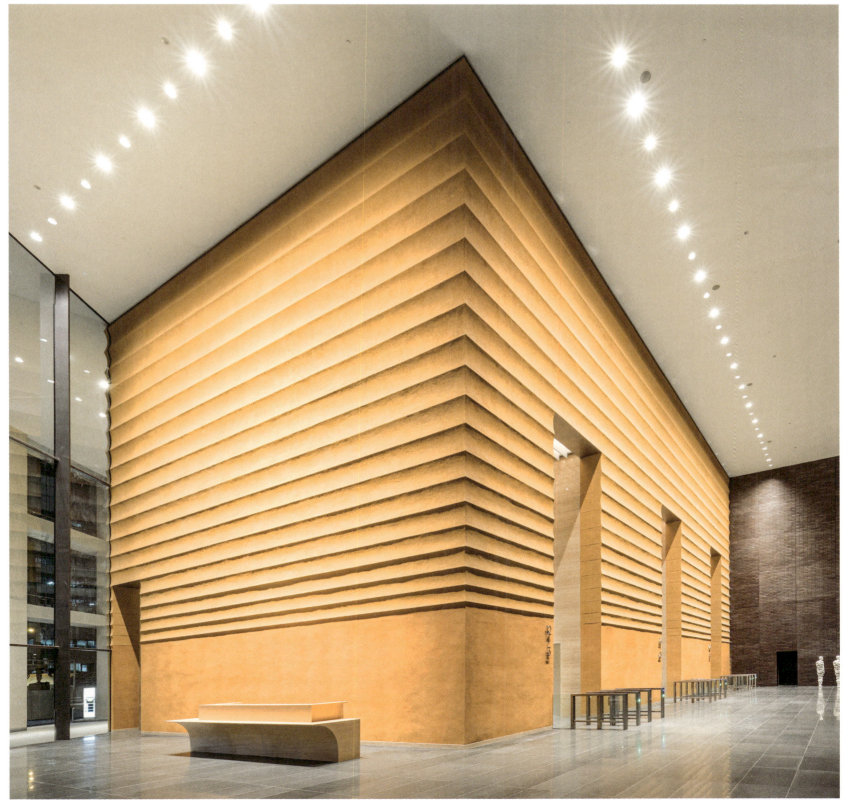

Contemporary Creativity: 1970 to the Present Day

Contemporary Art
Andy Goldsworthy
Richard Long
Robert Smithson
Mona Hatoum
Terunobu Fujimori

Many contemporary artworks have been inspired by earth. Two British artists in particular have been leading lights in this field. The works of Richard Long include circular murals made from soil from river banks. Several of these were made in France, including one in Bordeaux (**opposite, below**), and another in Paris, to accompany the 1989 exhibition *Les magiciens de la terre* (**below right**). The latter established a fascinating interplay with another artwork on the floor nearby, created on site by six Australian artists from the Aboriginal Yuendumu community, using sacred earth from their land. Juxtapositions of very different interpretations of the same natural material have led to the emergence of a progressive approach to the specificities and complementarities of global cultures. Andy Goldsworthy is another artist who makes earth murals that dry to form evocative motifs (**opposite, above**). Goldsworthy also produces land art: in *Lambton Worm* (1988), he arranged long, sinuous lines of earth along a disused railway track in the northeast of England (**above right**).

J.D.

Overleaf, above left: Japanese architect Terunobu Fujimori branched out into playful visual art in 2009 with his *Flying Mud Tea House*.

Overleaf, below left: In *Hanging Garden* (2008), Mona Hatoum stacked sacks of fertile earth planted with grass seeds. These eventually sprouted, transforming the work.

Overleaf, right: *Spiral Jetty*, created from gravel and earth in 1970 by Robert Smithson on the edge of the Great Salt Lake, Utah; it is considered a pioneering work in the field of land art.

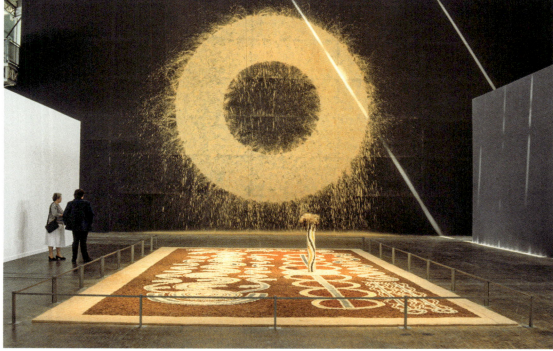

Contemporary Creativity: 1970 to the Present Day 463

Land Art
Hannsjörg Voth

Land art has two fundamental driving forces: firstly, the urge to break away from the institutional traditions of exhibiting and selling art (museums and galleries); and, secondly, the desire to establish a closer relationship with nature by making use of the locations, materials, and energy that it has to offer. This approach often focuses on plants and stones, but some practitioners of land art have also taken advantage of another local resource that would guarantee the longevity of their work: earth. Working within this tradition, the German artist Hannsjörg Voth (born 1940) has imbued his land art with an architectural dimension. This aspect has been heavily influenced by his time spent in Morocco; for two decades Voth spent six months of the year living there, on the edge of the Sahara. He established fruitful relationships with local artisans steeped in the ancient traditions of earth architecture, and with their collaboration he used rammed earth to build two striking pieces: *Stairway to Heaven* (*Himmelstreppe*, 1980–87) and *City of Orion* (*Stadt des Orion*, 1998–2003). The former (**opposite**) is an enormous 17-metre-high stairway of 52 steps, leading to an astronomical viewing platform, with a minimalist two-storey home occupying the space inside the structure. The latter (**above and below right**) is a representation of an ideal city, made up of high towers arranged in the pattern of the stars in the constellation of Orion, as described in the Mesopotamian epic of Gilgamesh. These rammed earth creations therefore establish a unique dialogue between the birthplace of earth architecture (in modern-day Iraq) and more contemporary uses of earth.

J.D.

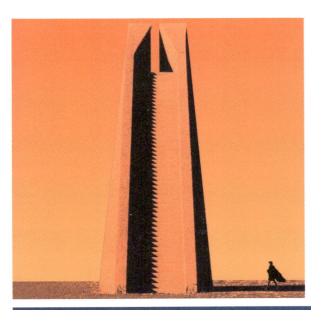
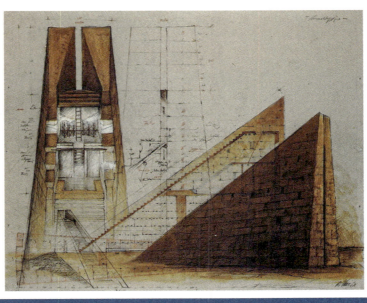

Contemporary Creativity: 1970 to the Present Day

Landscaping
The Netherlands

Apart from the wide range of architectural uses for earth, it has also played an important role in several innovative landscaping projects, some of which could be considered forms of land art. This symbiosis between the two disciplines is particularly evident in this striking intervention. Schiphol, to the south of Amsterdam, in the Netherlands, is one of the biggest airports in Europe, and as such is a significant source of noise pollution. To tackle this problem, H+N+S Landscape Architects joined forces with Paul de Kort, a land artist, to reconfigure the landscape between the runway and the homes affected by the noise. The team researched a variety of scientific phenomena including Chladni figures, the patterns of vibration created by sound waves. Eventually they designed a series of straight ridges of earth, 2 to 3 metres high, arranged in parallel lines (**right**). These earthworks were meticulously constructed and have proved successful in reducing the impact of aircraft noise. This inventive and socially relevant mixture of landscaping, science, urban planning, and land art involved considerable quantities of earth. The resulting site was named Buitenschot Land Art Park.

    J.D. & R.E.

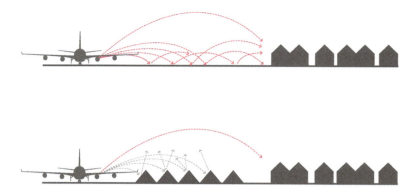

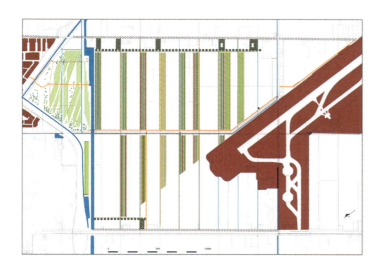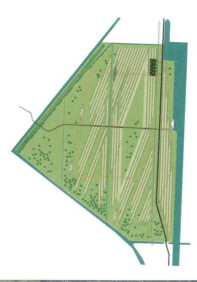

Landscaping
Great Britain

Several public and private gardens in Scotland feature striking earthworks created by American landscape artist and theoretician Charles Jencks (born 1939), who is also an advocate of postmodernist architecture. In the 1980s, he settled in the UK and turned his attention to landscaping. His most spectacular works include the grounds of the Scottish National Gallery of Modern Art in Edinburgh (*Landform*, 2002) and the 12-hectare Garden of Cosmic Speculation (1989–2007) in the grounds of his home in Dumfriesshire. The latter is a spatial transposition of his passion for cosmology, as well as an exploration and celebration of recent theories of complexity and chaos, using metaphors expressed through the landscape.

J.D. & R.E.

Right: Landscaped forms by Charles Jencks at Jupiter Artland (2003–2010), a contemporary sculpture garden outside Edinburgh, Scotland.

Chapter 7

Perspectives on the Future

Below: This large-scale project, on a 6-hectare brownfield site by the river in Ivry-sur-Seine, in the southern suburbs of Paris, is planned for construction in the 2020s. The innovative nature of this urban development stems from the economic, technological, and ecologically responsible choices that have guided its design, the breadth and diversity of its programme, and the skills of the team overseeing the project. Under the aegis of the real estate developer Quartus, the team includes Wang Shu (the 2012 Pritzker Prize winner) and Lu Wenyu, creators of the overall plan, as well as architects Lipsky & Rollet and Joly & Loiret. In 2015, the latter, with the aid of experts from CRAterre and Amàco, instigated a circular economy designed to reuse part of the enormous quantity of earth excavated from the urban subsoil during projects such as the digging of tunnels for the Grand Paris Express urban transit scheme. This valuable local resource, formerly ignored or treated as waste, will be turned into prefabricated *pisé* blocks, bricks, panels, and raw earth mortar, and used in the construction of a multi-use development covering some 50,000 square metres. It will include 350 housing blocks (40% of which will be public housing), accommodation for students and faculty, 20,000 square metres of offices and workshops, a hotel, urban allotments, and a centre for photographic art.

What is the Future of Earth Architecture?
Obstacles and Gains

Jean Dethier

All over the world, the practice of earth architecture has undergone a great many developments in recent years. Never before have so many innovations occurred in such a short space of time in the complementary fields of architecture and housing policy, engineering and scientific research, educational access and teaching skills, technology and culture. This creative ferment has given rise to possibilities beyond the wildest dreams of earlier generations. But what are the obstacles that may affect its future growth?

The Obstacles
- If earth architecture becomes more widespread, it could trigger a defensive reaction from lobbies promoting industrial building materials. Multinational corporations operating in this sector could become fearful of losing a portion of their market share and may adopt strategies to protect their interests, perhaps inspired by other powerful lobbies (e.g. the tobacco industry). These could include campaigns to discredit rivals and cast doubts on the validity of their scientific research and the legitimacy of their practice.
- The implementation of increasingly draconian regulations, often driven by technocratic interests, represents a real threat to the future of earth architecture.
- Politicians, who are often embroiled in the financial interests of heavy industry and only half-heartedly committed to ecological concerns, have myopically short-term vision and are instinctively suspicious of the benefits of earth architecture as an alternative approach.
- Furthermore, government policies that reward some sectors of industry with tax breaks already encourage the production of building materials that are incompatible with ecological transition, to the particular detriment of earth.
- Unlike other construction materials, earth has no pressure group on the international stage to promote its benefits and encourage its use.
- Educational institutions that train future architects, engineers, and artisans do not put sufficient emphasis on ecological issues or the specifics of earth architecture.
- The stabilization of earth with industrial additives such as cement reduces the ecological benefits of this natural material, even though the latest scientific research has demonstrated that this type of adulteration is not necessary and that similar effects can also be achieved with adjuvants from natural sources.
- When architects or designers use earth frivolously as a fashionable accessory, they detract from its ecological advantages.

The Gains
Despite these potential stumbling blocks, there are many positive factors that indicate an innovative dynamic in which earth architecture could thrive.

- In the 2010s, there has been a sea change within society, led by a new generation who are demanding ambitious ecological policy changes. This new movement is unequivocally criticising the inaction of political forces in this realm. Young people are determined to bring about the change that their elders had neither the foresight nor the courage to implement, and are developing new philosophies for living. These new ways of thinking and acting also challenge the paradigms of domestic architecture. Could this re-examination lead to a move towards the construction of cities, neighbourhoods, and homes that are genuinely ecologically responsible, by basing them on a healthy relationship with nature and natural materials?
- The considerable outreach of this new activism is largely the result of mobilization through social media. The internet has also allowed many aspiring builders to gather the information needed to construct their own homes with earth. This pragmatic dynamism, far removed from official channels, has given rise to a new informal economy.
- By 2015, there were signs that this circular economy was also being applied to earth architecture in urban contexts. Studies by CRAterre and Amàco have proved that much of the undersoil extracted for major construction projects in cities is compatible with the technical requirements of building with earth. Projects due to apply this innovative approach in

Paris and Brussels are scheduled for completion in the 2020s, indicating that the mistaken belief that this type of soil is useless for construction purposes has finally been banished. This situation represents not only a technical advance but also a conceptual revolution: earth is now no longer dismissed as a waste product but is instead valued as a resource.
- Other changes that have gradually taken hold in previous decades have led earth architecture to be seen in a more positive light, shedding many of the negative assumptions once associated with it. Nowadays, the benefits and unique features of earth arouse not only interest and curiosity but also enthusiasm.
- This trend is on the rise thanks to the increasing number of TV programmes, websites, books, and magazines that praise and promote earth architecture.
- Since the 1960s, several NGOs have successfully completed low-cost housing projects with raw earth in developing countries.
- The establishment of interprofessional networks has led to increased efficiency.
- There have been a growing number of meetings, seminars, and international congresses that have fomented the exchange of knowledge accumulated by both theoreticians and practitioners on the ground.
- An increasing number of internationally renowned architects have become involved in building with earth in Europe, Asia, and Africa.
- Since the dawn of the 21st century, hundreds of lesser-known architects and engineers have already created an impressive diversity of earth buildings, serving a wide range of functions.
- These buildings can now be found on every continent, in both rural and urban settings.
- This positive evolution is reflected in the number of earth buildings now listed as UNESCO World Heritage sites. Back in 1972, when the World Heritage scheme was created, the existence of this architectural legacy was largely unknown, but since then, the number of earthen sites included on this prestigious list has grown incrementally.
- In 1998, UNESCO set up a Chair on Earthen Architecture, Building Cultures and Sustainable Development, intended to fill any gaps in fields of study that had been previously overlooked. Since then, the Chair has been run by CRAterre at the Grenoble School of Architecture. It has trained almost a thousand specialists, who have subsequently passed on their knowledge in over a hundred countries.
- A growing number of universities and engineering schools are incorporating the specific subject of earth architecture into their curriculum, which represents a considerable investment in the future.
- This spirit of enquiry has provided the bedrock for scientific research that will be crucial to efforts to improve building techniques involving earth.
- The same research also gave rise, in 2001, to the creation of specialized professional training courses based on innovative and forward-looking teaching methods (see pp. 476–477).

This overview, albeit brief and non-exhaustive, shows that, despite the obstacles mentioned above, the gains that have been made in the last few decades are clearing the terrain for even more growth in the field of earth architecture. Recent advances have sometimes been so spectacular, however, that it is important to avoid interpreting them as a miracle solution. The methodologies of ecological construction, which have now grown to maturity, must continue to evolve through the input and passion of younger generations. This will allow earth architecture to become a key component in the ecological transformation that is now vital if we are to combat the increasing risks of climate change.

The Need for a Cultural and Educational Revolution

Patrice Doat

Promoting the universal right to build with raw earth is an enormous challenge. This vital freedom of action must be championed boldly and tenaciously. A radical approach is required to ensure that builders from future generations receive suitable training in its use. To make this transgressive philosophy a reality, a willing attitude must be developed in two spheres: active resistance against the ever-encroaching dominion of concrete, and defiance of the norms that impose this material on us. Such a far-reaching reappraisal of the world of building also implies a radical change in our approach to technical skills and the ways they are passed on. This ambition demands a true educational and cultural revolution. Theoretical teaching alone is insufficient: we must learn to think in a new way, in order to act and build in a new way. We must adopt a new educational paradigm based on lived experience, putting thought into action, and learning through experiment. Within the practice of this ethic, pleasure must play a role in making learning dynamic and attractive. Students must feel free to experiment without pressure or constraints and without fear of criticism, in order to fully explore the boundless construction potential of raw earth. Their imaginations should be free to create new concepts and applications that will stimulate their sense of invention. Experiments of this kind will help to foster a spirit of initiative and curiosity, so that the search for innovative solutions will be second nature once they start working professionally.

There is a glaring omission in the world of education: while construction with raw earth is still used extensively for housing all over the world, and has been for thousands of years, the field is rarely covered in universities or colleges, or even in architecture and engineering schools. Such widespread ignorance of the advantages of this ecological building material can no longer be tolerated. In fact, it effectively excludes a significant part of the world's population from high-quality housing. Furthermore, the culpable indifference on the part of so many architects, engineers, economists, and property developers has serious long-term consequences. It pushes builders to use and favour high-tech processes, pushing up energy costs to the detriment of local economies, job creation, and universal access to housing. It is therefore essential that all those involved in the construction industry receive a thorough professional training, complete with a qualification that recognizes their understanding of building with raw earth. This would allow the spread of contemporary forms of architecture that take full advantage of earth as an ecological building material. However, progress of this kind in not possible without a genuine cultural and educational revolution that questions the act of building itself, and its relationship with the necessary shift to renewable energy.

The negligible carbon footprint of raw earth makes it an ideal material that is more valuable than ever in the face of the environmental challenges ahead of us. Builders should now be guided by the maxim 'Do more and better with less.' Beyond the benefits of raw earth as an eco-material, we must take into account the societies of both tomorrow and today and the need to preserve and strengthen local architectural cultures. We must also promote a diverse range of building solutions that can be used in multiple contexts and on various scales. This requires an overhaul of our economic and social model, as well as a radical revision of the relationship between human beings and their environment.

Raw earth construction consumes very little grey energy and offers a sustainable solution for the future, as long as we understand that it demands not only an ecological way of building but a new way of living. Even now, in the early 21st century, building with raw earth is still a struggle. Huge determination is required to escape the constraints and overbearing rules imposed by the 'concrete above all' brigade. In this scenario, raw earth is a material that demands, in the words of Renzo Piano, the 'disobedience of the architect'. The spread of new production methods must be matched by a commitment to new working methods and a demonstration that raw earth adds an ethical dimension to the science of building. To quote Renzo Piano once again, 'a sublime stubbornness is needed to get things done'. The need for a social shift requires radical changes in human relationships and also between the various professions working together in the field of construction. The domination of engineering practices must be reconsidered, since it overrides the resources of creativity and imagination that are so necessary in architecture. Fortunately, however, raw earth constructions often display a deep understanding of materials. This type of progressive architecture, born from an ethic that combines humility with a spirit of resistance, restores meaning, dignity, and human value to the act of building.

Since the 1950s, there have been two conflicting philosophies in Europe regarding the supposed 'fragility' of raw earth. It is true that this material rarely passes the classic regulatory tests devised for concrete and other industrialized materials: compression, traction, durability, contraction, expansion, warping, freezing, thawing, etc. The technicians and engineers in testing labs view earth as part of the family of concrete aggregates. Accordingly, they try to make it sturdier and more resistant to their standard technical tests. They seek to 'stabilize' raw earth and improve its performance with additional processes and ingredients, such as lime and cement. This technocratic approach to the material, oblivious to its environmental context as a natural resource, undermines the normalization of its use. In contrast, builders accustomed to using raw earth approach the task more pragmatically, in the knowledge that evidence of its resistance and durability, when handled properly, can be found all over the world, stretching back thousands of years. The ancestral skill of generations of anonymous builders needs to be carefully re-examined as it provides a crucial foundation for a well-balanced appraisal of vernacular building practices. This traditional wisdom can be found in many parts of the world where earthen buildings have, for centuries, resisted storms, freezing, thawing, and even sometimes earthquakes. A realistic and functional approach would build in the architectural planning required to protect this inherently simple and vulnerable material. All raw earth architecture must take into account the relative fragility of its basic component while making the most of its advantages. 'Do more and better with less' has been the guiding ethic since the dawn of the 21st century for a new generation of talented, ecologically responsible builders that includes Wang Shu, Anna Heringer, Francis Kéré, Mariam Kamara, Martin Rauch, and many more. Their inspired and inspirational work is therefore featured heavily in this book.

Building with Earth in an Urban Context:
A Circular Economy for the Future

Hugo Gasnier

Every year, billions of tons of earth are extracted worldwide from building sites in large cities. This undervalued material represents an enormous potential resource for raw earth construction. Indeed, the challenges of energy transition are prompting research into the use of resources gathered sustainably in order to reduce the environmental impact of the construction industry. Earth seems to be the ideal material for this crucial transition, which demands a tectonic shift in the ways that we design and build our cities in order to encourage the reuse and recycling of materials. This approach requires ambitious policies designed to transform current practices, via training of the people involved and investment in the promotion of these resources.

The metropolis of Greater Paris, France, is home to 7.2 million inhabitants spread over 814 square kilometres (i.e. eight times the area of the city of Paris itself), and it is growing ever more dense. In total, its construction sites (for housing, shops, offices, and public transport infrastructure) generate 18 million tons of surplus earth every year. Furthermore, the construction of the new regional metro service, the Grand Paris Express, which began in 2016 and is due for completion in 2030, with its 200 kilometres of track and 68 brand-new stations, will require the extraction of a further 40 million tons of earth over a 10-year period. This earth is usually collected by specialist firms and then redistributed around the outskirts of the city. Some of it is taken to sites that separate out the aggregate that can be used as a base course for road building, but this process accounts for only a small proportion of the amount collected. Most of the earth is buried in some twenty landfill sites scattered across the outlying suburbs. This process fills vast tracts of land and disturbs the balance of the natural environments that provide the Paris region with food, water, and oxygen.

The use of this surplus earth for construction would have three advantages. First, its transformation into building material would counteract the negative ecological impact of treating it as landfill. Second, it would allow the production of healthy, natural materials with a small carbon footprint. Finally, it would reduce the dependence of Greater Paris on resources such as sand and gravel, which are growing rarer and have to be extracted ever farther afield. Since 2014, various strategies have been implemented in the Paris area to make use of this surplus earth. These could be used as political impetus to boost raw earth construction. An innovation of this magnitude would open up new horizons in city planning, bringing together two fields that have hitherto been separate: those engaged in urban planning for a changing metropolis, and those who understand the art of earth architecture, which is also in the throes of a major revival.

One fruit of this innovative approach is the ambitious project that won the 'Reinventing the Seine' competition in 2016. Situated in Ivry-sur-Seine, 2 kilometres to the southeast of Paris, it is due for completion in 2022 by the architectural firms Joly & Loiret and Lipsky & Rollet, in collaboration with the husband-and-wife team of Wang Shu (winner of the 2012 Pritzker Prize) and Lu Wenyu for city planning, and the property developer Quartus for financial backing. This pilot neighbourhood, spread over more than 2 hectares alongside the river, will be mixed use, combining 21,000 square metres of housing with 50,000 square metres of complementary facilities: offices, shops, hotels, cultural venues, sports centres, etc. This project will be the first of its kind in a major metropolis to demonstrate the advantages (environmental and otherwise) of using raw earth taken from its own subsoil.

In 2015, CRAterre analysed samples of earth taken from the subsoil of the Paris region. The results of the study recognized its potential as a construction material, which was further confirmed by the production of an initial series of 20,000 raw earth blocks.

Since 2010, strategies designed to make use of urban subsoil in construction projects have been launched elsewhere in Europe: in Geneva, Switzerland, via Terrabloc; and in Brussels, Belgium, via the cooperative BC Materials. Another French city, Rennes, is also the epicentre of a region dotted with traditional cob homes.

All of these recent initiatives reflect an ongoing ecological, political, and technological revolution that aims to develop new building strategies for cities by exploiting the vast wealth of the earth on which they stand. We are also witnessing the dawn of an urban revolution structured around a form of circular economy designed to transform 'waste' into an ecological building material, thereby paving the way for ecologically responsible architecture.

One of the streets in the urban neighbourhood due for construction in the early 2020s in Ivry-sur-Seine, near Paris, by the property development company Quartus (see pp. 472–473). The facades of the small housing blocks will feature a combination of prefabricated rammed earth and raw earth bricks. Architects: Joly & Loiret.

Perspectives on the Future

The Future of Earth Architecture
Six Viewpoints

The Housing Crisis in India and the Developing World: The Urgent Need for Raw Earth Architecture

S. K. Sharma*

As well as feeding its population, the developing world is faced with another major issue: its great need for public housing. In India, which has over a billion inhabitants, this glaring deficit has been calculated at more than 40 million homes, with 30 million of them in the countryside and the rest on the outskirts of cities. Africa also needs to build around 40 million homes for its poorer citizens. In India, 80%–90% of the rural population and 30%–40% of the urban population live in traditional raw earth dwellings. Given that a considerable proportion of the population is already living in homes of this kind, it is totally inappropriate to reject raw earth simply because the elite deems it outdated. On the contrary, this objective reality should make us aware that raw earth as a material is still used, still needed, and still relevant when producing cost-effective housing for tens of millions of people.

Raw earth construction must be integrated into our planning and development processes. Both government agencies and professionals must take responsibility for this change of focus and its practical application. As long as it continues to respond to the needs and lifestyles of its users, earth architecture will clearly seem more suitable than the options offered by industrial technologies. Used as a building material across the globe since time immemorial, earth has now become an object of new interest and is being incorporated into modernized building practices all over the world. It is vital to recognize this progressive evolution when formulating alternative strategies for public housing. It also requires the establishment of new institutional structures, new means of intervention, and new policies for action. More broadly, the suitability of traditional construction techniques and the benefits of natural materials such as earth need to be re-evaluated without negative assumptions.

Over the last few decades, the majority of traditional techniques – despite their efficiency and sustainability – have been ignored or disparaged by planners and architects. Many of the latter wrongly view earth architecture as a symbol of 'primitive' cultures. But within this crucial debate, with its social, cultural, technological, and economic implications, which arguments are fair and realistic, and which are incorrect? Who is guilty of arrogance and inefficiency here?

The importing of industrial rationalism and the architectural dogmas of a self-proclaimed 'International Style' from the West to the developing world, including India, has proved to be a less than useful response to the challenges of building low-cost housing for the masses. These doctrines – with all the industrialized materials and building philosophies that they imply – are not well suited to the specialized demands and limited financial resources of these countries. We must rediscover, re-evaluate, modernize, and disseminate valuable folk and vernacular wisdom so that its treasures are not irretrievably lost.

Among the natural local materials that are characteristic of these ancient traditions, earth should make a vital contribution to the rethinking of modernity in India, particularly in the light of new environmental concerns. This would mirror the experience of European countries in the 1970s and 1980s, when the ecological benefits of raw earth were rediscovered and its use was reintroduced, most notably in pilot programmes

The building of a raw earth vault on a construction site in India, overseen by the Auroville Earth Institute (see pages 384–385).

for public housing. India is not the only country that needs to create new earth architecture. This is a worldwide challenge, and it has begun to give rise to a new generation of thinkers and decision-makers, architects and builders. In India, the shift towards eco-construction with earth would also boost the so-called informal economy, whose importance is all too often overlooked by both technocrats and analysts. It is vital to redefine raw earth as a suitable bedrock for a forward-looking technological and cultural housing strategy. Doing so would also be an appropriate response to the new demands of sustainable development.

* Engineer and chairman of HUDCO (Housing and Urban Development Corporation), India

Text adapted by Jean Dethier

Vital Innovations in Raw Earth Architecture

Martin Rauch

For ten years I have lived in a three-storey house with load-bearing walls made of rammed earth. Every day I experience the advantages of this type of building through the quality of life it gives me. The solidity of the earth gives a sense of security. It has a balancing effect on interior temperature and humidity and its raw presence creates a feeling of ancient tradition. From the outside, the house sits discreetly within its natural and sociocultural environment. The earth, which was the residue of levelling work on the site, was rammed *in situ*, layer by layer. The colour of the local earth and the way the facade reacts to inclement weather add a sense of familiarity. If the building's function ever changed, the same material could be reused to produce a new structure on the same plot of land.

Building with earth requires a rigorous analysis of the material's properties, which are specific to each site. As with other projects that I have undertaken with my practice, Lehm Ton Erde, decisions about the structure and its details – from the geological composition of the chosen earth to the building's physical appearance – allowed us to move deeper into unexplored territory, considering chemical properties, the development of new tools, techniques, and finishes. But of course, because I was building my own home, the energy invested into researching construction processes became even more intense.

It is said that a third of the human race still lives in earth houses, but sadly this figure is falling day by day. If everybody lived in housing typical of industrialized countries, three planet Earths would barely be sufficient to provide all the materials necessary. In further industrializing construction worldwide, we are going down the wrong path. I am convinced that in three generations' time, half of humanity will be living in comfortable earth buildings. But to get to this stage, we need a global cost analysis that accurately factors in all the economic and social aspects of building materials.

It is not enough to talk and write about sustainable development and local resources; we must put these ideas into practice. We must make the unrivalled recyclability of earth buildings into a tangible advantage. Instead of contaminating clay with additives like cement or other chemical products, we must develop new tools and construction methods. In order to innovate, we must seek a suitable architectural language, with the aim of creating large-scale buildings from load-bearing earth, using forms suited to the properties of the material. An essential element of this approach is an acceptance of the calculated erosion of facades. To achieve this, long-term confidence must be re-established in techniques such as *pisé*, cob, and adobe, and it must be understood that a building's appearance will change over time. This will require the wide-scale training of raw earth specialists in all fields of construction.

In the absence of economic lobbying in favour of earth architecture, a political will is needed to promote research and development in this field. Initiatives are also required to spread expertise. The objective is to create a body of rules that can be continuously updated, making innovation easier than it is under the current stifling and overly rigid directives.

We are heirs to an historical legacy of earth buildings that range from the everyday to the spectacular. Western society may be prospering but it is faced with the challenge of proving that it can continue to do so. As the primary culprit behind the environmental crisis, it has a duty to aid in developing more eco-friendly construction methods. If the wealthy populations of industrialized countries can produce beautiful, comfortable buildings made of earth, then people in developing countries will be encouraged to follow suit. In this way, they will reconnect with their ancient skills and identities and will be empowered to create contemporary versions of raw earth architecture.

Better Living through Earth Architecture

Anna Heringer

Imagine a material:
 …that creates a healthy climate inside buildings.
 …that does not produce toxic emissions and creates a natural moisture balance.
 …that creates jobs, even for the unskilled.
 …that does not create CO_2 emissions during production.
 …that can be recycled without losing its advantages.
 …that can, at the end of its working life, be used to grow flowers or vegetables.

A material that is beneficial for human beings, for society, and for the planet. This material does not need to be invented. It is raw earth.

We can use it with no fear of long-term negative effects, as its virtues have been demonstrated all over the world for thousands of years. In the last few decades, however, the number of people living in earth houses has dropped. As soon as their finances allow, many residents of developing countries turn towards industrial materials such as concrete, baked clay bricks, and cement-stabilized earth blocks. Why? Because earth has the image of a flimsy material, a material for the poor. This image must be changed if we are to increase the quantity of raw earth constructions in order to safeguard our planet and its inhabitants.

We need demonstrations of the great beauty of earth architecture, the cultural wisdom embedded within this ancient building material, and the host of possible interpretations that it offers.

Earth is different in every area but it is always vulnerable to rain and bad weather. There are two ways to respond to this relative fragility: changing the material chemically or protecting it constructively.

Modifying the chemical composition of earth with stabilizers has many side effects. The addition of cement pushes up costs and, furthermore, its manufacturing process contributes to climate change. Stabilized earth does not create a balance of humidity inside a building, it cannot be recycled without a loss of quality, and it is more difficult to repair in the event of potential faults.

Although vulnerability is a natural phenomenon, our society tends to see it as something to fight against. If we are to build in a truly eco-responsible way, we must accept vulnerability, and even celebrate it. We must trust in this wonderful material by accepting it just as it is.

My work is deeply rooted in the characteristics of the local climate, the specific qualities of the soil (how stony it is, etc.), and the adapted building techniques I choose to use (cob, rammed earth, etc.) These are my sources of inspiration. With this as my starting point, every project quite naturally becomes unique and authentic.

Architecture should reinforce people's cultural identity and self-confidence, while sustaining the local economy and promoting ecological balance. Beauty is not a privilege of the rich. Aesthetic and ethical value are both defined by harmony between design, structure, technique, and use of materials.

All we need to do is rely on our own creativity, dreaming up houses and workplaces, villages and cities that are not only healthy and sustainable but also beautiful and human. My motivation is to design and erect buildings that make people happy.

Architecture is a tool to make life better!

The Philosophy and Future Strategies of CRAterre

Sébastien Moriset
in collaboration with Bakonirina Rakotomamonjy

Since its founding in 1979, CRAterre has spent more than forty years indefatigably championing the use of raw earth, a natural building material whose many benefits have been known to mankind for over 10,000 years. This local resource has made it possible to fight against poverty and cultural alienation by increasing the independence and self-sufficiency of individual communities. Our team seeks to expand and deepen this ethical commitment by passing on knowledge, skills, and principles of participatory governance that allow societies to plan their own future while also strengthening their cultural heritage. More than forty years of practice and research on the characteristics and techniques of building cultures all over the world (in 102 countries, to be exact) have convinced us of a self-evident but often overlooked truth: only a collective intelligence combined with an intimate knowledge of a region can create architecture that simultaneously improves lives, respects local cultural identities, and protects natural resources. In order to make knowledge about regional building cultures available to as many people as possible, CRAterre has developed a programme, in France and elsewhere, based around four axes: groundwork, research, training, and dissemination.

Groundwork
Through groundwork, we aim to challenge and adapt our preconceptions to fit local realities and deepen our skills by spending time with a community. This approach is also supported by on-site training programmes, which provide stimulating forums for debate. We adopt a humble and respectful attitude towards the members of a community and collaborate with them to find creative solutions that match their specific social context.

Research
Our research involves an in-depth analysis of each local building culture, undertaken in close collaboration with the local population, in order to discover the best that it has to offer, drawing from centuries of common sense, wisdom, and practical skill. It also takes into consideration the macro-territorial and architectural factors of scale (the physical and conceptual aspects of housing), as well as micro-territorial aspects such as locally available natural materials. In this way, we are able to pay tribute to local building cultures, and use them as true sources of inspiration for contemporary architecture.

Training
The training that we provide, at all levels and for all audiences, is an essential element of our work. It is vital for conveying our message across the world, particularly via the network of universities and educational bodies that are our partners in the UNESCO Chair in Earthen Architecture, Building Cultures and Sustainable Development, which we have run since 1998. Students who complete our programme are awarded a specialist diploma from the Grenoble School of Architecture. This training also provides a platform for exchange and debate that brings together researchers and teachers from different generations and disciplines. We also support the development of similar training programmes on other continents.

Dissemination
Raw earth is a natural and ecological material that is gaining ground in the field of construction, and the general public is becoming increasingly aware of its benefits. We seek to further this process by sharing our knowledge, particularly among professionals in the construction sector, and by taking advantage of new technologies and the collective intelligence of the many networks that are being formed every day, in order to strive for a better future.

The Philosophy and Vision of the Auroville Earth Institute

Lara K. Davis

It may seem surprising that earth architecture has not been more widely embraced in India, despite the recognition of its value as a means for building sustainable low-cost housing. It has not, for example, been incorporated into Pradhan Mantri Awas Yojana, a government project to construct 20 million affordable homes by 2022. Only the threat of climate change, which is already affecting the Indian regions with the greatest extremes of climate, and creative social solutions may be able reverse the status quo in the world's third largest – and most rapidly growing – carbon economy.

Bold policies are needed to speed up cultural change. Although they are supported by relevant data on demographic growth, the poverty index, and high housing costs, the quantitative arguments in favour of earth architecture remain misunderstood. Transfers of technology and changes of scale have proved insufficient. The same is true of the development of technology allowing the poor to aspire to the same architecture as the more affluent. Even when we acknowledge the real successes that have been achieved, there is still a need to move away from well-beaten paths and embrace models of collective social creation and empowerment.

We should take advantage of the long history of self-building in Indian villages by documenting the last surviving vernacular practices before they disappear completely. The country's varying climate and geophysical constraints have given rise to rich building cultures that display a remarkable capacity to adapt earth to suit local requirements – not only weather conditions but also natural resources, cultural values, and budgetary concerns. Modern India has developed so rapidly, however, that vernacular practices have not had time to catch up. Nevertheless, it is still possible to create new hybrid processes that can fulfil the needs of both the local population and outside decision-makers. This could spark an upsurge in traditional, small-scale building methods, practised by new artisans in a 'new vernacular'.

The Auroville Earth Institute (AVEI) forms part of an extensive network of influential building specialists in India that also includes COSTFORD, the Dharmalaya Institute, IISc Bangalore, and Biome. The primary mission of the AVEI is to revitalize the skills associated with earth construction by bringing together vernacular traditions and the modern technology of stabilized earth. It actively promotes research and development as well as spreading the word about earth architecture through publications and other means. Furthermore, for thirty years it has been organizing training programmes in house construction, using inexpensive, proven techniques that leave only a very small carbon footprint. The growing demand for eco-design that suits available resources and climate conditions is encouraging new generations of both self-builders and professionals to expand their skills through practical experience. A new culture of raw earth construction is beginning to emerge.

There is a huge demand for training in this field. More architects, engineers, and – above all – builders must be trained, and trained over longer periods. The AVEI aims to build on its already considerable achievements and raise public awareness, while extending its research and training programmes in order to influence multiple sectors of Indian society and the world at large. The AVEI has rejected the prevailing paradigm of courses for architects, engineers, and artisans by offering long-term continuous training. Its philosophy is based on creative, cross-curricular training for craftspeople that includes building materials and techniques from across the vernacular, historical, and contemporary domains. The school encourages a culture of creative solutions for real-world challenges, producing measurable results. It stresses the importance of adapting architectural concepts to match climate, ecology, culture, and people. The vernacular is one of the cornerstones of this approach, serving as an encyclopaedia, a living laboratory of local eco-conscious design. By examining sustainability issues in greater depth, this initiative is enabling a great leap forward for the younger generation of architects and builders. Solutions must spring from local cultures and communities if they are to give people the power to reimagine and reconstruct their own built environments.

An Ancient Material for Building the Future

Dominique Gauzin-Müller

For thousands of years, basic construction materials (earth, stone, wood, etc.) were difficult to transform and transport. The builders of vernacular dwellings and monuments therefore had to react instinctively to the limits imposed by their own particular geographical reality. It was the Industrial Revolution that turned this centuries-old balance upside down.

In the early 20th century, the architects of the modernist movement tried to resolve the problems of their age with the knowledge and resources at their disposal. The overriding issue at that time was the mass exodus of rural populations to cities (and their factories) in search of work. Concrete, which made use of the form panels invented in around 1800 by François Cointeraux for use in rammed earth buildings, seemed to be a miracle material. Who would have imagined that in just a few decades, concrete would come to play such a major role in global warming, pollution, and the depletion of natural resources?

Nowadays, the construction sector is responsible for around 40% of the world's consumption of energy and natural resources, 40% of its waste products, and 40% of its greenhouse gas emissions. Our task is to resolve the environmental crisis without creating new problems for the coming generations. The first step is to forswear environmental megalomania and stop plundering soils, raw materials, water, and energy sources. An ecologically responsible approach must focus on our real needs and give our actions meaning. Along with wood and fast-growing fibres (straw, hemp, bamboo, etc.), earth is one of the materials that possesses the necessary frugality and creative potential required to guarantee our survival on a planet with finite resources whose human population has multiplied by four over the last century.

Contemporary architecture in *pisé*, adobe, cob, wattle and daub, and compressed earth bricks is no longer confined to the fringes. There are several reasons for this upswing. The rediscovery of earth architecture's remarkable heritage and the spread of scientific understanding of granular materials have laid the foundations for this renaissance. Earth is abundant not only in rural areas but also in urban settings, as a byproduct of building excavations. While sand is becoming harder to find, the ready availability of earth, combined with new legal obligations to recycle waste, has aroused the interest of local authorities and major corporations alike. International commitments to reduce global warming have forced world leaders to look for viable solutions. The risks associated with environmental damage have tipped public opinion towards healthy materials derived from the circular economy, and this trend has been further encouraged by countless publications and exhibitions. All around the world, an ever-increasing number of builders, architects, engineers, researchers, artisans, and business people are making an active commitment to this field.

True environmental responsibility means using the right materials in the right quantities in the right place. Earth architecture is making a significant contribution to this crucial ecological and social shift.

Opposite: Domes built from raw earth blocks, supported by an elegant concrete structure, in the central mosque of the village of Dandaji, Niger, built in 2018. Architects: Mariam Kamara (founder of Atelier Masomi in Niger in 2014) and Yasaman Esmaili (founder of Studio Chahar in Iran). See pp. 490–491.

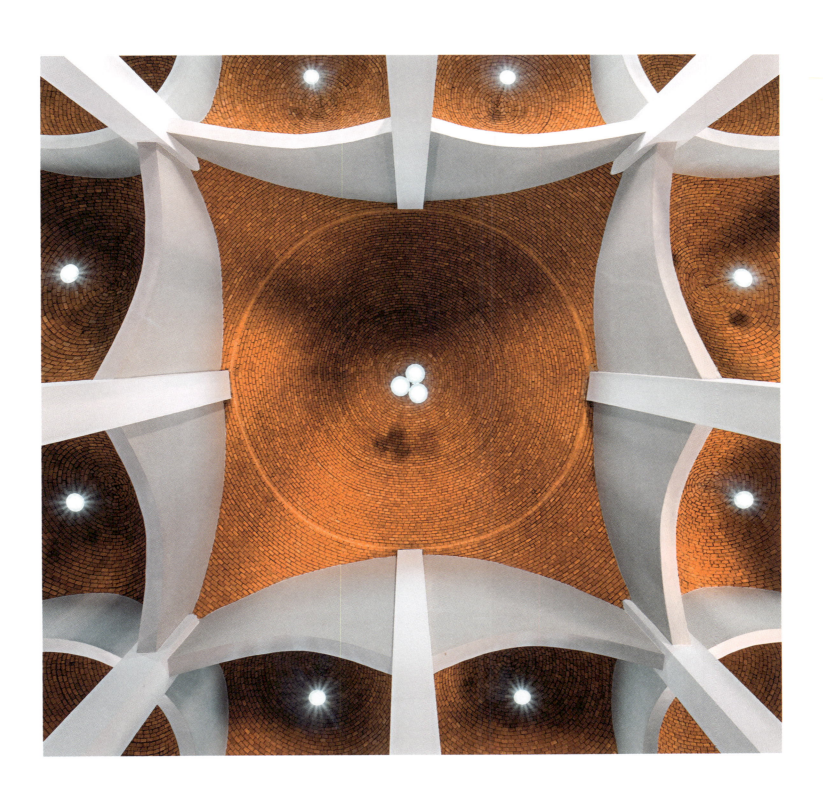

Warnings for the Future
Ron Cobb
Luc Schuiten

"Quand le dernier arbre sera abattu, la dernière rivière empoisonnée, le dernier poisson capturé, alors vous découvrirez que l'argent ne se mange pas." proverbe amérindien.

Left and opposite, above: Cartoons by Ron Cobb.

Opposite, below: 'When the last tree has been cut down, the last river poisoned, the last fish caught, you will discover that you cannot eat money.' Native American proverb. Cartoon by Luc Schuiten.

Below: 'I am the one omnipresent God. I am the fuel of all things, but soon I shall no longer be among you.' Cartoon by Luc Schuiten.

Perspectives on the Future

Conclusion

To conclude this international panorama of earth architecture, the image below is a union of the traditional and the contemporary. It shows the two primary elements of the Hikma complex, established in 2018 as a community hub for the village of Dandaji in Niger. This exemplary project is the work of award-winning architects Mariam Kamara and Yasaman Esmaili. In the field of African architecture, the talents of Mariam Kamara shine out as a powerful and encouraging sign of the emergence of a new generation of builders – now including young women – who are eagerly working and campaigning to promote a contemporary form of earth architecture that cleverly reconciles tradition and modernity without copying Western models. The long-awaited rise of this dynamic promises a thriving cultural and ethical legacy for the work of the African pioneers of earlier generations: Hassan Fathy, Elie Mouyal, and Francis Kéré.

J.D.

Below: On the left is the old mosque, built by the master mason El Hadji Falké Barmou (see his portrait on p. 43). He is one of the few artisans to have won the prestigious Aga Khan Architecture Award (awarded in 1986 for the raw earth Yaama Mosque, built in 1982 in Tahoua, Niger). Recently deconsecrated, the old mosque has been converted into a vibrant public library (see p. 444). On the right is the new mosque (see its interior on p. 487). The dialogue established between these two styles of earth architecture is of an exceptionally high quality.

About the Authors

Jean Dethier

Belgian-born Jean Dethier trained as an architect and city planner, but since the 1970s he has given priority to his work as a cultural mediator. He spent three decades curating exhibitions at the Centre Pompidou in Paris, and co-authored the books that accompanied them.

The Centre Pompidou is the only major museum of modern and contemporary art in Europe to have a department devoted to the art of building. It seeks to promote a form of architectural and urban culture that extends beyond specialist circles, in a democratic spirit that appeals to the general public, students, and the media. Dethier curated more than twenty exhibitions along these innovative lines, three of which won international acclaim by exploring previously ignored transdisciplinary subjects. The first charted the history of railway stations as a mirror of the epic global story of rail travel, while another examined the historical evolution of 'living bridges', seen as a fusion between engineering, architecture, and city planning. In 1981, Dethier curated an exhibition on earth architecture, which became a lasting passion that has marked the rest of his career.

1968: Co-director of the restoration project on the earthen *ksar* (village) of Tissergate, in the pre-Saharan Draa Valley in Morocco. **1979–1981:** Curates the exhibition *Des architectures de terre* at the Centre Pompidou, which recreated buildings from fifteen countries. This show was the first to survey global vernacular traditions in earth architecture and their modern adaptations, as well as advocating the continued use of earth as a natural building material. This pioneering, proselytizing spirit, along with the exhibition's extended lifespan of 16 years (at 24 venues on four continents), attracted three million visitors. The exhibition catalogue was translated into nine languages. **1981–1985:** Campaigned for construction of the experimental neighbourhood of the Domaine de la Terre, in Villefontaine, France. The exhibition *Des architectures de terre* was always intended to be coupled with a demonstration of the practicality and realism of its underlying ideas. The transition from theory to practice was made via the construction of this urban neighbourhood, containing 65 public housing units. CRAterre was heavily involved in the concept for the project and oversaw its technical details. In 2008, the Domaine de la Terre was classified by the Rhône-Alpes region as an 'exemplary display of sustainable development' and it is now recognized as having played a key role in the renaissance of earth architecture in Europe. **1987:** Wins the French Grand Prix of Architecture, in recognition of his achievements in 'democratizing the culture of architecture'. Dethier was also made a Chevalier des Arts et des Lettres by the French Minister of Culture, Jack Lang. **1988:** Co-authors the article 'Earth: architecture and ecological building material' for *Encyclopaedia Universalis*. **2002:** Curates an exhibition on raw earth mosques in Mali, with photographs by Sebastian Schütyser, at the Maison Européenne de la Photographie, Paris. **2013:** Co-founds the French National Prize for Earth Architecture, along with Dominique Gauzin-Müller and Patrice Doat. **2016:** Serves on the jury for the TERRA Award, an international prize for contemporary earth architecture, launched in 2000.

Text by Ruth Eaton

The Scientific Committee

From left to right: Jean Dethier and Patrice Doat; Hugo Houben; Hubert Guillaud.

A committee made up of the three co-founders of CRAterre was made responsible for checking the readability and relevance of this book, overseeing the expert contributions, writing a number of the essays, and reading all of the texts.

Patrice Doat

Architect. Professor Emeritus of Science and Technology in Architecture, co-founder of CRAterre and the Grands Ateliers. Author, in 1972, of the first scientific and technical handbook of earth architecture. In 1998, in conjunction with ENSAG in Grenoble, he launched the UNESCO Chair on Earthen Architecture, Building Cultures and Sustainable Development, designed to facilitate training and education in these subjects. In his quest to train architects in the realities of working with earth, Doat devised an original teaching programme based around practical workshops. This innovative approach, which sparks a desire to learn and a joy in understanding, led in 2001 to the founding of the Grands Ateliers, an educational space for production and experimentation. He also created the Grains d'Isère festival, a meeting point for scientific and technical exchange, open to all. He developed workshops for prototypes of affordable housing and a research centre for building materials (Amàco), under the auspices of the Grands Ateliers. Doat was made a Chevalier des Arts et des Lettres in 2009, and was awarded a medal for research and technique by the Académie d'Architecture in 2014 and a Global Award for Sustainable Architecture by the Locus Foundation and the Cité de l'Architecture et du Patrimoine in Paris in 2016.

Hubert Guillaud

Architect. Honorary professor of Science and Technology in Architecture at the École Nationale Supérieure d'Architecture de Grenoble (ENSAG). He discovered earth architecture on a trip to the United States (New Mexico, Arizona, California) in 1976, while still a student. There, he came into contact with the counterculture and visited solar adobe housing projects in Albuquerque and Santa Fe, as well as Indian pueblos in Taos, Acoma, and Isleta. Guillaud's thesis provided the first comprehensive list of extant earth architecture in rural and urban France. In 1984, he co-founded a specialist training course in earth architecture, culminating in the DSA Terre diploma. This course covers the history of vernacular building cultures and earthen habitats, as well as architectural conservation. In 1986, he co-founded the CRAterre-ENSAG research lab and was responsible for its scientific programme for many years. His many publications include Traité de construction en terre (which he co-authored). He has also taught earth construction in Nigeria, Cuba, Iran, and Peru. As a UNESCO World Heritage expert, he has helped to evaluate sites in Chogha Zanbil and Bam (Iran), and Bahla (Oman). He was formerly head of the UNESCO Chair on Earthen Architecture, Building Cultures and Sustainable Development and helped to develop its international network. He is also a committee member of ICOMOS-ISCEAH and the Proterra network.

Hugo Houben

Engineer and physicist. Research engineer at ENSAG. Co-founcer of CRAterre, after participating in the revival of earth construction in Algeria in the early 1970s. Co-author of Traité de construction en terre. He took part in establishing the DSA Terre diploma and the UNESCO Chair on Earthen Architecture, Building Cultures and Sustainable Development. In 1989, in collaboration with ICCROM in Rome and later the Getty Conservation Institute in Los Angeles, Houben launched the Gaia and Terra projects, which gave rise in the same year to international courses on the preservation of earthen architectural heritage (PAT courses). He has chaired the committee on CEB (compressed earth blocks) at RILEM (International Union of Laboratories and Experts in Construction Materials, Systems and Structures) and CIB (International Council for Building), which drew up a series of regulations in collaboration with ARSO (African Organisation for Standardisation), which were adopted by 21 African countries. Houben is also a consultant for several international organizations, including UN-Habitat, UNDP, UNIDO, the World Bank, and the European Union. He has developed a research programme on the physics of earth as a building material (Grains de Bâtisseurs), in collaboration with the Grands Ateliers and Amàco (both of which he co-founded).

Contributing Authors

To complement the texts written by Jean Dethier and the members of the scientific committee, ten experts were asked to contribute interdisciplinary views, and four more were asked to summarize their visions of the future. Two architects have also provided technical drawings.

Romain ANGER Engineer and academic, specializing in raw earth architecture. Co-author of the book *Bâtir en terre* (2009) and co-curator of the exhibitions *Ma Terre Première* (2009) and *Terres de Paris* (2016). He is the joint head of the Matter and Materials department at CRAterre-ENSAG. Since 2012, he has been educational and scientific director of Amàco.

Anne-Monique BARDAGOT Doctor of ethnology, teacher at ENSAG until 2017, focusing on inhabited space, qualities of use, and urban policy. Research associate with CRAterre.

Arthur BESNARD Qualified as an architect in 2017 at the École Nationale Supérieure d'Architecture de Paris-Belleville. His interest in earth architecture was sparked by studying the work of Hassan Fathy and continues via his kind contribution to this book, for which he created and coloured sixty architectural drawings.

Lara K. DAVIS Holder of a master's degree in architecture from the School of Architecture and Planning at MIT. Co-director of the Auroville Earth Institute (India), a resource centre that is part of the UNESCO Chair on Earthen Architecture, Building Cultures and Sustainable Development.

Ruth EATON Historian. Author of the book *Ideal Cities* (Thames & Hudson, 2000). Historical researcher for the exhibition *Des architectures de terre* (Centre Pompidou, Paris, 1981) and other architecture exhibitions in London (RAA), Paris (BNF), Barcelona (CCCB), New York (NYPL), Tokyo (MOT), and Frankfurt (DAM).

David GANDREAU Archaeologist, doctor of architecture, associate teacher at ENSAG, and researcher at CRAterre. Expert in Central Asia at UNESCO World Heritage Centre. Joint head of the UNESCO Chair on Earthen Architecture, Building Cultures and Sustainable Development since 2018.

Hugo GASNIER Doctor of architecture, research associate at CRAterre. As a technological specialist, he has developed a research programme on the use of earth excavated from major urban construction projects in order to build sustainable cities.

Dominique GAUZIN-MÜLLER Architect and researcher. Honorary associate professor of the UNESCO Chair on Earthen Architecture, Building Cultures and Sustainable Development. Founder and coordinator of the TERRA Award. Author of the book *Architecture en terre d'aujourd'hui* (2017) and curator of the tie-in touring exhibition.

Jean-Claude GOLVIN Architect with doctorate in history. Specialist in the architectural restoration of archaeological sites. Former head of research at the CNRS. Former director of both the Karnak Franco-Egyptian Center (CFEETK) and the Archaeological Mission in Tunisia. Author of many scientific papers and books.

Anna HERINGER She sums up her philosophy with the motto: 'Architecture is a tool for improving lives.' This approach is reflected in the various projects that she has undertaken in Asia, Africa, and Europe, which have won accolades including the Aga Khan Award and the Global Award for Sustainable Architecture.

Sébastien MORISET Architect and researcher at CRAterre. Specialist in the conservation of earth architecture. Expert on African countries at UNESCO World Heritage Centre. Recipient of a DSA Terre postgraduate diploma from ENSAG.

Bakonirina RAKOTOMAMONJY Architect and researcher at ENSAG. Educational coordinator of the DSA Terre programme. Head of the UNITWIN network for the UNESCO Chair on Earthen Architecture, Building Cultures and Sustainable Development. President of CRAterre. Member of the executive board of the international committee of ICOMOS-ISCEAH.

Martin RAUCH Specialist in building with rammed earth since 1984. In 1999, in his native Austria, he founded the company Lehm Ton Erde, which has been responsible for many pioneering buildings in Austria, Germany, and Switzerland, as well as outside Europe. Rauch has developed new techniques for prefabricating rammed earth elements without the use of cement. He is an honorary professor of the UNESCO Chair on Earthen Architecture, Building Cultures and Sustainable Development.

Nathalie SABATIER Doctor of ethnology and research associate at CRAterre. As a result of the Grains de Bâtisseurs project, she developed the ElemenTerre educational kit, which is designed to encourage a playful exploration of the scientific properties of earth as a building material.

Henri VAN DAMME Physicist and chemist, specializing in soft materials. Professor at ESPCI Paris and Massachusetts Institute of Technology (MIT). Scientific director of the central laboratory at the École des Ponts ParisTech and IFSTTAR. He helped to develop CRAterre's Grains de Bâtisseurs project.

Ariane WILSON Architect and historian, teacher at the École Nationale Supérieure d'Architecture de Paris-Malaquais. Her research and publications are largely focused on the cultural, symbolic, and political dimension of the use of materials – including raw earth – in the history of architecture.

Glossary of Institutions & Abbreviations

AE&CC: Architecture, Environment et Cultures Constructives Research unit at ENSAG, divided into two complementary laboratories: CRAterre and Cultures Constructives.

Amàco: Atelier Matières à Construire Sister organization of CRAterre, dedicated to research, training, and experimentation with raw materials, including earth, as well as biosourced and geosourced materials. Based at the Grands Ateliers in Villefontaine, France.

CNRS: Centre National de la Recherche Scientifique French national scientific research centre, founded in 1939.

CRAterre: Centre International de la Construction en Terre Both an association, founded in 1979, and a research lab at the École Nationale Supérieure d'Architecture de Grenoble (ENSAG), founded in 1986. Both are based in Grenoble.

DSA Terre: A professional qualification in earth architecture, established by CRAterre in 1984 and awarded on completion of a postgraduate course at ENSAG, Grenoble.

ElemenTerre: An educational kit created through the Grains de Bâtisseurs programme and distributed internationally to encourage scientific recognition of raw earth as a building material.

ENSAG: École Nationale Superieure d'Architecture de Grenoble Grenoble School of Architecture, part of the Université Grenoble Alpes (UGA).

ESPCI: École Supérieure de Physique et de Chimie Industrielles Engineering school and research centre founded in Paris in 1888. Several of its researchers have gone on to win Nobel Prizes.

Grains de Bâtisseurs: A research programme into the use of earth as a building material, developed by CRAterre at the Grands Ateliers since 2000. An annual international festival derived from this programme, Grains d'Isère, which also takes place at the Grands Ateliers, has helped raise awareness of earth architecture and building techniques in schools and universities.

Grands Ateliers: A public research institute founded in 2001 in Villefontaine, France. It includes a dozen architecture, engineering, and craft workshops, dedicated to teaching the art of building through practical experimentation.

ICOMOS: International Council on Monuments and Sites An international professional association devoted to the conservation and protection of heritage sites and monuments, founded in Paris in 1965.

IFSTTAR: Institut Français des Sciences et Technologies des Transports, de l'Aménagement et des Reseaux French public scientific and technological institution founded in 2010. Based in Marne-la-Vallée, near Paris.

ISCEAH: International Scientific Committee on the Conservation of Earthen Architectural Heritage Affiliated with ICOMOS and other international scientific committees.

ParisTech: Network of ten engineering schools in Paris and its outlying areas, focused on developing shared training, research, and innovation projects in the fields of science, technology, and management.

Proterra: An Iberian-American network (Spain, Portugal, and Latin American countries) of professionals involved in earth architecture and construction. Founded in 2006, as an offshoot of the CYTED public housing programme (Iberian-American programme of science and technology for development).

TERRA Award: International prize created in 2001 by Dominique Gauzin-Müller, CRAterre, and Amàco, recognizing outstanding earth architecture from all over the world.

UNESCO: United Nations Educational, Scientific and Cultural Organization Headquarters in Paris.

UNESCO Chair on Earthen Architecture, Building Cultures and Sustainable Development Founded in 1998 by the CRAterre-ENSAG research centre in Grenoble, France. By 2019, it included 41 academic and professional bodies in more than 20 countries with a focus on re-evaluating earth architecture and construction by means of research, training, and implementation of specific projects, especially in developing countries.

UNITWIN: The networking arm of the UNITWIN/UNESCO Chairs programme, founded in 1992, covering more than 700 teaching and research bodies in 116 countries. It encourages international cooperation between universities to facilitate the sharing of knowledge.

Bibliography

Ago 1982
Fabrizio Ago, *Moschee in adòbe, storia e tipologia nell'Africa occidentale*, foreword by Paolo Portoghesi, Rome: Kappa, 1982

Anger & Fontaine 2009
Romain Anger and Laetitia Fontaine, *Bâtir en terre, du grain de sable à l'architecture*, Paris: Belin/Cité des Sciences et de l'Industrie, 2009

Aurenche 1981
Olivier Aurenche, *La Maison orientale, l'architecture du Proche-Orient des origines au milieu du IVe millénaire*, Paris: Paul Geuthner, 1981

Aurenche et al. 2011
Olivier Aurenche, Alain Klein, Claire-Anne de Chazelles, and Hubert Guillaud, 'Essai de classification des modalités de mise en œuvre de la terre crue en parois verticales et de leur nomenclature', in Claire-Anne de Chazelles, Alain Klein, and Nelly Pousthomis (eds.), *Les Cultures constructives de la brique crue: Échanges transdisciplinaires sur les constructions en terre crue*, vol. 3, Montpellier: L'Espérou, 2011, pp. 13–34

Bardel & Maillard 2009
Philippe Bardel and Jean-Luc Maillard, *Architecture de terre en Ille-et-Vilaine*, Rennes: Apogée/Écomusée du Pays de Rennes, 2009

Bardou & Arzoumanian 1978
Patrick Bardou and Varoujan Arzoumanian, *Archi de terre*, Roquevaire: Parenthèses, 1978

Baridon, Garric, & Richaud 2016
Laurent Baridon, Jean-Philippe Garric, and Gilbert Richaud (eds.), *Les Leçons de la terre, actes du colloque 'François Cointeraux, pionnier de l'architecture moderne en terre'*, May 2012, Lyon: INHA; Paris: Éditions des Cendres, 2016

Beaudoin 1998
Gérard Beaudoin, *Soudan occidental, histoire et architecture*, Paris: BDT Éditions, 1998

Bedaux & Van der Waals 1994
R. M. A. Bedaux and J. D. Van der Waals, *Djenné, une ville millénaire au Mali*, Leiden: Rijksmuseum; Ghent: Martial, 1994

Bendakir et al. 2008
Mahmoud Bendakir et al., *Architectures de terre en Syrie, une tradition de onze millénaires*, Grenoble: CRAterre-ENSAG, 2008

Berge 2000
Bjørn Berge, *The Ecology of Building Materials*, Oxford: Architectural Press, 2000

Besenval 1984
Roland Besenval, *Technologie de la voûte dans l'Orient ancien*, 2 vols., Paris: Recherche sur les Civilisations, 1984

Boltshauser, Veillon, & Maillard 2019
Roger Boltshauser, Cyril Veillon, and Nadia Maillard, *Pisé: Rammed Earth, Tradition and Potential*, Zurich: Triest Verlag, 2019

Bourdier & Minh Ha 2005
Jean-Paul Bourdier and Trinh T. Minh Ha, *Habiter un monde, architectures de l'Afrique de l'Ouest*, Paris: Alternatives, 2005

Bourg & Fragnière 2014
Dominique Bourg and Antoine Fragnière, *La pensée écologique, une anthologie*, Paris: PUF, 2014

Bourgeois 1989
Jean-Louis Bourgeois, *Spectacular Vernacular: The Adobe Tradition*, photographs by Carollee Pelos, introduction by Basil Davidson, New York: Aperture, 1989

Brown 2007
Lester R. Brown, *Plan B 2.0: Rescuing a Planet under Stress and a Civilization in Trouble*, Washington, DC: Earth Policy Institute, 2006

Brundtland 1987
Gro Harlem Brundtland and the World Commission on Environment and Development, *Our Common Future*, Oxford: Oxford University Press/United Nations, 1987

Casel et al. 2000
Thomas Casel, Joseph Colzani, Jean-François Gardère, and Jean-Loup Marfaing, *Maisons d'argile en Midi-Pyrénées*, Toulouse: Privat, 2000

Chazelles, Klein, & Pousthomis 2011
Claire-Anne de Chazelles, Alain Klein, and Nelly Pousthomis (eds.), *Les Cultures constructives de la brique crue: Échanges transdisciplinaires sur les constructions en terre crue*, vol. 3, Montpellier: L'Espérou, 2011

Chesi 1995
Gert Chesi, *Architektur und Mythos: Lehmbauten in Afrika*, foreword by Dorothee Gruner, Innsbruck: Haymon, 1995

Cointeraux 1790
François Cointeraux, *École d'architecture rurale, premier cahier, dans lequel on apprendra soi-même à bâtir solidement les maisons de plusieurs étages avec la terre seule*, Paris: F. Cointeraux, 1790

Cointeraux 1791a
François Cointeraux, *École d'architecture rurale, second cahier, dans lequel on traite: 1. de l'art du pisé ou de sa massivation, 2. des qualités des terres propres au pisé, 3. des détails de la main d'œuvre [...]*, Paris: F. Cointeraux, 1791

Cointeraux 1791b
François Cointeraux, *École d'architecture rurale, troisième cahier, traité sur la construction des maisons de campagne*, Paris: F. Cointeraux, 1791

Cointeraux 1806
François Cointeraux, *École d'architecture rurale, quatrième cahier, dans lequel on traite du nouveau pisé inventé par l'auteur, de la construction de ses outils […]*, Paris: F. Cointeraux, 1806

Colleyn 2016
Jean-Paul Colleyn, *Architectures de terre dans l'Ouest africain*, photographs by Cécile Tréal and Jean-Michel Ruiz, Arles: Actes Sud; Paris: Imprimerie Nationale, 2016

Correia et al. 2014
Mariana Correia, Letizia Dipasquale, and Saverio Mecca (eds.), *VerSus, Heritage For Tomorrow: Vernacular Knowledge for Sustainable Architecture*, Florence: Firenze University Press, 2014

Correia & Fernandes 2005
Mariana Correia and Maria Fernandes (eds.), *Arquitectura de terra em Portugal/Earth Architecture in Portugal*, Lisbon: Argumentum/Escola Superior Gallaecia, 2005

Courtney-Clarke 1990
Margaret Courtney-Clarke, *African Canvas: The Art of West African Women*, New York: Rizzoli, 1990

CRAterre 1979
CRAterre (Patrice Doat, Alain Hays, Hugo Houben, Silvia Matuk, and François Vitoux), *Construire en terre*, Paris: Editions Alternatives, 1979

CRAterre 2004
CRAterre, *Navrongo Cathedral: The Merge of Two Cultures*, Grenoble: CRAterre; Accra: Ghana Museums and Monuments Board, 2004

CRAterre 2005
CRAterre, *Le Tombeau des Askia, Gao, Mali*, Grenoble: CRAterre, 2005

CRAterre 2006
CRAterre, *Cultural Heritage and Local Development: A Guide for African Local Governments*, Grenoble: CRAterre, 2006

CRAterre 2008
CRAterre, *La Cour royale de Tiébélé, Burkina Faso*, Grenoble: CRAterre, 2008

CRAterre 2009
CRAterre, *Dix années d'expérience de terrain, les projets de restauration du patrimoine architectural du programme 'Africa 2009'*, eds. Thierry Joffroy and Sébastien Moriset, Grenoble: CRAterre, 2009

CRAterre 2014
CRAterre, *Matières à construire, bilan du 12e Festival architectures de terre*, Grenoble: CRAterre, 2014

CRAterre 2015
CRAterre, *Assessing Local Building Cultures for Resilience & Development: A Practical Guide for Community-Based Assessment*, eds. Annalisa Caimi and Oliver Moles, Villefontaine: CRAterre Éditions, 2015

CRAterre 2017
CRAterre, *Argiles & biopolymères, les stabilisants naturels pour la construction en terre*, Grenoble: CRAterre, 2017

CRAterre 2018a
CRAterre, *Réhabiliter le pisé, vers des pratiques adaptées*, Arles: Actes Sud, 2018

CRAterre 2018b
CRAterre, *Réhabilitation et valorisation du bâti en pisé, guide à destination des collectivités territoriales*, Grenoble: CRAterre, 2018

CRAterre & Bardagot 1991
CRAterre and Anne-Monique Bardagot, *L'intelligence de l'Europe et le développement de l'habitat économique en terre des années 1920 à nos jours*, Grenoble: CRAterre, 1991

Dachverband Lehm 2006
Dachverband Lehm (Franz Volhard and Ulrich Röhlen), *Lehmbau Regeln: Begriffe, Baustoffe, Bauteile*, Wiesbaden: Vieweg+Teubner, 2006

Damluji 1992
Salma Samar Damluji, *The Valley of Mud Brick Architecture: Shibam, Tarim and Wadi Hadramut, Ancient to Contemporary Design*, Reading: Garnet Publishing, 1992

Damluji 2007
Salma Samar Damluji, *The Architecture of Yemen: From Yafi to Hadramut*, London, Laurence King, 2007

Damluji & Bertini 2018
Salma Samar Damluji and Viola Bertini, *Hassan Fathy: Earth & Utopia*, London: Laurence King, 2018

Dethier 1983
Jean Dethier, *Down to Earth: Adobe Architecture, An Old Idea, A New Future*, trans. Ruth Eaton, New York: Facts on File, 1983

Dethier 1985
Jean Dethier (ed.), 'Terre d'avenir', *H, revue de l'habitat social*, special issue, no. 111, October 1985, pp. 23–118.

Dethier 2017
Jean Dethier, '1789–1979, l'art moderne de bâtir en terre crue : une saga universelle initiée en France', *D'a*, no. 255, July 2017, pp. 43-71

Dewulf 2007
Michel Dewulf, *Le Torchis, mode d'emploi*, Paris: Eyrolles, 2007

Dingcheng 2014
Hong Dingcheng, *Les Tulou du Fujian*, Paris: Mirabilia Mundi, 2014

Dmochowski 1990
Z. R. Dmochowski, *An Introduction to Nigerian Traditional Architecture*, vol. 1, *Northern Nigeria*; vol. 2, *South-West and Central Nigeria*; vol. 3, *Eastern Nigeria*, London: Ethnografica, 1990

Duchert 2008
Daniel Duchert, *Gestalten mit Lehm*, Frammersbach: Farbe und Gesundheit, 2008

Dunzhen 1980
Liu Dunzhen, *La maison chincise*, Paris: Berger-Levrault, 1980

Écobâtir 2013
Écobâtir Network, *Enduits sur supports composés de terre crue*, Paris: Le Moniteur, 2013

Ecologik 2009
'Habiter la terre : manifeste pour le droit de construire en terre', *Ecologik*, special issue 'Architectures de terre', no. 12, December 2009, pp. 63–64

Ellington 1924
Karl Johan Ellington, *Modern Pisé: House Building with Compressed or Rammed Earth, a Revelation for the Farmer and Settler*, Lindsborg, KS: Taylor Publishing & Elk River Press, 1924

El-Wakil 2018
Leïla El-Wakil (ed.), *Hassan Fathy: An Architectural Life*, Cairo: American University in Cairo Press, 2018

Facey 1997
William Facey, *Back to Earth: Adobe Building in Saudi Arabia*, London: London Centre of Arab Studies, 1997

Fathy 1970
Hassan Fathy, *Construire avec le peuple, histoire d'un village d'Égypte: Gourna*, Paris: Sindbad, 1970

Fauth 1948
Wilhelm Fauth, *Der praktische Lehmbau*, Singen-Hohentwiel: Weber, 1948

Fiedermutz-Laun et al. 1990
Annemarie Fiedermutz-Laun, Dorothee Gruner, Eike Haberland, and Karl Heinz Striedter, *Aus Erde geformt: Lehmbauten in West- und Nordafrika*, Mainz: Verlag Philipp von Zabern, 1990

Fissabre & Wilson 2016
Anka Fissabre and Ariane Wilson, '*Lehmbaupropaganda*: On the Tradition of Earth Building Literature', in Hubert Feiglstorfer (ed.), *Earth Construction and Tradition*, vol. 1, Vienna: IVA, 2016

Fourel 2009
Christophe Fourel (ed.), *André Gorz, un penseur pour le XXie siècle*, Paris: La Découverte, 2009

Frey 2010
Pierre Frey, *Learning from Vernacular: Towards a New Vernacular Architecture*, Arles: Actes Sud, 2010

Frobenius 1894
Hermann Frobenius, *Afrikanische Bautypen*, Dachau, 1894

Galdieri 1982
Eugenio Galdieri, *Le meraviglie dell'architettura in terra cruda*, Rome: Laterza, 1982

Gardi 1973
René Gardi, *Indigenous African Architecture*, trans. Sigrid MacRae, New York: Van Nostrand Reinhold, 1973

Gardi 1975
René Gardi, *Auch im Lehmhaus lässt sich's leben*, Lausanne: Ex Libris, 1975

Gauzin-Müller 2002
Dominique Gauzin-Müller, *Sustainable Architecture and Urbanism: Concepts, Technologies, Examples*, trans. Kate Purver, Basel: Birkhauser, 2002

Gauzin-Müller 2016
Dominique Gauzin-Müller, *Architecture en terre d'aujourd'hui*, Paris: Museo Éditions/CRAterre, 2016

Goyon et al. 2004
Jean-Claude Goyon, Jean-Claude Golvin, Claire Simon-Boidot, and Gilles Martinet, *La Construction pharaonique, du Moyen Empire à l'époque gréco-romaine*, Paris: Picard, 2004

Gruner 1990
Dorothee Gruner, *Die Lehm-Moschee am Niger: Dokumentation eines traditionellen Bautyps*, Stuttgart: Franz Steiner, 1990

Guillaud 1997
Hubert Guillaud, *François Cointereaux (1740–1830): pionnier de la construction moderne en pisé*, Grenoble: CRAterre-ENSAG, 1997

Guillaud, Chazelles, & Klein 2007
Hubert Guillaud, Claire-Anne de Chazelles, and Alain Klein (eds.), *Les Constructions en terre massive, pisé et bauge, actes de la table ronde de Villefontaine, 28–29 May 2005*, Villefontaine/Montpellier: L'Espérou, 2007

Guillaud et al. 2008
Hubert Guillaud *et al.*, *Terra incognita, découvrir et préserver une Europe des architectures de terre*, 2 vols., Lisbon: Argumentum; Tervuren: Culture Lab Éditions, 2008

Guillaud & Houben 2011
Hubert Guillaud and Hugo Houben, 'Earthen Architecture and Sociocultural Challenges', in *Actes du 6º Seminario Arquitectura de terra em Portugal / 9º Seminario Iberoamericano sobre la construcción con tierra*, Coimbra, 17–23 February 2010, Lisbon: Argumentum, 2011

Guillaud & Zerhouni 2001
Hubert Guillaud and Selma Zerhouni (eds.), *L'Architecture de terre au Maroc*, Courbevoie: ACR Édition, 2001

Güntzel 1988
Jochen Georg Güntzel, *Zur Geschichte des Lehmbaus in Deutschland: Tekniken und Verbreitung*, 2 vols., Staufen: Ökobuch Verlag, 1988

Hallet & Samizay 1980
Stanley I. Hallet and Rafi Samizay, *Traditional Architecture of Afghanistan*, New York & London: Garland STPM Press, 1980

Hamid 2010
Ahmad Hamid, *Hassan Fathy and Continuity in Islamic Arts and Architecture: The Birth of a New Modern*, Cairo & New York: American University in Cairo Press, 2010

Heringer, Blair Howe, & Rauch 2019
Anna Heringer, Lindsay Blair Howe, and Martin Rauch, *Upscaling Earth: Material, Process, Catalyst*, Zurich: GTA Verlag, 2019

Holm, Kjeldsen, & Kallehauge 2017
Michael Juul Holm, Kjeld Kjeldsen, and Mette Kallehauge (eds.), *Wang Shu, Amateur Architecture Studio*, exhibition catalogue, Humlebaek: Louisiana Museum of Modern Art; Baden: Lars Müller, 2017

Houben & Guillaud 1994
Hugo Houben and Hubert Guillaud, *Earth Construction: A Comprehensive Guide*, London: Intermediate Technology Publications, 1994

Howard 1992
Ted Howard, *Mud and Man: A History of Earth Building in Australasia*, Melbourne: Earthbuild Publications, 1992.

Hulot 2015
Nicolas Hulot, *Osons, plaidoyer d'un homme libre*, Paris: Les Liens qui Libèrent/Fondation Nicolas Hulot pour la Nature et l'Homme, 2015

Illich 1982
Ivan Illich, *Gender*, New York: Pantheon Books, 1982

Jacques-Meunié 1962
Djinn Jacques-Meunié, *Architectures et habitats du Dadès*, Paris: Klincksieck, 1962

Jaquin & Augarde 2012
Paul Jaquin and Charles Augarde, *Earth Building: History, Science and Conservation*, Bracknell: IHS BRE Press, 2012

Jeannet et al. 1997
Jacky Jeannet, Bruno Pignal, Gérard Pollet, and Pascal Scarato, *Le Pisé, patrimoine, restauration, technique d'avenir, matériaux, techniques et tours de mains*, 3rd ed., Nonette: Créer, 1997

Joffroy & Guillaud 1994
Thierry Joffroy and Hubert Guillaud, *Éléments de base sur la construction en arcs, voûtes et coupoles*, Saint Gallen: SKAT, 1994

Joffroy, Guillaud, & Sadozai 2018
Thierry Joffroy, Hubert Guillaud, and Chamsia Sadozaï (eds), *Terra Lyon 2016, actes du XIIe Congrès mondial sur les architectures de terre*, Villefontaine: CRAterre Éditions, 2018

Joy 2002
Rick Joy, *Desert Works*, New York: Princeton Architectural Press, 2002

Kapfinger 2001
Otto Kapfinger, *Martin Rauch: Rammed Earth/Lehm und Architektur/Terra cruda*, Basel: Birkhäuser, 2001

Kapfinger & Sauer 2015
Otto Kapfinger and Marko Sauer (eds.), *Martin Rauch: Refined Earth Construction & Design with Rammed Earth*, Munich: Detail, 2015

Kassatly & Puett 2011
Houda Kassatly and Karin Puett, *De terre et de lumière, les maisons à coupoles du nord de la Syrie*, Beirut: Al-Ayn, 2011

Keable & Keable 2011
Julian Keable and Rowland Keable, *Rammed Earth Structures: A Code of Practice*, Rugby: Practical Action, 2011

Knapp 1986
Ronald G. Knapp, *China's Traditional Rural Architecture*, Honolulu: University of Hawaii Press, 1986

Knapp 2006
Ronald G. Knapp, *Chinese Houses: The Architectural Heritage of a Nation,* foreword by Jonathan Spence, photographs by A. Chester Ong, Honolulu: University of Hawaii Press, 2006

Krahn 2018
Tim Krahn, *Essential Rammed Earth Construction: The Complete Step-by-Step Guide*, Gabriola Island, BC: New Society Publishers, 2018

Kubler 1940
George Kubler, *The Religious Architecture of New Mexico in the Colonial Period and since the American Occupation*, Colorado Springs, CO: Taylor Museum, 1940

Lander & Niermann 1980
Helmut Lander and Manfred Niermann, *Lehm-Architektur in Spanien und Afrika*, Königstein: Langewiesche, 1980

Lasfargues 1985
Jacques Lasfargues (ed.), 'Architectures de terre et de bois. L'habitat privé des provinces occidentales du monde romain. Antécédents et prolongements: protohistoire, Moyen Âge et quelques expériences contemporaines', in *Actes du IIe Congrès archéologique de Gaule méridionale*, Lyon, 2–6 November 1983, Paris: Maison des Sciences de l'Homme, 1985

Lauber 1998
Wolfgang Lauber (ed.), *Architektur der Dogon: traditioneller Lehmbau und Kunst in Mali*, Munich: Prestel, 1998

Le Corbusier 1942
Le Corbusier, *Les constructions 'Murondins'*, Paris: Chiron, 1942

Le Corbusier 1946–52
Le Corbusier, 'La nouvelle cité de la Sainte-Baume, habitations en pisé', in *Oeuvre complète*, vol. 5, Basel: Birkhauser, 1994

Lefèvre 2009
Pierre Lefèvre, 'Retour d'expérience: le Domaine de la terre', *Ecologik*, 'Architectures de terre' issue, no. 12, December 2009, pp. 70–73

Lepik & Beygo 2016
Andres Lepik and Ayça Beygo (eds.), *Francis Kéré: Radically Simple*, Berlin: Hajte Cantz, 2016

Loubes 1998
Jean-Paul Loubes, *Architecture et urbanisme de Turfan, une oasis du Turkestan chinois*, Paris: L'Harmattan, 1998

Maas & Mommersteeg 1992
Pierre Maas and Geert Mommersteeg, *Djenné, chef-d'œuvre architectural*, Amsterdam: Tropenmuseum; Paris: Karthala, 1992

Marchand 2009
Trevor H. J. Marchand, *The Masons of Djenné*, Bloomington, IN: Indiana University Press, 2009

Marcom 2011
Alain Marcom, *Construire en terre-paille*, Mens: Terre Vivante, 2011

Maréchaux, Maréchaux, & Sautreau 2006
Pascal Maréchaux, Maria Maréchaux, and Serge Sautreau, *Cités du Yémen*, Paris: Imprimerie Nationale, 2006

Margueron 2013
Jean-Claude Margueron, *Cités invisibles: la naissance de l'urbanisme au Proche-Orient ancien*, Paris: Geuthner, 2013

Mauger 2002
Thierry Mauger, *Arabie, jardin des peintres, architecture et art mural du Asir*, Paris: Adam Biro, 2002

McCann 1983
John McCann, *Clay and Cob Buildings*, Album no. 105, Princes Risborough: Shire Publications Ltd, 1983

McHenry 1989
Paul Graham McHenry, *Adobe and Rammed Earth Buildings: Design and Construction*, Tucson, AZ: University of Arizona Press, 1989

Mellaart 1967
James Mellaart, *Çatal Hüyük: A Neolithic Town in Anatolia*, London: Thames & Hudson, 1967

Mester de Parajd & Mester de Parajd 1992
Corinne Mester de Parajd and Laszlo Mester de Parajd, *Regards sur l'habitat traditionnel au Niger*, Nonette: Créer, 1992

Mileto et al. 2018
Camilla Mileto, Fernando Vegas López-Manzanares, Lidia García-Soriano, and Valentina Cristini, *Vernacular and Earthen Architecture: Conservation and Sustainability*, London: CRC Press/Taylor and Francis Group, 2017

Minke 2000
Gernot Minke, *Earth Construction Handbook: The Building Material Earth in Modern Architecture*, Southampton: WIT Press, 2000

Minke 2006
Gernot Minke, *Building with Earth: Design and Technology of a Sustainable Architecture*, Basel: Birkhauser, 2006.

Moevus-Dorvaux et al. 2016
Mariette Moevus-Dorvaux, Lucile Couvreur, Basile Cloquet, Laetitia Fontaine, Romain Anger, and Patrice Doat, *Béton d'argile environnemental, résultats d'un programme de recherche tourné vers l'application*, Grenoble: CRAterre, 2016

Moréteau 2012
Sylvain Moréteau, *Enduits de terre crue, techniques de mise en oeuvre et conseils de professionnels*, Mens: Terre Vivante, 2012

Morgan 2008
William N. Morgan, *Earth Architecture: From Ancient to Modern*, Gainesville, FL: University Press of Florida, 2008.

Morin 1999
Edgar Morin, *Seven Complex Lessons in Education for the Future*, trans. Nidra Poller, Paris: UNESCO, 1999

Morris & Preston Blier 2004
James Morris and Suzanne Preston Blier, *Butabu: Adobe Architecture of West Africa*, New York: Princeton Architectural Press, 2004

Moughtin 1985
J.-C. Moughtin, *Hausa Architecture*, London: Ethnographica; Nottingham: Institute of Planning Studies, University of Nottingham, 1985

Naji 2001
Salima Naji, *Art et architectures berbères du Maroc*, Aix-en-Provence: Édisud, 2001

Nègre 2004
Valérie Nègre (ed.), *Terre crue, terre cuite, recueil d'écrits sur la construction*, Paris, Centre d'Histoire de Techniques, 2004

Niemeyer 1982
Richard Niemeyer, *Der Lehmbau und seine praktische Anwendung* (1946), Staufen: Ökobuch Verlag, 1982

Norberg-Schulz 1980
Christian Norberg-Schulz, *Genius Loci: Towards a Phenomenology of Architecture*, London: Academy Editions, 1980

Oliva & Courgey 2001
Jean-Pierre Oliva and Samuel Courgey, *L'Isolation thermique écologique*, Mens: Terre Vivante, 2001

Oliva & Courgey 2006
Jean-Pierre Oliva and Samuel Courgey, *La Conception bioclimatique, des maisons confortables et économes*, Mens: Terre Vivante, 2006

Oliver 1971
Paul Oliver, *Shelter in Africa*, New York: Praeger; London: Barrie & Jenkins, 1971

Oliver 1997
Paul Oliver (ed.), *Encyclopedia of Vernacular Architecture of the World*, Cambridge: Cambridge University Press, 1997

Patte 2009
Erwan Patte (ed.), *Architectures en terre, marais du Cotentin et du Bessin, inventaire général du patrimoine culturel, Région Basse-Normandie*, Cabourg: Cahiers du Temps, 2009

Patte & Streiff 2007
Erwan Patte and François Streiff (eds.), *L'Architecture en bauge en Europe*, Les Veys: Parc Naturel Régional des Marais du Cotentin et du Bessin, 2007

Petitjean 1995
Marc Petitjean, *Constructions en terre en Ille-et-Vilaine*, Rennes: Apogée, 1995

Piesik 2017
Sandra Piesik (ed.), *Habitat: Vernacular Architecture for a Changing Planet*, London: Thames & Hudson, 2017

Pignal 2005
Bruno Pignal, *Terre crue, techniques de construction et de restauration*, Paris: Eyrolles, 2005

Preston Blier 1994
Suzanne Preston Blier, *The Anatomy of Architecture: Ontology and Metaphor in Batammaliba Architectural Expression*, Chicago & London: University of Chicago Press, 1994

Prussin 1969
Labelle Prussin, *Architecture in Northern Ghana: A Study of Forms and Functions*, Berkeley, CA: University of California Press, 1969

Rael 2009
Ronald Rael, *Earth Architecture*, New York: Princeton Architectural Press, 2009

Richards, Serageldin, & Rastorfer 1985
J. M. Richards, Ismail Serageldin, and Darl Rastorfer, *Hassan Fathy*, Singapore: Concept Media; London: Architectural Press, 1985

Röhlen & Ziegert 2011
Ulrich Röhlen and Christof Ziegert, *Earth Building Practice: Planning, Design, Building*, trans. J. Reisenberger, Berlin: Bauwerk/Beuth, 2011

Romero & Larkin 1994
Orlando Romero and David Larkin, *Adobe: Building and Living with Earth*, photographs by Michael Freeman, Boston: Houghton Mifflin, 1994

Ruby, Ruby, & Janson 2014
Ilka Ruby, Andreas Ruby, and Nathalie Janson (eds.), *The Economy of Sustainable Construction*, Berlin: Ruby Press, 2014

Rudofsky 1964
Bernard Rudofsky, *Architecture Without Architects: A Short Introduction to Non-Pedigreed Architecture*, New York: MoMA, 1964

Sauvage 1998
Martin Sauvage, *La Brique et sa mise en œuvre en Mésopotamie, des origines à l'époque achéménide*, Paris: Recherche sur les Civilisations, 1998

Scherrer 2003
Olivier Scherrer, 2003, 'Actualité de la construction en bauge en Afghanistan, la technique du *pakhsa*', in Claire-Anne de Chazelles and Alain Klein (eds.), *Échanges transdisciplinaires sur les constructions en terre crue, 1. Terre modelée, découpée ou coffrée; matériaux et modes de mise en œuvre, actes de la table ronde de Montpellier 17–18 novembre 2001*, Montpellier: L'Espérou, 2003, pp. 213–230

Schreckenbach 2004
Hannah Schreckenbach, *Building with Earth: Consumer Information*, Weimar: Dachverband Lehm, 2004

Schroeder 2010
Horst Schroeder, *Lehmbau: mit Lehm ökologisch Planen und Bauen*, Wiesbaden: Vieweg+Teubner, 2010

Schuiten 2014
Marie Schuiten, *Oasis: Raw Earth Architecture, Dakhla Oasis in Egypt*, Brussels: ARP2 Éditions, 2014

Schütyser et al. 2003
Sebastian Schütyser, Jean Dethier, Ruth Eaton, and Dorothee Gruner, *Banco: Adobe Mosques of the Inner Niger Delta*, Milan: 5 Continents, 2003

Schwerdtfeger 1982
Friedrich W. Schwerdtfeger, *Traditional Housing in African Cities*, Chichester: Wiley, 1982

Schwerdtfeger 2007
Friedrich W. Schwerdtfeger, *Hausa Urban Art and Its Social Background: External House Decorations in a Northern Nigerian City*, Berlin: Lit Verlag, 2007

Seignobos & Jamin 2003
Christian Seignobos and Fabien Jamin, *La case obus, histoire et reconstitution*, Marseille: Parenthèses/Patrimoine sans Frontières, 2003

Shamir & Kounta 2007
Marli Shamir and Albakaye Ousmane Kounta, *Djenné-ferey, la terre habitée*, foreword by Joseph Brunet-Jailly, Brinon-sur-Sauldre: Grandvaux, 2007

Steele 1988
James Steele, *Hassan Fathy*, London: Academy Editions; New York: St. Martin's Press, 1988

Steele 1997
James Steele, *An Architecture for People: The Complete Works of Hassan Fathy*, London: Thames & Hudson, 1997

Stevens 1990
André Stevens, *Oman: Citadels Between Sand and Sea*, Brussels: Terra Incognita, 1990

Stevens 2015
André Stevens, 'Architecture de terre et patrimoine mondial', *Koregos, revue et encyclopédie multimédia des arts sous l'égide de l'Académie royale de Belgique*, 2015: http://www.koregos.org/fr/andre-stevens-architecture-de-terre-et-patrimoine-mondial

Szabo & Barfield 1991
Albert Szabo and Thomas J. Barfield, *Afghanistan: An Atlas of Indigenous Domestic Architecture*, Austin, TX: University of Texas Press, 1991

Terra 2000
Terra 2000, 8th International Conference on the Study and Conservation of Earthen Architecture, 11–13 May 2000, Torquay: James & James, 2000

Terrasse 2010
Henri Terrasse, *Kasbas berbères de l'Atlas et des oasis, les grandes architectures du Sud marocain* (1938), introduction by Salima Naji, Arles: Actes Sud, 2010

Turner 1976
John F. C. Turner, *Housing by People: Towards Autonomy in Building Environments*, London: Marion Boyars, 1976

UNESCO 2013
Earthen Architecture in Today's World: Proceedings of the UNESCO International Colloquium on the Conservation of World Heritage Earthen Architecture, 17–18 December 2012, Paris: UNESCO, 2013

Van Beek & Van Beek 2007
Gus Willard Van Beek and Ora Van Beek, *Glorious Mud! Ancient and Contemporary Earthen Design and Construction in North Africa, Western Europe, the Near East, and South Asia*, Washington, DC: Smithsonian Institution, 2007

Van Damme & Houben 2018
Henri Van Damme and Hugo Houben, 'Earth concrete: Stabilization revisited', *Elsevier Journal*, vol. 114, Amsterdam/London, December 2018, pp. 90–102

Varanda 1982
Fernando Varanda, *Art of Building in Yemen*, New York & London: MIT Press, 1982

Volhard 1983
Franz Volhard, *Leichtlehmbau, alter Baustoff – neue Technik*, Karlsruhe: Verlag C.F. Müller, 1983

Volhard 2015
Franz Volhard, *Light Earth Building: A Handbook for Building with Wood and Earth*, Basel: Birkhäuser, 2015

Volhard & Röhlen 2009
Franz Volhard and Ulrich Röhlen, *Lehmbau Regeln: Begriffe, Baustoffe, Bauteile*, 3 vols., Wiesbaden: Vieweg+Teubner, 2009

Wang Shu 2013
Wang Shu, 'Construire un monde différent conforme aux principes de la nature', trans. F. Ged, lecture given 31 January 2012 at the École de Chaillot, Paris: Cité de l'Architecture & du Patrimoine, 2013

Wienands 1983
Rudolf Wienands, *Die Lehmarchitektur der Pueblos: Eine Lektion in ökologischem Bauen*, Cologne: Dumont, 1983

Wilson 2014
Ariana Wilson, 'Objectif Terre', *Criticat 13*, Paris: Association Criticat, 2014, pp. 94–118

Williams-Ellis 1919
Clough Williams-Ellis, *Cottage Building in Cob, Pisé, Chalk and Clay: A Renaissance*, London: Country Life, 1919

Ziegert & zur Nieden 2002
Christof Ziegert and Günter zur Nieden, *Neue Lehm-Häuser International: Projektbeispiele, Konstruktionen, Details*, Berlin: Bauwerk Verlag, 2002

Index of Architects
and Other Creators

Page numbers refer to illustrations.
A: above, B: below, C: centre, L: left, R: right.

a

ABEY, Jackie & SMALLCOMBE, Jill (artisans, UK) 460 (C)
ABLINGER, VEDRAL & PARTNER (architects, Austria) 449 (A)
ACCETTA, André (structural engineer, France) 460 (BL)
ADAUA (architects association, Switzerland & West Africa) 388 (A)
AGO, Fabrizio (architect, Italy) 208–209
ALEPH ZERO see UTRABO, Gustavo
AMATEUR ARCHITECTURE STUDIO see WANG Shu
ANGULO, Dario (TierraTEC, architect & entrepreneur, Colombia) 402 (A+C), 403 (A)
AUROVILLE EARTH INSTITUTE (India) 51 (AL), 384–385, 481, 485
AUZET, Marc & GOUDY, Juliette (architects, France) 461

b

BAER, Steve (architect, USA) 342–343
BARMOU, El Hadji Falké (master builder, Niger) 43, 279 (A), 490–491
BARRIER, Jean-Yves (architect, France) 402–403 (B)
BC ARCHITECTS (architects association, Belgium) 446–447
BEAUDOIN, Gérard (artist, France) 190–191
BÉGUIN, Mathilde & BÉGUIN, Nicolas (designers France) 460 (BR)
BERLOTTIER, Jean-Vincent (architect, France) 25, 392 (BC), 394 (R)
BERTHIER, André & FRASSANITO, Joseph (architects, France) 426 (A+B)
BIANCIFIORI, Giuseppe (architect, Italy) 288–289 (B)
BILISIC, Vojtech (artist, Czech Republic) 416–417 (B)
BONNEVIE, Maxime (architect, France) 381 (B)
BORER, Pat (architect, UK) 428 (A)
BOUCHET, Boris (architect, France) 436 (C)
BRAURE, Élisabeth (artist, France) 378 (A)
BROWN, Capability (architect, UK) 260–261 (B)
BURGESS, Gregory (architect, Australia) 440–441, 454 (A)

c

CAMARA, Silla (artist, Mauritania) 42
CARACOL (architects association, France) 412 (B)
CASTEL, Corinne 76 (B)
CHAMBERS, William (architect, UK) 260–261
CHIANGMAI LIFE ARCHITECTS (Thailand) 411 (C+B), 423 (B)
COBB, Ron (cartoonist, USA) 488, 489
COINTERAUX, François (architect & entrepreneur, France) 309, 310–311
CONFINO, François (architect, France) 394 (L)
COQUARD, Denis (architect, France) 455 (A+C)
CORTÉS, Marcelo (architect, Chile) 52 (A), 388 (B)
CRAterre (interdisciplinary group, France) 30, 371, 374–375, 376–377, 378–379, 380–381, 382–383, 432–433

d

DAMLUJI, Salma Samar (architect, Iraq/UK) 112, 236
DELACROIX, Eugène (artist, France) 352
D'ERRICO, Enrico (architect, Italy) 288–289 (B)
DESIGN BUILD BLUFF (architecture programme, USA) 413 (A)
DETHIER, Jean (architect, Belgium) 282–283, 350–351, 390–391, 392
DIALOG (architects, Canada) 443 (A), 458
DODGE LUHAN, Mabel (art patron, USA) 325 (A)
DUBUFFET, Jean (artist, France) 353 (B)
DUCHERT, Daniel (artist, Germany) 379, 461 (AR)

e

EL-MINIAWY, Hany and Abdel Rahman (architects, Egypt) 341 (B)
ENCORE HEUREUX (architecture studio, France) 427
ESMAILI, Yasaman (architect, Iran) 444 (A), 487, 490–491
ESTEVE, Josep (architect, Spain) 44, 45, 371, 380 (B), 381 (A)

f

FATHY, Hassan (architect, Egypt) 50-51, 55 (A), 296–297, 335, 336–337, 338–339
FAMY, Adel (architect, Egypt) 340 (A)
FREITAS, Sébastien (architect, France) 434–435
FROBENIUS, Leo (ethnologist, Germany) 232 (C)
FUJIMORI, Terunobu (architect, Japan) 464 (A)

g

GOLDSWORTHY, Andy (artist, UK) 462 (A), 463 (A)
GOLVIN, Jean-Claude 64–65, 80–81 (B), 82 (B), 84–85 (B)
GRANIER, Thomas (master builder, France & West Africa) 389 (A+B)
GWANI, Mallam Mikhaila Babban (master builder, Nigeria) 222–223

h

H+N+S LANDSCAPE ARCHITECTS (Netherlands) 468–469
HAAS COOK ZEMMRICH (architects, Germany) 450 (B)
HATOUM, Mona (artist, Palestine) 464 (B)
HEIKKINEN, Mikko & KOMONEN, Markku (architects, Finland) 412 (C)
HENSENS, Jean (architect, Switzerland) 282–283
HERINGER, Anna (architect, Germany) 364, 365, 420–421, 429 (B), 483
HERZOG & DE MEURON (architects, Switzerland) 19
HESCO (company, UK) 457 (A)
HILL, Kerry (architect, Australia) 254

i

ICHTER, Jean-Paul (architect, Morocco) 428 (C)

j

JAY-ALLEMAND, Thomas (architect, France) 412 (B)
JENCKS, Charles (architectural theorist & landscape designer, USA) 470–471
JEQUIER, Pierre (architect, Switzerland) 450 (A), 451
JIMMEL, Steven (artist, France) 460 (AR)
JOLY, Serge & LOIRET, Paul-Emmanuel (architects, France) 18, 472–473, 479
JONES, Eddie (architect, USA) 399 (A+B)
JONES, Edward C. (architect, USA) 317
JOURDA, Françoise & PERRAUDIN, Gilles (architects, France) 393 (B), 395
JOY, Rick (architect, USA) 396–397, 448, 449 (B)

k

KAHLO, Frida (artist, Mexico) 453 (A)
KAMARA, Mariam (architect, Niger) 444 (A), 487, 490–491
KÉRÉ, Francis (architect, Burkina Faso & Germany) 368, 418–419, 424–425, 437
KLEIN, Alain (architect, France) 410 (C+B), 460 (BL)
KORT, Paul de (artist, Netherlands) 468–469
KUSUMI, Naoki (artisan builder, Japan) 461 (B)

l

LE CORBUSIER (Charles-Édouard Jeanneret, architect, France & Switzerland) 332–333
LE TIEC, Jean-Marie (architect, France) 434–435
LEA, David (architect, UK) 428 (A)
LEHM TON ERDE BAUKUNST (construction firm, Austria) 359, 406–407, 414–415, 449 (A), 450 (B), 459 (A+B)
LIPSKY, Florence & ROLLET, Pascal (architects, France) 380, 472–473
LONG, Richard (artist, UK) 462 (B), 463 (B)
LOUIS, Jean-Marie (artist, Switzerland) 350–351
LUMPKINS, William (architect, USA) 345 (A)
LUYCKX, Michel (architect, France) 328 (A)
L'VOV, Nikolai (architect, Russia) 314–315 (B)

m

MACGOWAN, John and Georgina (architects, USA) 345 (B)
MAÏNI, Serge (a.k.a. Satprem) & DAVIS, Lara K. (architects, India) 51 (AL), 384–385
MAJORELLE, Jacques (artist, France) 354–355
MARIELLE, Bruno (architect, France) 422 (B), 434–435
MARUYAMA, Kinya (architect, Japan) 378 (B)
MASTALKA, David (architect, Czech Republic) 416–417 (B)
MASSON, Alain (engineer, France) 348
MAURER, Yves-Marie (architect, France) 431 (A)
MÉAU, Rachel & CANNAT, Maude (Eskaapi Group, architects, France) 445 (A)
MINKE, Gernot (architect, Germany) 386–387
MISSE, Arnaud (architect, France) 434–435
MOUYAL, Elie (architect, Morocco) 404–405
MU Jun (architect, China) 423 (A)

n

NAMA ARCHITECTURE (studio, France) 434–435
NICOLAZZI, Marie (architect, France) 416–417 (A)
NG, Edward (architect, China) 423 (A)
NORTON, John (Development Workshop, architect, UK) 55 (A)

o

OLIVER, David (architect, Australia) 454 (C+B)
OSSART, Éric & MAURIÈRES, Arnaud (landscape architects, France & Mexico) 412 (A)

p

PALMER-JONES, William John (architect, UK) 320–321
PATHIRAJA, Milinda (architct, Sri Lanka) 444–445 (B)
PERREAU HAMBURGER, Odile (architect, France) 393 (C)
PERRET, Louis (architect, France) 316 (B)
PIANO, Renzo (RPBW, architect, Italy) 438–439
PIVIN, Jean-Loup (architect, France) 443 (B)
PREDOCK, Antoine (architect, USA) 346–347

q

QUARTUS (property developers, France) 472–473, 479

r

RAMA ESTUDIO (architects, Ecuador) 408–409
RAMÍREZ, Raúl (engineer, Colombia) 50
RATNAYAKE, Ganga (architect, Sri Lanka) 444–445 (B)
RAUCH, Martin (Lehm Ton Erde Baukunst, building specialist, Austria) 19, 359, 406–407, 414–415, 449 (A), 450 (B), 459 (A+B)
RAVEREAU, André & LAUWERS, Philippe (architects, France & Belgium) 436 (A)
REITERMANN, Rudolf & SASSENROTH, Peter (architects, Germany) 414–415
RIGASSI, Vincent (architect, France) 422 (B)
RIVERA, Diego (artist, Mexico) 94 (B)
ROBUST ARCHITECTURE WORKSHOP (Sri Lanka) 444–445 (B)
ROCHA, Mauricio (architect, Mexico) 431 (B), 436 (B)
ROSENBAUM, Marcelo & BENGUELA, Adriana (architects, Brazil) 10–11
ROSSELLI, Luigi (architect, Italy/Australia) 400–401
ROSWAG, Eike & JANKOWSKI, Guntram (architects, Germany) 289 (A), 420–421
ROWLAND, Richard (architect, France & Greece) 411 (A), 416–417 (A)

s

SCHINDLER, Rudolph (architect, Austria/USA) 326
SCHUITEN, Luc (architect, Belgium) 488, 489
SÉCHAUD, Laurent (architect, Switzerland) 450 (A), 451
SEDNAOUI, Olivier (architect, Egypt) 302, 340 (C)
SIREWALL (construction firm, Canada) 443, 458
SMITHSON, Robert (artist, USA) 465
SOMERS CLARKE, George (architect, UK) 320–321
STEFANOVA, Milena (architect, France) 422 (B), 434–435
STEINER, Peter (architect, Switzerland) 359

t

TAXIL, Gisèle (designer, France) 461 (AL)
TIERRATEC see ANGULO, Dario

u

URBINA & SANCHEZ (architects, Colombia) 402 (A+C), 403 (A)
UTRABO, Gustavo & DUSCHENES, Pedro (Aleph Zero, architects, Brazil) 10–11

v

VAN SOOM, Herwig (ORCA Group, architect, Belgium) 52 (A)
VANDERMEEREN, Odile (architect, Belgium) 429 (A+C), 450 (C)
VANNUCCI, Riccardo (architect, Italy) 428 (B)
VIER ARCHITECTOS (architects, Spain) 452–453
VIGUIER, Jean-Paul (architect, France) 422 (A)
VOLHARD, Franz & SCHAUER, Ute (architects, Germany) 410 (A)
VOTH, Hannsjörg (artist, Germany) 17, 47 (L), 292–293, 466–467
VOÛTE NUBIENNE, LA (AVN) (association, France & West Africa) 54–55, 366, 389 (A+B)

w

WANG Shu & LU Wenyu (Amateur Architecture Studio, architects, China) 14, 361, 369, 413 (B), 432–433, 472–473
WISSA WASSEF, Ramses (architect, Egypt) 341 (C)
WATANABE, Kikuma (architect, Japan) 422 (C)
WEBSTER-MANNISON, Marci (architect, Australia) 356–357, 430
WEINER, Paul (DesignBuild Collaborative, architect, USA) 398
WIMPF, Wilhelm Jacob (entrepreneur, Germany) 314 (A)
WOLFSON, Ricardo (artist, Argentina) 107
WRIGHT, David (architect, USA) 344 (B)
WRIGHT, Frank Lloyd (architect, USA) 327

Index of Illustrated Works
by Country

Africa
Algeria 233, 307, 328–329, 341, 350, 353
Benin 284–285
Burkina Faso 230, 231, 235, 291, 295, 389, 418–419, 424–425, 428, 437, 450–451
Burundi 446–447
Cameroon 228–229, 460
Egypt 55, 64–65, 80–81, 82–83, 84–85, 100, 168–169, 170–171, 276–277, 296–297, 302, 336–337, 338–339, 340–341
Ghana 234, 286–287, 320–321, 328, 445
Guinea 412
Ivory Coast 351
Libya 166–167
Madagascar 422
Mali 20, 33, 54–55, 59, 60–61, 62–63, 104, 155, 176–177, 178–179, 180–181, 182–183, 184–185, 186–187, 188–189, 190–191, 192–193, 194–195, 196–197, 198–199, 200–201, 292–203, 204–205, 206–207, 208–209, 210–211, 212–213, 214–215, 216–217, 234–235, 265, 267, 274, 278–279, 328, 351, 436, 443, 508
Mauritania 42, 45, 172–173, 174–175, 270–271, 388
Mayotte 382–383, 427
Morocco 17, 47, 55, 107, 144, 146–147, 150–151, 156–157, 158–159, 160–161, 162–163, 164–165, 268–269, 282–283, 292–293, 341, 348–349, 350, 352, 354–355, 404–405, 412, 428, 454–455, 460, 466–467
Niger 43, 58–59, 224–225, 233, 235, 266, 279, 280–281, 350, 366, 429, 444, 450, 487, 490–491
Nigeria 218–219, 220–221, 222–223, 224, 264–265, 350–351
Senegal 152, 411
Togo 48–49, 59, 226–227
Uganda 438–439

Asia
Afghanistan 100, 457
Bangladesh 364–365, 420–421, 429
Bhutan 254–255
China 14, 27, 46, 124–125, 126–127, 148–149, 250–251, 252–253, 361, 413, 423, 432–433, 457
India 6–7, 50–51, 128–129, 130–131, 248–249, 384–385, 386–387, 481
Indonesia 148–149
Iraq 71, 77, 79
Iran 56–57, 78, 101, 114–115, 116–117, 118–119, 120–121, 122–123, 277
Japan 132–133, 464
Jordan 363
Oman 288–289
Pakistan 87
Palestine 70, 464
Russia 314–315
Saudi Arabia 242–243, 244–245, 270–271
Singapore 461
South Korea 295
Sri Lanka 444–445
Syria 74–75, 76, 246–247, 442
Thailand 411, 422–423
Turkmenistan 87
Turkey 72–73
United Arab Emirates 288–289
Uzbekistan 68–69, 86–87
Vietnam 148–149
Yemen 28–29, 102–103, 108–109, 110–111, 112–113, 236–237, 238–239, 240–241, 272–273, 275

Australasia
Australia 40, 356–357, 400–401, 430, 440–441, 454
New Caledonia 426
New Zealand 316
Vanuatu 265

Europe
Austria 406–407, 449, 459
Belgium 52
Bulgaria 98–99
Czech Republic 416–417
France 18, 25, 26, 37, 46, 53, 256–257, 258–259, 309–310, 311–312, 313, 322–323, 330–331, 332–333, 371, 376–377, 378–379, 380–381, 390–391, 392–393, 394–395, 402–403, 410, 412, 416–417, 422, 431, 434–435, 436, 442, 456, 460–461, 452–463, 472–473, 479
Germany 52, 262–263, 314–315, 322–323, 386–387, 410, 414–415, 450, 461
Great Britain 27, 260–261, 428, 460, 462–463, 470–471
Luxembourg 456
Netherlands 468–469
Romania 98
Spain 28, 52, 144–145, 452–453
Sweden 98
Switzerland 19, 315, 359, 407

North America
Canada 443, 458
United States 50–51, 96–97, 134–135, 136–137, 316–317, 324–325, 326–327, 335, 342–343, 344–345, 346–347, 396–397, 398–399, 413, 448–449, 465

South America
Brazil 10–11, 40, 140–141
Bolivia 138–139
Chile 53, 388
Colombia 140–141, 402–403
Ecuador 408–409
Guatemala 142, 386
Mexico 94–95, 143, 353, 431, 436
Paraguay 139
Peru 88–89, 90–91, 92–93, 318–319
Venezuela 138, 142–143

Member Institutions of the UNESCO Chair on Earthen Architecture

The UNESCO Chair on Earthen Architecture, Building Cultures and Sustainable Development was founded in 1998 at the Grenoble School of Architecture, under the aegis of CRAterre. Its mission is to promote the international dissemination of scientific, technical, and cultural knowledge. Along with its 41 partners, it facilitates the running of teaching, research, and experimental projects. Over two decades, several projects have been developed, including a specialist diploma in earth architecture, as well as courses in Europe, North and South America, Asia, and Africa. The Chair is represented in more than 20 countries and is part of a global network that establishes training and information centres that grow bigger every year.

https://terra.hypotheses.org

Algeria: Centre Algérien du Patrimoine Culturel Bâti en Terre (CapTerre).

Angola: Department of Architecture, Lusíada University.

Argentina: [1] Regional Centre for Research into Raw Earth Architecture, Faculty of Architecture, National University of Tucumán (CRIATIC-FAU-UNT). [2] The Mario J. Buschiazzo Institute of Art, Faculty of Architecture, University of Buenos Aires.

Austria: BASEhabitat, Linz.

Brazil: Faculty of Engineering and Architecture, Methodist University of Piracicaba.

Chile: The Arcot Network (Arquitectura y Construcción con Tierra), run by the Fundación Joffre, with universities affiliated with the UNESCO Chair. Network member institutions: [1] Fundación Joffre. [2] Faculty of Architecture and Construction, Catholic University of the North (UCN), Antofagasta. [3] University of Bío-Bío (UBB), Talca. [4] Arturo Prat University (UNAP), Iquique. [5] University of La Serena (ULS). [6] University of Concepción (UDEC). [7] Technical University of Federico Santa María (UFSM), Valparaíso. [8] University of Santiago de Chile (USACH), Santiago.

China: [1] School of Architecture and Urban Planning, Beijing University of Civil Engineering and Architecture, Beijing. [2] Architecture Department, China Academy of Art, Hangzhou.

Colombia: [1] Faculty of Architecture, National University of Colombia, Bogotá. [2] Pontifical Bolivarian University, Medellín. [3] Tierra Tech, Bogotá.

Democratic Republic of Congo: Amicale des Autoconstructeurs Ruraux (Amicor).

France: [1] Association CRAterre, Grenoble. [2] Laboratoire CRAterre-ENSAG.

India: [1] Auroville Earth Institute (AVEI), Auroville. [2] SECMOL.

Iran: [1] University of Art, Tehran. [2] Iran's Cultural Heritage Handicrafts and Tourism Organization (ICHHTO). [3] Vernacular Architecture Research Center (VARC), University of Yazd.

Italy: Department of Architecture, Faculty of Engineering, University of Cagliari (UNICA).

Mexico: [1] CIPTEV Centre of Research and Production of Eco-Technology for Living. [2] Faculty of Architecture, Autonomous University of Tamaulipas (FADU/UAT). [3] Metropolitan Autonomous University (UAM), Xochimilco.

Morocco: [1] National Schools of Architecture of Rabat and Marrakech, in association with the PATerre research centre. [2] CERKAS Centre of Conservation, Restoration, and Rehabilitation of Ksour and Kasbahs, Ouarzazate.

Peru: Pontifical Catholic University of Peru (PUCP).

Portugal: Escola Superior Gallaecia (ESG), Vila Nova de Cerveira.

South Africa: Earth Unit, Department of Architecture, University of the Free State.

South Korea: Department of Architecture, Mokpo National University (DOA-MNU), and Terra Korea (Korea Earth Architecture Institute).

Spain: Escuela Técnica Superior de Arquitectura, Polytechnic University of Valencia.

United Kingdom: Earth Building UK and Ireland (Ebuki).

Uruguay: North Region Department of Architecture, Salto, University of the Republic (UDELAR), Montevideo.

Honorary professors of the UNESCO Chair on Earthen Architecture: Anna Heringer (Germany), Martin Rauch (Austria), Dominique Gauzin-Müller (France), Rowland Keable (UK).

The authors are responsible for the selection and presentation of all the information in this book and for all the opinions expressed, which are not necessarily those of UNESCO and for which UNESCO is not liable.

Acknowledgments

I dedicate this book to my children, to the pioneers and artisans of the earth architecture revival, and to the young people campaigning for a transition to a greener way of life.

Jean Dethier

Since this book is the culmination of research and engagement carried out in phases over several decades, it is both a large and pleasing task to thank all of those who have contributed, in one way or another, to its completion.

My deepest gratitude goes first of all to the three founders of CRAterre – Patrice Doat, Hubert Guillaud, and Hugo Houben – who, as part of this book's scientific committee, made four crucial contributions: overseeing the overall coherence and relevance of the work, coordinating the contributions from other experts, providing a critical reading of all the texts, and writing a dozen essays themselves.

Thanks to the other writers whose complementary fields gave this book the interdisciplinary approach that I wanted: Anne-Monique Bardagot, Ruth Eaton, Dominique Gauzin-Müller, Nathalie Sabatier, Henri Van Damme, Ariane Wilson, and from CRAterre, Romain Anger, David Gandreau, Hugo Gasnier, and Sébastien Moriset.

Thanks also to those who shared their beliefs about the future of earth architecture: Lara K. Davis, Anna Heringer, Bakonirina Rakotomamonjy, Martin Rauch, and S. K. Sharma.

Thank you to all the photographers whose work constitutes the beating heart of this book, capturing the beauty and harmony of earth architecture. For their very generous contributions, I must express particular gratitude to Marie Schuiten and to Dorothee Gruner. Thanks also to Alain Klein, André Stevens, Jacques Evrard and Christine Bastin, James Morris, Deidi von Schaewen, Dominique Gauzin-Müller at CRAterre, and Thierry Joffroy.

Thanks to the illustrators whose work has enriched and diversified this book, and especially to Jean-Claude Golvin, Luc Schuiten, and Jean-Marie Louis.

Thanks to all the architects, designers, artists, landscape gardeners, and other creators – as well as to the relevant institutions and associations – who contributed photographs and illustrations for use in this book.

Thanks to young architects Nicolas Genest, and in particular Arthur Besnard who took care of the scanning and colouring of over a hundred illustrations.

Thanks to the publishers for turning a dream into concrete reality. Special thanks to the team at Flammarion who oversaw the culmination of my two decades of research: Julie Rouart, head of art and architecture books; Marion Doublet, project editor, assisted by Manon Clercelet; Clémentine Bougrat, proofreader; Marie Audet, picture researcher; and Jana Navratil-Manent, who sold translated editions of this book to four publishers: Thames & Hudson in the UK, Princeton Architectural Press in the USA, Detail in Germany, and Blume in Spain.

Thanks to Patrice Doat, François Perrin, and Anne Moreau for reading my texts.

Special thanks to Hubert Guillaud: he took on this important task with a critical eye for detail and exceptional thoroughness. I must once again stress my gratitude for his great contribution.

Thanks to the two designers who came up with the conceptual approach and elegant layout of this book: my gratitude goes to Marc Walter, who began this creative process – sadly interrupted by his early death – and to Pierre-Yann Lallaizon, who continued and completed the task, meeting all my expectations and demands.

Thanks to everyone who encouraged me throughout the making of this book: Marie Schuiten, François Perrin, Joseph Brunet-Jailly, and Anne Van Loo, as well as, in my own family, Sophie, Anne, Pierre, Manuel, Ruth, Éloïse, and Julien.

Special thanks to my faithful friend Patrice Doat for his constant encouragement and support. I owe him my deepest gratitude for his fierce and brotherly generosity.

Last but not least, thanks to Ariane Braillard and to Isabelle Ducimetière, board members of the Fondation Braillard Architectes in Geneva, whose contributions helped to cover the costs of picture research and repro for the many images in this book. Thanks to the agency A2RC Architects in Brussels for their support. Thanks also to Guy Rothier. Thanks to the Centre National Français du Livre for awarding me a writer's grant as part of their programme to promote the publication of innovative works about architecture.

Mosque in the village of Nando,
Dogon Country, Mali (see pp. 180-183).

Picture Credits

Key: A: above, B: below, C: centre, L: left, R: right

Adaptation and colorization of illustrations by architects Arthur Besnard and Nicolas Genest: 40 (A, after Mitchell and Stein), 46 (AR), 52 (C), 55 (AR, after John Norton / Development Workshop), 70, 72 (after James Mellaart), 78 (A), 81 (AR), 82 (A), 84 (A, after Jean-Claude Golvin / Editions Errance), 85 (A, after Walter Emery), 86 (A), 89 (AR), 94 (AR, after Coe), 98 (BL, BR), 109 (A), 112 (BL, BC, BR), 122 (BL), 124 (BL), 127 (A, CL, CR, after Michaël Bier), 134 (BL), 136 (A), 139 (AL, AR), 141 (AL, AR), 162 (AL, AR, after Jean Hensens), 180 (BL), 184 (AR, after Gérard Beaudoin), 192 (BL, after Pierre Maas), 208–209 (after Fabrizio Ago), 210 (A, after Fabrizio Ago), 222 (AL, BL, after Fabrizio Ago), 228 (A, after Christian Seignobos), 229 (AL, AR, after Christian Seignobos), 232 (A), 234 (BL), 235 (AL, HM, after Corinne & Laszlo Mester de Parajd), 253 (AL, AR, after Jean-Paul Loubes), 258 (AL, AR), 261 (AR, after Thomas Sharp), 273 (AL, after Salma Samar Damluji), 309 (after François Cointeraux), 310 (C, B, after Jean-Baptiste Rondelet), 311 (after François Cointeraux), 317 (A), 320 (A, C, after Somers Clarke and Palmer-Jones), 339 (AL, AR, after Aga Khan Architecture Award, Geneva), 344 (AL, AR, after David Wright), 346 (A, after Antoine Predock), 381 (A, after Josep Esteve), 386 (AL, AR, after Gernot Minke), 393 (AR, after Alain Leclerc), 408 (A, after Rama Estudio), 415 (A, after Reitermann & Sassenroth), 420 (A, after Anna Heringer), 442 (B, after André Stevens), 450 (A, after Pierre Jequier & Laurent Séchaud).

6–7 © Satprem Maïni (Auroville Earth Institute); 10–11 © Cristóbal Palma; 14 © Amateur Architecture Studio; 17 © Marion Tabeaud; 18 © Joly & Loiret; 19 © amàco - Gian Franco Noriega & Zoé Tric; 20 © Yann Arthus Bertrand / Hemis.fr; 25 © CRAterre / Thierry Joffroy; 26 (AL) © CRAterre / Arnaud Misse; 26 (AC) © CRAterre / Hubert Guillaud; 27 (AC) © Terra Incognita; 27 (AR) © Mu Jun / Chaire UNESCO de CRAterre en Chine; 26–27 (B) © CRAterre / Arnaud Misse; 28–29 © Pascal & Maria Maréchaux; 30 © CRAterre / Arnaud Misse; 33 © Dorothée Gruner; 34 © Tomas Griger / Alamy / Photo12; 35 © Jürg Donatsch; 37 (L, R) © Alain Klein architect; 40 (C) © Bert Kitchen; 40 (B) © Luiz Claudio Marigo / Nature Picture Library / Getty Images; 41 © imageBROKER / Photo12; 42 © Margaret Courtney-Clarke; 43 © Aga Khan Trust for Culture / Kamran Adle (photo); 44, 45 (A, B) © Josep Esteve; 46 (L) © British Library Board. All Rights Reserved / Bridgeman Images; 46 (CR) © Jean Dethier; 46 (BR) © Andreas Krewet / AKTERRE; 47 (L, R) © Ingrid Amslinger; 49 (A) © Malagasy View / Alamy / Photo12; 48–49 (B) © Paule Seux / hemis.fr; 50 (A), 51 (AL) © Satprem Maïni (Auroville Earth Institute); 51 (AR) © CRAterre / Hugo Gasnier; 50–51 (B) © Bastin & Evrard SPRL / Adagp, Paris 2019; 52 (AL, AR) © Herwig Van Soom / ORCA Architectuur & Stabiliteit (orcaarchi.be); 52 (B) © Guillermo Maestro Casado; 53 (AL) © Roland Schweitzer; 53 (AR) © Marcelo Cortes; 53 (B) © Bastin & Evrard SPRL / Adagp, Paris 2019; 54–55 (B) © Association la Voûte Nubienne (AVN); 55 (CR) © ADAUA; 55 (BR) © Charlie Sheppard; 56–57 © André Stevens; 58 (AL) © Dominique Lenclos; 58 (CL) © NSP-RF / Alamy / Photo12; 58 (BL) © Alain Klein architect; 58–59 (C) © Tuul & Bruno Morandi; 59 (AR) © Clayarch Gimhae Museum; 59 (ACR) © Lucille Reyboz; 59 (BCR) © CRAterre / Thierry Joffroy; 59 (BR) © CRAterre / Romain Anger & Laetitia Fontaine; 60–61, 62–63 © James Morris; 64–65 Watercolour by Jean-Claude Golvin. Musée Départemental Arles Antique © Jean-Claude Golvin / Éditions Errance; 68–69 © Tuul & Bruno Morandi; 71 © Jean Dethier; 72–73 (C) © Marcel Socías; 73 (A) © Mauricio Abreu / AWL Images / Getty Images; 74 © Harold Hill; 75 (A) © Musée du Louvre, Dist. RMN-Grand Palais / Christian Larrieu; 75 (B) All Rights Reserved; 76 (A) © Walter Andrae; 76 (B) © Al-Rawda Archaeological Survey; 77 Drawing by Maurice Bardin. Courtesy of the Oriental Institute of the University of Chicago; 78 (B) © Gilles Barbier / Imagebroker / Photo12; 79 (A, B), 80–81 (B) Watercolour by Jean-Claude Golvin. Musée Départemental Arles Antique © Jean-Claude Golvin / Éditions Errance; 80 (A), 81 (B) © Luisa Fumi / Shutterstock.com; 82 (B), 83 (B), 84–85 (B) © Jean-Claude Golvin / Éditions Errance; 86 (B) © Stephan Lippmann / Oneworld Picture / Alamy / Photo12; 87 (A) © Agencja Fotograficzna Caro / Alamy / Photo12; 87 (B) © Calle Montes / Photononstop; 88–89 (B) © Jon Arnold Images Ltd / Alamy / Hemis.fr; 89 (AL) © André Stevens; 90 © marktucan / Shutterstock; 91 (A) © Trujillo, Proyecto Huaca de la Luna-Museo Huacas del Valle de Moche, Universidad Nacional de Trujillo, Ministry of Culture of Peru; 91 (B) © Matyas Rehak / Shutterstock; 92 (A) © CRAterre / Hubert Guillaud; 92 (B) © Watchtheworld / Alamy / Photo12; 93 © Toño Labra / Agefotostock / Photo12; 94 (AL) © Luis Covarrubias; 94 (B) © 2019 Banco de México, Diego Rivera Frida Kahlo Museums Trust, Mexico, D.F. / Adagp, Paris 2019. Photo © De Agostini Picture Library / G. Dagli Orti / Bridgeman Images; 95 © Granger / Bridgeman Images; 96 (A, B) © Jon Gibson; 97 (A) Courtesy of The Ancient Ohio Trail; 97 (B) © Lloyd Townsend; 98 (A), 99 © Giovanni Caselli; 100 (A) All Rights Reserved; 100 (B) © Jean Dethier; 101 © RMN-Grand Palais (musée du Louvre) / Hervé Lewandowski; 102–103 © Yann Arthus-Bertrand / Hemis.fr; 104 © Dorothée Gruner; 107 © Ricardo Wolfson. Photo © Jean Dethier; 108 © Pascal & Maria Maréchaux; 109 (B) © Yann Arthus-Bertrand / Hemis.fr; 110–111 (A) © Paule Seux / Hemis.fr; 110–111 (B) © Aga Khan Trust for Culture / Anne De Henning (photo); 112 (A) © Pascal & Maria Maréchaux; 113 (A) © Aga Khan Trust for Culture / Anne De Henning (photo); 113 (B) © Jon Arnold Images / Hemis.fr; 114 (A) © Tina Manley / Alamy / Photo12; 114 (C) © Jean-Philippe Lenclos; 114 (B) © CRAterre / Sébastien Moriset; 115 © Roland & Sabrina Michaud / akg-images; 116 (A) © Aliaksandr Mazurkevich / Alamy / Photo12; 116 (B) © Tuul & Bruno Morandi; 117 (A) © Paule Seux / Hemis.fr; 117 (B) © Tuul & Bruno Morandi; 118, 119 © M. Khebra / Shutterstock; 120–121 (A) © Mauritius images GmbH / Alamy Stock Photo / Hemis.fr; 120–121 (B) © Georg Gerster / Gamma-Rapho; 122 (A) © EmmePi Travel / Alamy / Photo12; 122 (BR) © Robert Harding / Alamy / Hemis.fr; 123 (A) © EmmePi Travel / Alamy / Photo12; 123 (B) © CRAterre; 124–125 (A) © Tuul & Bruno Morandi; 124–125 (BR) © Keren Su / Getty Images; 126 (A, B), 127 (B) © Marie Schuiten; 128–129 © Geoff Wiggins / Alamy / Photo12; 130–131 © travelib india / Alamy / Photo12; 132 (A) © John Lander / Alamy / Photo12; 133 (A) © Picture Partners / Alamy / Photo12; 132–133 (B) © Sean Pavone / Alamy / Photo12; 134 (A) © RGB Ventures / SuperStock / Alamy / Photo12; 135 (A) © Everett Historical / Shutterstock; 134–135 (B) © Dennis Frates / Alamy / Photo12; 136 (B) © Robert Fried / Alamy / Photo12; 137 © Steven Milne / Alamy / Photo12; 138 (A); © Bildagentur-online / Alamy / Photo12; 138–139 (B) © Marica van der Meer / Arterra Picture Library / Photo12; 140 (A) All Rights Reserved; 140–141 (B) © StockBrazil / Alamy / Photo12; 142 (A) © Keren Su / China Span / Alamy / Photo12; 142 (B) © Jordi Cami / Alamy / Photo12; 143 (A) © Wendy Connett / Alamy / Photo12; 143 (B) © Robert Harding / Alamy / Photo12; 144 (A) © CFimages / Alamy / Photo12; 144 (C) © Jacques Sierpinski / Hemis.fr; 144 (B) © Jordi Cami / Alamy / Photo12; 145 © Ken Welsh / Alamy / Photo12; 146 (A) © Jack Sullivan / Alamy / Photo12; 146 (C) © Jean Dethier; 146 (B) © Lucas Vallecillos / Alamy / Photo12; 147 (A) © Goran Bogicevic / Alamy / Photo12; 147 (B) © Hope Production / Hemis.fr; 148 © Stefan Auth / ImageBROKER / Photo12; 149 (A) © Lin Yiguang / Xinhua / Alamy / Photo12; 149 (B) © Sean Pavone / Shutterstock; 150–151 © Jean Dethier; 152 (A) © CRAterre / Thierry Joffroy; 152 (B) © CRAterre / Thierry Joffroy; 155 © Jordi Cami / Alamy / Photo12; 156 (A), 157 (AL) All Rights Reserved; 157 (AR) © Robert Fried / Alamy / Photo12; 156–157 (B) © Rob Crandall / Alamy / Photo12; 158 (A, B), 159 (A, B) © Jean Dethier; 160 (A) © Jam World Images / Alamy / Photo12; 161 (AL) © Karl Heinz Striedter; 161 (AR) © Charles O. Cecil / Alamy / Photo12; 160–161 (B) © Tuul & Bruno Morandi; 162 (B) © Karl Heinz Striedter; 163 (A) © Tuul & Bruno Morandi; 163 (B) © Ellen McKnight / Alamy / Photo12; 164 © Travel4pictures / Alamy / Photo12; 165 (A) © Jean Dethier; 165 (B) © Franck Charton / Hemis.fr; 166 (AL, BL,), 167 © CRAterre / Grégoire Paccoud / Thierry Joffroy; 166–167 (C) © CRAterre / Grégoire Paccoud; 167 (BR) © Susanna Wyatt / Getty Images; 168, 169 © Marie Schuiten; 170 (BL) © Bastin & Evrard SPRL / Adagp, Paris 2019; 170–171 (R) © Yann Arthus Bertrand / Hemis.fr; 172–173, 174 (A) © Deidi von Schaewen; 174 (B), 175 © Ruiz / Tréal / Gamma-Rapho; 176 (A) © CRAterre / Romain Anger & Laetitia Fontaine; 176 (C) © Claude Lefèvre / www.claudelefevre.fr; 176 (B) © Tuul & Bruno Morandi / Hemis.fr; 177 © Gert Chesi; 178 © Marie Schuiten; 179 (A) © Alioune Ba; 179 (B) © Alfred Wolf / Gamma-Rapho; 181 (A) © Marie Schuiten; 180–181 (BR) © Alfred Wolf / Gamma-Rapho; 182–183 © Marie Schuiten; 184 (AL) Collection Jean Dethier; 185 (A), 184–185 (B) © Yann Arthus Bertrand / Hemis.fr; 186 (A) © F. Nansen; 186 (C, B) Collection Alain Klein architect; 187 © René Gardi; 188 Collection Alain Klein architect; 189 © Gert Chesi; 190, 191 © Gérard Beaudoin; 192 (A) © Andrault; 192–193 (BR) © CRAterre / Thierry Joffroy; 193 (A) © Aflo / Hemis.fr; 194–195 © Yann Arthus-Bertrand / Hemis.fr; 196 © Marli Shamir; 197 © Jon Arnold Images / Hemis.fr; 198 (A, B) © Peeyush Sekhsaria; 199 © Aga Khan Trust for Culture / Anne-Hélène Decaux (photo); 200–201 © Yann Arthus-Bertrand / Hemis.fr; 202, 203, 204, 205, 206 (A) © Dorothée Gruner; 206 (B) © Bert de Ruiter / Alamy / Photo12; 207 (A) © Marie Schuiten; 207 (B) © Roberto Nencini / Shutterstock; 210–211 (B), 211 (A) © CRAterre / Thierry Joffroy; 212–213 © Catherine de Clippel; 214–215 © Dorothée Gruner; 216 (AL) © Andrault; 216 (AR) © Deidi von Schaewen; 216 (B) © Marli Shamir; 217 (AL) © Andrault; 217 (AR) All Rights Reserved; 217 (B) © Marie Schuiten; 218 (A) © René Gardi; 219 (A) © Steven Ehrlich; 218–219 (B) © CRAterre / Thierry Joffroy; 220 (A) All Rights Reserved; 220 (B) © René Gardi; 221 © Deidi von Schaewen; 222–223 (R) © Z. R Dmochowski; 224 (A, BL) © Steven Ehrlich; 224 (BR) © RMN-Grand Palais (musée du Quai Branly - Jacques Chirac) / Jean-Gilles Berizzi; 225 © René Gardi; 226 (A, B) © CRAterre / Thierry Joffroy; 227 (AL, AR) © CRAterre / Arnaud Misse; 227 (B) © Lucille Reyboz; 228–229 (B) © René Pauleau. Collection Alain Klein architect; 230 © Marie Schuiten; 231 (AL, AR) © CRAterre / Romain Anger & Laetitia Fontaine; 231 (B) © Marie Schuiten; 232 (C) © F. Nansen; 232 (B) Collection Alain Klein architect; 233 (A) © CRAterre / Thierry Joffroy; 233 (B) © Mohand Abouda; 234–235 (B) © Gert Chesi; 235 (A) © René Gardi; 236–237 © javarman / Shutterstock.com; 238 (BL) © Christophe Boisvieux / Hemis.fr; 238 (AR) © Bastin & Evrard SPRL / Adagp, Paris 2019; 239 (AR) © Trevor H. J. Marchand; 238–239 (BR) © Nick Ledger / Alamy / Photo12; 240 (AL) © Harper Collins / TAA / Aurimages; 240 (BR) © Pascal & Maria Maréchaux; 240–241 © Christian Darles; 242 (AL) © Eric Lafforgue / Alamy / Photo12; 242 (BL) © John Warburton-Lee Photography / Alamy / Hemis.fr; 243 (AR), 242–243 (B) © Patrice Doat / CRAterre; 244 (A, B), 245 © Thierry Mauger; 246 (A) © Urs Flueeler / Alamy / Photo12; 246–247 (B) Collection: André Stevens; 247 (A) © Houda Kassatly; 248 (A) © Tuul & Bruno Morandi; 248 (B) © Purepix / Alamy / Photo12; 249 (A) © Tuul &

Bruno Morandi; 249 (B) © Dinodia photos / Alamy / Photo12; 250 (A), 250–251 (B) © Marie Schuiten; 251 (A) © Henry Westheim Photography / Alamy / Photo12; 252 (A) © Ana Flasker / Alamy / Photo12; 252–253 (B) © Tuul & Bruno Morandi; 254 © Ana Flasker / Alamy / Photo12; 255 (A, B) © Marie Schuiten; 256 (A) © CRAterre / Thierry Joffroy; 256 (C) © Christian Lignon; 256 (B) © CRAterre / Romain Anger & Laetitia Fontaine; 257 (A) © CAUE du Gers; 257 (B) © CRAterre / Patrice Doat; 258 (B) © Gilles Targat / Photo12; 259 (A) © Richard Weil; 259 (C) © CRAterre / Philippe Bardel; 259 (B) © Mark Jones / Alamy / Photo12; 260 (A) All Rights Reserved; 261 (AL) © travelib prime / Alamy / Photo12; 260–261 (B) © Incamerastock / Alamy / Photo12; 262–263 © Bahnmueller / Alamy / Photo12; 264–265 © Lesley Lababidi; 265 (AR) © MCLA Collection / Alamy / Photo12; 265 (BR) © Musée du Quai Branly - Jacques Chirac, Dist. RMN-Grand Palais / Patrick Gries / Bruno Descoings; 266 © Alberto Arzoz.Design Pics / Alamy / Photo12; 267 © Jean-Pierre De Mann / AGE / Photo12; 268 (A) © Jean Dethier; 268 (C) © Chris Mellor / Lonely Planet / Getty Images; 268 (B) © Andrew Wilson / Alamy / Photo12; 269 © Juergen Ritterbach / Alamy / Photo12; 270 (BL) © Jean Dethier; 270–271 © René Burri / Magnum Photos; 272 (A) © Trevor H. J. Marchand; 273 (AR) © Christian Heeb / Alamy / Photo12; 272–273 (B) © Pascal & Maria Maréchaux; 274 All Rights Reserved; 275 (A) © Pascal & Maria Maréchaux; 275 (B) © Aga Khan Trust for Culture / Courtesy of Salma Samar Damluji; 277 (AL) © Design Pics Inc / Alamy / Photo12; 277 (AR) © Bastin & Evrard SPRL / Adagp, Paris 2019; 276–277 (B) © Deidi von Schaewen; 278 (A) All Rights Reserved; 278 (B) © Jordi Cami / AGEfotostock / Photo12; 279 (A) © Design Pics Inc / Alamy / Photo12; 279 (B) © Marie Schuiten; 280–281 © James Morris; 282 (A) © Rob Crandall / Alamy / Photo12; 282 (B), 283 (A,B) © Bart Deseyn; 284 (A) © Marica van der Meer / Alamy / Photo12; 284 (B) © Eric Lafforgue / AGEfotostock / Photo12; 285 (AL, CL, BL) © Aldo Pavan / AGEfotostock / Photo12; 285 (AR) © Louise Batalla Duran / Alamy / Photo12; 285 (CR) © Eric Lafforgue / Alamy / Photo12; 285 (BR), 286 (AL, BL), 287 (A) © CRAterre / Thierry Joffroy; 287 (B) © Ariadne Van Zandbergen / Alamy / Photo12; 288 (AL) © Leonid Andronov / Alamy / Photo12; 288 (BL) © Michele Burgess / Alamy / Photo12; 288–289 (B) © Tuul & Bruno Morandi; 289 (AL) © Fabian von Poser / ImageBROKER / Photo12; 289 (AR) © Robert Harding / Alamy / Photo12; 291 © CRAterre / Thierry Joffroy; 292–293 © Marion Tabeaud; 295 (A) © Gimhae Clayarch Museum; 295 (B) © Kéré Architecture; 296–297 (A) © Aga Khan Trust for Culture / Hassan Fathy (architect), Gary Otte (photographer); 296–297 (B) © Aga Khan Trust for Culture / Albek A. & Niksarli M.; 302 © Bastin & Evrard SPRL / Adagp, Paris 2019; 307 © Clara Eyckerman; 310 (AL, AR) © Jean-Baptiste Rondelet; 312 (A, B) © Christian Lignon; 313 (A) © CRAterre; 313 (C) © Bastin & Evrard SPRL / Adagp, Paris 2019; 313 (B) © Christian Lignon; 314–315 (B) © Irinia Afonskaya / Alamy / Photo12; 316 (A), 317 (B) © Library of Congress; 316 (B) © Greg Balfour Evans / Alamy / Photo12; 318 (A, B), 319 (A, B) © Marie Schuiten; 320 (B) © Association Égyptologique Reine Élisabeth; 321 (A) © Nicholas Warner; 321 (B) © The Metropolitan Museum of Art, Dist. RMN-Grand Palais / image of the MMA; 322 (A) © Mary Evans Picture Library / Photononstop; 323 (AL, AR) © Jean Dethier; 322–323 (B) © Ministère de la Culture et de la Communication, Médiathèque de l'Architecture et du Patrimoine, Dist. RMN-GP; 324 (A) © Ivo Roospold / Alamy / Photo12; 324 (C) © America / Alamy / Photo12; 324 (B) © Oliver Gerhard / ImageBROKER / Photo12; 325 (A) © Cannon Photography LLC / Alamy / Photo12; 325 (B) © Jay Goebel / Alamy / Photo12; 326 (A, B) © R. M. Schindler papers, Architecture & Design Collection. Art, Design & Architecture Museum; University of California, Santa Barbara; 327 (AL, AR, C, B) © Adagp, Paris, 2019. © The Frank Lloyd Wright Foundation Archives (The Museum of Modern Art / Avery Architectural & Fine Arts Library, Columbia University, New York); 328 (A, B) © Jean Dethier; 328 (C) © CRAterre / Thierry Joffroy; 329 (A) © Richard Mayer / Alamy / Photo12; 329 (B) © Frans Lemmens / Alamy / Photo12; 330 (A, B), 331 (A) Collection Alain Klein architect; 331 (BL, BR) All Rights Reserved; 332 (A, B), 333 (A, B) © F.L.C. / Adagp, Paris, 2019; 335 © Bastin & Evrard SPRL / Adagp, Paris 2019; 336 (A), 337 (AL, AR) All Rights Reserved; 336 (B) © Deidi von Schaewen; 337 (C), 338 (A, B) © Bastin & Evrard SPRL / Adagp, Paris 2019; 337 (B) © Aga Khan Trust for Culture /Albek A. & Niksarli M; 338 (C) © B. O'Kane / Alamy / Hemis.fr; 339 (B) © Aga Khan Trust for Culture / Christopher Little (photo); 340 (A) © Adel Famy; 340 (C) © Olivier Sednaoui; 340 (B), 341 (B) © Bastin & Evrard SPRL / Adagp, Paris 2019; 341 (A) © Bruno Ruffini; 341 (C) © Aga Khan Trust for Culture / Chant Avedissian (photo); 342 (A), 343 (AL, AR) All Rights Reserved; 342–343 (B), 344 (B), 345 (A, B) © Bastin & Evrard SPRL / Adagp, Paris 2019; 346 (C) All Rights Reserved; 346 (B), 347 (A, B) © Bastin & Evrard SPRL / Adagp, Paris 2019; 347 (C), 348 (A, AC, BC, B), 349 (A, B) © Jean Dethier; 350, 351 © Jean-Marie Louis; 352 © Musée des Augustins, Toulouse, France / Bridgeman Images; 353 (A) © 2019 Banco de México Diego Rivera Frida Kahlo Museums Trust, Mexico, D.F. / Adagp, Paris 2019. Photo © Alamy / Photo12; 353 (B) © Adagp, Paris, 2019. Photo © RMN-Grand Palais / René-Gabriel Ojéda; 354–355 © Adagp, Paris, 2019. Photo © Artcurial; 356–357 © Germain Rozo & Claire Guyet; 359 © Bruno Klomfar; 361 © Marc Auzet / Juliette Goudy; 363 © Blaine Harrington III / Alamy / Photo12; 364 © Kurt Hoerbst; 365 © Studio Anna Heringer; 366 © Association la Voûte Nubienne (AVN); 368 © Astrid Eckert / TUM; 369 (BL, BR) © Gino Maccarinelli; 371 © CRAterre / Pierre Eric Verney; 376 (A, B), 377 (A, B), 378 (A, C, B), 379 © CRAterre / Patrice Doat; 380 (A) © Florence Lipsky & Pascal Rollet; 380 (C, B) © CRAterre / Patrice Doat; 381 (B) © AE&CC / Maxime Bonnevie; 382 (A) © Vincent Liétard; 382 (AC, B) © CRAterre / Patrice Doat; 382 (BC), 383 (A, B) © CRAterre / Thierry Joffroy; 384 (AL, BL), 385 (AR, BR) © Satprem Maïni (Auroville Earth Institute); 384–385 (C) © CRAterre / Sébastien Moriset; 386 (C, B), 387 (A, B) © Gernot Minke; 388 (A) © Josep Esteve / ADAUA; 388 (B) © Marcelo Cortes; 389 (A, B) © Association la Voûte Nubienne (AVN); 390 (A) © Dominique Appia; 390 (B) © Ruth Eaton; 391 (A) © Jean-Claude Planchet; 391 (B) © Jean Dethier; 392 (A), 393 (C, B) © CRAterre / Thierry Joffroy; 392 (AC, BC, B) © Dominique Pidance & Alain Lebahl; 393 (AL) © CRAterre / Patrice Doat; 394 (AR, AL) © CRAterre / Thierry Joffroy; 395 (A, B) © Gilles Perraudin & Françoise Jourda; 396 (AL), 396–397 (B) © Bill Timmerman / Studio Rick Joy; 396–397 (HM) © Undine Pröhl; 397 (AR) © Wayne Fuji / Studio Rick Joy; 398 © Paul Weiner / Design Build Collaborative; 399 (A) © Low Compound by Tim Hursley; 399 (B) © Johnson-Jones Residence by Tim Hursley; 400 (A, B), 401 © Luigi Rosselli Architects; 400 (C) © Edward Birch / Luigi Rosselli Architects; 402 (A, C), 403 (A) © Dario Angulo; 402–403 (B) © Andrei S.; 404 (AL, AR, B), 405 (CL, CR, B) © CRAterre / Thierry Joffroy; 405 (A) © Elie Mouyal; 406 (A), 407 (A) © Dominique Gauzin-Muller; 406 (B) © Bruno Klomfar; 407 (B) © Ralph Feiner; 408 (C, B), 409 (A, B) © Rama Estudio / JAG; 410 (A) © Thomas Ott / www.o2t.de; 410 (C, B) © Pierre Mignot; 411 (A) © By Reg› - Régis L›Hostis; 411 (C, B) © Alberto Cosi / Chiangmai Life Architects; 412 (A) © Ossart+Maurières, architects. Photo © Nicolas Schimp; 412 (C) © Onerva Utriainen; 412 (B) © Thomas Jay - Caracol Architectures; 413 (A) © Bluff Design Build; 413 (B) © Amateur Architecture Studio; 414 (A) © Lothar Steiner / Alamy / Photo12; 414 (B) © Ingo Jezierski / Alamy / Photo12; 415 (B) © Adam Eastland / Alamy / Photo12; 416–417 (A) © Richard Rowland / Justine Girard / Marie Niccolazi; 416–417 (B) © David Mastalka / A1 architects; 418 (A) © Francis Kéré; 418 (C) © Architectural Review; 418 (B) © Francis Kéré; 419 (A, B) © Erik-Jan Ouwerkerk; 420 (C), 421 (A), 420–421 (B) © Kurt Hoerbst; 422 (A) (c) © Adagp, Paris 2019. Photo © Faly Randrianjatovo; 422 (AC, BC, B) © Kikuma Watanabe; 423 (A) © Mu Jun; 423 (B) © Chiangmai Life Architects; 424–425 © Erik Jan Ouwerkerk; 426 (A) © Christophe Malecot / Yann Letenier SCB / André Berthier & Joseph Frassanito Architects; 426 (B) © Guillaume Lavesvre / André Berthier & Joseph Frassanito Architects; 427 (A, C, B) © Encore Heureux & Co-Architectes; 428 (A) © Keith Morris / Alamy / Photo12; 428 (C) © Pascal & Maria Maréchaux; 428 (B) © Cariddi Nardulli; 429 (AL, AR) © Odile Vandermeeren; 429 (C) © Gustave Deghilage; 429 (B) © Kurt Hoerbst; 430 All Rights Reserved; 431 (AL, AR) © Michel Denancé; 431 (B) © Sandra Pereznieto; 432–433 (B), 433 (A) © Amateur Architecture Studio; 434–435 (A, B) © Miléna Stefanova; 436 (A) © Manuelle Roche / Adagp, Paris 2019; 436 (C) © Jean Dethier; 436 (B) © Luis Gordoa; 437 (A) © Andrea Maretto for Kéré Architecture; 437 (B) © Kéré Architecture; 438 (A, B) © RPBW; 438–439 (AR, BR) © Archivio Emergency; 440 (A) © Craig Lamotte; 440 (B) © Ben Wrigley; 441 (A) © Gregory Burgess Architects; 441 (C) © Gregory Burgess; 441 (B) © Trevor Mein; 442 (A) © Frédéric Hédelin; 443 (A) © Nic LeHoux / DIALOG; 443 (B) © CRAterre; 444 (A) © James Wang; 445 (A) © Eskaapi; 444–445 (B) © Robust Architecture Workshop; 446 (AL, AR, B), 447 (A, B) © BC Architects; 448, 449 (B) © Bill Timmerman / Studio Rick Joy; 449 (A) © Bruno Klomfar; 450 (AC, BC) © Renaud Leblevenec; 450 (B) © Alnatura / Marc Doradzillo; 451 (A) © Aga Khan Trust for Culture / Amir-Massoud Anoushfar (photo); 451 (B) © Laurent Séchaud (architect & photographer). Source: Aga Khan Trust for Culture; 452–453 (B), 453 (A) © Héctor Santos-Díez; 454 (A) © John Gollings; 454 (C) © Greenway Architects; 454 (B) All Rights Reserved; 455 (AL) © Denis Coquard; 455 (CL, B) Charlie Sheppard; 455 (AR, CR) Bruno Ruffini; 456 (AL) © EDF / Dominique Guillaudin; 456 (AR, B) All Rights Reserved; 457 (A) © MC2 Patrick W. Mullen III; 457 (B) © Felix Beato; 458 © Nic LeHoux / DIALOG; 459 (A, B) © Bruno Klomfar; 460 (A) © Steven Jimel; 460 (C) © Abey-Smallcombe; 460 (BL) © Alain Klein architect; 460 (BR) © Mathilde and Nicolas Béguin / Atelier Alba; 461 (AL) © Gisèle Taxil; 461 (AR) © Daniel Duchert, 2016 ; 461 (B) © Tim Nolan 2014; 462 (A) Andy Goldsworthy, *Lambton Worm* earthwork, County Durham, UK, 1988 © Andy Goldsworthy; 462 (B) Richard Long, *Red Earth Circle*, 1989 (vertical wall), river Avon clay on wall, 12 x 20 m © Adagp, Paris 2019. Paddy Japaljarri Sims, Paddy Cookie Japaljarri Stewart, Neville Japangard Poulson, Francis Jupurrurla Kelly, Paddy Jupurrurla Nelson, Franck Bronson Jakamarra Nelson, Towser Jakamarra Walker, members of the Yuendumu community, *Yarla* (*Yam Dreaming*), 1989 (on ground) © Warlukurlangu Artists of Yuendumu. Photo © Centre Pompidou, MNAM-CCI Bibliothèque Kandinsky, Dist. RMN-Grand Palais / Béatrice Hatala / Konstantinos Ignatiadis; 463 (A) Andy Goldsworthy, *Clay Wall*, Musée Départemental de Digne, Digne-les-Bains, Haute Provence, France. June 1999 © Andy Goldsworthy. Photo © Camille Moirenc / Hemis.fr; 463 (B) © Adagp, Paris, 2019. Photo © Eloïse Dethier-Eaton; 464 (A) © Terunobu Fujimori. Photo © Alamy / Photo12; 464 (B) © Mona Hatoum. Courtesy Galerie Chantal Crousel (Photo: Marc Domage); 465 © Holt / Smithson Foundation/ ADAGP, Paris, 2019. Photo © Nathan Allred / Alamy / Photo12; 466 (A), 467 (AL) © Ingrid Amslinger; 466 (B), 467 (B) © ImageBROKER / Photo12; 467 (AR) © Hannsjörg Voth; 468 (A), 469 (AL, AR) © H+N+S Landscape Architects; 468–469 (B) © Irvin van Hemert; 470–471 © KCphotography / Alamy / Photo12; 472–473, 479 © Joly & Loiret, L+R, Amateur Architecture Studio; 481 © Satprem Maïni (Auroville Earth Institute); 487 © James Wang; 488 (A), 489 (A) © Ron Cobb; 488 (B), 489 (B) © Luc Schuiten; 490–491 © James Wang; 493 (L, C, R) © Gino Maccarinelli; 510 © Marie Schuiten.

This book was produced with the support of Quartus, as part of its commitment to the circular economy and to raw earth construction.

Published by
Princeton Architectural Press
202 Warren Street
Hudson, New York 12534
www.papress.com

Translated from the French *Habiter la terre*
by Matthew Clarke

Original edition © 2019 Flammarion, Paris
This edition © 2020 Princeton Architectural Press
All rights reserved.
Printed in Slovenia
23 22 21 20 4 3 2 1 First edition

ISBN: 978-1-61689-889-2

No part of this book may be used or reproduced in any manner without written permission from the publisher, except in the context of reviews.

Every reasonable attempt has been made to identify owners of copyright. Errors or omissions will be corrected in subsequent editions.

From Princeton Architectural Press:
Editor: Kristen Hewitt

Special thanks to: Paula Baver, Janet Behning, Abby Bussel, Jan Cigliano Hartman, Susan Hershberg, Stephanie Holstein, Lia Hunt, Valerie Kamen, Jennifer Lippert, Sara McKay, Parker Menzimer, Wes Seeley, Rob Shaeffer, Sara Stemen, Jessica Tackett, Marisa Tesoro, and Joseph Weston of Princeton Architectural Press —Kevin C. Lippert, publisher

Library of Congress Cataloging-in-Publication Data available upon request.

On the cover:
Front: Domed rooftops in Iran.
Photograph © André Stevens
Back: Mosque in the village of Nando, Mali.
Photograph © James Morris